WHAT'S ON THE INTERNET

ERIC GAGNON

Peachpit Press

What's on the Internet
Winter 1994/95

Previously published under the title *Internet Field Guide: What's on the Internet* by Internet Info

Peachpit Press, Inc.
2414 Sixth Street
Berkeley, CA 94710
(510) 548-4393
fax: (510) 548-5991

Author: Eric Gagnon, INTERNET: p00553@psilink.com
Cover design, page design, layout and graphics: Chris Gagnon
Copy editor: Liz Sizensky

Distribution

Peachpit Press books are distributed to the U.S. book trade by Publishers Group West, 4065 Hollis, P.O. Box 8843, Emeryville, CA 94609, phone (800) 788-3123 or (510) 658-1834. Peachpit books are also available from wholesalers throughout the United States, including Baker & Taylor Books, Golden-Lee Book Distributors, and Ingram Book Company. Bookstores can also order using Wordstock or IBID (SAN 2028522). Resellers outside the book trade can contact Peachpit directly at (800) 980-8999.

ISBN 1-56609-162-4

0 9 8 7 6 5 4 3 2 1

Printed and bound in the United States of America

 Printed on Recycled Paper

WHAT'S ON THE INTERNET

Contents

In the next five minutes, where else on Earth could you:

■ *Trade information and comments with almost 23 million people around the world?*

■ *Get a fast answer to any question on a scientific, computing, technical, business, investment or other subject?*

■ *Join almost 8,000 electronic conferences, anytime, on any subject imaginable, "broadcasting" your views, questions and information to millions of other participants?*

It's all on the Internet!

Your first stop along the Information Highway: newsgroups devoted to the mechanics of using the Internet and to its unique Net Culture.

Newsgroups for business, entrepreneurship, personal investment advice, legal and consumer issues comprise a small but rapidly growing collection of information exchange and person-to-person communications resources on the Internet.

▲ *U.S. Liberty gold coin, downloaded from University of Iowa photo archives via Internet FTP at* **grind.isca.uiowa.edu**

Contents

▲ Bicycle shop PIXAR computer graphic, downloaded from **grind.isca.uiowa.edu**

Chapter 4: Politics 43

Politics-oriented newsgroups satisfy the innate desire of many of us to stand up and speak our mind in the best tradition of the old-time New England town hall meeting.

▲ Student facing down tanks, Tiananmen Square massacre, Beijing, China, 1989, downloaded from Asian photo archives via Internet FTP from **sunsite.unc.edu**

Chapter 5: Support Groups, Culture, Religion & Philosophy 55

While the Internet represents a triumph of the individual, giving each of us a direct channel to millions, use of the Net by specific social interest groups is also a strong attraction.

▲ Cute baby photo, image file downloaded from Internet photo archives at **grind.isca.uiowa.edu**

Contents

▲ *Formula I race car, downloaded from* **wuarchive.wustl.edu**
◄ *Terrier photo image, downloaded via Internet FTP from* **grind.isca.uiowa.edu**

Chapter 6: Hobbies, Travel & Tourism 72

If you're devoted to any one of dozens of interesting crafts or hobbies—woodworking, photography, sewing, car restoration and more—you'll find thousands of like-minded people who share your interest. Also, if you're into collectibles, antiques, art objects or most anything else, you can find your own special obsession among a rich and varied collection of newsgroups devoted to collectors and art lovers.

▲ *Boy with northern pike caught with lure made from 256K computer memory chips, downloaded via Internet FTP from* **grind.isca.uiowa.edu**

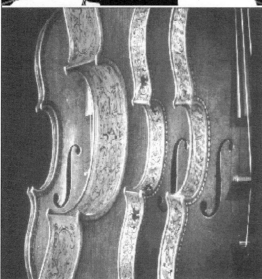

▲ *(Top) Max Headroom, downloaded via Internet FTP from* **wuarchive.wustl.edu**
▲ *Stradivarius violins, downloaded from Smithsonian FTP archives at* **sunsite.unc.edu**

▲ *Marilyn Monroe, and* ▶ *David Letterman,*
both downloaded via Internet FTP from
wuarchive.wustl.edu

▲ *Sharon Stone, downloaded from*
wuarchive.wustl.edu ▲ *Sean Connery as James*
Bond in "Never Say Never Again," downloaded
from **grind.isca.uiowa.edu**

Chapter 9: Science, Technology & Education   123

Connecting our schools, colleges and companies to the Information Highway may be the single most important thing we do this decade to maintain this country's economic vitality.

Contents

Chapter 10: Computers & Telecommunications   140

Millions of computer experts access the Internet's computer and software-related newsgroups each day, making it by far the largest and best source for valuable technical help on computers, peripherals, software, applications and troubleshooting for novices, power users and developers alike.

▲ *Astronaut Buzz Aldrin of Apollo 11, photo downloaded from* **wuarchive.wustl.edu**

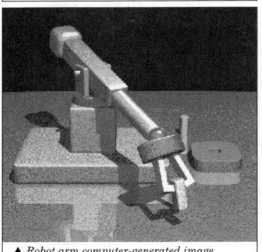

▲ *Robot arm computer-generated image, downloaded via Internet FTP from* **wuarchive.wustl.edu**

Contents

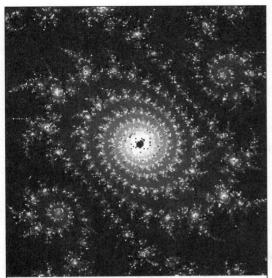

▲ *"Fascination," fractal image downloaded from* **grind.isca.uiowa.edu**

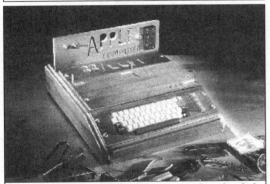

▲ *First Apple I personal computer, downloaded via Internet FTP from Smithsonian photo archives at* **sunsite.unc.edu**

Chapter 11: Sports, Sports Talk & News 175

When it comes to talk on the Net, fans of any sport can find a newsgroup devoted especially to them. There are newsgroups for all American professional sports—baseball, football, basketball, hockey (and their college counterparts) plus international sports such as soccer, rugby and cricket.

▲ *Bowling computer graphics PIXAR image, downloaded from* **grind.isca.uiowa.edu**

Contents

▲ *Winston Churchill commemorative stamp, downloaded from* **grind.isca.uiowa.edu**

▲ *"UPC Bar Code Conspiracy" graphic, downloaded from* **wuarchive.wustl.edu**

Preface

The catchphrase Information Superhighway has taken America by storm. You can hardly watch the nightly news without seeing video clips of happy couch potatoes—pioneers on the Information Superhighway— using the latest prototype of Interactive TV remote clickers to play video games, order pizza and send couch-to-couch video mail on a cable TV test system somewhere in Anytown, U.S.A.

Our Vice President, Al Gore, promises to commit thousands of Washington bureaucrats and regulators to the task of insuring that no one will be left on the shoulder of tomorrow's brave new Information Superhighway.

What most of the popular media doesn't understand is that the origins of the Information Superhighway have been with us since the 1950s. Started as a nuclear war-proof computer communications network by the Defense Department, based on a RAND Corporation study dating way back to the Eisenhower years, with additional R&D efforts by the government and corporations such as Xerox during the 1960s and 1970s, this network gradually evolved into what is known today as the **Internet**—basically, a nationwide (and now global) backbone of ultra-high-speed telephone wires linking thousands of computer facilities around the world.

The method of computer-to-computer communications that grew out of this 1960s Cold War research is called the **Internet Protocol**. It has become the *de facto* international standard for connecting computers to high-speed communications links and to other computer facilities anywhere else in the world.

The Internet Protocol is what the computer techies are using today to connect their big-time computer systems to the Information Superhighway of tomorrow. So whenever you hear someone talking about the Information Superhighway, what they're *really* talking about is the Internet.

In 1991, while working with a small online start-up, I took my first look at a strange computer network called the Internet. Back then, the Internet was a collection of university-owned computer facilities, funded by a National Science Foundation grant and consisting of 100,000 or so computer science students and scientific researchers who used it for electronic mail and remote university computer access.

At the time, the Internet was accessible only if you knew how to use UNIX, a terse and irritating, unforgiving operating system that only the phone company could love (it was, in fact, developed at Bell Laboratories and *given away* to universities—that's one of the reasons it became so popular).

In just a few short years, but after decades of lingering in the ivory towers and basement research labs of academia, use of the Internet has exploded beyond anyone's expectations. The Internet Protocol has been adopted by large corporations as the standard for low-cost electronic mail, fueling a surge in use of e-mail. The federal government withdrew its funding of the Internet in 1992, forcing it to open up to hundreds of new private companies providing access to larger numbers of individuals each year (best current estimates are 15 to 23 *million* users worldwide, increasing at a rate as high as 15% per *month*).

Another big change in the Net is its rapidly improving ease of use. A growing number of companies that sell access to the Internet are also providing easy-to-use graphical interfaces, such as Mosaic and PSILink, which are making online access to the Internet as easy, efficient and fun as any user-friendly commercial online service, such as America Online and Compuserve (both of which are now providing access to many of the Internet's most important features, such as electronic mail and newsgroups).

For all of its present day idiosyncracies and Wild West-style chaos, the Internet will form the core of the emerging global Digital Age that will restructure entire industries, governments and cultures, destroying the old-line structures that cannot adapt and creating entirely new industries, cultures—and possibly, even governments—in the process.

As a veteran network user and active participant in the business side of information companies and interactive online services, I've always believed that the most important element of the Information Superhighway will be its content. So, unlike most Internet books, **What's on the Internet** focuses on the *content* of the Net, not the mechanics of using it.

I hope my book will open many new and exciting possibilities for you, just as it did for me—by connecting you to an interactive, global Net of millions of other interesting, thoughtful and resourceful people—every one of us pioneers in the Digital Age.

Special thanks to Christina Gagnon (my wife and partner of 14 years) for her cover design and the graphics you'll see throughout this book, and to Linda Barrera, for her excellent transcription work. Thanks also to Ted Nace and the staff of Peachpit Press for their support, enthusiasm and responsiveness in helping to produce this edition in record time.

Eric Gagnon (p00553@psilink.com) Fairfax, VA   June 11, 1994

Chapter 1: Introduction

In the next five minutes, where else on Earth could you:

- *Trade information and comments with millions of people around the world?*

- *Get a fast answer to any question imaginable on a scientific, computing, technical, business, investment or other subject?*

- *Join almost 8,000 electronic conferences, anytime, on any subject, "broadcasting" your views, questions and information to millions of other participants?*

It's all on the Internet!

The Internet is a free-wheeling, global network of more than 34,000 smaller computer networks, public and private. It works like a nonprofit food co-op; it has no owner, is managed by volunteers and derives operating costs from its members, who pay connection fees to large regional computer hubs that direct the system's traffic or to local-access providers that tie into the hubs.

Steve Stecklow, "Internet Becomes Road More Traveled as E-Mail Users Discover No Usage Fees," *The Wall Street Journal* (9/2/93)

The Global Electronic Information Highway

There's never been anything like the Internet—the amazing "network of networks" consisting of super high-speed telephone communications links binding together as many as 35,000 smaller computer networks, 350,000 host computer systems, and up to 23 *million* individual online users around the world!

Growing at a rate of 15% per month, the Internet has captured the public imagination as the Information Superhighway. It's always mentioned in the same breath as the numerous mega-mergers now occurring between telephone and cable TV companies, newspapers and other media corporations, and all headed for the same goal: the futuristic vision of an interactive global village where hundreds of millions of people have instant, easy access to each other, to any business or corporation, to huge collections of information stored on host computers and to conventional libraries online—a future where, literally, a database of any and all information ever created in history will be built.

"Within five years," said William M. Bluestein, at Forrester Research Inc., **"a barrage of new technologies will radically change your relationship with customers, product features and service delivery, and the structure of manufacturing, sales, service and distribution."**

Peter H. Lewis, **"The Next Tidal Wave? Some Call It 'Social Computing,'"** *The New York Times* (9/19/93)

The Internet phenomenon, which has come from nowhere, has now taken on a life of its own: Witness the many front page articles, major network TV news items and magazine articles published on a daily basis describing various aspects of the Net. The Internet is even starting to make substantive changes to conventional ways of doing business (such as the Internet's electronic mail), of accessing and exchanging information (access to databases and extensive information retrieval on the Internet) and communicating interpersonally (the vast number of special-interest Internet discussion groups).

What Is the Internet?

Let's start to describe the Internet by explaining what it *isn't*: The Internet isn't an online service in the traditional sense, like America Online, CompuServe or Prodigy. There is no Internet Company, no Internet CEO, no slick Internet TV commercials or chrome-and-glass Internet building. The Internet is not really any one computer facility, but a network of networks, a sprawling collection of over 35,000 individual and independent computer networks, each owned by separate universities, corporations, government research organizations and individuals—a network that has grown steadily since the late 1960s.

Think of the Internet as a national and global electronic interstate highway system connecting you to an astronomical number of computer facilities worldwide. Just as you'd get in your car and pull out onto the interstate to drive to a distant city, you log onto the Internet to connect to various online features on distant computers, like those owned and operated by:

Universities and Research Labs: Practically every college and university in the U.S, Europe and many foreign countries is connected to the Internet. Any student, professor, researcher or staffer connected with these universities can usually obtain free or low-cost access to the Internet through the university's computer center.

Major Corporations: Executives, employees and entrepreneurs in many businesses large and small are connected to the Internet, including most high-tech companies.

Individuals, Professionals and Business Owners: Rapid commercialization of the Internet by companies providing access for profit is making it possible for anyone to get local Internet access at affordable cost.

What's on the Internet?

In brief, the three major features of the Internet are:

Online Discussion Groups: At current count there are over 7,400 special-interest discussion groups, called **newsgroups**, on most any topic you can imagine. When you're on the Net, you can participate in any of the discussions in any of these newsgroups.

Cheap and Universal Electronic Mail: The cheapest and biggest e-mail system anywhere is one of the Internet's main attractions. Since all commercial online services now have "gateways" for sending and receiving electronic mail mesages on the Internet, you're able to use e-mail to send messages to anyone else who's online, anywhere in the world, in seconds.

Files and Software: All told, the thousands of individual computer facilities connected to the Internet are also vast storage repositories for hundreds of thousands of software programs, information text files, video/sound clips and other computer-based resources, all accessible in minutes from your personal computer through the **anonymous FTP** (File Transfer Protocol) feature of the Internet.

The Birth of the Internet: Your Tax Dollars at Work

The Internet can trace its origins to the late 1960s when its predecessor, the ARPAnet, was established by the U.S. Department of Defense as a computer communications research project for defense contractors and universities.

The purpose of the ARPAnet was to create a defense and research-oriented computer network that could still function reliably even if damaged by military attack. The developers of the ARPAnet assumed that the many miles of phone lines, wires and switching connections between the various computers on the networks were inherently vulnerable, and, therefore, unreliable.

To solve this problem, they devised a standardized, reliable and redundant way for computers of different types to communicate with each other, called the **Internet Protocol** (also called **IP**, or **TCP/IP**). This method of computer-to-computer communications enables any computer on a network to communicate with any other computer on an equal basis by putting its data into an electronic "envelope" (called a **packet**), and shipping it electronically across the network to any other computer. IP soon became a standard, and was incorporated into many of the mainframes and minicomputers of the day.

That thought [the rise of new business opportunities from the growth of the Internet] was echoed by John C. Malone, chief executive of TeleCommunications, Inc. "The overwhelming majority of revenues we get by the end of the decade will be from services and products that have not yet been invented," he said.

Edmund L. Andrews, "When We Build It [the information superhighway], Will They Come?" *The New York Times* (10/17/93)

Every 10 minutes another computer network joins the Internet, according to Jayne Levin, editor of the *Internet Letter*.

Kent Gibbons, "Above a Greenbelt Chinese eatery is an International Internet Menu," *The Washington Times* (10/25/93)

As computers became smaller, cheaper, faster and more powerful, this communications protocol expanded to accommodate Local Area Networks (LANs), consisting of large numbers of personal computers, minicomputers and mainframe computers linked to each other (usually within a company, a university or other specific organization). The Internet Protocol lets one company's LAN communicate with any other LAN on the network.

The modern-day version of the Internet started in 1982, when the National Science Foundation (NSF) created a high-speed communications network designed to permit widespread access by researchers and scientists to five supercomputer centers spread across the country.

Over time, more and more companies and organizations found it productive (and profitable) to link their groups of computers together in networks. Since it was already in place (and supported by your tax dollars), the Internet became a way for a company to link up with a university to allow its product developers to communicate inexpensively and efficiently with campus researchers; or, for computer programmers at a high-tech company (many of whom first started using the Internet when they were computer science students) to access libraries of computer software programs stored on university computers. Eventually, in helter-skelter fashion, this government-funded electronic communications backbone evolved into the Internet as we know it today: a high-speed global communications net with virtually unlimited potential for expansion.

What's So Good About the Internet?

The idea of global community—an electronic marketplace of ideas and information, where each individual has instant access (and an equal voice) to every other individual in a worldwide network—has tremendous appeal. Witness the hundreds of Internet-related features and stories appearing in the media over the past year.

The rise of cheap, ubiquitous communications has been fueled by cheap computing power. Ever-cheaper prices with exponential increases in power have fueled the explosive growth in sales and use of PCs, fax machines, modems, cellular telephones and other high-tech gear, dramatically compressing the amount of work that can be done in a day, slashing deadlines and product development cycles, and increasing the average person's access to vast quantities of information and access to one another.

Add cheap computing horsepower to the innate human desire to compress time, increase productivity, make more money and increase

The Internet Is a Network Of Networks

The Internet

©GAA GRAPHICS

Newsgroups are thousands of organized online conferences consisting of hundreds of individual messages, or **postings**, which are continuously broadcast over the Internet 24 hours à day. Newsgroups and their associated messages are organized according to a computer program called **Usenet**, which transmits newsgroups and their new messages to thousands of individual servers on the Internet.

Colleges And Universities were the first organizations to use the Internet for exchange of scientific research and for use by Computer Science departments. Many students who used the Internet in college now push their employers in private industry to link to the Net, fueling a rapid growth in its business use.

Electronic Mail is one of the Internet's major attractions. E-mail messages are flashed in seconds across the Net and end up on a single server where the recipient's Internet account resides (sort of like a home address).

The Internet consists of a central network, or **backbone**, of high-speed telephone lines designed specifically to carry an extremely high volume of computer data at an extremely high speed. It was created by the Department of Defense in the 1960s as a scientific research and military contractor's network. Universities, government agencies and defense contractors were the first groups to connect to these high-speed computer links, but now commercial access providers can lease their own high-speed lines to get access to the Internet.

Servers are individual **host computers** owned and operated by corporations, universities, government agencies and (sometimes) private individuals, all connected by special high-speed telephone lines to the Internet. You may connect to a server to download files, such as **FAQ**s (using a process called **FTP**) or send mail messages to an individual whose Internet mail address resides there.

Commercial Internet Access Providers such as America Online, Delphi, PSI and others connect to the Internet via high-speed lines. Most people gain access to the Internet this way, since government and university funding and sponsorship of the Internet is rapidly giving way to ownership by many different telecommunications companies both large and small.

Who's On The Net? individuals who work for corporations, universities or other organizations; students; and private individuals who purchase access from **commercial Internet public access** providers

freedom and you'll always get more technological innovation. It started in the 1920s, when the telephone became essential in business, then continued in the 1970s, with overnight express delivery, and then passed on to the fax machine in the 1980s. Personal (and now, wireless hand-held) computers, combined with high-speed data communications, now seem poised to become the next great wave of innovation for instant communications and information access in business and society.

It's not too far-fetched to imagine that, by the end of this decade—or even sooner—businesspeople will have their Internet electronic mail addresses printed on their business cards, right below their phone and fax numbers (it's already happened in many high-tech companies!).

Why should this be so? What's so great about the Internet that it should attract all this interest? And most importantly, what's it good for?

What the Internet Means to You

Answer Number One: It's REALLY BIG

Its sheer size, volume of messages and explosive monthly growth rate (best estimates put this growth at well over 15% per month) makes the Internet the "800-pound gorilla"—a force to be reckoned with *in and of itself*, which ought to get the attention of any smart, forward-thinking person who uses technology to improve his or her life.

Best estimates say there are currently up to 23 *million* people who use the Internet worldwide. To put that number in perspective, that's ten times the size of CompuServe, America Online, Prodigy and all other commercial online information services *combined*. Or, more than the combined populations of New York City, London and Moscow. When something becomes this big, no wonder people take notice.

Answer Number Two: It's Contagious

Now that the Internet has captured the attention and imagination of the popular media, vast numbers of personal computer users (which probably includes most everyone you know under the age of forty) are getting interested in the Internet.

All this excitement has also captured the attention of hundreds of entrepreneurs in the software, hardware, communications and publishing businesses, so you can be sure there will be many new and exciting services, products and technologies that will make using the Internet cheaper, faster and better.

The Internet is rapidly becoming the de facto information utility in this country—and the world—making many of today's commercial online services pale by comparison (in fact, all commercially oriented online services now provide Internet access).

The Internet is well on its way to fulfilling the prophecies of Marshall McLuhan and other visionaries of the media age who have predicted the coming of the "global village." And, like all other dramatic changes to society, the Internet phenomenon will be compelling, irresistible and here to stay.

Just like most people in business today wouldn't think of doing business without a fax machine, it's not too hard to imagine that most business executives will be at a disadvantage without Internet access five years from now.

The Internet's Changing Face: "The Rest of Us" Take Over

Just a few years ago, the Internet was the exclusive domain of a small band of computer science students, university researchers, government defense contractors and computer nerds, all of whom had cheap or free access through their universities or research labs. Because of this widespread free use, many people who used the Internet as students have since demanded—and received—connections to the Internet from their employers as they got jobs in the outside world. As a result, use of the Internet has exploded among knowledge workers in many high-tech companies and major corporations.

The Internet is rapidly achieving a state of critical mass—attracting interest from huge numbers of personal computer users from non-technical backgrounds.

These new Internet users are rapidly transforming the nerd-oriented culture of the network and opening up the Internet to many more new and exciting possibilities.

What Can the Internet Do for You?

Here is what's good about the Net and why you should be using it:

Connections: The best current estimates put the number of individuals on the Internet at 23 million and growing exponentially. People in all kinds of businesses and industries, sharing a wide spectrum of professional, business and personal interests are now "on the Net." Most share the same high level of enthusiasm for the Internet and want to

> Until a few years ago, business interest on the Internet was largely limited to companies' research and development departments. But commercial use is now growing faster than research and development use, with businesses rushing to hook up their own computer networks. Four years ago, hardly any commercial enterprises used the Internet. But as of March, 51% of the 34,400 networks that had registered to join belonged to private businesses, versus 29% identified as research institutions and 4% that are educational, according to the Internet Society, a year-old group whose founding members include more than two dozen major corporations.
>
> Steve Stecklow, "Computer Users Battle High-Tech Marketers Over Soul of Internet," *The Wall Street Journal* (9/16/93)

send and receive e-mail messages. Also, one-to-one communications by newsgroups or electronic mail is different and better than conventional letter-writing or voice phone conversations in that the people you communicate with by e-mail seem more accessible and more willing to share their ideas in an informal way. Because of this, once you start using the Internet—by joining its special-interest online conferences, asking questions or giving answers—you'll strike up new connections with people you'd have a hard time communicating with in any other way.

Information: Instant access to such a large, varied and intelligent base of individuals on the Net gives you the power of being able to get *good information*. When you ask a question on the Internet you stand an excellent chance of getting at least one intelligent answer from someone who's gone through the same experience. Whether it's advice on getting a home mortgage, starting a consulting business or building furniture, there's always someone on the Internet willing to share their experience with you.

Profit: A rapidly increasing number of companies and entrepreneurs are using the Internet to market and sell their products and services. When it's done in an informative way, in good taste and in the online areas designated for advertising-oriented messages, most Internet users like to see information and announcements of new products and services on the Internet. A growing number of companies are generating substantial sales of their products and services by posting promotional announcements and information files in specially designated online areas. For example, a manufacturer of video imaging boards for the Macintosh derives almost 35% of its sales volume from Internet referrals. As the Internet grows even larger, its use as a marketing channel will increase dramatically.

Fun: There are almost 8,000 special-interest online conferencing areas called **newsgroups**, on the Internet. Many of these groups feature large, active and (sometimes) raucous discussions on the widest imaginable range of interests, hobbies and activities—from antique cars, new business opportunities and personal investing to politics, gun control, sex, and "The Simpsons." Participating in these newsgroups is a lot more fun than watching TV, because when *you* throw in your two cents' worth, *you* become part of the action!

What's Bad About the Internet?

The Internet is like the Wild West of the 1870s—lawless, individualistic, brutal and chaotic. And like any new frontier, the Internet is not without its problems. Before you decide on how you want to connect to the Internet, there are a few things you should know.

RULE ONE: "Raw" Internet Can Be Pretty RAW

Forget about user friendliness, graphic user interfaces and pull-down windows—a raw connection to the Internet lags behind modern personal computer interface technology by about 15 years. Without a good PC or Macintosh **graphical software interface** (more on these later), to use all features of the Internet you'd need to learn UNIX, a terse computer operating system command language that's a throwback to timesharing computer systems of the 1970s.

If the prospect of having to learn a twenty-year-old computer operating system with a well-deserved reputation for difficulty doesn't seem appealing (and we understand why it wouldn't), the good news is that America Online, Delphi, CompuServe, and a growing number of Internet public access providers now offer friendlier, menu-based software packages, such as PSILink and Mosaic, to connect you to the Internet.

A Look at Internet Usenet Newsgroups

The Internet has many powerful capabilities and an almost infinite range of information and communications power, all of which can never be adequately covered in any one book. In *What's on the Internet*, we focus exclusively on the content, power and utility of the 7,400 special-interest Usenet discussion groups available to anyone on the Net. What makes *What's on the Internet* different from other Internet books is that we focus here on content and benefits to (mostly) non-technical people—"the rest of us." For the most part we leave the job of describing the mechanics of Internet access to any one of the other excellent Internet books, such as *The Internet Starter Kit* books for the PC and the Macintosh, and *The Whole Internet Users Guide & Catalog* by Ed Krol (a comprehensive technical manual for Internet access via the old, computer timesharing-oriented method of direct UNIX access commands).

For Internet access, we recommend one of the small but rapidly growing number of off line news readers—easy-to-use communications software packages specially designed for easy, intuitive Internet access to

---

"What's bad about the Internet is that its chaos," said Brad deGraf, director of digital media at Colossal Pictures, Inc., a San Francisco company that is working with several cable operators to design the look and feel of new interactive video services. "We think the hardest part in all this is giving people a sense of where they are."

To meet that challenge, companies as diverse as Microsoft and *TV Guide* are working on computer "navigators" or "agents" that help people find their way. Agents are usually software programs that search through streams of programming or data and select the things a customer wants.

Edmund L. Andrews, "When We Build It [the information superhighway], Will They Come?" *The New York Times* (10/17/93)

■ Internet networking standards, called TCP/IP, are now widely adopted by businesses of all kinds and sizes as a way for companies to interconnect their computer systems

■ Benefits of standardization: Internet networking gives companies access to the cheapest and most widely available electronic mail service

newsgroups. A listing of providers of this method of Internet access is found on pages 27, 28 and 255.

Whichever way you choose to go, toughing it out with arcane UNIX commands on "raw" Internet host systems or with much easier access to newsgroups via a PC/Mac-based offline news reader (sometimes available as shareware or from commercial Internet service providers), let *What's on the Internet* be your roadmap to locating, organizing and getting the most from the thousands of active, informative and exciting discussion groups on the Internet's Information Superhighway.

What's a Newsgroup?

Today's special-interest discussion groups on the Internet can trace their ancestry to UNIX-based message posting and conferencing programs written in the 1970s by computer science and graduate students, originally cobbled together to distribute information on the **UNIX** computer operating system, a popular computer operating system now in use at nearly all computer facilities in colleges and universities around the world. From the late 1970s onward, this conferencing software and discussion group content gradually evolved into what are now known as **Usenet** newsgroups. The predecessor to Internet discussion groups, known as **Bitnet**, a format organized around electronic mail mailing lists, has now largely been converted to the Usenet newsgroup format.

If you've ever used a computer-based electronic mail or inter-company e-mail system, right away you'll see that Usenet newsgroups look a lot like organized batches of electronic mail messages. First of all, newsgroups have a descriptive name that usually identifies that specific newsgroup's topic. Messages posted by newsgroup participants are gathered into a specific newsgroup through the use of standardized **Internet Protocols (IP)** that have been developed over the years and that are used to organize access to the Internet and its thousands of connected computer facilities. Messages for a specific Internet newsgroup are kept on a specific, individual computer called a **host**, or **server**, and are distributed far and wide across the Internet on a frequent basis to other host systems, ending up where you have access to them (your Internet service access provider). If you've already used a computer-based electronic mail system or **BBS** (Bulletin Board System), you'll immediately recognize that individual newsgroup items are posted as a series of individual text messages from other participants on the Net.

A newsgroup's individual messages are organized by date and time posted, and contain a **From:** (Internet electronic mail address) and a brief one-line **Subject** describing the content of the message. If the message is a participant's response to another participant's message, that message's particular subject line will show a **Re:** (in regard to) tag. In this book, we show you a raw feed of **Subject:** lines for many newsgroups taken directly from the Internet to give you a flavor of the discussion content within that group.

Individual posted messages under a specific newsgroup look exactly like e-mail messages and contain a participant's comment, opinion, text excerpt, quote or any other information that the user has entered into that message or response. Most newsgroups continue *ad infinitum* in a continuous discussion-based format; these streams of discussion are called **threads**. Ongoing discussions in a single newsgroup can be a lot like multiple conversations at a cocktail party: Beneath the noisy din of conversation, individual dialogues are taking place between two, three or four partygoers with a much higher number of people just standing there, listening—it works the same on the Net, too.

Internet Newsgroups: YOU Are the Media!

In Netspeak, the phenomenon of multiple, ongoing discussions under a single newsgroup is called a **thread**. In popular, active newsgroups there may be several ongoing threads, each one a unique conversation that goes on and on, twisting and turning until it either runs out of steam or evolves into a new thread. For example, many of the politics-oriented newsgroups on the Net have continuous threads on the controversial issue of abortion, where pro and con participants argue their views on this issue forever with apparently no end in sight. Another notable thread on the Net is the ongoing gun control debate, where participants, each holding their own extreme view, take over many discussion groups with their intensely spirited pro and con discussions.

The most exciting aspect of an Internet newsgroup is YOU: You have the power to participate in any of the 7,400+ individual special-interest discussion groups on the Net as an equal of any other Net discussion group participant. You decide whether or not to stand on the sidelines, passively reading the comments and information supplied by other newsgroup participants, or to become a full and active contributor. You are in full control of what you say and how you say it. Remember, usually there is no one else standing between your posted message and the millions of other readers and participants of a particular newsgroup.

This brings up another intriguing prospect. Newsgroups on the Internet can be thought of as an entirely new form of media, wholly unlike today's traditional forms of mass media— what's different in this media is that, as *individuals*, Net participants determine the context, form and style of

How A Newsgroup Works...

Conversations In Cyberspace Newsgroups are a running sequence of electronic messages organized under a specific topic. They are accessible to millions of Internet users around the world and cover most any topic imaginable.

You can use newsgroups to ask questions, make new contacts and participate in online dialogues with other Net users—or, you can simply read the messages posted by others without participating in online discussions—it's all up to you.

Here's a typical example of an actual newsgroup dialogue, picked up from the newsgroup **rec.travel**...

```
                        Newsgroups
Wed, 16 Feb 1994 02:55:59      rec.travel        Thread   69 of  433
Lines 15                Monument Valley questions.      3 Responses
rickc@news.NeoSoft.com  Rick Campbell at NeoSoft Internet Services -- +1 713 68

I'm planning a trip to Grand Canyon and Monument Valley for the middle of
March and would like some recommendations on where to stay while in the
Monument Valley area.

I've talked to the Wetherill Inn in Kenyeta, Ariz., and the San Juan Inn
in Mexican Hat, Utah. The prices are right, but how about the places?

Also, I'm interested in taking a Jeep tour if I have time. Any
recommendations on guides?

If you can help. post or e-mail is just fine with me.

thanks,

    <n>=set current to n, TAB=next unread, /=search pattern, ^K)ill/select,
        a)uthor search, B)ody search, c)atchup, f)ollowup, K=mark read,

    2:03:25 PM
```

1. **A User Writes And Posts A Message**
Here, someone who is planning a Utah and Arizona vacation writes a short electronic message online and posts it to the newsgroup **rec.travel**...

```
                        Newsgroups
>with steps so that you can go down and swim (river's cold in non-summer).
>They can also arrange rafting expeditions on the San Juan. The restaurant
>is quite good, and serves Navajo dishes, though for me a little fry bread
>goes a long way.
>
>I'd suggest if you're going to Monument Valley to take a horse rather
>than a jeep tour. Stables and guides are near the park entrance; I remember
>the figure of $40 per day, which seemed to me a real bargain, and
>the pace on a horse seemed exactly right for what I was seeing.
> Eric Mankin
>
Just a few additional observations.  My wife and I took the San Juan
rafting day-trip run by Wild River Expeditions a few years ago and it
was just great.  It was not the rollercoaster kind, but it had its own

    <n>=set current to n, TAB=next unread, /=search pattern, ^K)ill/select,
        a)uthor search, B)ody search, c)atchup, f)ollowup, K=mark read,
        l=pipe, m)ail, o=print, q)uit, r)eply mail, s)ave, t)ag, w=post

                                                          -More -
    2:08:26 PM
```

```
                        Newsgroups
Thu, 17 Feb 1994 16:04:20      rec.travel        Thread   69 of  433
Lines 51               Re: Monument Valley questions.    Respno   2 of   3
KAPLAN@YaleADS.CIS.Yale.Edu            Reid Kaplan at Yale University

In article <2jttt4$90s@mizar.usc.edu>
mankin@mizar.usc.edu (Eric Mankin) writes:

>
>In article <2jsjif$jlc@uuneo.NeoSoft.com> rickc@news.NeoSoft.com (Rick Campbel
>>I'm planning a trip to Grand Canyon and Monument Valley for the middle of
>>March and would like some recommendations on where to stay while in the
>>Monument Valley area.
>>
>>I've talked to the Wetherill Inn in Kenyeta, Ariz., and the San Juan Inn
>>in Mexican Hat, Utah. The prices are right, but how about the places?
>>Rick
>

    <n>=set current to n, TAB=next unread, /=search pattern, ^K)ill/select,

    2:06:52 PM
```

4. **Participants Share Experiences, Opinions And Advice** by responding to questions posted to the Net—ever
(windows above and below).These running dialogues, called **threads**, are a common and quirky feature of Net newsgroup discussions
directions. just like real-life conversations sometimes do. Respondents to this sample vacation question (above and below) share thei

```
                        Newsgroups
                                    --More--(59%) [1881/3188]
Thread 69 of 433, Resp 2/3 (page 3):  Re: Monument Valley questions

sort of drama, including 30 Bighorn sheep, petroglyphs, ruins, and a bunch
more.  (WR was actually mentioned in one of Tony Hillerman's novels about
the Navaho.) We stayed at Goulding's and it was breathtaking sitting on
our patio and watching the sunset on the rock formations.  Goulding's has
a decent restaurant serving southwestern style food (I had to get used to
the deep fried chicken steak, though).  About the horseback trip: think
about it a little before you do it.  How are your calluses?  We took a
horseback trip with guide in Canyon de Chelly just before we went to
Monument Valley (we spent a month touring the Four Corners).  6 hours long
and after the second hour I was in agony.  Thighs and butts just don't
get enough action when you sit in front of a computer.  It made my
bicycle butt break-in period every Spring seem like a picnic.  Also, can
you handle a horse?  Rental horses are not well behaved.  My wife's horse tried
to roll over on her and only her marvelous reflexes got her out of the saddle
and stirrups in time.  Finally, bring your own water.  Don't depend on
the guide to do it.  We packed 4 quarts and shared with the guide; gone

    <n>=set current to n, TAB=next unread, /=search pattern, ^K)ill/select,

    2:10:36 PM
```

```
                        Newsgroups
and stirrups in time.  Finally, bring your own water.  Don't depend on
the guide to do it.  We packed 4 quarts and shared with the guide; gone

    <n>=set current to n, TAB=next unread, /=search pattern, ^K)ill/select,
        a)uthor search, B)ody search, c)atchup, f)ollowup, K=mark read,
        l=pipe, m)ail, o=print, q)uit, r)eply mail, s)ave, t)ag, w=post

                                    --More--(95%) [3049/3188]
Thread 69 of 433, Resp 2/3 (page 4):  Re: Monument Valley questions

by the time we got back.

But, what the hay...  enjoy it any way you want to; it is beautiful.

        ...Reid Kaplan

    2:12:30 PM
```

There Are Almost 8,000 Internet Newsgroups...And Dozens More Added
How To Use Newsgroups
roll fan's groups and philosophical discussions. Internet newsgroups are an invaluable communications
networking ■ Engaging in political discussions and debate ■ Reading interesting and thought-provokin

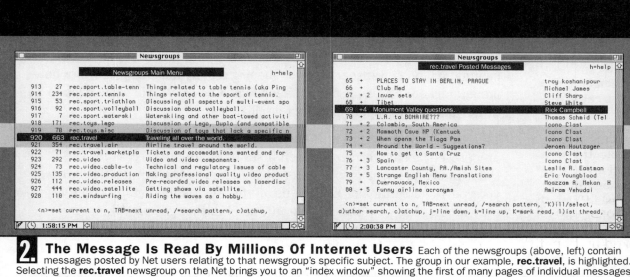

2. The Message Is Read By Millions Of Internet Users

Each of the newsgroups (above, left) contain messages posted by Net users relating to that newsgroup's specific subject. The group in our example, **rec.travel**, is highlighted. Selecting the **rec.travel** newsgroup on the Net brings you to an "index window" showing the first of many pages of individual messages posted to that group, their subjects and who posted them to the group (above, right). The message we're following is highlighted...

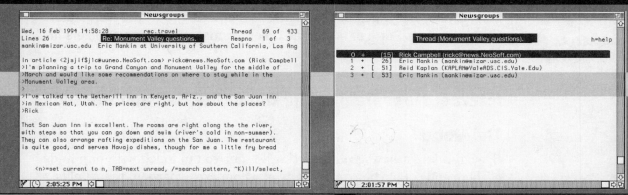

commenting on responses posted by others to the same question here the dialogue often meanders into other strange and interesting personal experiences and advice...

3. Other Readers Respond Over The Net

within minutes, hours, days, even weeks. In our example above, the message has generated three responses in a day...

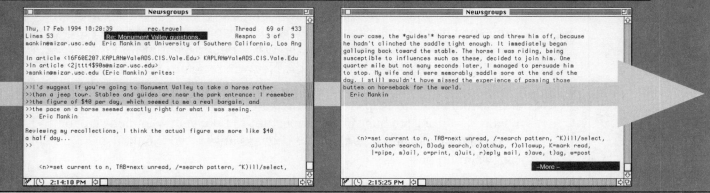

Every Week covering every subject you could ever imagine, from Bonsai gardening to business opportunities, engineering, computer software, rock 'n' roll for: ■ Seeking out information ■ Getting referrals and advice on products and services ■ Asking for how-to advice on just about anything ■ Business comments ■ Friendly online conversation ■ Contacting others who share your specific interests.

Cable companies will connect to
the Internet, information pathway
to millions of personal-computer
users world-wide, early next year
through a direct link-up via
Continental Cablevision Inc., one
of the nation's largest cable
operators.

The service, which could greatly
alter the delivery of electronic
information, would allow
Continental's customers to plug
PCs and a special modem directly
into Continental's cable lines,
said William Schrader, president
of Performance Systems
International Inc., a Herndon, Va.,
network services company that is
Continental's partner in the
project.

Mary Lu Carnevale and John J.
Keller, "Cable Company Plans to
Connect to the Internet,"
The Wall Street Journal
(8/24/93)

the information that is created, distributed and disseminated under a specific discussion group.

On Net discussion groups, there's no blow-dried, insipid TV anchorperson trying to spoon-feed watered-down soundbites as a substitute for useful information, no newspaper reporter shaping a story according to his or her predetermined, politically correct agenda and no MTV-style video clips to rattle your eyeballs and insult your intelligence.

This new medium of Internet special-interest discussion groups, unlike any present media form, gives you instant, *interactive* access to thousands and thousands of other people around the world who share your particular interest. Each of us on the Net, as intelligent, creative individuals, can now provide instant, helpful, thought-provoking and substantive information to all other participants in a newsgroup, anywhere else in the world.

All of this is done by each of us without interference by editors, publishers, shamans, packagers, promoters, spin doctors, politicians, government bureaucrats, Hollywood actors/actresses/phonies/activists, rock stars, Madonna, Ross Perot or any of the other functionaries, icons or fakers in today's mass media.

Internet Newsgroups: The Good, the Bad and the Ugly

The Good

Special-interest newsgroups on the Net put you in touch with hundreds of thousands of participants, many of whom are experts in their fields. There are many participants in discussion groups who also happen to be intelligent, well-read individuals with something to say. More often than not, reading newsgroup postings and participating in newsgroup discussions will give you useful new information or an interesting perspective on an issue. Where else could a twelve-year-old boy posting a question on black holes under an astronomy discussion group get an answer from the head of the Astrophysics Department at MIT? Examples like these abound on the Net, where some of the world's smartest and most interesting people seem to be generous with their time and effort to help other participants with their questions. People who are either too busy or too important to take your telephone call or respond to your letters will almost always answer your e-mail or newsgroup posting.

Newsgroups can also be used to make new business contacts, get referrals to specific products and services, or specific advice on most any arcane, technical or specialized problem. For example, if you restore classic cars, there is someone in the **rec.autos.antique** newsgroup who can tell you everything you'd want to know about polishing the stainless steel trim on your classic car. Have a tax question about a home mortgage? There's probably a CPA under **misc.invest.real-estate** who can answer that question. Got a problem with a specific software package or laser printer? There are scores of newsgroups where you'll find a good answer.

There are also hundreds of Net newsgroups covering any cultural and personal interest: pop culture-oriented newsgroups for musical recording artists and groups, newsgroups for literally any current or classic TV series or movie, book and literary discussion groups and hundreds of groups whose sole purpose is for discussions of political issues or social interaction. It's guaranteed that you will find dozens of groups in this book that appeal to *your* specific needs, interests, political viewpoints and obsessions.

Individual newsgroups also can serve as useful pointers to other indispensable subject-specific files and information resources available elsewhere on the Net. Newsgroup **moderators**, individual volunteers who sometimes screen the messages that get posted to a specific newsgroup, also usually maintain a **FAQ** file related to that specific newsgroup's interest area. (FAQ stands for Frequently Asked Questions, and is pronounced: "FAK.") These FAQs are a compilation of commonly asked questions, useful insider information, resources, contacts and referrals (such as book reading lists) specifically related to the newsgroup's subject area. FAQ files are an invaluable resource on the Net and give you the inside scoop on the newsgroup's subject area. For example, there's an excellent FAQ, posted under **rec.travel.air**, on how to buy low-cost airline tickets.

For the most part, newsgroup participants have done an excellent job of writing and maintaining the many FAQ files available on the Net—and it is all the more amazing that this high volume of material has been created by unpaid volunteers who do it to keep their name out in front of thousands of potentially valuable contacts.

What's on the Internet lists the currently available FAQs that can be found in each newsgroup on the Net.

The Bad and the Ugly

The freedom-of-speech, the chaos and the hyper-participatory nature of Net newsgroups does, however, bring its own share of problems. What most first-time Net newsgroup visitors find most offensive is the Net

Howard Rheingold, author of *The Virtual Community* (Addison-Wesley, October 1993), says that online communication via discussion groups is "a new kind of culture...a virtual village where there's always another mind." He likens the huge Unix Users Network, or Usenet, to "a giant coffee house with a thousand rooms...a worldwide digital version of the Speaker's Corner in London's Hyde Park, an unedited collection of letters to the editor, a floating flea-market, a huge vanity publisher...a vast electronic Chautauqua."

Tom Peters, "Electronic Link Gets Everyone Together," *On Excellence* (10/5/93)

phenomenon known as **flaming**—constant, intense and (mostly) insulting ad hominem attacks carried out by hothead Netters against one or more other Net newsgroup participants over seemingly trivial slights. It seems that instant electronic communication provides for little cooling-off time, so there are many Net users whose tempers compel them to respond heatedly and instantly to any message or other little thing that bothers them. This could be something as simple as a reasonable disagreement under a political discussion newsgroup, or anything that might be perceived as an attack on the flamer's right to freedom of speech. The rudeness and downright pinheadedness of many Net flame messages provokes hurt feelings and irritation on the part of many first-time Internet users. In time, you'll get used to seeing flames and learn to accept them as both an integral part of Net culture, as well as a dead giveaway which exposes many of the flamers for the jerks they are.

Also, since the Net is cheap, easy to access and uncensored, you'll encounter a much wider spectrum of topics and viewpoints than is normally allowed by the mainstream media. Everyone's online, including gays, revolutionaries, Marxists, militant environmentalists, sprout-eaters, S&Mers, polygamists, animal rights activists and abortion protesters. So, if any of these groups offend you, don't say you haven't been warned! Otherwise, if you have something to say about anything that's within a newsgroup's charter, don't hesitate to jump right in (go ahead—everyone else does, why shouldn't you?).

Information Superhighways, Cyberspace and Other Internet Lingo

If you're new to the Internet you'll probably be puzzled by the many references in books, newspaper and magazine articles to its being described as an electronic community. The buzzwords used to describe the Internet: **cyberspace**, **global village**, **information superhighway**, **aether**, **infobahn** and **virtual community** may seem strange or sensationalistic if you're new to the Net. But, with a little experience reading and participating in Net newsgroups you'll soon realize that there *is* something to all of this: Many popular newsgroups actually do begin to resemble communities, where Net citizens go about their business, obey certain rules of decorum, help newcomers, play and work. Active Net newsgroup participants soon begin to talk to each other on a first-name basis as a result of the bonds that are formed out of the group's mutual interest.

The Internet can also be thought of as an electronic highway, with many roadside stops—newsgroups—along the way. Driving along this highway, you can pull off at any exit ramp and visit any newsgroup you like—for a minute or two, or longer. In a flash, you can go to dozens, hundreds or thousands of other locations on the Net to read and join in other newsgroup discussions, too.

Since its birth more than twenty years ago, the Internet has evolved its own unique culture, customs, terminology and rules of the road. Fact is, the Internet shares the same characteristics as any other large community of individuals. Just as any conventional community has its share of opinionated blowhards, jerks and fools, it also has many more fine, upstanding people you'd be proud to call "friend." It's the same on the Net, with its virtual communities. If you use the Net to your advantage, you, too will make helpful contacts, acquaintances and friends.

Internet Usenet Newsgroup Basic Organization

There are nearly 8,000 newsgroups on the Internet. This number grows daily as new newsgroups are created. Like many other aspects of the Internet, establishing new newsgroups is a democratic process with defined rules and procedures. If sufficient interest is generated for a newsgroup, then a place for it is found in any one of the following general newsgroup categories, or **hierarchies**:

alt. The largest category of newsgroups—focusing on pop culture, music, media, controversial issues and off-the-wall discussions;

bit. Newsgroups that started out as Bitnet mailing lists, the forerunner of the Usenet newsgroup structure. Most Bitnet mailing lists have been converted to Usenet format, so they can be read and accessed like any other Usenet newsgroup.

comp. Newsgroups focusing on computer hardware, systems and software.

de. A large number of German-language newsgroups on a wide variety of subjects.

fj. Japanese-language newsgroups covering a range of topics.

misc. Newsgroups covering many topics related to consumers and business and legal issues.

news. Newsgroups about newsgroups. Contains news and information about all Internet Usenet newsgroups, technical information for newsgroup managers and sysops and announcements of new Usenet newsgroups.

The [Internet] systems' dispersed users are bound by a sense of community. "Virtual communities are social aggregations," Mr. Rheingold [author of *The Virtual Community*] writes, "that emerge from the Net when enough people carry on...public discussions long enough with sufficient human feeling, to form webs of personal relationships in cyberspace."

Tom Peters, "Electronic Link Gets Everyone Together," *On Excellence* (10/5/93)

The Internet, the world's largest computer network, is poised to become a staple of modern business communications. Since June 1991, the Internet has jumped from 2,982 interconnected networks supporting about 130,000 computers to more than 10,500 networks with more than 8 million users. By 1998, the total number of users is expected to top 100 million. Rapid communication over the Internet is helping to shorten the development cycle for new medicines and chemicals.

Jayne Levin, "Businesses are Making the Internet Connection," *InfoWorld* (5/24/93)

A penny tossed from the Empire State Building can crack the sidewalk, or a pedestrian's skull.

It won't bother the alligators, though; they are underground, stalking New York's sewer system.

Speaking of plumbing, try bathing in Rio. Water drains the opposite way than it does in the Northern Hemisphere.

Most people have heard such anecdotes, perhaps even passed them around. But are they urban fact or are they urban legend?

Figuring that out is the self assigned task of people such as Charles Lasner, a computer consultant from Queens, New York. Clipping through textbooks and old news clippings, they sift fact from fallacy and blast their findings over the best technology available—the Internet computer network [in the newsgroup alt.folklore.urban]—so others can confirm, refine or quibble with their verdict.

Jared Sandberg, "When a Penny Falls from Heaven, Can It Kill a Pedestrian?,"
The Wall Street Journal
(9/22/93)

rec. A large category containing many newsgroups related to recreation, hobbies, games, cultural and musical interests, sports and video.

relcom. A large number of Russian-language newsgroups. The Russian version of the Internet.

sci. Newsgroups related to science, technology, medicine and biology.

sfnet. Newsgroups from Finland.

soc. Newsgroups for discussions relating to cultures of specific foreign countries, religions and politics.

talk. Political-and controversial-issue-based discussion newsgroups.

zer. More German-language Internet Usenet newsgroups.

In addition to the above broad categories, there are dozens of "mini-hierarchies" of Usenet newsgroups that focus on regional or local metropolitan area news; info and discussion newsgroups affiliated with specific universities, colleges, corporations, specialized educational newsgroups; and commercially oriented newsgroups available on a fee basis or containing advertising and promotional messages.

How to Use *What's on the Internet*

The Internet's sheer volume of content and its chaotic nature also wreaks havoc on newsgroups. It is estimated that the hundreds of thousands of people posting messages on the Internet load up to 25,000,000 new characters *each day*—that's over 7,000 single-spaced typewritten pages every 24-hour period. Another challenge for new Net newsgroup users is getting a handle on the thousands of different newsgroups available. How can you tell which newsgroups might be of interest to you? Which newsgroups are worth your time?

Most Internet access providers don't give you much advice when it comes to selecting newsgroups. True, a handful of helpful Netters have posted lists of newsgroups and their descriptions but, at best, their content does little to define *what the newsgroup does, what's in it* and, most importantly, *how you can use it.*

Another problem with the (dis)organization of Net newsgroups is that there are many, many different newsgroups relating to a single subject spread out all across the Internet. For example, there are scores of political discussion newsgroups spread far and wide, and, even worse, many newsgroups are actually used for discussions that are entirely unrelated to that particular newsgroup's name or charter.

Many times, this Wild West-style chaos on the Internet can be one of its most endearing features. You can spend months poking around thousands of interesting newsgroups (like we have), reading through the sheer volume of postings and files and observing the fascinating discourse and debate that occurs over time—that is, if you have this much time.

But what do you do when you need a fast answer relating to a business, technical or scientific question? Where do you post your inquiry? How can you be sure that you've selected the best newsgroups for your information need? Aside from a couple of broadly descriptive computer files on the Net, there's really no information source that truly describes what's in the major newsgroups, what subjects they cover and, if you're in the business world with a tight schedule and operating under deadline pressure, exactly which ones to access—fast.

However you decide to use Internet newsgroups (and we bet you'll find many new and unintended uses for them once you start), its disorganization and overwhelming online volume truly stands in the way of getting the most productivity, information, communication and enjoyment value from using the Internet. ***What's on the Internet*** provides detailed descriptions of all significant newsgroups on the Internet. Newsgroups have also been classified into numerous categories within ***What's on the Internet***. Chapter 15 contains a "Master Newsgroup Subject Index and Finder," where newsgroups have been sorted and classified by subject, newsgroup name and page number reference.

Newsgroup Descriptions in *What's on the Internet*

In compiling ***What's on the Internet***, we've accessed, downloaded, read and surveyed every significant Usenet newsgroup on the Internet. Descriptions in this book cover all newsgroups that (when reviewed) contained ten or more posted messages over a consecutive three-day period. In our experience using newsgroups on the Net, we found that newsgroups with fewer than ten postings are less useful, in that activity is often (but not always) a good indicator of a newsgroup's value. The exception to this rule occurs in **moderated** newsgroups, whose content is screened by a newsgroup **moderator**, a sort of editor and traffic cop for a specific newsgroup. Generally, moderated newsgroups contain fewer posted messages, but with far higher *quality of content* due to the fact

"Just the FAQs, Ma'am"

FAQ: Acronym for "Frequently Asked Question" file that is used in many newsgroups to answer the common questions posed by newcomers to the group.

As a side bonus, many FAQs also contain excellent, comprehensive information on a newsgroup's subject.

For example, the FAQ for the newsgroup rec.travel contains valuable information on getting the lowest air travel, lodging and rental car rates.

FAQs are sometimes written by a newsgroup's "moderator"—an unpaid volunteer who also screens newsgroup messages (for relevancy to that group's particular subject) and performs other Net housekeeping functions. Other times the role of "keeper of the FAQ" is assigned to another involved newsgroup participant.

that the moderator filters and hand-picks the messages to be posted to the group.

How *What's on the Internet* is Organized

What's on the Internet contains over 1,600 detailed descriptions of the most worthwhile and popular newsgroups on the Internet. Newsgroups in *What's on the Internet* have been organized into general subject areas covering the widest possible range of personal, business, technical and professional interests. Within each individual subject chapter, we've also further organized newsgroups by subchapters (for example: *Chapter 8*—"Entertainment & the Media"—is further organized into the *Arts, Books, Games, Music, Science Fiction* and *TV* subchapters).

Each of the chapters in this book make it easy to find the newsgroups that appeal to your personal interests. You'll be amazed at the large number of newsgroups and the range of extremely specific topics they cover, as well as the depth of content that can be found in newsgroups relating to many esoteric subjects.

The "Master Newsgroup Subject Index & Finder" in Chapter 15 of *What's on the Internet* is an aid to locating any Internet newsgroup by subject—quickly, accurately and efficiently. Chapter 14, the "Newsgroup Alpha Directory," is an alphabetical listing of all Internet newsgroups (up to the book's publication time—more newsgroups are being added daily). Newsgroups that have generated enough usage to be listed in *What's on the Internet* have been printed in boldface type, along with their reference page number.

The "Master Subject Index & Finder" organizes the 1,600+ significant newsgroups covered in *What's on the Internet* under nearly 4,000 subject/topic reference terms, listing all relevant Internet newsgroups under each subject/topic phrase. For instance, if you're looking for newsgroups about conservative politics, the word "conservatism" contains cross-references to a variety of newsgroups, with each newsgroup listing followed by the page number where its description can be found in *What's on the Internet*. The "Master Subject Index & Finder" helps you solve one of the Internet newsgroup novice's biggest problems: selecting the newsgroups available on the Net that relate to a very specific subject.

Newsgroup Descriptions in *What's on the Internet*

What's on the Internet contains detailed descriptions of about 1,600 of the most popular newsgroups on the Internet. A typical description contains the following information:

Title: The newsgroup's subject, as defined by us.

Name: The exact name of the Internet Usenet newsgroup. This is the "official" newsgroup name you would use to access that newsgroup through your Internet service provider.

Usage Symbol: HI M L Three symbols indicate the level of usage for a newsgroup:

HI **High Usage** (**14 or more messages posted daily**) indicates a higher-than-average level of usage for a newsgroup, showing that 14 or more messages from Internet users were posted per day to that newsgroup during the period it was reviewed.

M **Medium Usage** (**4-13 messages posted daily**) indicates a usage level between 4 and 14 posted messages daily, a moderate level of ongoing usage for that newsgroup during the time it was reviewed.

L **Low Usage** (**less than 4 posted messages per day**) indicates that less than 4 messages were posted daily when the group was reviewed.

Usage ratings for *What's on the Internet* were compiled from a variety of sources, including rankings posted on the Net by Internet host operators, or **sysops**. Bear in mind that quantity (i.e., level of usage) is not always the sole indicator of quality, but as a general rule we've noticed that the more messages and postings a newsgroup has, the more incentive its participants have to make their messages more informative. An active newsgroup is much like a crowded, raucous party, in that the active flow of conversation (messages) feeds upon itself and (hopefully) leads to better and better *quality* of information. This is not to say, however, that a specialized newsgroup with low usage might not provide value to you if you were interested in its subject.

You should view usage indicators as simply one basic indicator of a newsgroup's value because, just as in real life, the most popular things are not always the best.

Newsgroup Description: Newsgroup listings in *What's on the Internet* feature individual description paragraphs. These descriptions tell you, in a general sense, what the particular newsgroup is all about, who it's for, what it does, and how we think you might be able to benefit from using it. In many listings, we also provide you with a few **Sample Subjects**, raw feeds of information discussed in a particular newsgroup during the time it was reviewed. Given the fact this is an electronic, *interactive* medium, the content of Net newsgroups will change constantly. Wherever possible, we have attempted to make the descriptions in ***What's on the Internet*** as generalized as possible in an effort to make its descriptions as accurate over time as possible.

Sample Subjects: Many descriptions in ***What's on the Internet*** also contain subject lines, which are sample **Subject:** lines excerpted from actual Net newsgroup discussions for that particular Net newsgroup. Subject lines give you a small flavor of a newsgroup's content, over and above our description.

FAQs: Many newsgroups also feature informative FAQ (Frequently Asked Question) files containing useful supplemental info relating to a newsgroup's subject. We've listed many of the FAQs relating to specific newsgroups, plus the directories on the Net, and where they can be found using **FTP** (**File Transfer Protocol**), the Internet's method for sending and receiving files or software via computers (also called **servers**) connected to the Internet. (Refer to the instructions supplied by your specific Internet service provider for retrieving FAQ files via Internet FTP).

Other Details About Newsgroup Descriptions in *What's on the Internet*

In some cases, we discovered that many Net newsgroups have a central theme. For example, the dozens of popular music recording artist's fans' groups, each containing essentially the same general information but relating specifically to that artist or group (latest albums, concert dates, fan talk, etc.). In ***What's on the Internet***, these newsgroups have been organized under a single description.

What's on the Internet also features **ClariNet** news wire feeds that have been incorporated under the Usenet newsgroup format. ClariNet, a company based in California, provides Associated Press and Reuters news wire services to various commercial Internet access providers. Since they are essentially "read-only," ClariNet newsgroups do not provide for two-way communications among Internet users, but do provide you with up-to-the-minute news and information from around the world. You'll find ClariNet news features relating to a specific subject chapter at the last section of many chapters. ClariNet newsgroups are also featured exclusively in Chapter 7, "Headline News."

Graphics Resources Available on the Internet

Newsgroups are but one of many interesting and useful aspects of the Internet. Inexpensive, global electronic mail is the Internet's most popular feature, providing users with the ability to send text messages around the world at a fraction of the cost of long distance, fax or overnight courier services. You can also get access to massive archives of computer software programs and digital picture files stored on distant computers (usually owned by major academic institutions such as the University of Iowa) through a UNIX feature called **FTP** (File Transfer Protocol). FTP takes a little bit of effort to learn but allows you to use your Internet account to connect to another computer facility, or **FTP site**, also connected to the Internet.

Once connected, you can transfer shareware programs, utilities, sound files, picture files, even video clips from a distant computer archive, to your Internet access provider's computer, and then download these files direct to your own personal computer.

To "illustrate" this point (*and* this book) we've included actual picture and graphic samples downloaded from various Internet photo archives in order to further demonstrate the vast array of all the information—even visual information—available. As you can see, there's a truly immense variety of interesting, informative and entertaining image files available.

For the lowdown on downloading image files from various computer archives on the Net, check out the newsgroup **alt.binaries.pictures.d** for their excellent FAQ (Frequently Asked Question) files. These well-written and easy-to-understand text files, maintained by Jim Howard (whose Internet e-mail address is **deej@cadence.com**), tell you everything you need to know to explore the Internet's young but rapidly expanding collection of multimedia resources.

Graphics image files are just the first wave of a multimedia explosion that will occur on the Internet over the next few years. As line transmission speeds increase, you will soon be able to exchange video e-mail and view video clips online.

Your Special Bonus Disk: Internet Newsgroup Finder Software for Windows and Macintosh Personal Computers

Your copy of **What's on the Internet** includes a card that you can mail in to receive a diskette for either the Windows or Macintosh version of our program called the **Newsgroup Finder**.

The **Newsgroup Finder** is a useful desktop accessory that allows you to keyword search for the newsgroups on the Internet relating to a specific subject. For example, you can type the word "motorcycle" in the Finder's window and see a listing of all Net newsgroups having to do with discusssions of motorcycles, plus their usage rating (high, medium or low).

There are more features to the **Newsgroup Finder**. Read the descriptive information on the back cover flap of *What's on the Internet*, and on the "Read Me" files contained on the disk.

Getting Access to the Internet

The most common way to get access to the Internet is to sign up with an access provider in your area, or with one of the major consumer online services offering Internet access, such as America Online and Delphi (by the time you read this, CompuServe will be offering expanded access as well). This way, your online phone connection is a local (toll free) phone call. A cottage industry of new companies has also sprung up in every major city to provide cheap Net access (see the listing of Internet public access providers sorted by area code on page 255). For the most part, these companies give you "raw Internet"—that is, access that requires you to know at least a handful of UNIX commands to read newsgroups or send electronic mail.

If you're like most people, the majority of your use of the Internet will be for newsgroup access and cheap electronic mail and, as you learn more about the Net, an occasional file download via FTP. Fortunately, the UNIX commands required to do this are easy to learn and remember. There are several books that cover the mechanics of raw Internet access, but we strongly recommend *Internet—Complete Reference* by Harley Hahn, published by Osborne. You don't need to be a UNIX expert to navigate around the Net, but your travels will be easier with some basic understanding of UNIX. Hahn's book tells you exactly what you need to know to work the Internet from the raw UNIX level.

Internet the Easy Way

The real value of the Internet is the ability to meet people with similar interests and exchange information via newsgroups, plus cheap and unlimited e-mail and the occasional FTP file transfer. Most people do not care—nor should have to care—about having to learn UNIX commands to use the Internet. Since the personal computing world has progressed to graphic user interfaces like Windows and Macintosh, we asked ourselves, why should using the Internet still require having to type in those damnable, cryptic UNIX commands? The good news is, it doesn't.

When we started writing this book we scratched out some simple requirements for the ideal basic Internet public access provider system/interface:

■ The system should provide the three basic Internet services everyone needs: e-mail, newsgroup access, and file transfer. The e-mail system should have a simple, PC-based text editor that anyone can use immediately, without having to be connected to the Internet.

■ For newsgroup reading and writing, the system should have a complete list of current newsgroups and provide an intuitive means of subscribing or unsubscribing. The editing functions for creating and posting messages should be the same for the e-mail module and the newsgroup writing module.

■ The FTP or file transfer function should allow a user with a specific FTP site address, directory and file name to retrieve the file using a "fill-in-the-form" approach.

■ Finally—and most importantly—the system should allow the user to do most of the basic functions like responding to mail, posting responses to newsgroups and preparing FTP requests while offline, or while their PC is not connected to the public access provider's host computer. Then, when the user does connect to the host, all the mail, newsgroup postings and file requests are exchanged automatically in one short, efficient session. This method eliminates that nasty feeling that "the meter's running" because you're wasting money online in per-minute connect time charges—a problem that has plagued online customers for many years.

We looked at scores of "easy-to-use" systems and interfaces while completing this book and only one consistently met our requirements, **PSILink** from **Performance Systems International**, Reston, VA (800-827-7482). There are DOS, Windows and Macintosh versions available and PSI has one of the largest networks of local telephone numbers available. You can get a PSI local access number in most of the top metropolitan areas.

Raw Internet Access Providers

When you're ready to explore some of the other aspects of the Net, such as **Interactive Relay Chat** (**IRC**), **World-Wide Web** (**WWW**), and **telnet**, you'll want to try one of the countless "public access providers"

Internet Access Via Well-Known Consumer Online Services

The major proprietary online services such as CompuServe, America Online and Delphi have recognized the existence of Internet for some time, and have provided e-mail "gateways" to and from their systems and the Internet. Prodigy, the largest of these services, does not currently provide a gateway.

Two of the systems—Delphi (800-695-4005) and America Online (800-327-7265) have gone further. Delphi provides full Internet connectivity for its subscribers. Their users can send and receive Internet e-mail, read and post to newsgroups and do file transfers. America Online, the fastest growing online service, has demonstrated an Internet newsgroup module at various trade shows, and has announced plans to introduce access to additional Internet tools such as Gopher and WAIS.

Introduction

Graphical Front End Software Packages for the Internet

In the last year several new PC- and Mac-based interfaces to the Internet have been introduced. The most exciting, Mosaic, developed at the National Center for Supercomputing Applications (NCSA) at the University of Illinois, allows the exchange of not only text but also sound and video. Versions of Mosaic have been introduced for MS Windows, the Macintosh and Unix X-windows environments, but there's a catch: To use Mosiac you need to be linked directly to the Internet via a TCP/IP connection. Installing such a connection is not a task for a typical end-user.

On a more down-to-earth level, there have been several Windows-based software packages introduced, mostly in connection with a specific public access provider's systems such as Pipeline and Winnet. Our conclusion is that if you live in the area codes covered by any one of these systems and are a Windows user, you should give them a try. However, if you live outside of these areas, the incremental cost of a long distance phone call may not be worth the added convenience of the Windows interface.

that have sprung up around the country in the last couple of years (see chart on page 255 for a listing).

Most of these vendors will provide three basic services: full newsgroup feeds, FTP and telnet capability. Vendors typically will provide any one of three newsreading programs—**nn**, **rn**, or **tin**. FTP (**File Transfer Protocol**) is the capability to retrieve files from remote FTP sites. **Telnet** is the capability to log on to remote sites anywhere on the Net. Monthly charges for basic services range from a low of $15 per month to a high of $50. There are some free public access sites called **Freenets**, but, as you would anticipate, their lines are always busy.

Some of the public access providers we experimented with while compiling this book were: **Netcom**, good basic service with a wide network of access nodes throughout the country, great if you're a road warrior; **World**, based in Boston, which has great customer support and a very low $2.00 per hour variable pricing plan; and **Digital Express** of Greenbelt, MD, which has a $25 per month "all you can eat" plan that is great if you feel yourself getting addicted to the Net or have to do a lot of file transfer.

Chapter 2: The Internet

Your first stop along the Internet Information Highway: Newsgroups devoted to the mechanics of using the Internet and to its unique Net Culture.

Internet Resources

If you're new to the Net, the online discussion groups relating to the Internet will give you a look at current controversies concerning its use (such as: should advertising be permitted?) and the issue of Net etiquette—the right and wrong ways of posting messages and engaging other Netters in online discussions. You will also get helpful tips on the nuts and bolts of using the Internet, helpful advice on access software, and referrals to public access providers found in many of the groups in this Chapter.

There are also Internet-related newsgroups which give you a first look at proposed, upcoming and newly announced newsgroups. Since Internet users themselves actually vote on whether a proposed newsgroup can be established on the Net, you, too, can have a voice in helping to establish a new Internet newsgroup. Given this highly participatory environment, it's always exciting to see what people have to say about the newsgroups being proposed for the Internet.

What's a FAQ?

FAQs (Frequently Asked Question) files are an added bonus to newsgroup access, and (to the outside world at least), one of its best kept secrets. A FAQ can best be thought of as the "100 Proof" informational content of a specific newsgroup's subject. As their name implies, FAQ files are intended to bring novice Internet newsgroup users up to speed quickly on that particular newsgroup's "charter"—subject areas covered, a newsgroup's appropriate use and, most importantly, the fundamental background information relating to a newsgroup's subject.

Over 21,000 FAQs for relevant Internet newsgroups have been listed throughout **What's on the Internet**; there are a handful of Internet-related newsgroups which feature nothing but announcements of new FAQs as well as the actual FAQs themselves. Let these Net-related newsgroups be your online guideposts to productive and efficient use of all Internet newsgroups.

Wilmer Cutler & Pickering, a District law firm, signed on to the Internet about two months ago. David Johnson, a partner at Wilmer, said the firm mainly uses the Internet to communicate with colleagues and clients. Having an Internet connection, he said, was the deciding factor in winning one new client.

Jayne Levin, "Getting Caught Up In The Internet,"
The Washington Post
(5/17/93)

Carl Malamud thinks he has a better idea: desktop broadcasting. Starting March 31, and then weekly, Internet Talk Radio will be on the virtual airwaves. That is, it will be "broadcast" to computers...[He] explained that the program could be stopped, started, rewound or forwarded like a tape recorder, but from virtually any desktop computer.

Joshua Quittner, "Desktop Radio For Computer Users,"
New York Newsday
(5/5/93)

Internet Resources

Smart PC Software for the Net
alt.usenet.offline-reader **M**

"Offline news readers" are the latest hot setup on the Net—and its future. What an offline reader does is help you pull down newsgroup messages from the Internet, using your PC, in a "batch" mode: That is, it uses software that pulls down all the newsgroup messages under all the topics you're interested in, all at once, storing them to your PC's hard disk for your review after you've disconnected ("offline"). There's really no easier, better or more efficient way to view online newsgroup messages (or anything else on the Net) than this! Participants in this newsgroup discuss their experiences using various offline news reader software packages (many of which have been made freely available as shareware by their authors on the Internet). Discussion areas include updates and fixes to popular offline reader programs, usage tips and questions on availability of offline reader software for various personal computer systems. Definitely a category that will become increasingly popular as more and more non-techies come on to the Net.

Sample Subjects:
VMS/News readers select subjects offline/New versions of the Zip News door

Help for Novice Internet Users
alt.newbie **L**

A small newsgroup with a lot of potential: alt.newbie is set up to help novice Internet users—**Newbies**—with the basics of using Internet newsgroups. If you're brand new to the Net, this newsgroup, although rather small when reviewed, would be worth a look.

Newsgroups: Software News Readers
news.software.readers **HI**

General discussion group for various types of UNIX-based online Internet newsgroup readers.

Internet: News, Philosophy & Direction
alt.amateur-comp **M**

Current-events discussions about the Internet, its direction, political perspective, and future. Features information from key Internet experts and backers.

Sample Subjects:
Internet town meeting/Nation article on Internet/The Net and the labor movement/Internet testimony to U.S. Congress/Internet access to Congress

New Newsgroups (Mailing Lists)
bit.listserv.new-list **L**

Features announcements of new Internet **bit.net** mailing lists (the predecessor to newsgroups and, for

▲ *First commercial Bell telephone, image downloaded via Internet FTP from Smithsonian picture archives at* **sunsite.unc.edu**

purposes of this book, functionally the same in that they both put you in touch with other users in online Net discussion areas), this newsgroup contains the latest new mailing lists (newsgroups) under the **bit.**newsgroup category and should be on your short list of groups to check relating to information about Net newsgroups. Also a good place to post your questions about where to find newsgroup discussion groups on specific subjects.

Internet Samples & Comments
alt.best.of.internet **L**

This group, which doesn't quite live up to its name, contains some excerpts of postings from all Internet newgroups categories, plus various comments from people on the Net. A good place to get a sampling of messages from a wide variety of newsgroups.

Sample Subjects:
Pave or destroy the Earth?/Knocking off your wife/ Economic warfare?/Math hooligans

How To Start An Internet Discussion Group

alt.config `HI`

Got an idea for a new online discussion group on the Internet? Post it here! **alt.config** handles all new submissions for suggestions on new newsgroups for the Internet. Various network system operators then reach consensus on which newsgroup ideas should be adopted. Plenty of discussion and debate on various proposed newsgroup ideas and online voting to decide whether or not proposed newsgroups get adopted to the Net.

Sample Subjects:
Proposal: alt.creative.writing/Proposal: alt.execution

`FAQ` ▶ The following FAQs are available via FTP from RTFM.MIT.EDU in the directory:
pub/usenet/alt.config:
Another_listing_of_newsgroups_in_the__alt__hierarchy,_Part_1_of_2
Another_listing_of_newsgroups_in_the__alt__hierarchy,_Part_2_of_2
Another_listing_of_newsgroups_in_the__alt__Usenet_hierarchy
Creating_a_new__alt__group_—_guidelines

Internet Online Culture

alt.culture.usenet `M`

Random discussions on Internet newsgroup issues and online culture for hardcore devotees of the Internet, but probably not very interesting for those who aren't.

Sample Subjects:
Netizens/The Net and Netizens

Internet Training Info

bit.listserv.nettrain `L`

Contains announcements and information files primarily of interest to Internet insiders: announcements of upcoming Internet user group meetings and training sessions held in local cities, questions by system operators of local Internet servers, academic use of the Internet and more.

Internet Netiquette

alt.culture.internet `M`

Place for discussion related to flaming, newsgroup conduct and a wide and wild assortment of other topics related to the culture of the Net.

Net Newsgroups: Issues, Ethics & Net Civility

news.misc `HI`

The place to post your inquiries and questions concerning newsgroup Netiquette. The role of the Internet in today's culture and political system and personal views on newsgroup messages and conflicts.

Net Newsgroups: Administration

news.admin.misc `HI`

Net participants, Net server administrators and newsgroup moderators discuss general newsgroup freedom-of-speech issues and current newsgroup controversies, of which there are always many.

`FAQ` ▶ The following FAQs are available via FTP from RTFM.MIT.EDU in the directory:
pub/usenet/news.admin.misc:
arbitron_data_from_these_sites_has_expired
Articles_rejected_at_news.uu.net_during_the_past_week
BIONET_BIOSCI_Checkgroups_message
Changes_to_How_to_Construct_the_Mailpaths_File
Changes_to_How_to_Create_a_New_Usenet_Newsgroup
Checkgroups_message_(without_INET_groups)
Checkgroups_message_(with_INET_groups)
How_to_become_a_USENET_site
How_to_Construct_the_Mailpaths_File
How_to_Create_a_New_Usenet_Newsgroup
Idle_USENET_groups_(no_traffic_the_last_60_days)
Known_Geographic_Distributions
Known_University_Distributions
News_Administration_Macros_for_Geographic_Distributions
Public_Organizational_&_Logical_Network_Distributions
Sites_honoring_invalid_newsgroups_(by_group)
Sites_honoring_invalid_newsgroups_(by_site)
USENET_FLOW_ANALYSIS_for_SEP_93:_Who_stores_how_much_news
USENET_FLOW_ANALYSIS_REPORT_FOR_AUG_93
USENET_FLOW_ANALYSIS_REPORT_FOR_SEP_93
USENET_READERSHIP_SUMMARY_REPORT_FOR_AUG_93
USENET_READERSHIP_SUMMARY_REPORT_FOR_SEP_93

Net Newsgroups: Policies & Complaints

news.admin.policy `L`

Newsgroup for posting your comments and complaints on Net newsgroup usage. Covers Net policies, freedom of speech, libel issues and other general Internet newsgroup concerns.

Net Newsgroups: Technical Issues

news.admin `M`

Technical, telecommunications and software issues of interest mainly to Net administrators and developers.

Newsgroups: ANU-News Software (Technical)

news.software.anu-news `M`

Technical news discussion group for users of the ANU-News newsgroup reader software package.

`FAQ` ▶ The following FAQ is available via FTP from RTFM.MIT.EDU in the directory:
pub/usenet/news.software.anu-news:
FAQ:_news.software.anu-news

Newsgroups: Netnews Software

news.software.b **HI**

Technical question-and-answer software discussion group for users of the Netnews software used for Internet newsgroups (Usenet).

FAQ ▶ The following FAQs are available via FTP from RTFM.MIT.EDU in the directory:
pub/usenet/news.software.b:
Changes_to_FAQ:_FAQ:_Norman_s_INN_quick-start_guide_(Part_3_of_3)
Changes_to_FAQ:_INN_General_Information_(and_compiling)_(Part_1_of_3)
Changes_to_FAQ:_The_INN_Tutorial_(plus_Debugging_FAQ)_(Part_2_of_3)
Changes_to_INN_FAQ_Part_1_3:_General_Information,_how_to_compile,_how_to_operate
Changes_to_INN_FAQ_Part_2_3:_Tutorial_on_installing
Changes_to_INN_FAQ_Part_3_3:_Tutorial_on_debugging_and_adding_options
FAQ:_INN_General_Information_(and_compiling)_(Part_1_of_3)
FAQ:_Norman_s_INN_quick-start_guide_(Part_3_of_3)
FAQ:_The_INN_Tutorial_(plus_Debugging_FAQ)_(Part_2_of_3)
INN_FAQ_Part_1_3:_General_Information,_how_to_compile,_how_to_operate
INN_FAQ_Part_2_3:_Tutorial_on_installing
INN_FAQ_Part_3_3:_Tutorial_on_debugging_and_adding_options

Newsgroups: NN Software

news.software.nn **M**

Technical software discussion group for users of UNIX-based nn newsreader software for newsgroups.

FAQ ▶ The following FAQ is available via FTP from RTFM.MIT.EDU in the directory:
pub/usenet/news.software.nn:
NN_Frequently_Asked_Questions_(FAQ)_with_Answers

Newsgroups: NOV Newsgroup Database Software

news.software.nov **L**

Technical software discussion group for users of News OverView database software for newsgroup control and access.

Internet: Local Access Via Computer BBS Systems

alt.bbs.internet **HI**

For personal computer users who need access to the Internet for their local area. Contains discussions on various telecommunications and personal communications issues of interest to people who use online services and general information on the Internet.

Sample Subjects:
Internet in Northern Virginia/White House Internet address/Cleveland Freenet!/Internet provider in New York City

FAQ ▶ The following FAQ is available via FTP from RTFM.MIT.EDU in the directory:
pub/usenet/alt.bbs.internet:
Updated_Internet_Services_List

Internet & Commercial Online Services: How-To

alt.online-service **M**

A well-travelled, interesting discussion group focusing on access to the Internet through commercial online services such as CompuServe, Genie and PC Pursuit. Discussions relate to using various features of the Internet (for example, online chat) and to reducing the cost of Internet dial-up through the use of low-cost data communications networks such as PC Pursuit. Includes general discussions on various Net issues and the growth of the Internet.

Sample Subjects:
Use of Internet Relay Chat/Internet luxury/Genie and ZModem

Internet Technical Standards

info.big-internet **M**

A technically oriented group for discussions of Internet networking standards and protocols.

FAQ Files

FAQs: Frequently Asked Question Files on the Net

rec.answers **HI**

The catch-all area for large and highly informative files written by other Net users describing some of the other newsgroups in the **rec.** categories. These files, which are called FAQs (Frequently Asked Questions) give you basic information on what a particular newsgroup is all about, as well as factual answers to the most-asked questions by new users to that group. As a general rule, it's always a good idea to look for a newsgroup's FAQ whenever you first access that particular group. Doing this gives you a mental basis for determining the kinds of questions that are appropriate to ask on that newsgroup and can also provide you with other useful information on that newgroup's particular subject. **rec.answers** also contains a number of interesting and highly informative files of an "insider info" nature. When reviewed, there were excellent files on such subjects as how to get cheap airline tickets, frequently asked questions on satellite TV, etc. An eclectic, interesting and fun to read newsgroup, with new files added daily. Highly recommended.

FAQ ▶ The following FAQ is available via FTP from RTFM.MIT.EDU in the directory:
pub/usenet/rec.answers:
index

FAQ Files Give Good Answers

misc.answers **L**

Online Net repository containing many interesting Frequently Asked Question (FAQ) files relating to **misc.** newsgroups. Examples include FAQs on investment topics, writing, copyright law, electrical wiring and more.

FAQ ▶ The following FAQ is available via FTP from RTFM.MIT.EDU in the directory:
pub/usenet/misc.answers:
index

FAQs: Frequently Asked Questions Files: .alt groups

alt.answers **L**

A catch-all newsgroup category containing files of FAQs (Frequently Asked Questions and their answers) for newsgroups, as well as announcements of new newsgroups.

FAQ ▶ The following FAQs are available via FTP from RTFM.MIT.EDU in the directory:
pub/usenet/alt.answers:
index
usenet-univ-FAQ

Government Publications

bit.listserv.govdoc-l **M**

Librarian-oriented group for exchanging lists of publications, documents, files and other information produced by the U.S. government. A rather specialized and arcane interest group.

Test Newsgroup Posting

alt.test **HI**

A test newsgroup used by new Internet users for posting sample or test messages to the Net.

ClariNet News Services

Announcements for News Admins at ClariNet Sites
clari.net.admin

Monthly Journal on the Internet
clari.matrix_news

Announcements for All ClariNet Readers
clari.net.announce

Online Info about ClariNet
clari.net.newusers

FAQ ▶ The following FAQs are available via FTP from RTFM.MIT.EDU in the directory:
pub/usenet/clari.net.newusers:
ClariNet:_How_it_works_(Jul_92)
ClariNet_Electronic_Newspaper_Introduction_(Oct_92)
ClariNet_frequently_asked_questions_(Jul_92)
ClariNet_news_reading_basics_(Jul_92)
Decoding_ClariNet_special_article_headers_(Oct_92)

▲ *First transatlantic undersea cable sample (l), compared to modern cable (r), downloaded via FTP from Smithsonian Internet picture archives at* **sunsite.unc.edu**

Description_of_ClariNet_newsgroup__Standing_stories___(Jul_92)
Picking_which_ClariNet_newsgroups_you_wish_to_read_(Jul_92)

New ClariNet Products
clari.net.products

Discussion of ClariNet—Only Unmoderated Group
clari.net.talk

Milestones: Commercialization Of The Internet

■ Mid-1991: Number of corporate/industrial connections to the Internet exceeds total number of connections in colleges and universities for the first time

■ March, 1993 To June, 1993: Number of corporation-owned computer networks connecting to the Internet jumps dramatically, from 485 to 1,590

Chapter 3: Business, Investment & Consumer Issues

Newsgroups for business, entrepreneurship, personal investment advice, legal and consumer issues comprise a small but rapidly growing collection of information exchange and person-to-person communications resources on the Internet.

Business and Entrepreneurship

On the Net, use of business- and investment-related newsgroups has increased dramatically in recent months as greater numbers of "non-computer" people have begun to discover the Net. There's no doubt this trend will continue—making business- investment- and consumer-related newsgroups one of the Internet's hottest and most rapidly expanding interest areas.

In these Net newsgroups you'll find experienced, streetwise entrepreneurs and small business owners onhand to provide useful advice to anyone who's thinking about starting a business or seeking to answer a nuts-and-bolts question about marketing, finance or new business opportunities. We've often observed that a small number of Net users in these groups—who have clearly been around the block when it comes to starting up and running successful businesses—contribute the best answers to questions asked by less-experienced newsgroup participants.

For the most part, a unique quality of the answers given in these newsgroups is that they reflect the benefit of the respondent's entrepreneurial experience (read: "hard knocks"). As a result, the answers given tend to be frank, direct and remarkably free of the generalities and squishiness generally found in the thousands of books and articles published on the subject of starting and building a new business.

Participating in entrepreneur-related newsgroups on the Net, for the business neophyte, is like having access to dozens of wise old uncles who can take you aside and tell you the "Real Deal" on your start-up's particular problem.

Resources for Experienced Entrepreneurs, Business Owners and Professionals

If you're already running your own business, the newsgroups in this chapter are worth a good look from time to time, but we'd also suggest you look closely at many of the newsgroups covered in other chapters of *What's on the Internet* as well. For example, if you run a business in the technology field, many of the newsgroups featured in Chapter 9: "Science, Technology & Education," and Chapter 10: "Computers and Telecommunications" can provide you with access to a vast array of useful contacts, resources, referrals and answers to any question related to computers, electronics, software, applications and other information or manufacturing technology.

We suggest using the large number of these specialized technical groups on the Net to make the contacts and get the answers you need for your particular business challenge. For example, if you had a question on manufacturing plastic products, you'll get some excellent answers and advice in the **sci.engr** newsgroup (Engineering—see Chapter 9, "Science, Technology & Education" under "Science & Technology, Engineering"). In this way, you should think of the Internet newsgroups covered in *What's on the Internet* as being potential resources for high quality specialized business information, online contacts, referrals, "inside info" and more.

But don't just take our word for it—there are already thousands of savvy entrepreneurs and business owners swarming onto the Net and using it exactly this way.

Personal Investment and Legal Advice

A number of solid and informative newsgroups are available to help you with a wide variety of questions related to personal investment strategies and legal, tax and homebuying advice. As with all newsgroups on the Internet, the information, comments and opinions expressed among participants reflect their real-life experiences in buying stocks, developing personal investment strategies, getting a mortgage, doing their taxes and resolving legal issues. On the Net, you can benefit from this experience.

Institute for the Future fellow Paul Saffo thinks that in the next 5 years, computer networks will support a shift to business teams from individuals as the basic unit of corporate productivity. In 20 to 30 years, there will be a shift so fundamental that it will mean the end of corporations as they are now known.

Saffo insists that corporations have already started down a path to the sort of pervasive interconnectivity that will give rise to a new virtual corporate structure.

Two indicators are the personal computer (PC) and the Internet. The PC has already begun a transformation from processing to accessing that will eventually replace the traditional PC with hand-held information appliances and desktop communications computers.

Margie Wylie, "Will Networks Kill The Corporation?" *Network World* (1/11/93)

Business, Investment & Consumer

When it absolutely, positively has to get there, John Shore wouldn't think of using an overnight delivery service. It takes too long. Instead, Shore, president and chief executive of Entropic Research Laboratory Inc. in the District, sends documents using his computer linked to the world's largest computer network, the Internet.

By using the Internet, Shore was able to meet a recent deadline for sending the first commercial release of a new software product to reviewers at Cambridge University in Britain. "The Internet gave us the power to do something significant and the ability to do it quickly," Shore said. "In business terms, it's a first-quarter success...."

Via the Internet, companies can swap information, develop new products, offer customer support, collaborate, take orders for merchandise, receive electronic publications, edit documents and retrieve data from specialty databases.

Jayne Levin, "Getting Caught Up In The Internet," *The Washington Post* (5/17/93)

Consumer and Privacy Issues

The Internet also features an eclectic collection of consumer-oriented newsgroups from the mundane to the exotic. Netters are eager to share their opinions and experiences with specific products and services and can also tell you how to defend your privacy by keeping your personal electronic files away from the prying eyes of commercial and government databases. Advice on health food and nutritional supplements, electronic computer encryption, tips on good self-help books and homesteading advice for rural residents round out this interesting batch of newsgroups.

Online Help Wanted and Electronic Classifieds

There are also many good newsgroups on the Internet for career and job search advice, help wanted listings (mostly for jobs in the computer/electronics field) as well as online classified advertising for used household items, cars, computers and anything else Netters want to sell. Online help-wanted listings are also numerous among regional newsgroups, so check Chapter 12: "Local, Regional, University & International Newsgroups," for listings of positions available in your city.

Business/Economic News

We've also listed a couple dozen ClariNet business-related news feeds which (while not newsgroups in that they aren't set up for two-way discussion) have been implemented on many Internet commercial access services in the Usenet newsgroup format. Check with your commercial Internet access vendor to see if ClariNet news services are available. ClariNet news services contain up-to-date AP and Reuters news wire feeds for business and economic subjects and can provide you with convenient access to business information that may not have been picked up by your local newspaper.

Business & Entrepreneurship

Business Opportunities & Connections
alt.business.misc **L**

Starting a new business? Need a new business connection? Or, would you like to learn more about some new business opportunities? A small-business-owners-oriented newsgroup, covering a wide range of business-related topics. Everything from multi-level marketing, announcements from people starting their own new businesses and looking for connections on the Net, to ongoing and very interesting discussions of new business opportunities. Often this group will feature good analysis and common-sense perspectives on business opportunities and new business ideas. The value of this group is that you will often get a more objective opinion from someone who has already faced the same business challenge you are now facing.

Sample Subjects:
New import/export business starting/Want to sell? buy?/New 900 numbers/Success article/Products wanted to export

Business Opportunities & Advice: Multi-Level
alt.business.multi-level **HI**

A newsgroup devoted to people currently involved or interested in getting involved in multi-level marketing. Full of inside information concerning various multi-level marketing companies, such as Amway and other lesser known multi-level opportunities (some of which have been exposed by Net participants as scams). As with any online discussion group, you will find many opinions on various multi-level opportunities here—some useful and some not so useful. But if you'd like to know more multi-level marketing or about multi-level marketing businesses, or if you need to check out an opportunity that's been presented to you, there are people in this newsgroup who can give you help and good advice. Recent topics have included discussion on marketing and selling techniques for multi-level products, reviews and evaluations of new multi-level marketing business opportunities, with many personal comments on all these topics.

Sample Subjects:
Amway distributors mailing list/Tape prices/Cold contacts/Motivational tapes

FAQ ▶ The following FAQ is available via FTP from RTFM.MIT.EDU in the directory:
pub/usenet/alt.business.multi-level:
alt.business.multi-level_FAQ_(Frequently_Asked_Questions)

Business Research Q & A
bit.listserv.buslib-1 **M**

Got a question about a particular line of business or industry? Need a company name or contact? This newsgroup is a useful forum for exchanging business information of all kinds, such as industry data, statistical data, government data on business and economic activity, phone numbers of companies in various industries and other across the Net questions relating to business. Since it is frequented by many helpful business librarians at major well-known corporations, it's also a good place to post your business question and (possibly) get a speedy reply.

▲ *U.S. Liberty gold coin, downloaded from University of Iowa photo archives via Internet FTP at* **grind.isca.uiowa.edu**

Entrepreneur's Resource Group
misc.entrepreneurs **M**

A useful newsgroup, oriented more toward beginners, **misc.entrepreneurs** can put you in touch with thousands of other aspiring-to-experienced entrepreneurs and small business owners who can answer your questions about what it takes to start a business, marketing, financing and other practical advice for launching a new venture. Also used by small business owners wanting to locate materials or components or with products or excess inventory to sell.

Sample Subjects:
Working at home/Internet Coffee Shops/Books and resource suggestions?

Manufacturing Questions & Resources
alt.manufacturing.misc **L**

Questions and answers to manufacturing and product development questions, from prospective entrepreneurs wishing to get information on how to manufacture their specific products.

■ **Business, Investment & Consumer**

Business Opportunities: Miscellaneous

biz.misc **M**

Listings of bulk manufactured products available for sale; products/ services wanted.

Investment & Legal

Personal Investment Strategies

misc.invest **HI**

General-interest savings, investment and speculation group for investors of all ages, incomes and skill levels. Netters discuss a wide spectrum of investment opportunities; tout their favorite investment vehicles and company stocks; trade advice on company future earnings prospects, fixed income yields and mutual funds; and swap referrals on information resources available to individual investors.

Sample Subjects:
Stock Market correction/Rumors of G.E. buying Boeing/T-Bills versus CDs/Stock spread question

FAQ ▶ The following FAQs are available via FTP from RTFM.MIT.EDU in the directory:
pub/usenet/misc.invest:
diffs_for_misc.invest_general_FAQ
misc.invest_FAQ_on_general_investment_topics_(part_1_of_3)
misc.invest_FAQ_on_general_investment_topics_(part_2_of_3)
misc.invest_FAQ_on_general_investment_topics_(part_3_of_3)
misc.invest_FAQ_on_general_investment_topics_(Table_of_Contents)
Pointer_to_misc.invest_general_FAQ_list

Investment Software & Technical Theories

misc.invest.technical **HI**

Intense, highly motivated technical stock traders discuss advanced charting and mathematical modeling stock price prediction systems, computer software, stock quote information services and other trading tactics and strategies for more advanced technical analysis-oriented investors.

Real Estate Investing & Legal Issues

misc.invest.real-estate **M**

Participants discuss the ins and outs of home buying, financing and legal liability issues. Experienced home buyers relate their personal experiences and help first-time home buyers select the best mortgage types and terms; additionally, highly experienced real estate investors "run the numbers," helping fellow Netters solve tricky refinancing or other legal problems.

▲ *Roman gold coin, downloaded from* **grind.isca.uiowa.edu**

Sample Subjects:
Paying off mortgage/First right of refusal/ Help a confused first-time homeowner

Tax Questions & Advice

misc.taxes **M**

Netters help each other out on their personal tax-related questions. Good place to get fast answers to basic personal tax return questions. Includes question-and-answer info on home mortgages and other deductions.

Legal Advice & Discussion

misc.legal **HI**

This group can provide you with useful, streetwise advice on basic everyday legal problems, as Netters share their personal experiences on legal problems with police, auto accidents, landlord/tenant issues, etc. Also contains a good deal of discussion of national legal and constitutional issues, with a decidedly conservative/ libertarian attitude.

Sample Subjects:
Homeowners associations/Collision damage waivers/Car rental responsibility/Finding credit worthiness of tenants

Immigration Info

alt.visa.us **HI**

A useful and very active resource group for U.S. visa holders and other would-be immigrants. Participants (mostly college and graduate students) share information on the ins and outs of visa status, green cards and other info of interest to citizens of foreign countries wanting to extend their stays in this country or apply for U.S. citizenship.

Sample Subjects:
Green card application/Tax for H-1 holders/Status change

Copyright Discussion Group

misc.int-property **M**

Detailed but rather legalistic discussions by Netters on copyright, trademark and other intellectual property issues, focusing on copyright, distribution and use of information posted on the Internet. Also contains several in-depth FAQs on the subject of copyright law.

FAQ ▶ The following FAQs are available via FTP from RTFM.MIT.EDU in the directory:
pub/usenet/misc.int-property:
Copyright_Law_FAQ_(1_6):_Introduction
Copyright_Law_FAQ_(2_6):_Copyright_Basics
Copyright_Law_FAQ_(3_6):_Common_miscellaneous_questions
Copyright_Law_FAQ_(4_6):_International_aspects
Copyright_Law_FAQ_(5_6):_Further_copyright_resources
Copyright_Law_FAQ_(6_6):_Appendix_(a_note_about_legal_citation_form)

Consumer Issues

Consumer Products Reviewed On the Net

misc.consumer **HI**

Need fast advice on which product brand to buy? Need help resolving a customer service complaint? Have a problem trying to a fix a product? Net participants offer all kinds of great advice on good (and not so good) products to buy, based on their own experiences. Covers a wide range of products and consumer issues from cars to electric shavers to telephone scams and small claims court. Good, down-to-earth recommendations and advice that can save you time, money and trouble on major product purchases.

Consumer Advice for Homeowners & Buyers

misc.consumers.house **HI**

Extremely useful Net resource, chock-full of useful tips for homeowners and prospective home buyers, **misc.consumers.house** gives you access to thousands of other Net homeowners and their recommendations, based on their own hard knocks and home improvement experiences. Practical down-to-earth tips cover every aspect of home improvement—painting, basic repairs, renovation and refinishing, landscaping/lawn care and much more—making this group the electronic equivalent of the friendly neighborhood hardware store. Also includes good advice on home mortgage financing, legal property/title issues, and resolving real estate disputes.

Sample Subjects:
Staining decks/Refinishing cast iron bathtubs/Fireplace mantles/When are building permits needed?/Paying off mortgage

FAQ▶ The following FAQs are available via FTP from RTFM.MIT.EDU in the directory:
pub/usenet/misc.consumers.house:
Electrical_Wiring_FAQ
Electrical_Wiring_FAQ_[Part_1_2]
Electrical_Wiring_FAQ_[Part_2_2]
rec.woodworking_Electric_Motors_Frequently_asked_Questions

Electronic Privacy & Personal Security Info

alt.security **HI**

It seems that Net participants are more concerned about their personal privacy in today's increasingly Net-connected world (and perhaps rightly so). If you're concerned about maintaining privacy in your daily and personal communications and are interested in seeking advice on ways to keep your personal and business affairs away from the prying eyes of big corporations, or "Big Brother," there's good, practical advice here—everything from private post office boxes and personal ID security to more esoteric

▲ *3-D computer-generated scene of living room by PIXAR, downloaded via Internet FTP from* **grind.isca.uiowa.edu**

discussions on electronic computer encryption and the NSA.

Sample Subjects:
Post Office security/FBI versus Secret Service/ Product info. request

FAQ▶ The following FAQs are available via FTP from RTFM.MIT.EDU in the directory:
pub/usenet/alt.security:
FAQ:_Computer_Security_Frequently_Asked_Questions
RIPEM_Frequently_Noted_Vulnerabilities

Electronic Privacy Issues & the Government

alt.privacy.clipper **L**

Ongoing discussions relating to the Clipper data encryption controversy. Current topics include discussion relating to whether or not the government should have the right to decode computer encrypted data, ostensibly for purposes of investigating criminal and national security threats. Also, discussion of related new product announcements and media articles.

Sample Subjects:
Compromising escrow/Free markets alternative to clipper/Various articles on clipper

Health Foods & Alternative Health Resources

misc.health.alternative **M**

Contains many valuable bits of information and resources, focusing mainly on natural health food supplements, vitamins, herbal treatments and nutrition. Knowledgeable, helpful Netters are happy to provide you with good information—based on their own personal experiences—on just about any medical/ health self-help and nutrition question. Also includes references to helpful suppliers of alternative nutritional products and resources.

How to Plan a Wedding
alt.wedding **M**

Planning a wedding? Need advice on how to work with a caterer? This very active group, used mostly by future brides and their families, offers good advice and suggestions on the ins and outs of planning a wedding—everything from how to dress a "tomboy" flower girl, to photographers, wedding dresses for sale and dealing with future in-laws.

Sample Subjects:
Most unusual ceremonies/Wedding help/Elegant wedding gown for sale/Laura Ashley wedding dress catalog

▲ *GM's Impact electric car prototype, downloaded via Internet FTP from* **grind.isca.uiowa.edu**

Saturn Car Owners Group
csn.ml.saturn **M**

Enthusiastic Saturn owners trade tips on maintenance, dealer service and pricing and car care. Lots of chit chat about this popular U.S. car line.

Street-Smart Safeguards for Your Personal Privacy
alt.privacy **HI**

The amount of personal information recorded about each of us on computer databases by government and business increases every year as do our concerns about our personal privacy. That's what **alt.privacy** is all about: This very active group discusses all aspects of your privacy—privacy of your personal information on the Net, commercial and government computer databases, the IRS and FBI, credit reports and state records. Lots of valuable and useful tips and advice on preserving your privacy and alternative methods. One of the good things about this group is that it can help

you gain the benefit of someone else's experience in dealing with a personal privacy issue, while at the same time allowing you to protect your privacy without revealing personal information. For example, recent discussions in this newsgroup have addressed problems relating to renting apartments and opening bank accounts without having to provide social security numbers (an important way to preserve privacy). Participants relate their own experiences in dealing with government bureaucracies and large corporations to protect their own privacy. Other discussions have included talk about computer privacy on the Internet, encryption keys and data network privacy.

Sample Subjects:
SSN/Drivers license miscellaneous/War on Drugs/ Anonymity on the Internet frequently asked questions/ Social Security frequently asked questions

FAQ ▶ The following FAQs are available via FTP from RTFM.MIT.EDU in the directory:
pub/usenet/alt.privacy:
Anonymity_on_the_Internet_FAQ_(2_of_4)
Anonymity_on_the_Internet_FAQ_(3_of_4)
Anonymity_on_the_Internet_FAQ_(4_of_4)
Privacy_&_Anonymity_on_the_Internet_FAQ_(1_of_3)
Privacy_&_Anonymity_on_the_Internet_FAQ_(2_of_3)
Privacy_&_Anonymity_on_the_Internet_FAQ_(3_of_3)
RIPEM_Frequently_Asked_Questions
Social_Security_Number_FAQ
The_Great_Usenet_Piss_List_Monthly_Posting

Tips on Good Self-Help Books & Instructions
alt.self-improve **M**

Quite a useful online group for those of us interested in various forms of self-improvement, from talk of various popular books to exchange of personal advice. Recent discussions have included feedback and comments on books by Anthony Robbins and Wayne Dyer, to comments on Toastmasters International meetings and handwriting analysis. A good place for advice on self-improvement books, video and audio tapes, with feedback from others from a "try before you buy" perspective.

Sample Subjects:
Your Erroneous Zone/Speaking, nervousness/What's a Toastmasters meeting like?/Handwriting analysis

Homesteading Advice
misc.rural **M**

Tons of good advice for homesteaders, rural residents and other lovers of the country life. Back-to-the-land Net participants trade pointers on every aspect of country homestead living, repair and maintenance, making the Net an excellent way for people who live in the boonies to get good information fast. Topics discussed cover everything from which tractor to buy to poison ivy control, septic systems, wells and how to get rid of bats. A good and useful Information Age companion for anyone trying to make it in a country home.

Sample Subjects:
How to preserve fence posts/Garden tractor—best size?

Ultimate Miscellany
misc.misc **HI**

This quirky little category contains all the postings that don't fit anywhere else—everything from how to clean your bathtub to the perfect Irish Coffee recipe. A novel, interesting newsgroup with a lot of personality!

FAQ ▶ The following FAQs are available via FTP from RTFM.MIT.EDU in the directory:
pub/usenet/misc.misc:
USENET_Readership_summary_for_Aug_93_posted
USENET_Readership_summary_for_Sep_93_posted

Help Wanted & Careers
Employment Advertising on the Net

The Net features a handful of very active professional employment posting newsgroups, mostly focused on computer, electronics and engineering careers. There are, however, a growing number of help wanted listings now being posted for product development, sales and marketing and other less technically oriented positions—as well as a growing number of entry-level positions. So, if you're contemplating a job change, it'll be well worth it for you to check out the following employment opportunity newsgroups on the Net.

Help Wanted: Contract Programming
misc.jobs.contract **HI**

Ads for short-term contract software development jobs, technical writing jobs and specialized CAD operator positions.

FAQ ▶ The following FAQs are available via FTP from RTFM.MIT.EDU in the directory:
pub/usenet/misc.jobs.contract:
Misc.jobs.contract:_Frequently_Asked_Questions_(FAQs)
Misc.jobs.contract:_Text_of_USA_IRS_Section_1706;_the_Twenty_Questions
Misc.jobs.contract:_Welcome_to_misc.jobs.contract
Welcome_to_misc.jobs!

Job Hunting Tips
misc.jobs.misc **HI**

Job hunters help each other in this useful career discussion group by trading information on resume writing, interviewing, positioning work skills and general morale-boosting. Highly recommended for getting inside information on what it's like to work for specific companies, for career ideas and for interviewing tips.

Help Wanted: Job Postings
misc.jobs.offered **HI**

Programming, software, engineering and sales jobs, mostly posted by executive recruiters.

FAQ ▶ The following FAQs are available via FTP from RTFM.MIT.EDU in the directory:
pub/usenet/misc.jobs.offered:
***REMINDER:put_JOB-
TITLE_COMPANY_LOCATION_in_subject***
—>[l_m_6_29_93]——
>Read_BEFORE_posting:_stylistic_consensus

Help Wanted: Entry Level Positions
misc.jobs.offered.entry **M**

Help wanted listings for entry-level positions in high-tech companies, such as customer service reps, sales reps, part-time jobs, work-at-home jobs, etc. A good resource for recent college graduates and college students.

FAQ ▶ The following FAQ is available via FTP from RTFM.MIT.EDU in the directory:
pub/usenet/misc.jobs.offered.entry:
_READ_BEFORE_POSTING:__SPECIAL_FAQ_on_using_m.j.o.e

Help Wanted: Post Your Resume Online
misc.jobs.resumes **HI**

Post your own resumes online in this helpful employment newsgroup. Also includes requests for jobs wanted.

FAQ ▶ The following FAQs are available via FTP from RTFM.MIT.EDU in the directory:
pub/usenet/misc.jobs.resumes:
—>[l_m_2_4_91]—
>Read_BEFORE_posting:_Resume_Style_Consensus

Help Wanted: Computer Careers
biz.jobs.offered **HI**

Postings of computer software/hardware and electrical engineering positions, mostly from executive recruiting firms.

Electronic Classifieds
Merchandise Wanted/For Sale: General
misc.wanted **M**

Broad-based newsgroup for posting items or merchandise wanted, focusing mainly on computers, software and related accessories, with some for-sale items featured.

For Sale: Merchandise Wanted
misc.forsale.wanted **L**

Miscellaneous ad postings for a wide variety of items wanted by Netters: computers, peripherals, household items, stereos, airplane tickets, etc.

ClariNet News Services

Newsbytes Business & Industry News
clari.nb.business

Aerospace Industry & Companies
clari.tw.aerospace

Computer Industry, Applications & Developments
clari.tw.computers

Newsbytes New Product Reviews
clari.nb.review

Newsbytes New Developments & Trends
clari.nb.trends

Newsbytes Legal & Government Computer News
clari.nb.govt

Newsbytes General Computer News
clari.nb.general

Defense Industry Issues
clari.tw.defense

Stories Involving Universities & Colleges
clari.tw.education

Electronics Makers & Sellers
clari.tw.electronics

Environmental News, Hazardous Waste, Forests
clari.tw.environment

Disease, Medicine, Health Care, Sick Celebs
clari.tw.health

General Technical Industry Stories
clari.tw.misc

General Science Stories
clari.tw.science

NASA, Astronomy & Spaceflight
clari.tw.space

Regular Reports on Computer & Technology Stocks
clari.tw.stocks

Phones, Satellites, Media & General Telecom
clari.tw.telecom

Commodity News & Price Reports
clari.biz.commodity

Economic News & Indicators
clari.biz.economy

Economy Stories for Non U.S. Countries
clari.biz.economy.world

Business Feature Stories
clari.biz.features

Finance, Currency, Corporate Finance
clari.biz.finance

Earnings & Dividend Reports
clari.biz.finance.earnings

Personal Investing & Finance
clari.biz.finance.personal

Banks & Financial Industries
clari.biz.finance.services

News for Investors
clari.biz.invest

General Stock Market News
clari.biz.market

American Stock Exchange Reports & News
clari.biz.market.amex

Dow Jones NYSE Reports
clari.biz.market.dow

NYSE Reports
clari.biz.market.ny

NASDAQ Reports
clari.biz.market.otc

General Market Reports, S&P, Etc.
clari.biz.market.report

Mergers & Acquisitions
clari.biz.mergers

Other Business News
clari.biz.misc

Important New Products & Services
clari.biz.products

Top Business News
clari.biz.top

Breaking Business News
clari.biz.urgent

Chapter 4: Politics

Politics-oriented newsgroups satisfy the innate desire of many of us to stand up and speak our mind in the best tradition of the old-time New England town hall meeting.

> Very fond we were of Argument, and very desirous of confuting each other. Which disputacious Turn, by the way, is apt to become a very bad Habit, making People often extremely disagreeable in Company...and thence, besides souring and spoiling the Conversation, is productive of Disgusts and perhaps Enmities where you may have occasion for Friendship.
>
> **Benjamin Franklin**

The Online Equivalent of Talk Radio

When it comes to politics, talk, and MORE TALK about current controversies and news events, the Internet is a beehive of activity, promoting the same kind of grassroots participation heard on radio talk shows. Like many other things about the Internet, content found in politically oriented newsgroups tends to be both diverse and extreme: The views of participants always seem to polarize to either the extreme right or extreme left on any issue—moderation is *not* a virtue on the Internet. Given the fact that most Internet newsgroup participants are well read and highly intelligent, they also employ generous amounts of empirical reasoning, facts, factoids, refutations, points and counterpoints to buttress their views in debates on the Net.

The Internet also serves as soapbox and safe harbor for proponents of an almost infinite range of views spanning the political spectrum (and some going way, *way* beyond!). Some Net participants, having equal access to this new electronic medium, also tend to have a voice on the Internet that is far out of proportion to their actual numbers among the citizenry. Adding to all this the fact that many Net political discussions degrade to vicious personal attacks, and you have all the ingredients for one very spicy cyberspace gumbo!

Everyone Has an Opinion

The chaotic, freewheeling and hyper-participatory nature of political discussion groups on the Internet is, in the final analysis, the natural outgrowth of its existence as an online electronic communications *medium*. On the Net, anyone with a PC, an Internet account and an attitude has equal voice with any one of millions of similarly equipped Net participants.

There are no TV network anchors, newspaper editors or other filters to stand in the way of a participant's opinion and its instant projection to millions of other "viewers" on the Net. Conversely, each and every one of

Flamers

A small number of Net users seem to take offense at the slightest provocation—be it a too-simple question posed by a newsgroup novice, or a gentlemanly disagreement in a political discussion. The resulting message is usually a tirade of unbelievably grotesque personal insults flung onto some hapless Netter from a total stranger, or "flamer."

Flaming is an established and notorious part of Net Culture and the bane of the new user unfortunate enough to take the receiving end of a Flame War.

There's just something about the anonymity provided by a computer screen that turns some mild-mannered Net users into raging a**holes.

If *you* ever get flamed on the Net, just remember that your flamer is probably some computer geek who is *sorely* in need of a life.

So resist that urge to snap his little pencil neck: Tell the little wang to turn off his computer and shrug it off as one of those quaint little eccentricities of the Net.

the millions of "viewers" on the Internet has an equal opportunity to respond to any comment made in any newsgroup.

Despite their chaotic tendencies, online political discussion groups on the Internet mark the beginning of an entirely new computer-based *electronic medium* where opinions and dialogue are traded at lightning speed and people are freer than ever to express their own opinions—however extreme they might be.

Using political newsgroups on the Net gives you access to a virtually limitless spectrum of political opinions and viewpoints, many of which are not (or could never be) publishable in any current mass media channel.

Conservative and Liberal Politics

When it comes to the purely political, discussion groups on the Internet are highly polarized to the extreme right and extreme left of the political spectrum. Within this polarization lies a vast quantity of interesting, informative and highly contentious political discourse as staunch believers cross over to newsgroups reflecting the other sides of their political ideologies to do battle over the Net. For example, you'll see a few brave conservative souls crossing over to liberal-oriented groups to debate Marxist ideologies, and liberal ideologues engaging their conservative counterparts on the abortion issue in a conservative group. Debates in these groups go on endlessly, with online conversations between the same participants occurring over a period of days, weeks, even months, without resolution. These "threads" are a common occurrence on the Internet, since all may speak their mind freely without a referee to end the fight, or a TV host who breaks for a commercial.

Surprisingly enough, all this political "heat" does (from time to time) shed some light on political issues. Reading the intense back-and-forth on political discussion groups will give you new and useful facts to reinforce your own values and political points of view or interesting and eye-opening observations from an opposing viewpoint that may force you to buttress (or even rethink) your position.

Currently, the most popular political talk newsgroups on the Internet are the ones for fans of popular talk show host Rush Limbaugh and those for strong supporters of constitutional Second Amendment rights to keep and bear arms.

Closely behind the conservative groups are the Net groups used as information exchanges by members of environmental groups such as Greenpeace and the American Green Party.

Discussion Groups: The White House and the Clinton Presidency

If you have something you want to say about how President Clinton is doing, there's intense debate going on, right now, in a variety of political Internet newsgroups. When reviewed, participant's comments were overwhelmingly anti-Clinton, with surprisingly few defenders.

The White House has also discovered the Internet, establishing a handful of newsgroups that, disappointingly, have become mere online dumping grounds for canned White House press releases, speech transcripts and other Clinton/Gore boilerplate. Let's hope that some day we'll get a President who'll put a medium as promising as the Internet to better use for this country (but then again, given the low esteem many of us have for the government, maybe that's not such a good idea).

Conspiracies and Cover-Ups

Given the wide-open nature of the Internet, it's no surprise you'll find lively discussion newsgroups for many of the usual (and unusual) conspiracy theories, government cover-up speculations and other political notions that might be called "fringe."

You'll see a wide array of intense speculations on a variety of off-the-edge political issues and current events, from intense discussions of the ATF/FBI raid and subsequent firestorm of the Branch Davidian compound in Waco, Texas, to historical revisionist's attempts to deny the occurrence of the Holocaust, and that moldy old dog of the conspiracy buff's world—the JFK assassination. The material and comments found in these newsgroups can be informative—and occasionally provocative.

Let's just say there's a lot said here that you won't be reading in your hometown newspaper.

Political discussion groups on the Internet will provide you with a refreshing change of pace from the squishy soundbites, *USA Today*-style factoids, and political axes-to-grind that all too often pass for honest political discourse from today's media.

George Gilder thinks the Washington policy-wonks should wake up and pay attention to the real world. If they did, he says, they'd see that their vision of the future is here now. An electronic data highway already exists. "America's networking industry doesn't need fixing," Gilder, author of *Life After Television* and other tele-techno books, insists. Networks are the fastest-growing part of the computer industry and double their cost-effectiveness every year. "Although connecting government labs, libraries and researchers with supercomputers by cable is desirable, a massive government network is not," Gilder said in an interview. Let the marketplace of users "build" the network, as it already has done. "Networks are driven by public demand, shaped by human needs and rooted in a moral universe of growth through sharing. Experience creates the expertise to maintain and use it," Gilder says in a special article in *Forbes* magazine.

Dinah Zeiger, "Electronic Data Networks Already Positioned," *Denver Post* (6/6/93)

Conservative Politics

Rush Limbaugh Dittohead Fan Club

alt.rush-limbaugh **HI**

Group for fans (and foes) of America's most popular conservative talk show personality. Want to comment on Rush's comments for the day? Go here and you'll find raucous, intense debate on many of the issues addressed on Rush's daily radio show. Given the rather polarized nature of Net partici-pants (viewpoints expressed seem to be heavily weighed on both the extreme left and extreme right sides of the political spectrum), expect a tremendous volume of intense debate on both sides of any issue. Topics include daily summaries of Rush's broadcasts written by Net participants and lengthy, intense debates on issues brought up by Rush in his daily broadcast.

▲ *Rush Limbaugh, C-SPAN video capture image, Internet image file downloaded from* **wuarchive.wustl.edu**

Sample Subjects:
Summary Wednesday, 7-14-93/Snapple boycott/Clinton jokes list/Social insecurity

Libertarian & Conservative Comment and Debate

alt.politics.libertarian **HI**

Extremely busy online group featuring many discus-sions from a libertarian point of view relating both to current issues and general libertarian philosophy. Present-day political and economic news events and issues are discussed and solutions are proposed from a libertarian point of view, stressing the advantages of government detachment from peoples' lives and the benefits of allowing individuals to make their own choices. Consistent, high-quality discussions make this a must-read if you are a conservative, hold libertarian views or are a moderate who's grown tired of television soundbites.

Sample Subjects:
The trouble with Democracy/Historical crimes and grudges/Libertarians and the military/The State of the Union—2009

FAQ The following FAQ is available via FTP from RTFM.MIT.EDU in the directory:
pub/usenet/alt.politics.libertarian:
Libertarian_Platform_Change_Re_Drug_Legalization?

Gun Owner's Activist Group

talk.politics.guns **HI**

Overwhelmingly pro-gun Netters advance the cause of Second Amendment rights, providing a wide variety of background material of interest to anyone wanting to know more about gun control issues, facts and fallacies.

Conservative Values & Philosophy

alt.society.conservatism **M**

Conservatives on the Net engage in high-level discussions on conservatism in American society, politics and government. Topics include media distortion, gun control as despotism, censorship of conservative philosophy in the media and the Fairness Doctrine in radio and TV broadcasting.

Dan Quayle Fan Club

alt.fan.dan-quayle **M**

He's gone now, but his notoriety lingers on the Net. Discussion in this group is evenly divided between Dan Quayle ridicule and more serious conservative debate. Catch the very funny col-lected quotes of Vice President Quayle and other stories featured here. Since the Democrats took the White House, this group has also become another Net forum for conservative pro-and-con discussions.

Sample Subjects:
New Quayle quote list/Cartoon conservatives/Still worrying about the Panama Canal

Liberal Politics

Left-Wing Political Activism

alt.activism **HI**

Discussion group devoted to exchange of resources for local and national political activist groups. Includes spirited discussions of many political issues from a (mostly) left-wing perspective.

Sample Subjects:
Cold War/Jane Fonda/Pirate FM transmitters/Not guilty at Nuremberg/Bible and sexuality/Current job climate/Iraqi bombing: Unanswered questions

FAQ The following FAQs are available via FTP from RTFM.MIT.EDU in the directory:
pub/usenet/alt.activism:
GROUPS:_Anti_War-on-Drugs_Activists__List
Libertarian_FAQ:_Frequently_Asked_Questions
Libertarian_FAQ:_Organizations
Libertarian_FAQ:_World_s_Smallest_Political_Quiz
Libertarian_Frequently_Asked_Questions
Libertarian_Organizations
Libertarian_World_s_Smallest_Political_Quiz_[periodic_posting]

Left-Wing Political Debate

alt.activism.d **M**

The sister newsgroup to the **alt.activism** group, with

far-ranging debates and discussions of many current political issues from a mainly left-wing perspective.

Sample Subjects:
Saddam/No MSG/FBI trustworthiness/Homelessness discussion/Greenpeace budget/Elitism activism

Radical Left Politics & Dissent

alt.politics.radical-left **HI**

A discussion group for left-wing political activists consisting of largely pro-left comments and debates, interspersed with dissent from conservative posters. Also features press release materials from left-wing activist groups, some of which go *far* left.

Sample Subjects:
Roll over Stalin/Republicans vote against working people/Neo-Nazi ban

Resources for Environmentalists

alt.save.the.earth **L**

For hardcore environmental activists and related groups, this newsgroup is a gathering place for activists and others interested in various environmental issues—save the whales, rainforests, old growth forests, etc. Contains news releases from various activist groups, comments on recent current events and environmental news.

Sample Subjects:
Highway litter/Whaling, IWC rejection/Environmental justice

Green Party Political Discussions

alt.politics.greens **M**

A surprisingly active newsgroup for U.S. and international-based members of the Green Party. This pro-environmentalist political movement uses this newsgroup as a means to update Green Party events around the world and distribute other organizing information. Also used as a forum for debate on topics such as air pollution restrictions, energy conservation and genetic engineering in agriculture.

Pro-Marxism Discussion Group

alt.society.revolution **L**

Even though it's been three years since the fall of Communism, it seems the last remaining defenders of Marxism exist in and around U.S. universities using the Internet, which is, ironically, a product of U.S. Cold War military technology research. This newsgroup is a forum for Marxists who debate various theoretical points relating to socialism and how they may be applied to reforming capitalist society.

The White House

Clinton: Current Debate & Comments on Policies

alt.president.clinton **HI**

A spirited and busy roundtable discussion about President Clinton and his policies. A hotbed of dissent and debate, whether it's talking about Clinton's economic policies, gays in the military, his foreign policy or his handling of today's hottest issue. Participants in this newsgroup feel strongly about their positions and back them up with plenty of facts, statistics and references. When reviewed, sentiment in this group was running strongly against Clinton and his policies, but there were also a fair number of Clinton defenders. Whenever there's another controversy in the White House (and you can bet there will be), this will be the place you can go online to express your views.

Sample Subjects:
President's poll numbers/"Slick"/Small business taxes

Talk Back to the White House I

alt.politics.clinton **HI**

If you've got something you want to say to the president, this is probably the quickest way to say it. And, judging from the intensity and overwhelming anger of the comments posted to this discussion group, we would say President Clinton shouldn't be planning on another term in the White House. Always an active discussion group for comments and debate about today's hot political, economic and national issues with a lot of well-reasoned debate, most of it anti-Clinton. Includes postings of official Clinton statements, press releases and transcripts direct from the people in the White House basement. Given the spin doctoring by this White House, it's unlikely you will ever see President Clinton responding to "flamers" on the Net.

Sample Subjects:
If Clinton left everything alone/Transcript of flood response/Bombing Iraq is stupid

■ Politics

Talk Back to the White House II

alt.dear.whitehouse 🄷🄸

There has been a lot of talk recently by the Clinton White House about making itself accessible on the Internet. So far, though, this "interaction" has been little more than low-level functionaries in the White House basement posting canned press release announcements to various Internet newsgroups (some might say that a president has better things to do than spend time in front of a computer anyway). Even though this newsgroup does not live up to its title, it does contain spirited debate on Clinton policies from all points of view. Current topics have included: taxing the rich, role of government in our daily lives, legalization of drugs and user fees.

Sample Subjects:
Why not tax the rich?/Problems and solutions/ Suggestions/ Resource redirection

Clinton White House Info I

alt.politics.org.misc 🄻

Monopolized by canned, boilerplate press releases, transcripts and other propaganda from the Clinton White House.

Clinton White House Info II

alt.politics.reform 🄷🄸

Yet another newsgroup monopolized by Clinton White House propaganda in the form of press releases, briefing transcripts and other non-interactive boilerplate (at least that's how it was when we reviewed it). Includes sporadic comment from Perot volunteers.

Clinton Pro & Con Discussion & Comment Group

alt.politics.usa.misc 🄼

Despite its being used as yet another bucket for dissemination of Clinton White House press releases and other official flackery, this newsgroup does keep up some spirited discussions, pro and con, about current political topics. Discussions focus on current

Clinton White House policies, congressional legislation, tax increases and government economic programs.

Current Controversies

Political Discussion & Debate Groups

The Net is well known for its many extremely active political discussion groups covering most any imaginable topic. As a rule, Net participants are highly educated and extremely knowledgeable, providing voluminous facts to buttress their rhetoric under various Net political discussion groups. In addition to their smarts, Netters are also quite passionate in their individual beliefs, sometimes going well past the point of hot headedness. In Net political discussion groups, this often leads to *ad hominem* attacks and street-level insults which tend to degrade the debate, but certainly add to the fun (so don't say we didn't warn you!). If you're like most people, there's at least one political issue you feel strongly about—and on the Net there's a political newsgroup that's just right for you. So, if you're ready, strap on your flak jacket and wade into any of the following Net groups.

▲ *You-know-who, downloaded via Internet FTP from* **grind.isca.uiowa.edu**

Abortion: Scientific & Medical Debates

alt.abortion.inequity 🄼

A spirited and informative online forum on the abortion debate from a scientific and medical perspective.

Sample Subjects:
Abortion methods/Cranial decomposition/Fetal brain activity/Innocent life/Zygote=homo sapien abortion

Abortion: Discussions

talk.abortion **HI**

Highly charged pro and con abortion discussion and debate among opinionated Netters. Emotional debate in this group often spills over into personal attacks.

▲ *"Gender" computer graphic, downloaded from* **wuarchive.wustl.edu**

Racism, Sexism & Gay & Lesbian Controversies

alt.discrimination **HI**

Raging debates on current discrimination-related topics in the news, including racial and cultural discrimination, sexism, the *Sports Ilustrated* swimsuit issue, and whether or not a landlord should rent an apartment to a homosexual. Participants in this group make great efforts to define their terms and positions, with strong feeling displayed by both sides of any argument.

Sample Subjects:
Why whites attack affirmative action/*Sports Illustrated* discrimination

Gay & Lesbian Discussion Group

alt.politics.homosexuality **HI**

Pro-gay newsgroup for discussing various related political issues. Also features debate from those opposing the gay political agenda, but, since the majority of these newsgroup participants are gay, the balance of opinion (at least in this group) goes their way most of the time.

Sample Subjects:
Gays in the military/Gay and lesbian BBS/Gays: What will Clinton do?

Sexism, Gay Rights & Feminism Debate

alt.politics.sex **M**

Might be worth a look for those interested in engaging in discussions on issues involving sexism, gay rights, and feminism or other related issues.

Environmental Activism

talk.environment **M**

Netters discuss current environmental news stories, argue various sides of environmental policy questions and exchange ideas and resources for environmental action, local protest and high-tech environmental cleanup options.

Pesticide-Free Farming & Alternative Agriculture

alt.sustainable.agriculture **M**

Theoretical and academic discussions on the concept of sustainable agriculture, a farming concept that promotes environmentally sound growing practices, such as farming without pesticides, natural plant selection and other farming methods. Recent discussions have included genetic plant engineering, bovine growth hormone and European agricultural policies.

Political Debates: Right Vs. Left

alt.politics.usa.republican **M**

Spirited conservative/liberal debate. Current discussion topics have included global warming, Patrick Buchanan's culture war, and the teaching of controversial subjects in public schools. Although the discussions tend to get personal here from time to time (at least the personal attacks appear to be well thought out!) this would be a good group for those who like to debate the usual right-vs.-left political issues.

Sample Subjects:
Global Warming/Vermont Public Radio News/ Population growth/Culture war

Current Events & Political Talk

talk.politics.misc **HI**

Covers a wide spectrum of current political discussion issues in the news, incorporating many topics and subjects from other **talk.politics** newsgroups.

More Political Discussions

bit.listserv.politics **HI**

Yet another political discussion group on the Net; however, this one is less interesting and diverse than many other discussion groups and (when reviewed) was dominated by endless flames between Turks and Armenians in their eternal blood feud.

Hot Debates on Political Correctness

alt.politics.correct **HI**

Ongoing debates about political correctness, with comments evenly divided both left and right. Debate topics range from discussions of racism in the 1990s, sexism, population control and censorship issues. Participants sometimes make too fine a point of things in an attempt to support their arguments, but they *are* passionate about their views.

Sample Subjects:
Population growth/Culture war/Laws and norms

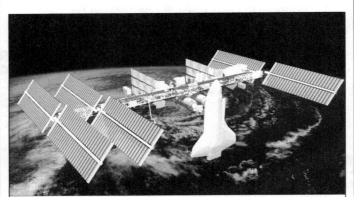

▲ *Artist rendering of space station "Freedom," downloaded from* **wuarchive.wustl.edu**

Space Program Political Discussions
talk.politics.space **HI**

Very active and interesting discussion group on the political and technical aspects of the U.S. space program. Discussion topics have included the test flights of the DC-X VTOL rocket, economics of various rocket launch vehicles, congressional funding probabilities for various individual space programs and speculation on the future of the U.S. space program. The more technically oriented Netters in this group can't help throwing in a fair number of their own pet space-tech ideas, too.

Sample Subjects:
DC-X...help us save it!/Why have humans in space?/SETI project funding

Political Theory
talk.politics.theory **HI**

An intellectual newsgroup with high-level discussions and comments on "big picture" political issues: school vouchers, libertarian theory, the U.S. educational system and more, featuring well-reasoned analyses with detailed, academic explanations.

Talk about Economics, Taxes & Clinton
alt.politics.economics **HI**

Another political discussion group specializing in comments on economic issues of the day. Includes discussion of popular business/economic books and their theories, Clinton economic policies, taxation and the deficit.

Sample Subjects:
Equality and coercion/How many homeless are there?

Politics: Talk and Organization
alt.politics.elections **M**

Organized to help people in the process of running for political office, this newsgroup has recently been co-opted by spillover from other political debate groups. For example, recent comments on this newsgroup have been mostly about Rush Limbaugh's opinions. However, before and during elections, we suspect this newsgroup really comes into its own.

Politics & Media Talk
alt.politics.media **L**

When we reviewed this newsgroup, we found that it was completely monopolized by a heated discussion of revisionist attempts to deny the Holocaust, which, while an important historical and emotional issue, seemed to be somewhat irrelevant to this newsgroup's charter: to discuss the media's handling of various political news and issues.

Ross Perot Fan Club
alt.politics.perot **HI**

A clearinghouse for those involved in the United We Stand America party backed by Ross Perot. Background information, semi-official pronouncements, schedule postings and other inside information posted by UWSA members and other assorted "Perotistas." Also features occasional comments and debates on Perot political and economic opinions.

Sample Subjects:
Grassroots/Perot on Education/Perot doomed?/UWSA brief update

Healthcare Policy
talk.politics.medicine **M**

Informative discussion and debate on U.S. healthcare policy and proposed healthcare reform, with comparisons to healthcare systems in other countries and discussions of healthcare costs, the medical establishment and health insurance issues.

Drugs, Politics & the Law
talk.politics.drugs **M**

A mixture of pro-illegal drug legalization and libertarian discussion of current FDA policies relating to prescription drugs and vitamins.

Soviet Politics
talk.politics.soviet **HI**

Russian students discuss and debate major political and nationalist issues in their home country.

▲ *Student facing down tanks, Tiananmen Square massacre, Beijing, China, 1989, downloaded from Asian photo archives via Internet FTP from* **sunsite.unc.edu**

Asian & Indian Politics & Culture

alt.culture.us.asian-indian **HI**

An active newsgroup whose participants (mainly Asian and Indian students) discuss a wide range of political and cultural topics.

Sample Subjects:
South Asian immigrant films/Stranger in a strange land/ Western NY's first Hindu temple

China & Asian Politics

talk.politics.china **HI**

Chinese students studying in U.S. universities discuss the latest political events and government actions in China, Hong Kong and other Asian countries.

Mideast Politics

talk.politics.mideast **HI**

Highly charged discussions among Arabs and Jews concerning Israeli-Palestinian relations, peace in the Middle East and first-hand news from the region.

Censorship, Media & Free Speech Debates

alt.censorship **HI**

The freedom of expression found on the Net makes its participants extremely sensitive to any attempts at online censorship: Participants in this discussion group do battle on both sides of the censorship issue on a variety of current topics of the day. Censorship issues discussed relate not only to Net content, but also to recent newspaper editorials, other online services, and state/local First Amendment-related news items. This newsgroup is living proof of one of the things the Internet does best: provide a forum for opinionated people to debate the topics on which they

hold strong opinions. One of this group's side benefits is that it shows you how Net users think about various important and evolving online network censorship issues.

Sample Subjects:
Letter to the Oregonian/Anti-gay rights measures/My view on kiddie porn/BBC porn documentary/Reclaiming the airwaves

FAQ▶ The following FAQ is available via FTP from RTFM.MIT.EDU in the directory:
pub/usenet/alt.censorship:
Libernet:_an_electronic_forum

Freedom of the Press on the Net

alt.comp.acad-freedom.talk **HI**

A busy newsgroup featuring many comments on academic censorship, freedom, and communications issues related to computer networks, specifically the Internet. Focuses on current controversies, newspaper media reportage and the academic policies of various universities concerning censorship on the Internet. Includes discussions on sexual harrasment online, newsgroup posting policies, and other issues relating to freedom of expression on the Net.

Sample Subjects:
Censorship/Computer lab sexual harrasment/ Online advocate

International Development

bit.listserv.devel-l **L**

Resource group for government and academic specialists in infrastructure development in Third World countries. Participants exchange ideas relating to sustainable growth, Internet access to Third World countries and philosophies of global development.

Peace Corps Volunteer Talk Group

bit.org.peace-corps **L**

Present and former Peace Corps volunteers provide inside advice to students interested in joining. Subjects include languages, training, locations and overall Peace Corps policy discussions.

Prisons & Criminal Justice: What Should We Do?

alt.prisons **M**

Discussion and debate on the U.S. prison system, crime and just punishment. Includes brief references to publications and groups organized by and for prison inmates, but no direct participation by prison inmates, since it appears obvious that prison inmates do not yet have access to the Internet (and, given

▲ *U.S. troops on patrol in Vietnam and* ▶ *Huey helicopter discharging troops at Vietnam landing zone, both downloaded from* **wuarchive.wustl.edu**

recent examples of inmates committing wire fraud just by using prison pay phones, it's probably *not* a good idea to give them online access to the Net, either!) The tenor of the discussion here ranges from Ghengis Khan conservative ("commit three crimes and we'll fry ya") to bleeding-heart liberal.

Sample Subjects:
Prison legal news/Age-old debate/Prison overcrowding

History, Policy & War

Historical Controversy Discussion Group

soc.history **HI**

Intense debates featuring discussion on historical events from World War I to World War II. Current controversies include holocaust revision attempts, World War I propaganda and military history.

Fight Back Against Historical Revisionism

alt.revisionism **HI**

Group dedicated to discussing, revealing, debating and debunking *ex post facto* attempts to revise historical events. Oriented toward debunking recent writings that claim the Holocaust did not occur. Other topics include media bias, the Middle East, religious beliefs and discussions of background information on writers who promote such controversial revisionist theories.

Sample Subjects:
Control of the media/The Germans of America/Not guilty at Nuremburg

FAQ ▶ The following FAQs are available via FTP from RTFM.MIT.EDU in the directory:
pub/usenet/alt.revisionism:

```
HOLOCAUST_FAQ:_Auschwitz-Birkenau:_Layman_s_Guide_(1_2)
HOLOCAUST_FAQ:_Auschwitz-Birkenau:_Layman_s_Guide_(2_2)
HOLOCAUST_FAQ:_Operation_Reinhard:_A_Layman_s_Guide_(1_2)
HOLOCAUST_FAQ:_Operation_Reinhard:_A_Layman_s_Guide_(2_2)
HOLOCAUST_FAQ:_The__Leuchter_Report__(1_2)
HOLOCAUST_FAQ:_The__Leuchter_Report__(2_2)
```

Law Enforcement Discussion Group

alt.law-enforcement **L**

Originally intended for use by police and other law enforcement officers, this group is dominated by participants (most of whom do not seem to be in the law enforcement field) engaging in high-level philosophical discussions on gun control, the role of police in the community, constitutional rights, etc.

Military History Discussions

alt.war **M**

Students of military history discuss past wars, battles, armies and strategies and speculate on current conflicts in the news. Topics also range to discussions of hypothetical insurrections by private citizens against tyrannical governments, personal firearms and the role of the military in a democracy.

Sample Subjects:
American strafing of Japanese/History Army Airborne 82nd/Armed insurrection

Vietnam War Discussions

alt.war.vietnam **L**

Discussion of various aspects of U.S. involvement in Vietnam during the 1960s and 1970s, and current U.S. position toward Vietnam and Vietnam military history. Also features comments between former Vietnamese nationals and Vietnam vets.

Sample Subjects:
More questions on tactics/Escape from tyranny/A good book/Napalm

Civil War Discussions
alt.war.civil.usa **M**

Civil War buffs engage in active and interesting discussion of Civil War battles, political issues and military/political lessons learned. Book reviews and current political issues relating to slavery and the Confederacy have also been discussed.

Sample Subjects:
CSA and slavery/Questions about slaves in free states/ UDC and the Flag

Conspiracies & Cover-Ups

Government Conspiracies, Cover-Ups & Theories
alt.conspiracy **HI**

An active, lively and informative online discussion group focusing on alleged present-day conspiracies. Current discussions have included the assault by the ATF on the Branch Davidian compound in Waco,

▲ *JFK in Dallas, seconds before his assassination, November 22, 1963, image file downloaded via Internet FTP from* **ftp.netcom.com**

Texas, including posted letters written by Branch Davidian survivors now being held in jail. Also includes intriguing, thought-provoking firsthand accounts alleging conspiracy and/or other restrictions on personal freedom. The overall tone of this group is decidedly libertarian: If you feel your personal liberty is increasingly under threat by your government, you will find much of interest here. Also includes the usual conspiracy theory discussion on JFK, AIDS, etc.

Sample Subjects:
Waco and the intimidated press/Is AIDS manmade/ Judgement day for America

FAQ ▶ The following FAQs are available via FTP from RTFM.MIT.EDU in the directory:
pub/usenet/alt.conspiracy:
HOLOCAUST_FAQ:_Willis_Carto_&_The_Institute_for_Historical_Review_(1_2)
HOLOCAUST_FAQ:_Willis_Carto_&_The_Institute_for_Historical_Review_(2_2)

JFK Assassination Conspiracy Talk
alt.conspiracy.jfk **M**

The event occurred over thirty years ago, but the debate continues. Did Oswald act alone? Was the JFK assassination a CIA plot? Maybe these questions will never be answered conclusively, but they're debated endlessly in this popular Net group. Discussions, comments and debate on recently published JFK assassination books, postings of new theories, observations on events surrounding the JFK assassination and a clearinghouse for exchange of other newly published information. Postings are often thoughtful and always interesting. A valuable resource for those interested in JFK conspiracy theories, since there is also a high volume of JFK assassination information stored on Internet computers, such as film clips, book and radio program transcripts, etc.

Sample Subjects:
Warren commission reports/LBJ role in conspiracy/Rethinking Camelot/Deadly secrets

A Little Revolution Now & Then Is a Good Thing
alt.politics.usa.constitution **M**

Spirited and decidedly right-wing discussion group oriented toward Second Amendment issues relating to private ownership of firearms, definition and discussion of militias, and the present and potential future oppression of individuals by the federal government. Ample discussion on gun ownership rights, contemporary citations, court cases and writings related to concepts of individual rights and the power of the citizenry as set forth in the Constitution. Discussions on how the original intent of the Constitution and Bill of Rights has been corrupted by liberals and the federal government and speculation on citizen-inspired means to restore true representative government by overthrow of the current power structure. Not for the fainthearted, this group does raise many intriguing issues.

Sample Subjects:
Police state advocates are on the move/Feds tried to silence lone voice/The second amendment

Politics

▲ *American flag photo, downloaded via Internet FTP from* **wuarchive.wustl.edu**

Discussions of U.S. Government Oppression

alt.society.civil-liberties **M**

Discussions of current news events and other issues relating to real and perceived infringements on individual freedoms. Participants express their views on the news of the day and, when reviewed, were talking about Waco and the Branch Davidians, and the child molester in Washington state who was burned out of his home. Participants also share their tips and advice for protecting personal privacy and discuss "big picture" views on whether or not society is becoming less protective of individual civil liberties.

Sample Subjects:
Waco video/Felons on Fargo, North Dakota, Police Department/Pro-gun local op-ed piece

ATF Watch Group

alt.politics.org.batf **L**

Net participants engage in both sides of heated online debates concerning abuses by the Bureau of Alcohol, Tobacco and Firearms and subsequent threats to individual liberty. Participants discuss recent news items and policy concerning issues of improper assault by government law enforcement organizations on cult groups and investigations, including comments on the recent high profile debacles by federal law enforcement at Waco and in the Randy Weaver case. Given the highly individualistic and freedom-loving nature of Net participants, you can expect discussions here to be overwhelming anti-ATF.

Anarchist's Debate Group

alt.society.anarchy **M**

In-depth discussions on the subject of anarchism and its related effects: private property ownership and medical care in an anarchist society, anarchy versus capitalism, etc. Discussions in this group always tend to boil down to age-old conservative-versus-liberal debates, since the proponents of anarchy in this group have a decidedly left-wing/borderline Marxist attitude. Think of this group as the other end of the political spectrum from the **alt.libertarian** newsgroup.

Sample Subjects:
We won the cold war/What are the rules/Anarchism and property rights

Political Fringe Discussions

alt.revolution.counter **M**

A very strange newsgroup: Depending on when you access it, this group swings widely both right and left, and is home to many far-out theories, off the wall political views and odd religious beliefs. Recent topics have included discussions on neo-paganism.

Rumor Central

talk.rumors **M**

Want to hear a juicy rumor? Better yet, want to start one? **talk.rumors** is a slightly out-of-control newsgroup where Netters dish the dirt on the latest speculations of the hour—everything from who's gay in Hollywood to satirical hoaxes (is Pepsi *really* developing an edible container for its products?).

"What If" History Scenarios

alt.history.what-if **M**

Net history buffs provide extensive factual detail and well-argued support on a variety of historical speculations. What if the Japanese attack on Pearl Harbor had failed? What if the Confederacy had won the Civil War? Could Italy have existed as a Papal State in the 1930s? Participants in this group take great relish in showing off their personal knowledge of their own pet historical events and speculations; such attention to detail and extensive documentation makes this group not only enjoyable to read, but very educational as well.

FAQ The following FAQs are available via FTP from RTFM.MIT.EDU in the directory:
pub/usenet/alt.history.what-if:
LIST:_Alternate_History_Stories_(1_7,_780_lines)
LIST:_Alternate_History_Stories_(1_8,_825_lines)
LIST:_Alternate_History_Stories_(2_7,_780_lines)
LIST:_Alternate_History_Stories_(2_8,_825_lines)
LIST:_Alternate_History_Stories_(3_7,_780_lines)
LIST:_Alternate_History_Stories_(3_8,_825_lines)
LIST:_Alternate_History_Stories_(4_7,_780_lines)
LIST:_Alternate_History_Stories_(4_8,_825_lines)
LIST:_Alternate_History_Stories_(5_7,_780_lines)
LIST:_Alternate_History_Stories_(5_8,_825_lines)
LIST:_Alternate_History_Stories_(6_7,_675_lines)
LIST:_Alternate_History_Stories_(6_8,_725_lines)
LIST:_Alternate_History_Stories_(7_7,_850_lines)
LIST:_Alternate_History_Stories_(7_8,_950_lines)
LIST:_Alternate_History_Stories_(8_8,_110_lines)

Chapter 5: Support Groups, Culture, Religion & Philosophy

While the Internet represents a triumph of the individual, giving each of us a direct channel to millions of others, use of the Net by specific social interest groups is also a strong attraction.

Advantages of Internet Online Social Newsgroups

Computer networking and online discussion groups are especially suited to use by special-interest groups. First, participants in these groups are bound together by their shared interest or need. Second, the instantaneous nature of online discussion groups means that messages posted to that group may be read or responded to at the user's convenience—no meetings to attend or deadlines to meet. Third, online group interaction is, at each participant's option, fully anonymous, giving each user the opportunity to share views, thoughts or feelings that might not be shared so easily around a meeting table. Socially oriented groups on the Internet also have the unique and important advantage of being wide open to potential joiners from anywhere in the world.

The Internet's social, affinity and support discussion groups run the full range of human emotions and social involvement, from online discussion groups oriented toward specific professional occupations and friendly chat groups for foreign nationals and students, to serious and emotion-filled support groups for childhood sexual abuse survivors.

Social and Affinity Groups

A useful, eclectic and interesting collection of social and affinity-oriented newsgroups are here on the Net. There are groups for would-be novelists, military veterans, Quakers, bikers, feminists and Boy Scouts—each providing participants with valuable tips, information and contacts, plus the benefit of informal online conversation and camaraderie that can be shared only by those having a common interest.

Chris Glover switched on his computer Thanksgiving Eve and tapped into a global communications network called Internet. He noticed a message from a University of Denver student who was threatening to kill herself.

When he realized it was not a joke, Mr. Glover spent two hours communicating with the woman from his town house in Fredericksburg (MD). The woman told him she was diabetic and was taking a new medicine but thought something might be wrong with it. Others from around the country then got involved as well, he said.

The woman eventually told Mr. Glover she was in the computer lab in the campus's engineering building, and he was able to call campus security around 9 p.m. They found her, unharmed, a short time later, and she is now getting medical care.

"College Student Stops Suicide Via Computer," News Item, *The Washington Times* (11/27/93)

■Support Groups, Culture, Religion & Philosophy

She was pregnant with her first child and especially nervous one morning, so Mikki Barry decided to chat with a few other expectant mothers. After plugging her portable computer into a telephone socket near her bed, Barry typed a few words and waited for a connection. Then a comforting sight flashed across her computer screen: an electronic "bulletin board," where mothers-to-be exchange concerns and ideas. "I would write in and say: 'Oh, gee, I'm feeling awful. Is this normal?'" And they would write back and say, "Yes, of course, you're fine," or, "Call your doctor," said Barry, 32, a lawyer from Great Falls.

"Computer-Friendly Homes Increasing," Robert O'Harrow Jr., *The Washington Post* (12/27/92)

Online Support and Counseling Groups

An array of serious discussion groups are available on the Internet to address a wide range of serious emotional, physical, medical and psychological problems, crises and challenges. There are online Internet support groups specifically devoted to adult victims of child sexual abuse and their spouses, groups for co-dependency and rape victims, father's rights in child custody divorce cases and couples wishing to adopt. These online groups allow participants to lend moral and emotional support to one another. Participants who are currently in crisis with a particular emotional, psychological, medical or addictive problem are often helped along by other online participants who have experienced—and overcome—the same challenges in their own lives.

Since these newsgroups often deal with emotionally charged, life-and-death personal issues, they are free of the clutter and triviality that sometimes plagues other newsgroups on the Internet. These groups have an extremely serious purpose and exist to provide troubled individuals with the means to overcome their problems.

Cultural Talk and News

The Internet contains a large number of social groups devoted to residents of foreign countries around the world and expatriates abroad. These groups are a handy medium of exchange for home-country talk, news, discussions, banter and cultural information, providing a useful base for residents of a particular country, no matter where else they are in the world. If you're planning to travel abroad, these cultural groups can often provide you with interesting and unique travel advice for your destination country, making them a useful inside information supplement to the various tourism and travel-related newsgroups on the Net.

Religion and Philosophy Discussion Groups

Newsgroups covering the entire spectrum of religious beliefs and philosophies attract thousands of serious, intense believers who engage in conversation and debate in these areas. Although discussion threads in a few of these philosophical newsgroups can become tedious at times, participants do conduct their discussions with intelligence, grace and dignity.

▲ *"UPC Bar Code Conspiracy" graphic, downloaded via Internet FTP from* **wuarchive.wustl.edu**

Social & Affinity Groups

Modern Folklore Newsgroups on the Net
alt.folklore.urban **HI**

Do albino alligators lurk in the New York City subway system? Would a mouse be killed in a fall down a mineshaft? Does tapping a Coke can keep it from overflowing? Join over 60,000 Net users who contribute, research, refute and document the odd myths and urban folklore we all know and love. Netters submit their own personal urban legends (UL's) for review by die-hard amateur Net sleuths, who exhaustively research and disprove or document the wide array of off beat stories and supposed facts that many accept as true. In **alt.folklore.urban**, Netters relate and discuss odd stories heard from friends or in the office—stories like "Are there really microscopic spider eggs in bubble gum?" Other Netters then take turns discussing, researching and either proving or disproving the speculation. The urban folklore category has proven so popular it has spawned four other specialized (and just as active) newsgroups—**alt.folklore.college**, **alt.folklore.computers**, **alt.folklore.ghost-stories** and **alt.folklore.science**. **alt.folklore.science** features speculations on such topics as the "Full Moon Phenomenon" (are we more accident-prone during a full moon?) and how sailors are killed in submarine accidents. In **alt.folklore.ghost-stories**, Netters speculate on ghost sightings, ghost tours and ghost

legends. In **alt.folklore.computers**, aging hackers fondly reminisce about vintage hacking gear and "incompetent users." Netters relate their personal college stories and hi-jinks in **alt.folklore.college**, with stories about Animal House-style fraternities, cafeteria tray tobogganning and classroom antics. Urban folklore groups are the Internet equivalent of stories told 'round the campfire and promote a sense of Net community among the thousands of people who use them. So go ahead and post your own personal stories or overheard modern-day legends to any of these groups; or just enjoy reading the voluminous postings added everyday.

Sample Subjects:
666, The Bible and the UPC bar code/ Computer problems with 1999-2000/ Velcro and the space program/Apocalypse real soon now/The origins of religions/

FAQ▶ The following FAQ is available via FTP from RTFM.MIT.EDU in the directory:
pub/usenet/alt.folklore.urban:
alt.folklore.urban__Frequently_Asked_Questions

Hackers Talk Group
alt.hackers **L**

Hackers with aliases like Craig Powderkeg DeFo, Sean Captain Napalm and The Prophet trade stories and information on breaking into networked computer systems and more innocent (and definitely more legitimate) computer pursuits.

FAQ▶ The following FAQ is available via FTP from RTFM.MIT.EDU in the directory:
pub/usenet/alt.hackers:
(17aug93)_Welcome_to_alt.hackers_-_automated_posting.

Online Singles & Pen Pals
soc.penpals **HI**

An active and fun-loving group for Netters wishing to link up with pen pals via Internet electronic mail. The tone runs from the innocent to the risque—so don't say you haven't been warned.

FAQ▶ The following FAQs are available via FTP from RTFM.MIT.EDU in the directory:
pub/usenet/soc.penpals:
Email-Pal_Address_Book_[non-US_list][A-M]
Email-Pal_Address_Book_[non-US_list][N-U]
Email-Pal_Address_Book_[US_list][A-M]
Email-Pal_Address_Book_[US_list][N-W]
Email-Pal_Address_Book_[US_list][N-Z]

Relationships: Men & Women
soc.couples **HI**

The battle of the sexes continues online in this

popular Net group: In characteristically intense and obsessive Net fashion, participants discuss all aspects of relationships from their own male and female points of view. Participants also provide advice on specific relationship situations posted by others on the Net. Typical discussion topics include: nice guys versus flashy guys—who wins?, women who give backrubs, and romantic fantasies. If you have a problem in a relationship, a question posted here would provide you with dozens of messages to wade through.

Missing Person Finder
soc.net-people **M**

Looking for a long-lost college classmate? A former co-worker who moved to another city? This intriguing newsgroup contains numerous inquiries from Netters searching for long-lost contacts and old friends, announcements of college reunions and information on how to locate a particular person's Internet electronic mail address.

FAQ ▶ The following FAQ is available via FTP from RTFM.MIT.EDU in the directory:
pub/usenet/soc.net-people:
Tips_on_using_soc.net-people_[l.m._10_04_92]

Human Rights Discussion Group
soc.rights.human **HI**

Current news announcements from various human rights organizations (including Amnesty International) and other activist groups, plus a small number of discussions from Netters around the world concerning human rights issues and human rights abuses in their home countries.

Quaker & Peace Activist Group
soc.religion.quaker **M**

Discussion, comment and announcement group for Quakers, pacifists and peace activist groups such as Food Not Bombs. Contains information on recent protest announcements and activities, methods of peaceful civil disobedience, help for the homeless and pacifist ideology.

FAQ ▶ The following FAQ is available via FTP from RTFM.MIT.EDU in the directory:
pub/usenet/soc.religion.quaker:
soc.religion.quaker_Answers_to_Frequently_Asked_Questions

Women's Issues
soc.women **HI**

A more generalized discussion and comment group covering an expanded range of women's issues and going beyond the usual fare on the Net.

Medical Librarians
bit.listserv.medlib-l **M**

Useful resources, information and professional advice for information specialists at medical and hospital libraries. Librarians exchange references on specific medical article requests, tips on computer software/hardware and information printed in medical journals and other medical publications.

Reference Librarians
bit.listserv.libref-l **L**

Reference librarians on the Net from universities and corporations talk shop on library information technology, software and other products and services for information retrieval in libraries.

Librarians Talk Shop
bit.listserv.circplus **M**

Although the purpose of this newsgroup is to provide a place for librarians to discuss the ins and outs of running a library (like how much to charge for photocopying), a sneaky, lazy information-seeker might want to post a research question here for an answer from a friendly, charitable librarian on the Net.

Librarians Resource Exchange Group
soc.libraries.talk **M**

Informal talk group for librarians interested in exchanging reference tips and library management advice, along with some light hearted chitchat.

School Libraries Association Group
bit.listserv.slart-l **L**

Discussions among SLA members concerning various aspects of running school libraries.

Conferences, Workshops & Symposia
news.announce.conferences **HI**

Technical-oriented newsgroup, mostly for academics, containing postings of upcoming scientific/technical/computing conferences, background information, dates, etc.

Writer's Talk Group
misc.writing **HI**

A social, friendly and informational group for moonlighting and freelancing writers, serving as an online coffee klatsch. Writers discuss issues important to them: how to make money writing, good markets for writers and complaints/problems that only writers know.

FAQ ▶ The following FAQs are available via FTP from RTFM.MIT.EDU in the directory:
pub/usenet/misc.writing:
misc.writing_FAQ
misc.writing_FAQ:_Recommended_Reading
the_Internet_Writer_Resource_Guide

Computers & Writing

bit.listserv.mbu-l **M**

Close-knit discussion group for tech writers and others interested in computer-oriented writing, hypertext and hypermedia for academics in university settings.

Technical Writers Tips & Resources

bit.listserv.techwr-l **HI**

This group is a must for all technical writers, providing invaluable desktop publishing software information and how-to tips. Net participants and professional tech writers at computer and software companies also provide sound advice on tech writing employment opportunities, freelancing and breaking into the tech writing field, as well as useful tech writing style and publication-structuring advice.

Word Lovers' & Linguists' Group

bit.listserv.words-l **M**

English and Latin language lovers converge to discuss word meanings and engage in comical inside language conversations on the Net.

Farmer's News & Info Group

alt.agriculture.misc **L**

Discussions of current farm and agricultural techniques, government programs, crops and recent news events relating to farming and agriculture.

Sample Subjects:
Milk prices/Honey support programs/Farming on life-support/Evolution of farming/Fruit crops agriculture

Kids School Pen Pals Group

csn.ml.kids **M**

Fun group that lets elementary and junior high school students at schools on the Net write to other online pen pals via school computers. Also accessible from any online service providing Internet access.

Emergency Rescue Services Professionals Group

misc.emerg-services **M**

Discussion group for news, topics and resources of interest to Emergency Medical Technicians (EMTs) and other volunteer or professional rescue and emergency medical service providers. Covers EMT procedures, new equipment, training, etc.

Military Service News

soc.veterans **M**

Extensive and detailed daily reprints of Army, Air Force, Navy, NATO and other news and press release announcements from military/government organizations. Also includes text files from the Veterans Administration concerning veterans assistance programs.

Scouting Online

rec.scouting **HI**

Newsgroups used by Cub Scouts, Boy Scouts, Eagle Scouts and other scouting organizations around the world. Features info on major scouting events, activities, scout pen pals and computer merit badge.

FAQ ▶ The following FAQs are available via FTP from RTFM.MIT.EDU in the directory: **pub/usenet/rec.scouting:**
rec.scouting_FAQ#1:_Skits,_Yells_&_Creative_Campfires_(1_2)
rec.scouting_FAQ#1:_Skits,_Yells_&_Creative_Campfires_(2_2)
rec.scouting_FAQ__#0:_Welcome_to_rec.scouting_-_General_questions
rec.scouting_FAQ__#2:_Sco
rec.scouting_FAQ__#2:_Scouting_around_the_World
rec.scouting_FAQ__#3:_Games_(1_3)
rec.scouting_FAQ__#3:_Games_(2_3)
rec.scouting_FAQ__#3:_Games_(3_3)
rec.scouting_FAQ__#4:_Unit_Administration
rec.scouting_FAQ__#5:_Silk_Screen_Techniques
rec.scouting_FAQ__#6:_Cub_Scout_Leader_Hints
rec.scouting_FAQ__#7:_Fund_Raising_Ideas
rec.scouting_FAQ__#8:_BSA_GSUSA_official_policies_(gays_in_scouting)

▲ *Boy Scout symbol, image file downloaded via Internet FTP from* **wuarchive.wustl.edu**

Illuminati & Freemasonry Talk Group

alt.illuminati **M**

Netters discuss secret societies such as the Illuminati, Masons, etc. Lots of speculation and mis-information, some of which is corrected from time to time by members of various Masonic groups.

Literary Discussion Group

bit.listserv.literary **M**

Highly intelligent discussion on classic novels, authors, thinkers and poetry, with many specialized Net participants who are knowledgeable in their specific literary interests. Discussion usually consists of long, analytical threads relating to a single novel or other literary work.

Motorcycle Riding Group

ne.motorcycles **M**

Die-hard riders talk about bikes, upcoming rides, recent accidents and other chitchat in this small newsgroup.

Historian's Discussion Group

bit.listserv.history **L**

Resource group for historians and other academics for exchanging research information and addressing various administrative matters related to historical societies and/or organizations.

Feminism Discussion Group

soc.feminism **HI**

Discussions of feminist theory, experiences and opinions for those wishing to learn more about feminism. Discussion and direction is mostly from a left-wing perspective.

FAQ ▶ The following FAQs are available via FTP from RTFM.MIT.EDU in the directory:
pub/usenet/soc.feminism:
soc.feminism_Information
soc.feminism_References_(part_1_of_3)
soc.feminism_References_(part_2_of_3)
soc.feminism_References_(part_3_of_3)
soc.feminism_Resources
soc.feminism_Terminologies

Feminism from the Male Perspective

soc.men **HI**

Largely pro-male discussion group (with a smaller number of female/feminist participants) debating the issues of sexism, men's rights and feminism.

GayNet

bit.listserv.gaynet **L**

Compilation of voluminous messages, news articles, observations and miscellany of interest to gays and lesbians.

Bisexuality

soc.bi **HI**

Online conversations and other discussions on issues of interest to bisexuals.

FAQ ▶ The following FAQs are available via FTP from RTFM.MIT.EDU in the directory:
pub/usenet/soc.bi:
Bisexual_Resource_List_(monthly_posting)
soc.bi_FAQ

Gay & Lesbian Talk

soc.motss **HI**

Another gay and lesbian discussion group.

FAQ ▶ The following FAQs are available via FTP from RTFM.MIT.EDU in the directory:
pub/usenet/soc.motss:
Gay_and_Lesbian_BBS_List_-_July_1993

Support Groups

Help & Support for Adult Victims of Child Abuse

alt.abuse-recovery **L**

A sensitive and serious online discussion and support group for people overcoming childhood and present-day psychological and physical abuse.

Help for Adult Victims of Child Sexual Abuse

alt.sexual.abuse.recovery **HI**

Active, serious, helpful group for survivors of childhood sexual abuse. Includes many serious participants who do their best to provide meaningful support and good advice. Provides a healing service by making the most of the anonymous nature of using the Net.

Sample Subjects:
My friend anger/Getting old psychologist's records/ Forgiveness

FAQ ▶ The following FAQs are available via FTP from RTFM.MIT.EDU in the directory:
pub/usenet/alt.sexual.abuse.recovery:
bi-weekly_asar_faq_list_posting,_part_1_3
bi-weekly_asar_faq_list_posting,_part_2_3
bi-weekly_asar_faq_list_posting,_part_3_3

Co-Dependency & Child Sexual Abuse Support Group

alt.recovery.co-dependency **M**

Support group for those seeking to recover from co-dependency, child and/or adult sexual abuse and the grief of losing a loved one. Participants are quite sincere in their offerings of support and advice to one another, making this an extremely useful resource for sharing experiences and aiding in self-healing.

For Partners of Abuse Survivors

alt.support.abuse-partners **L**

Participants share their experiences in dealing with relationship problems arising from spouses who suffered sexual or physical abuse as children. Participants provide valuable support, advice and encouragement to each other based on their own heartfelt personal experiences.

Rape Discussion Group

talk.rape **HI**

Participants discuss current rape trials in the news, date rape and rape self-defense issues.

For Couples Wishing to Adopt & Birth-Parent Seekers

alt.adoption **M**

A useful and informative group focusing on discussions, resources and contacts for adopted persons wishing to find birth parents. Also includes information resources for couples wishing to adopt.

Sample Subjects:
Baby Jessica/Birth mother's searching rights/State law questions/Books about adoption/Search and support groups

Divorce and Child Support Resources

alt.child-support **HI**

Devoted to issues, resources and facts relating to child custody issues, court-ordered financial support requirements and personal experiences related to divorce, custody and child support issues. This group's participants relate their personal experiences, ask for advice or access to information and trade their personal experiences for the benefit of others. Recent discussions have included father's rights, legal issues relating to custody at time of divorce and what happens when the mother moves out of state with the children.

Sample Subjects:
Establishing precedence/North Carolina child support guidelines/Pennsylvania child support/Long term effects of divorce on children

Father's Rights Resources in Child Custody Cases

alt.dads-rights **HI**

An online support and information sharing group for husbands involved in divorce proceedings and child custody battles. Contains discussions on state-by-state custody laws and procedures and a high volume of debate about related issues concerning marriage, abortion and child custody.

Sample Subjects:
Establishing precedence/The myth of male power/Abortion and child support

Fathers' Rights & Equality Exchange

bit.listserv.free-l **M**

Rambling discussions on numerous child support, divorce and custody issues, dominated by fathers exchanging information and advice on child custody, support and visitation issues in divorce.

Help & Advice for Parents of Teenagers

alt.parents-teens **L**

A wide variety of discussions on raising teenage children, focusing primarily on education. Current topics discussed have included home schooling, peer pressure relating to teens and issues oriented to education of teenagers.

Autism Support Group

bit.listserv.autism **M**

An active, substantive and highly informative support group both for parents of autistic infants and children as well as autistic adults. Participants discuss aspects of various aspects of autism: behaviors, schooling and education, books, medical resources and discussion of current and past research in the field of autism. An especially touching and noteworthy aspect of this newsgroup is its inspirational stories and direct personal experiences told by adults who were diagnosed as autistic children; they relate their extraordinary educational achievements and progress in overcoming this learning disability. Also features many postings from learning disability specialists in academia. An invaluable Net resource as well as a source of comfort and inspiration for parents of autistic children and others affected by this condition.

Resources for the Blind

bit.listserv.blindnws **L**

Compilation of interesting and informative resources, products, services and other Net user messages of interest to the blind.

Support Group for Members of Twelve-Step Programs

alt.recovery **M**

The ability of people to access the Net anonymously makes this a good online support group for participants involved in various Twelve-Step recovery programs for alcoholism, drug abuse or psychological problems. Participants offer mutual comfort and support, interspersed with comments and suggestions to improve participation in Twelve-Step recovery programs. Members of Twelve-Step programs who have been successful to date in overcoming their addictions also use this forum to offer their words of encouragement. A useful resource for those having problems with alcohol, drugs or smoking addictions as well as those looking for a place to start.

Sample Subjects:
Twelve steps versus religion/One solid year of sobriety today/Sociophobia

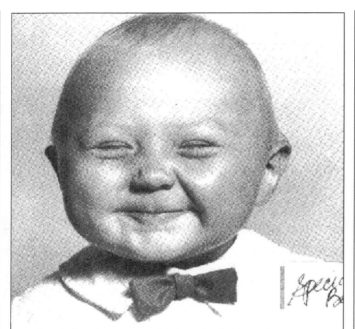

▲ *Cute baby photo, image file downloaded from Internet photo archives at* **grind.isca.uiowa.edu**

Pregnancy, Infant Care & Toddlers
misc.kids **HI**

A friendly and useful support group for expectant parents and parents of infants and small children, **misc.kids** can connect you instantly with good advice on most any question you might have about pregnancy, childbirth, and especially, the art of being a parent. Discussions range from cute baby names to pediatric care and good all-around advice for parents of newborns and young children. The large number of cute baby stories in this group also add a special touch of humor and humanity to the Net.

Sample Subjects:
Morning sickness at end of first trimester/Bedtime stories/Not my morning/My daughter the tom-boy

FAQ ▶ The following FAQs are available via FTP from RTFM.MIT.EDU in the directory:
pub/usenet/misc.kids:
Welcome_to_Misc.kids_FAQ_File_Index_(Updated
Welcome_to_Misc.kids_FAQ_File_Index_(Updated_10_4_93)
Welcome_to_Misc.kids_FAQ_File_Index_(Updated_9_13_93)

Deafness Resources & Information
bit.listserv.deaf-l **M**

Information exchange, discussion and support group for deaf students and teachers from universities around the world. Discussions on various issues in deaf education, resources and services for the deaf, "mainstreaming," and general conversations among hearing impaired persons on the Net.

Diabetic Resource Group
misc.health.diabetes **M**

Perhaps the most compelling use of the Net is its bringing together of persons with like interests and conditions: If you're a diabetic or know someone among your friends and family who is, this Net group should be a regular and frequent visit for the great many benefits it can provide. Diabetics share referrals and information on a wide variety of subjects, including: blood monitoring, insulin dosages, providers of testing supplies and equipment and advice on dealing with doctors, diabetic children, nutrition and exercise programs for diabetics, and the latest medical developments in diabetes treatment and related medical conditions.

Sample Subjects:
Comparing your blood/Glucose Meter/Energy level/Alternative to Insulin

More Support Groups: Cancer, MS, Obesity & Step-parents

The Net provides many useful online support groups that cover a variety of emotional and health-related problems. **alt.support.big folks** is a support group for overweight individuals and people with "body visualization" problems; **alt.support.cancer** is a forum for discussing various conventional and unconventional cancer-fighting therapies; **alt.support.diet** is primarily a clearinghouse for exchange of dieting information, health tips while dieting and miscellaneous dieting recipes; **alt.support.mult.sclerosis** is an online social group for those afflicted with MS; and **alt.support.step-parents** contains discussions among step-parents and is primarily concerned with issues involving those who have recently become step-parents to teenagers.

Support for Overweight People
alt.support.big.folks

Cancer Survivor's Support Group
alt.support.cancer

Dieting Health Tips & Support
alt.support.diet

Multiple Sclerosis Support Group
alt.support.mult.sclerosis

Step Parents' Support Group
alt.support.step-parents

Support: Miscellaneous
alt.support **L**

When reviewed, this group was monopolized by a rather frenetic and disorganized rant concerning the ongoing battle of the sexes that occurs on the Net quite frequently. If you are seeking support for whatever emotional or health problems you might be having, you would be better served by going to a Net support group specifically oriented to your particular problem (check out the other support groups in this book, or our Index/Finder).

Resources for the Disabled
misc.handicap **M**

Useful, informative newsgroup for persons with disabilities, **misc.handicap** focuses on the resources and technology available to make everyday life more enjoyable. Topics include computer-based speech for the blind, accessibility issues, employment resources, therapy, social interaction, books and treatment.

Sample Subjects:
Meeting friends/Deaf BBS/Braille and audio books wanted

▲ *Chinese river village in Malaysia, downloaded via Internet FTP from* **grind.isca.uiowa.edu**

Cultural Talk & News

Social & Cultural FAQs
soc.answers **M**

Contains a large number of extensive and frequently updated FAQ (Frequently Asked Question) files relating to all of the **soc.** newsgroups. The FAQs in **soc.answers**, when related to a specific foreign country, usually address questions of interest to expatriates living in the U.S., such as how to get news and sports scores from that particular country, resources relating to that particular country on the Net, etc. FAQs relating to social-oriented newsgroups (such as **soc.feminism**) are often organized in the usual question-and-answer FAQ format. These newsgroups also contain general FAQs detailing how to locate the electronic mail address of someone else on the Net, college electronic mail addresses and extensive files of book reading lists.

Afghanistan News & Culture
soc.culture.afghanistan **M**

Afghan natives discuss current news, human rights issues, Afghan reconstruction efforts and Middle East peace efforts.

African News & Culture
soc.culture.african **HI**

African students discuss current events related to their specific African home countries, portrayals of Africans in U.S. media and postings of news releases and other announcements from African governments and political organizations.

Argentina News & Culture
alt.culture.argentina **L**

A Spanish language discussion group covering cultural, sporting and recreational events in Argentina.

Black Issues & Controversies
soc.culture.african.american **HI**

An even number of whites and blacks share their opinions on affirmative action programs in colleges, violence on TV, portrayal of blacks in the media and the emerging black conservative movement.

Arab Talk & Culture
soc.culture.arabic **HI**

Citizens of various Arab countries discuss issues relating to conflicts of Western culture with Islam, human rights in Arab countries and peace efforts in the Middle East.

Southeast Asian News & Talk
soc.culture.asean **HI**

Expatriate citizens of Indonesia, Malaysia, Singapore, The Philippines and other countries in the region discuss current Asian news events and post announcements from various ASEAN social and political groups.

Asian American Talk Group
soc.culture.asian.american **HI**

Wild talk group mostly dominated by endless discussions of Asian American romances and Asian racism issues.

FAQ▶ The following FAQ is available via FTP from RTFM.MIT.EDU in the directory:
pub/usenet/soc.culture.asian.american:
soc.culture.asian.american_FAQ

Australian Chat & News
soc.culture.australian **M**

Casual chatter about current Australian news and political issues, sports and the advantages of living in Australia.

FAQ▶ The following FAQs are available via FTP from RTFM.MIT.EDU in the directory:
pub/usenet/soc.culture.australian:
soc.culture.australian_FAQ_(Part_1_of_2)_(monthly_posting)
soc.culture.australian_FAQ_(Part_2_of_2)_(monthly_posting)

Baltics News & Talk
soc.culture.baltics **HI**

Talk of current struggles, outbreaks of fighting, business opportunities and political issues in the Baltics (Latvia, Lithuania and Estonia) with additional discussions on Russia and Georgia.

Bangladesh News & Talk
soc.culture.bangladesh **HI**

Bangladeshis engage in spirited informal debate with each other and with Indian and Pakistani nationals on human rights, religious issues, current news and making it in the U.S.

Balkan News & Disputes
soc.culture.bosna-herzgvna **HI**

The bitter, thousand-year-old conflict between Serbs, Bosnians and Croats continues online. A mixture of foreign-language comments and debate, postings of news items from the region and many hostile online exchanges between Serbs and Bosnians. Those interested in gaining more insight into the Bosnian crisis will find good information here; however, the overall amount of strife in this group does become tiresome.

British Talk & Culture
soc.culture.british **HI**

Brits engage in spirited debate with their American counterparts over the Net. Topics include American versus U.K. food, curious national customs, manners and gun control in America.

▲ *River barges on the Thames, London, downloaded from Internet photo archives at* **grind.isca.uiowa.edu**

Brazilian News & Talk
soc.culture.brazil **HI**

Mostly foreign-language (Portuguese) talk of news, sports and chatter for Brazilians and expatriates.

Bulgaria/Macedonia News & Talk
soc.culture.bulgaria **HI**

Bulgarian expatriates from around the world discuss various items and issues of interest. Also includes daily reports from news services in the region, Radio Free Europe/Radio Liberty daily news excerpts and discussions of sporting events.

Canada Talk & News
soc.culture.canada **HI**

Canadians and Canadian expatriate students and professionals engage in spirited discussions of national Canadian issues, the current Prime Minister, the Canadian healthcare system and more. Also includes daily news summaries reprinted from one of Canada's top newspapers, *The Globe & Mail*.

Caribbean Talk & News
soc.culture.caribbean **HI**

Expatriates from Jamaica, Barbados and other Caribbean island countries discuss local issues, politics, local media and living in the U.S.

Irish, Welsh & Scotch News & Talk
soc.culture.celtic **HI**

Discussion of political events in Northern Ireland,

living in Ireland, Welsh nationalism, Gaelic language and news from Ireland, Wales and Scotland.

Chinese Student Talk & News
soc.culture.china **HI**

Chinese students discuss and comment on current news concerning China and Chinese politics.

FAQ ▶ The following FAQ is available via FTP from RTFM.MIT.EDU in the directory:
pub/usenet/soc.culture.china:
soc.culture.hongkong_FAQ,_Part_II

Croatia News & Talk
soc.culture.croatia **HI**

Continuing, intensely heated debates between Croats and Serbs on the Net, featuring extensive reprints from books and articles posted by Serb and Bosnian Netters promoting their views on the Balkan crisis.

Czech News & Comment
soc.culture.czecho-slovak **HI**

Czech nationals and expatriates discuss current issues of interest to the Czech people and provide helpful travel and tourism advice to American students wishing to live and work in that country.

Czech & Slovak Politics
bit.listserv.slovak-l **L**

Intense and focused discussions on current news and political issues of interest to Czechs and Slovaks, such as the recent partitioning of this country.

Esperanto Language Talk
soc.culture.esperanto **HI**

Esperanto language discussion and practice group for this "good idea" of a language that never caught on. Participants engage in analytical discussion concerning various aspects of this language.

FAQ ▶ The following FAQ is available via FTP from RTFM.MIT.EDU in the directory:
pub/usenet/soc.culture.esperanto:
soc.culture.esperanto_Frequently_Asked_Questions_(Oftaj_Demandoj)

European Culture
soc.culture.europe **HI**

Group for question-and-answer dialogue concerning visits to European countries.

FAQ ▶ The following FAQ is available via FTP from RTFM.MIT.EDU in the directory:
pub/usenet/soc.culture.europe:
Hungarian_electronic_resources_FAQ

Philippine Talk & Culture
soc.culture.filipino **HI**

Spirited discussions between Philippine nationals and American students concerning cross-cultural

differences, relationships, jokes and current news from the Philippines.

French Culture & Travel Info
soc.culture.french **HI**

French nationals provide helpful travel and tourism tips to inquiring tourists. Also contains French-language discussions on places of interest, current issues and sporting events in France.

FAQ ▶ The following FAQs are available via FTP from RTFM.MIT.EDU in the directory:
pub/usenet/soc.culture.french:
FAQ:_soc.culture.french_-_Contents_[monthly]
FAQ:_soc.culture.french_-_French_language_[monthly]
FAQ:_soc.culture.french_-_Introduction_[monthly]
FAQ:_soc.culture.french_-_Intro_[monthly]
FAQ:_soc.culture.french_-_Medias_[monthly]
FAQ:_soc.culture.french_-_Miscellaneous_[monthly]
FAQ:_soc.culture.french_-_Networking_1_2_[monthly]
FAQ:_soc.culture.french_-_Networking_2_2_[monthly]
FAQ:_soc.culture.french_-_Restaurants_[monthly]

German Talk & Debate
soc.culture.german **HI**

Mostly discussions relating to World Wars I and II and the pressures of reunification, with a small amount of German-language comment and discussion among students in Europe and the U.S.

FAQ ▶ The following FAQ is available via FTP from RTFM.MIT.EDU in the directory:
pub/usenet/soc.culture.german:
FAQ:_soc.culture.german_Frequently_Asked_Questions_(posted_monthly)

Greek News & Talk
soc.culture.greek **HI**

Participants discuss and compare Greek politics to politics in the U.S. and post news items reprinted from Greek newspapers and news wires.

FAQ ▶ The following FAQs are available via FTP from RTFM.MIT.EDU in the directory:
pub/usenet/soc.culture.greek:
(10_Oct_93)_Soc.Culture.Greek_FAQ_-_Culture
(10_Oct_93)_Soc.Culture.Greek_FAQ_-_Linguistics
(10_Oct_93)_Soc.Culture.Greek_FAQ_-_Technical_Information
(10_Oct_93)_Soc.Culture.Greek_FAQ_-_Tourist_Information
(26_Sep_93)_Soc.Culture.Greek_FAQ_-_Culture
(26_Sep_93)_Soc.Culture.Greek_FAQ_-_Linguistics
(26_Sep_93)_Soc.Culture.Greek_FAQ_-_Technical_Information
(26_Sep_93)_Soc.Culture.Greek_FAQ_-_Tourist_Information
(9_Sep_93)_Soc.Culture.Greek_FAQ_-_Culture
(9_Sep_93)_Soc.Culture.Greek_FAQ_-_Linguistics
(9_Sep_93)_Soc.Culture.Greek_FAQ_-_Technical_Information
(9_Sep_93)_Soc.Culture.Greek_FAQ_-_Tourist_Information

Hong Kong Talk
soc.culture.hongkong **HI**

A noisy group with many random comments on life in Hong Kong, reprinted articles from local news feeds and other comments among Chinese Net users.

Support Groups, Culture, Religion & Philosophy

FAQ ▶ The following FAQs are available via FTP from RTFM.MIT.EDU in the directory:
pub/usenet/soc.culture.hongkong:
Chinese_BIG5_environment:_FAQ_of_alt.chinese.text.big5
soc.culture.hongkong_FAQ,_Part_I
soc.culture.hongkong_FAQ,_Part_III
soc.culture.hongkong_FAQ,_Part_IV

India Digest
bit.listserv.india-l **L**

A forum for discussion of issues of interest to the Indian community, India Digest consists of a large volume of relevant news articles, comments and discussions of interest to Indian nationals.

Indian Talk & News
alt.culture.karnataka **HI**

An English-language discussion for and about India and current in-country events.

▲ *Japanese television news anchorwoman Karuna Shinsho, downloaded via Internet FTP from* **wuarchive.wustl.edu**

Indian Keralan Talk & Culture
alt.culture.kerala **HI**

An English-language discussion group relating to the Indian Keralan subculture.

Indonesian Talk, News & Info
alt.culture.indonesia **HI**

An Indonesian language newsgroup for exchanging notes, jokes and news for people from Indonesia.

Indian Students Group
soc.culture.indian **HI**

Indian students talk about news and political events back home, trade jokes and discuss cultural differences about life in the U.S.

FAQ ▶ The following FAQ is available via FTP from RTFM.MIT.EDU in the directory:
pub/usenet/soc.culture.indian:
[soc.culture.indian]_FREQUENTLY_ASKED_QUESTIONS

Indian (Telugu) Culture & Talk
soc.culture.indian.telugu **HI**

News, talk and discussion among Indian nationals and students from the Indian Telugu subculture.

Indonesian News & Talk
soc.culture.indonesia **HI**

Indonesian-languages chat group for Indonesian students in the U.S., Canada and Europe.

Iranian Talk & Comment
soc.culture.iranian **HI**

Anti-Khomeini Iranian nationals in the U.S., Canada and Europe discuss Islamic Fundamentalism, human rights in Iran, the Middle East peace process and principles of civil disobedience, such as those followed by Dr. Martin Luther King. Participants in this group are openly concerned that their comments are being monitored by the Iranian government secret police, while other participants hold the view that the Iranian secret police aren't even smart enough to use computers. And so it goes...

FAQ ▶ The following FAQ is available via FTP from RTFM.MIT.EDU in the directory:
pub/usenet/soc.culture.iranian:
soc.culture.iranian:_Frequently_Asked_Questions_[monthly_posting]

Italian Talk & Comment
soc.culture.italian **HI**

Italian-language discussion group from Italy. Paisano Netters discuss Italian politics, latest government crises and soccer.

FAQ ▶ The following FAQs are available via FTP from RTFM.MIT.EDU in the directory:
pub/usenet/soc.culture.italian:
s.c.italian_Frequently_Asked_Questions_(FAQ)_[1_3]
s.c.italian_Frequently_Asked_Questions_(FAQ)_[2_3]
s.c.italian_Frequently_Asked_Questions_(FAQ)_[3_3]

Japanese Chat & Culture
soc.culture.japan **HI**

Japanese nationals and Americans living and working in Japan share comments and advice on getting along in Japan, the Japanese language, current news events in Japan and a wide variety of other topics.

FAQ ▶ The following FAQ is available via FTP from RTFM.MIT.EDU in the directory:
pub/usenet/soc.culture.japan:
Soc.culture.japan_references_[Monthly_Posting]

Jewish Culture, Comment & News
soc.culture.jewish **HI**

American Jews and Israelis share information on

Jewish religious practices, customs and current events concerning Israel and the Middle East.

FAQ ▶ The following FAQs are available via FTP from RTFM.MIT.EDU in the directory:
pub/usenet/soc.culture.jewish:
Judaism_Reading_List:_Antisemitism_and_Christian_Relations_(Pt._IX)
Judaism_Reading_List:_Conservative_Judaism_(Pt._V)
Judaism_Reading_List:_Humanistic_Judaism_(Pt._VII)
Judaism_Reading_List:_Intermarriage_(Pt._X)
Judaism_Reading_List:_Introduction_and_General_(Pt._I)
Judaism_Reading_List:_Kabbalah_and_Chasidism_(Pt._III)
Judaism_Reading_List:_Periodicals_(Pt._XI)
Judaism_Reading_List:_Reconstructionist_Judaism_(Pt._VI)
Judaism_Reading_List:_Reform_Judaism_(Pt._IV)
Judaism_Reading_List:_Trad._Lit._and_Practice_(Pt._II)
Judaism_Reading_List:_Zionism_(Pt._VIII)
soc.culture.jewish_FAQ:_Holocaust,_Antisemitism,_Missionaries_(9_10)
soc.culture.jewish_FAQ:_Introduction_to_the_FAQ_and_s.c.j_(1_10)
soc.culture.jewish_FAQ:_Jewish_Thought_(6_10)
soc.culture.jewish_FAQ:_Jews_and_Israel_(8_10)
soc.culture.jewish_FAQ:_Jews_As_A_Nation_(7_10)
soc.culture.jewish_FAQ:_Miscellaneous_and_References_(10_10)
soc.culture.jewish_FAQ:_Observance,_Marriage,_Women_in_Judaism_(4_10)
soc.culture.jewish_FAQ:_Torah_and_Halachic_Authority_(3_10)
soc.culture.jewish_FAQ:_Who_We_Are_(2_10)
soc.culture.jewish_FAQ:_Worship,_Conversion,_Intermarriage_(5_10)

▲ *Drawing of Aztec figure Xochiquetzal, downloaded from* **grind.isca.uiowa.edu** ▶ *Sitting Bull, image downloaded via Internet FTP from Smithsonian photo archives at* **sunsite.unc.edu**

Korean Talk & News
soc.culture.korean **HI**

Korean students (mostly) engage in lighthearted discussion, most of it rather unrelated to this group's intended subject. However, this group does contain daily Korean-language news summaries taken from Korea-based wire services.

Latin America Comment & News
soc.culture.latin-america **HI**

Discussion and some foreign language talk on political issues, news and ideologies of Central and South American countries and Cuba.

FAQ ▶ The following FAQs are available via FTP from RTFM.MIT.EDU in the directory:
pub/usenet/soc.culture.latin-america:
soc.culture.mexican_FAQ
soc.culture.mexican_FAQ_(Monthly_Reposting)

Lebanese Talk & Comment
soc.culture.lebanon **HI**

Lebanese expatriates discuss current Middle East news events, homesickness and rebuilding efforts in their country.

FAQ ▶ The following FAQs are available via FTP from RTFM.MIT.EDU in the directory:
pub/usenet/soc.culture.lebanon:
soc.culture.lebanon_FAQ,_part_1_2
soc.culture.lebanon_FAQ,_part_2_2

Hungarian Chat, News & Resources
soc.culture.magyar **HI**

Comments and discussions relating to various subcultures and peoples of Hungary. Includes Hungarian news wire digests and references to other Hungarian information services on the Internet.

Malaysia Talk & News
soc.culture.malaysia **HI**

Malaysian Muslim nationals and Chinese Malaysians engage in numerous and random discussions and try to locate friends on the Net.

Mexico Talk & Comment
soc.culture.mexican **HI**

In this mostly Spanish-language discussion group, Mexican nationals and U.S. citizens discuss many issues of concern to both countries, such as immigration, trade, etc.

Native American Talk & Culture
soc.culture.native **HI**

Discussions of Native American history, culture and current events largely from a left-wing point of view. Comments from Native American activists and other activist groups. Also features inquiries and answers posted by academics studying Native American and Western history.

Nepalese Tourism & Talk
soc.culture.nepal **HI**

Nepalese nationals discuss local issues and provide advice to Americans, Canadians and Australians wishing to visit and climb mountains in this country.

Netherlands Culture & Talk
soc.culture.netherlands **HI**

Mostly Dutch-language talk group for nationals and students discussing current news events as they affect the Netherlands.

▲ *Russian President Boris Yeltsin emerges victorious from the Russian Parliament building after failed Soviet coup, 1991, downloaded via Internet FTP from photo archives at* **wuarchive.wustl.edu** ▲ *Moscow church spires, downloaded from* **grind.isca.uiowa.edu**

New Zealander Talk & News

soc.culture.new-zealand **HI**

New Zealanders engage in lighthearted, humorous discussions and talk of news from home.

Swedes, Finns & Norwegians

soc.culture.nordic **HI**

Citizens of various Nordic countries discuss U.S. news items of concern to their countries, answering interesting and humorous Nordic-language questions posed by Americans.

Pakistan Talk & Culture

soc.culture.pakistan **HI**

Extremely active discussion group for Pakistani nationals and students residing in the U.S. Discussions of current Pakistan home news issues, politics and resources.

Polish Comments, Talk & Culture

soc.culture.polish **HI**

A mix of Polish-language comments and discussions of recent and World War II Polish/German history, plus discussions of Polish/German relations.

Portuguese News & Talk

soc.culture.portuguese **HI**

Active discussion group for Portuguese nationals and U.S.-based Portuguese students. News wire digests, sports news and scores and discussions of current events in Portugal.

Romanian Comments

soc.culture.romanian **HI**

News summaries from Radio Free Europe/Radio Liberty relating to Romania, plus comment and discussion on Eastern European controversies.

Singapore Talk Culture & News

soc.culture.singapore **HI**

Informative and humorous discussions on things to do in Singapore, current events, sports and social activities.

Soviet & Eastern European Talk

soc.culture.soviet **HI**

Bitter and intense discussions between nationals of formerly occupied Eastern European countries and Russian nationals. Also a smattering of humorous Russian-language comments.

Spain: News & Talk

soc.culture.spain **HI**

Spanish nationals and students residing in the U.S. discuss Spanish news media items, sporting events and Spanish metropolitan items of interest in this Spanish-language group.

Social & Support

Sri Lankan Talk & Culture

soc.culture.sri-lanka **HI**

Tourism, travel advice and local color discussions from Brits and Sri Lankan nationals.

Taiwan News & Talk

soc.culture.taiwan **HI**

Chinese residents of Taiwan discuss Beijing politics and Chinese cultural freedom issues.

Sri Lankan Tamil Cultural Discussion

soc.culture.tamil **HI**

Group for current event discussions and political views of the Tamil subculture of Sri Lanka.

Thailand: Travel, Tourism, News & Talk

soc.culture.thai **HI**

Thai nationals discuss current news articles and provide useful travel, tourism and sightseeing advice to prospective tourists from the United States, Great Britain and Australia.

Turkish News & Culture

soc.culture.turkish **HI**

Turkish nationals discuss recent events in the region, relations with former Soviet states and other topics of interest.

American Cultural Debates

soc.culture.usa **HI**

Netters from England, Canada and the U.S. engage in humorous debate on all things American: ketchup, french fries, American planes, the Second Amendment, and more—so join this newsgroup and defend your country against cultural attack.

Vietnamese Talk & Social Group

soc.culture.vietnamese **HI**

Extremely active social group for Vietnamese residents and citizens in the U.S. Participants express their views on political change in Vietnam, post announcements for local Vietnamese communities and talk sentimentally about their home country.

Southeast Asia News & Comment

bit.listserv.seasia-l **M**

More discussion and reprints in news digest form pertaining to Thailand, Vietnam and other Southeast Asian countries.

Crisis in Yugoslavia

soc.culture.yugoslavia **HI**

Bitter arguments between Serbs, Croats, Bosnians and Turks serving as another channel in the seemingly endless thousand-year-old Balkan ethnic conflict.

Culture: Miscellaneous Talk

soc.culture.misc **M**

Catch-all group for generalized discussions on various cultures from an historical perspective, including disappearance of past cultures, assimilation, emigration and health issues.

Religion & Philosophy

Christian Discussion Group

soc.religion.christian **HI**

Active, intense, yet dignified discussion group offering a range of viewpoints for Christians and others interested in Western religions. Sample topics include debates on New Age-versus-Christian religious issues, the Second Coming, and open questions to atheists.

Christian Bible Study Discussion

soc.religion.christian.bible-study **HI**

Christian Netters discuss meaning and interpretations of Biblical references, exchange computer-based Bible resource information and debate other Bible-related citations in a highly focused and dignified way.

Catholic Discussion Group

bit.listserv.catholic **HI**

Laypeople and academics discuss the current major debates in the Catholic church and offer serious, well-considered, literate comment on Vatican policy, books, abortion and prayer.

Sample Subjects:
Joseph and the Holy Family/New quotation question/Organ donation

Religious Discussions & Prayer Requests

bit.listserv.christia **M**

Participants discuss many different aspects of Christianity, the Bible, morality and civility. This newsgroup is also used as a place for personal prayer requests and replies for participants currently experiencing emotional, spiritual or physical trials in their lives. Heavily focused on Roman Catholicism; also a fair number of Protestant participants.

Support Groups, Culture, Religion & Philosophy

Sample Subjects:
Prayer requests/Perpetual virginity of Mary/On the intelligent life thread

Unitarian & Universalist Discussions
bit.listserv.uus-l **L**

Members of the Unitarian/Universalist faiths engage in discussions on assisted suicide, inherent human rights, religion and Unitarian/Universalist local and national events.

Buddhism, Hinduism & Eastern Religions
soc.religion.eastern **HI**

Comprehensive discussion group featuring multiple discussions on all Eastern religions and philosophies from Buddhism to Sikhism, and numerous other lesser-known Asian- and Indian-based religions. Followers of these religions are extremely polite and quite helpful as they assist Netters wishing to learn more about these particular religions.

Islamic Religion Discussions
soc.religion.islam **M**

Islamic followers and those interested in Islam participate in wide-ranging discussions on the Qur'an, Islamic Fundamentalist belief, the treatment of women in Islam and Islamic historical references. Also includes numerous announcements of activities of interest to followers of Islam.

Baha'i Faith Group
soc.religion.bahai **M**

Discussion group for followers of the Baha'i faith.

FAQ ▶ The following FAQs are available via FTP from RTFM.MIT.EDU in the directory:
pub/usenet/soc.religion.bahai:
Baha_i_Faith_Annotated_Bibliography
Baha_i_Faith_Introduction
Welcome_to_soc.religion.bahai

Atheism Debates
alt.atheism **HI**

Intense discussion group covering the contradictions, controversy and debates surrounding atheism.

Sample Subjects:
New religious trends/Burden of proof/Free will/Logic has its limits/Few female atheists?

Atheism Debates II
alt.atheism.moderated **M**

Moderated, more structured version of the **alt.atheism** newsgroup.

Sample Subjects:
Atheism frequently asked questions/Is he not God?/Contradictions in the Bible

FAQ ▶ The following FAQs are available via FTP from RTFM.MIT.EDU in the directory:
pub/usenet/alt.atheism.moderated:
Alt.Atheism_FAQ:_Atheist_Resources
Alt.Atheism_FAQ:_Constructing_a_Logical_Argument
Alt.Atheism_FAQ:_Frequently_Asked_Questions
Alt.Atheism_FAQ:_Introduction_to_Atheism
Alt.Atheism_FAQ:_Overview_for_New_Readers

Myths & Legends from around the World
alt.mythology **M**

A discussion group consisting mostly of college students and graduate students, **alt.mythology** features discussions on a wide variety of mythologies from both Western and Eastern cultures. Participants in this group are very helpful, answering each other's questions and providing useful literature references to myths and mythological characters.

Sample Subjects:
Olympian ancestry/The Fisher King/Babylonian mythology

Witches Group
alt.pagan **HI**

We bet you thought witches and warlocks didn't know how to use computers. Well, they do, and this group proves that there's room for just about anything on the Net. Frightfully detailed discussions, comments and information on many aspects of paganism, witchcraft, satanism, etc.

Sample Subjects:
Goddesses and ducks/Flaming fundamentalists/Good witch movies

FAQ ▶ The following FAQ is available via FTP from RTFM.MIT.EDU in the directory:
pub/usenet/alt.pagan:
ALT.PAGAN_Frequently_Asked_Questions_(FAQ)

Ayn Rand & Objectivism Resource Group
alt.philosophy.objectivism **HI**

Who is John Galt? If you know who he is, then you've read *Atlas Shrugged*, *The Fountainhead* and other books by Ayn Rand, the founder of Objectivism. An active and information-packed newsgroup for believers and others interested in the Objectivist tenets of reason, selfishness as a virtue and individual achievement. Thought-provoking discussion and intellectual discourse on Objectivism in today's society. Current discussions have included new planned Objectivist communities, modern-day taxation issues, Objectivist humor, Ayn Rand vs. the Positivists and the theory of humor. Good place to go for both beginning and advanced students of this philosophy.

Sample Subjects:
Guide to philosophy-related resources/Atlantis project/Privatization of police/Objectivists and sports

Scientology Discussion Group
alt.religion.scientology **HI**

An intense and detailed discussion group for adherents to the philosophy of Scientology. Participants discuss consciousness, religion, self-awareness and thought processes.

FAQ ▶ The following FAQs are available via FTP from RTFM.MIT.EDU in the directory:
pub/usenet/alt.religion.scientology:
alt.religion.scientology_Users__FAQ2_(Frequently_Asked_Questions)
alt.religion.scientology_Users__Frequently_Asked_Questions_(FAQ)

Scientology: Religious Discussions

alt.clearing.technology **M**

An online group discussion of the Scientologists' goal of "getting clear." Also includes a number of other Scientology-related discussions.

Sample Subjects:
Questions I care to ask/Beliefs, disbeliefs and doubts/Lifesprings?

Debates Against Satanism

alt.satanism **HI**

This chaotic newsgroup is what you get when you throw a handful of satanic cult worshipers into a large group of mostly conservative Net participants. A strange combination of in-depth information about satanism (more than you'd want to know, really), mixed in with conservative-versus-liberal debate on current political issues.

Evolution Vs. Creationism

talk.origins **HI**

Extensive and (sometimes) educated discussion and debate on all subjects related to evolution, dinosaurs and prehistoric events; cosmic creation; and the role of religion in scientific debate. Heavily laden with scientific facts, new theories and spirited discussions mixing physics, biology and religion into the argument.

FAQ ▶ The following FAQ is available via FTP from RTFM.MIT.EDU in the directory:
pub/usenet/talk.origins:
talk.origins_Welcome_FAQ_v.1.1

Philosophy Talk Group

talk.philosophy.misc **HI**

You'll find many wildly polarized discussions in this catch-all philosophy talk group. The main debates here usually revolve around Ayn Rand's philosophy of Objectivism (pro and con), new thoughts on feminism (Camille Paglia) and grad-school-level general philosophy.

▲ *Buddha statue, image file downloaded from Smithsonian photo archives at* **sunsite.unc.edu**

Religious Debate Group

talk.religion.misc **HI**

Members of diverse religions answer questions, debate and defend their particular religious beliefs.

New Age Religions

talk.religion.newage **M**

Covers all aspects of New Age philosophy, resources, lifestyles and a wide variety of New Age theories promoted by their adherents. Recent topics include sex in the New Age, ancient civilizations, ethics, enlightenment and Vedic thinking.

Chapter 6: Hobbies, Travel & Tourism

If you're devoted to any one of dozens of interesting crafts or hobbies—woodworking, photography, sewing, car restoration and more—you'll find thousands of like-minded people who share your interest. Also, if you're into collectibles, antiques, art objects or most anything else, you can find your own special obsession among a rich and varied collection of newsgroups devoted to collectors and art lovers.

Collectibles, Arts, Crafts and Do-it-Yourself

The Internet features a vast number of online newsgroups covering an amazing range of personal interests, hobbies and other enthusiasms and many groups for travel, tourism and food/dining information and advice as well.

The spirit of community that is pervasive on the Internet is full and rich among the craft, hobby and special-interest newsgroups featured here. Participants in any newsgroup are always eager to provide beginners with a wealth of advice and useful pointers relating to that newsgroup's particular interest. This advice usually includes referrals to good, lowest-cost suppliers of materials, pointers on what tools to buy and loads of "how to get started" information on that particular newsgroup's craft or hobby subject.

Hobbies and Pets

There are also many interest groups for hobbies as popular (and arcane) as antique auto restoration, genealogy, bonsai gardening, winemaking and marching bands. The American spirit of individual ingenuity and do-it-yourself confidence is alive and well among these Net newsgroups.

If you can fly an airplane (or would like to), there are a dozen or so newsgroups covering every aspect of aviation, from homebuilt aircraft to technical tips on flying.

Travel, Tourism, Drinking and Dining

Useful travel and tourism newsgroups are also on hand to provide you with valuable travel advice, places to see and good recommendations from seasoned Net travellers. (For additional travel and tourism information; check the **soc.** newsgroups in Chapter 5.)

And so the new wave of computer users includes people such as Charlotte Berg, 71, of Alexandria. She said that she has no professional experience with computers and that the idea of tapping into a computer network was science fiction when she was a girl. But now, Berg regularly sends electronic letters, known as E-mail, to a grandson in Evanston, Ill., a daughter in Colorado and a son in Fort Worth. Other seniors in this area and across the country use computer networks to keep in contact with elderly friends who are unable to leave their homes. "It keeps me in touch with family members I want to feel close to," Berg said. "It's so clean. You don't have to hunt up an envelope or stamp."

Robert O'Harrow Jr., "Computer-Friendly Homes Increasing; Electronic Bulletin Boards Provide Many Residents With Comfort, Communication," *The Washington Post* (12/27/92)

Arts

Fine Arts Discussion & Comment
rec.arts.fine **HI**

More of a forum for amateur art critics and flame wars about "What Is Art?" than anything substantive about art, **rec.arts.fine** consists mainly of people expressing their own opinions about the state of today's art world. It does contain a small number of art workshop announcements and tips on various art, painting and sculpture techniques—if you're able to wade through the sheer mass of highly politicized and (sometimes) personal attacks by different posters (also includes newsgroup **rec.arts.misc**).

Sample Subjects:
**$1.8 million for this "art"?/
Redneck reevaluates Rothko/
Understanding and Appreciation/
Joan Miro's constellation series**

Art Talk & News
alt.artcom **M**

Discussions related to art, art and personality, and other aesthetic issues.

Art & Postmodernism Debate
alt.postmodern **M**

Some say that Postmodernist thought throws away 5,000 years of Western culture. Others say it can be an intellectual guidepost for the next century. A small but dedicated group of participants discuss the role, effects and other aspects of Postmodernism in art, culture, literature, politics and current events. Highly intellectual debate covering a wide range of topics, and not necessarily those restricted to art.

Sample Subjects:
Postmodernism and political ideology/Examples of Postmodernism in literature/Conservativism and Postmodernist thought

Collectibles

Postcard Collectors
bit.listserv.postcard **M**

Quirky little group for collectors of old and new postcards of all kinds. Netters post their want lists and exchange postcards with others from around the world.

Autograph Collector's Group
alt.collecting.autographs **L**

A clearinghouse for trading insiders' tips on autograph collecting; getting in touch with celebrities, actors and other notables; and discussing of autograph values and sources. Collectors participating in this group describe their latest autograph acquisition, how they got it, and how you can get autographs from celebrities and leading figures, too.

Sample Subjects:
Autographs/Diane Keaton/Got my first actor by mail/Need addresses/Sale autographed baseball bats

Collectibles Chat Group
rec.collecting **M**

A general-interest newsgroup that covers a wide range of collectible items, such as old toys, matchbooks, comics, coins, train sets, advertising specialties and assorted bric-a-brac.

Collectible Cards & Online Auctions
rec.collecting.cards **HI**

Newsgroup specializing in card collectibles of all types: baseball cards, non-sports cards (such as those for movies, TV shows, etc.) and online auctions where newsgroup participants can bid on posted listings of collectible cards.

Antiques & Collectibles
rec.antiques **M**

rec.antiques covers the entire range of (mainly moderate-to low-priced) collectibles, nostalgia items and antiques. Accessed by knowledgeable amateur collectors, it's also a good place to get authoritative pricing appraisals on many collectible items. Also features a good number of buy-and-sell messages to and from collectors of various items.

Sample Subjects:
Ceramic tile fireplace/G. Stickley chairs/Cookie jar value

▲ *The Mona Lisa, image file downloaded via Internet FTP from art image file archives at* **grind.isca.uiowa.edu**

Hobbies & Crafts

Fashion Tips & Talk
alt.fashion (M)

A useful group for the clothing-conscious Netter. Participants talk about this season's fashion trends, advice on building a wardrobe, best clothing for various body types and advice on where to buy high quality, hard-to-find clothing and accessories. Netters also provide their own recommendations on good mail order clothing sources, items and workmanship.

Sample Subjects:
Versac's photos/Icelandic sweaters/J.Crew/Buying clothes for my girlfriend

Sewing Skills & Crafts: Beginner to Expert
alt.sewing (HI)

We were surprised to find an extremely active group on the Net devoted entirely to sewing. This Net discussion group is for you if you're interested in learning how to sew, or already know how to sew but need some tips or advice. There are lots of experienced sewing mavens on the Net to help you. Everything from advice on sewing sueded silk to stretch needles and user feedback on sewing machine brands.

Sample Subjects:
How did you learn to sew?/Fitting classes/Truly portable sewing machine/Help with adhesive on suede

FAQ ▶ The following FAQs are available via FTP from RTFM.MIT.EDU in the directory:
pub/usenet/alt.sewing:
Historical_Costuming_FAQ
Textiles_FAQ
Textile_Related_Books_FAQ:_Part_1_of_2
Textile_Related_Books_FAQ:_Part_2_of_2

Help for Bonsai Gardeners
alt.bonsai (L)

If you're into bonsai gardening (or would like to get started), here's a group for you. Tips, tricks and good advice on anything related to bonsai gardening.

FAQ ▶ The following FAQs are available via FTP from RTFM.MIT.EDU in the directory:
pub/usenet/alt.bonsai:
The_rec.arts.bonsai_alt.bonsai_FAQ:_Part1
The_rec.arts.bonsai_alt.bonsai_FAQ:_Part2
The_rec.arts.bonsai_alt.bonsai_FAQ:_Part3
The_rec.arts.bonsai_alt.bonsai_FAQ:_Part4
The_rec.arts.bonsai_alt.bonsai_FAQ:_Part5

Dance Discussion Group
rec.arts.dance (HI)

For anything related to the art of dancing. Covers everything from ballroom dancing events and two-step techniques to how to moonwalk.

Sample Subjects:
New York City dance announcement/How to moonwalk/

Place to dance in Hawaii?/Ballroom dancing in Atlanta, Georgia

▲ *Locomotive, "The City Of San Francisco," downloaded via Internet FTP from Smithsonian photo archives at* **sunsite.unc.edu**

Railroad Fans
rec.railroad (HI)

Enthusiasts discuss their favorite yesteryear railroads as well as modern rail lines, locomotives, engines, local/regional railroads and other railroad memorabilia. (Note: model railroading is not discussed in this newsgroup.)

Beer Brewing at Home
rec.crafts.brewing (HI)

A growing number of beer drinkers prefer more expensive small-brewery brands and a smaller number of these people go the ultimate step: They make and bottle their own beer at home. **rec.crafts.brewing** contains everything you'd ever want to know about making beer at home, with extensive, detailed discussion, comments and information by experienced home beermakers on brewing techniques, ingredients, different types of beer (like stout, mead, and even pineapple beer!), and any other info you would ever need to bottle your own brew.

Sample Subjects:
Brewlab yeast update/Wort aeration/Bottle labels

FAQ ▶ The following FAQ is available via FTP from RTFM.MIT.EDU in the directory:
pub/usenet/rec.crafts.brewing:
rec.crafts.brewing_Frequently_Asked_Questions_(FAQ)

Beer Drinker's Paradise
alt.beer (HI)

An online Oktoberfest. If you like beer (and who doesn't?) this is the group for you! Very

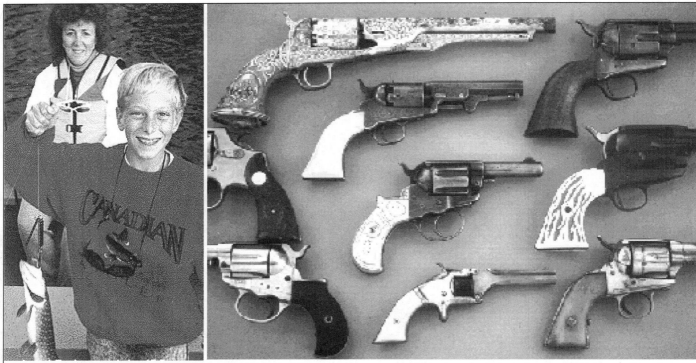

▲ *Boy with northern pike caught with lure made from 256K computer memory chips, downloaded via Internet FTP from online photo archives at* **grind.isca.uiowa.edu** ▲ *Smithsonian display of antique revolvers, downloaded from Smithsonian photo archives at* **sunsite.unc.edu**

popular discussion group that's always filled with the latest information about the sport of beer drinking. Wide variety of interesting facts from beer festivals, recommendations of new beer brands and local breweries and anything else you can think of related to beer drinking.

Sample Subjects:
Guinness cans in Oregon/New Jersey microbrew pubs/ New York City brew pubs/My trip to Alburquerque/Best beer names

Fisherman's Paradise

alt.fishing **M**

Die-hard fishermen swap extensive reports on their latest fishing trips and exchange information on top fishing areas, equipment, tackle, boats and more. Also features a small number of buy/sell listings.

Sample Subjects:
Fly fishing near Sacramento/Rock fishing/Boat for sale

Gun Owners Talk & Resources

rec.guns **HI**

Very active newsgroup for all aspects of gun owner-ship and use from specific recommendations of good handguns, rifles, shotguns and accessories to buy, to

discussion of recent news items and opinions relating to guns and gun control. Experienced, informed gun owners are happy to provide prospective first-time gun owners with solid advice on such topics as types of firearms most suitable for home defense, shooting skills and gun safety. If you're already an enthusiastic gun owner, you'll find many good bits of information and comment on various new gun models, ammunition, ballistics, reloading and accessories posted here. A highly recommended information source and talk group for all gun owners on the Net.

Sample Subjects:
Recommendations for a rifle/Most accurate and reliable 9mm/Advice on .357 magnum/Bullet seating/Glaser bullets

FAQ ▶ The following FAQ is available via FTP from RTFM.MIT.EDU in the directory:
pub/usenet/rec.guns:
charter_for_rec.guns

Firearms Tips & Resources

info.firearms **M**

A hands-on newsgroup devoted to addressing specific gun owner questions concerning marksmanship, gun purchase, reloading specifications and parts. A good place to throw out any type of practical or technical gun-related or ammo-related question for fast answers by many fellow Net firearms enthusiasts.

Sample Subjects:
Pump shotgun jam?/Practice ammo for S & W/Dillon Square Deal tip

Metalworking Crafts & Techniques
rec.crafts.metalworking **M**

Good and useful tips and techniques for all different kinds of metalworking projects—welding, metal finishing, polishing, blacksmithing and various metal fabrication projects for hobbyists.

Sample Subjects:
Titanium wire/Anvil polishing/Expanding metal

Leather, Pottery & Miscellaneous Crafts
rec.crafts.misc **M**

Useful discussion group for crafts not fitting into any other category. Topics include pottery, calligraphy and British crafts.

Textile Crafts
rec.crafts.textiles **HI**

Useful resource for weavers, knitters and quilters. Knowledgeable participants offer useful tips, techniques and resources on a wide range of specialized weaving craft topics.

Sample Subjects:
Russian lace/Spinning wheels/Celtic cross-stitch/Mile-a-Minute Quilt

Photography Tips, Gear, & Techniques
rec.photo **HI**

Tremendous resource for photographers of all types and skill levels! **rec.photo** always contains great information and tips on all facets of photography, from better photo techniques in all film formats to darkroom skills and cameras/accessories to buy/for sale, etc. Highly skilled amateur photographers are also ready and willing to provide great picture-taking advice to amateur Net photographers.

Sample Subjects:
Going to Antarctica—What should I take?/Photobook recommendations/Canon and Nikon for sale/High contrast B&W film

FAQ ▶ The following FAQs are available via FTP from RTFM.MIT.EDU in the directory:
pub/usenet/rec.photo:
Photographic_Mail_Order_Survey
rec.photo_FAQ_and_answers

Woodworking
rec.woodworking **HI**

Useful, interesting and fun discussion group for

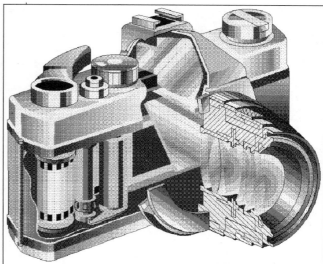

▲ *35 mm camera cutaway image, downloaded via Internet FTP from* **wuarchive.wustl.edu**

woodworking hobbyists of all skill levels, **rec.woodworking** is a handy resource for any home woodworking shop. Netters provide their enthusiastic comments and support on many woodworking techniques, materials, tools or accessories question you might have. Advice on what woodworking power tools to buy, good project plans and resources, hard-to-find woodworking project hardware, fittings, accessories, veneers, etc. Also features extensive power tool and woodworking equipment reviews written and posted by Net woodworking enthusiasts.

Sample Subjects:
Tabletop band saw questions/Shop lighting/Oak flooring—how to/Baby crib plans

FAQ ▶ The following FAQs are available via FTP from RTFM.MIT.EDU in the directory:
pub/usenet/rec.woodworking:
rec.woodworking_Changes_to_Frequently_Asked_Questions
rec.woodworking_Changes_to_Frequently_Requested_Addresses
rec.woodworking_Frequently_Asked_Questions
rec.woodworking_Frequently_Requested_Addresses
rec.woodworking_Frequently_Requested_Tool_Reviews

Brainteasers & Puzzles
rec.puzzles **HI**

If you're into solving tricky math problems, conundrums and other brain twisters, check out this group where Net participants trade and solve each others' favorite trick math problems and online "bar bets." Hours of puzzling fun!

FAQ ▶ The following FAQs are available via FTP from RTFM.MIT.EDU in the directory:
pub/usenet/rec.puzzles:
index
rec.puzzles_Archive_(analysis),_part_02_of_35

```
rec.puzzles_Archive_(arithmetic),_part_03_of_35
rec.puzzles_Archive_(arithmetic),_part_04_of_35
rec.puzzles_Archive_(combinatorics),_part_05_of_35
rec.puzzles_Archive_(competition),_part_06_of_35
rec.puzzles_Archive_(competition),_part_07_of_35
rec.puzzles_Archive_(competition),_part_08_of_35
rec.puzzles_Archive_(competition),_part_09_of_35
rec.puzzles_Archive_(competition),_part_10_of_35
rec.puzzles_Archive_(cryptology),_part_11_of_35
rec.puzzles_Archive_(decision),_part_12_of_35
rec.puzzles_Archive_(geometry),_part_13_of_35
rec.puzzles_Archive_(geometry),_part_14_of_35
rec.puzzles_Archive_(group),_part_15_of_35
rec.puzzles_Archive_(induction),_part_16_of_35
rec.puzzles_Archive_(Instructions),_part_01_of_35
rec.puzzles_Archive_(language),_part_17_of_35
rec.puzzles_Archive_(language),_part_18_of_35
rec.puzzles_Archive_(language),_part_19_of_35
rec.puzzles_Archive_(language),_part_20_of_35
rec.puzzles_Archive_(language),_part_21_of_35
rec.puzzles_Archive_(logic),_part_22_of_35
rec.puzzles_Archive_(logic),_part_23_of_35
rec.puzzles_Archive_(logic),_part_24_of_35
rec.puzzles_Archive_(logic),_part_25_of_35
```

▲ *Table, glass and wine bottle 3-D computer graphics scene downloaded via Internet FTP from* **wuarchive.wustl.edu**

Crossword Puzzles

rec.puzzles.crosswords **M**

In this intriguing newsgroup, Net participants conduct People's Clue Writing Competitions (PCWC)—online weekly crossword puzzle tournaments created and solved by Net participants.

FAQ ▶ The following FAQs are available via FTP from RTFM.MIT.EDU in the directory:
pub/usenet/rec.puzzles.crosswords:
FAQ_rec.puzzles.crossword_part_1_3
FAQ_rec.puzzles.crossword_part_2_3
FAQ_rec.puzzles.crossword_part_3_3

Food, Drink & Dining

Cooking, Eating, Drinking & Dining

Whether you're a bachelor struggling to learn to cook for yourself or a kitchen wizard searching for the perfect Alfredo Sauce recipe, the Net has a variety of categories that will make anyone hungry.

Dining Out Guide

rec.food.restaurants **M**

Diners on the Net share their experiences at local restaurants all around the U.S. and answer your specific requests for good out-of-town places to dine.

Cooking Talk Group

rec.food.cooking **HI**

Net participants share general information about various recipes, cooking utensils, food preservation, preparation and nutrition in this general-interest newsgroup.

FAQ ▶ The following FAQ is available via FTP from RTFM.MIT.EDU in the directory:
pub/usenet/rec.food.cooking:

rec.food.cooking_FAQ_and_conversion_file

Liquor, Whiskey & Wine

rec.food.drink **M**

Participants in this popular newsgroup discuss their favorite whiskey, bourbon, wines and cordials.

Winemaking at Home

rec.crafts.winemaking **M**

An interesting group, featuring a large number of active participants ready to tell you anything you ever wanted to know about making wine at home. Tips for good sources of winemaking supplies by mail, fermentation tips, recipes for all types of wines and other fermented products, ongoing discussions about the details of home winemaking, and more. Participants, whether spirited amateurs or highly skilled experts in the craft of do-it-yourself winemaking, seem anxious to help with beginners' questions.

Cooking: Historic Dishes & Baking

rec.food.historic **M**

Discussions on regional, old-style cooking and baking techniques around the country.

Recipes Exchange

rec.food.recipes **M**

Contains large numbers of interesting recipes of dishes from around the world, posted by Net users. Also a good place to post your request for recipes wanted (or your own personal favorites).

Sourdough Bread Baking

rec.food.sourdough **L**

Tips and recipes for baking the perfect sourdough bread.

Vegetarian Cooking

rec.food.veg **HI**

Vegetarian cooking and baking recipes, food ingredients, cooking/baking techniques and general vegetarian lifestyle issues are discussed here.

FAQ ▶ The following FAQs are available via FTP from RTFM.MIT.EDU in the directory:
pub/usenet/rec.food.veg:
rec.food.veg_FREQUENTLY_ASKED_QUESTIONS_LIST_(FAQ)
rec.food.veg_World_Guide_to_Vegetarianism_-_Airlines
rec.food.veg_World_Guide_to_Vegetarianism_-_California1
rec.food.veg_World_Guide_to_Vegetarianism_-_California2
rec.food.veg_World_Guide_to_Vegetarianism_-_Canada1
rec.food.veg_World_Guide_to_Vegetarianism_-_Canada2
rec.food.veg_World_Guide_to_Vegetarianism_-_Europe
rec.food.veg_World_Guide_to_Vegetarianism_-_Other
rec.food.veg_World_Guide_to_Vegetarianism_-_USA2
rec.food.veg_World_Guide_to_Vegetarianism_-_USA3

Aviation

Newsgroups for Aviation Enthusiasts

As technology buffs, private pilots were one of the earliest enthusiast special-interest groups to use personal computers and online services, so it's really no surprise that you would find over 53,000 active and enthusiastic pilots, plane-builders, students and aviation buffs on the Net's very popular aviation newsgroups. There is an excellent chance that somewhere among these groups you'll find the aviation-related information you're looking for: From homebuilt and kit airplane building construction techniques, to IFR instruction/examination tips and personal experiences, to the inside dope on aviation products, accessories and systems to WW II-vintage aircraft—it's all here. In addition to the top-notch info and advice, you'll find thousands of fellow pilots to swap your flying tales and plenty of good-natured camaraderie.

▲ *(Top) WWII-era Corsair fighter, downloaded via Internet FTP from* **grind.isca.uiowa.edu** ▲ *Biplane, downloaded via Internet FTP from* **wuarchive.wustl.edu**

Aviation General Info

rec.aviation.answers 🇱

Newsgroup containing FAQs on aviation and aviation-related newsgroups, plus a few other interesting files such as an index of aviation fuel prices across the U.S., info on ultralight and homebuilt aircraft, and extensive online indexes of aviation-related publications and trade associations.

FAQ ▶ The following FAQ is available via FTP from RTFM.MIT.EDU in the directory:
pub/usenet/rec.aviation.answers:
index

Homebuilt Aircraft

rec.aviation.homebuilt 🇲

Useful information center for homebuilt plane builders and dreamers. Good resource for plans, components, engines and home building techniques, such as use of new composite plane building materials. A great resource for sharing tips on homebuilt plane assembly and finishing, with fast answers available from other users on most any construction problem.

Aviation IFR

rec.aviation.ifr 🇲

Useful tips, techniques, scenarios and product reviews for instrument-rated private pilots. Participants help each other with FAA test prepara-tions and discuss various IFR trip planning scenarios and new avionics products on the market.

Military & Vintage War Aircraft

rec.aviation.military 🇭🇮

Very active group with lots of fascinating information, mostly about World War I and II-vintage aircraft and air weaponry, plus discussion of air show schedules, modern-day military fighter jets, aviation weapons and museums. A large number of participants in this group are former military pilots, which adds a considerable amount of color and credibility to the stories, facts and historical information related here.

■ **Hobbies, Travel & Tourism**

▲ *SR-71 Blackbird spy plane, downloaded from Smithsonian photo archives at* **sunsite.unc.edu** ▶ *B17 bomber, downloaded via Internet FTP from* **grind.isca.uiowa.edu**

Private Pilots Chat Group

rec.aviation.misc [M]

Private pilots trade flying tips and share their comments on local airports, aviation news and personal flying war stories in this informal aviation discussion group.

Flying Trips & Stories

rec.aviation.stories [L]

Long files posted by pilots relating their recent plane trips, events and interesting stories.

Student Pilots' Group

rec.aviation.student [M]

Students and novice pilots receive tips and trade information with experienced pilots. Great beyond-the-classroom resource for budding private pilots.

Aircraft Buyers Tips/Buy & Sell

rec.aviation.owning [M]

Good resource for prospective plane buyers. Useful tips from plane owners, planes wanted-to-buy/planes for sale, maintenance, overhaul info and price discussions.

Flying Tech Tips

rec.aviation.piloting [M]

Flying techniques from mild to wild—ranging from where to rent a plane in Phoenix to crossing the Rocky Mountains with a new engine. Pilots trade their flying tips on their own plane types and models and comment on tips contributed by fellow pilots.

Aircraft Product Advice

rec.aviation.products [L]

Lots of good inside dope on any plane gear, from an "I've used it and here is what's good about it" point of view. Everything from avionics to composite wing coverings to which oxygen system is the best to buy.

Flight Simulator Software

rec.aviation.simulators [M]

Good info for users and fans of PC-based flight simulation programs (Microsoft Flight Simulator, Falcon 3, etc.), tips on new releases, scenery packages and troubleshooting.

Gliders & Soaring

rec.aviation.soaring [M]

Glider enthusiasts trade soaring techniques, maintenance and restoration tips and soaring school locations and events.

Consumer Electronics

Big-Buck Television & VCR Buffs Group

rec.video [HI]

Talk group for high-end VCR, camcorder, TV and video recording buffs. Video product advice and comments, recording tips, troubleshooting, etc.

Cyber Tech: First Look at Hot New Technology

alt.cyberpunk.tech [M]

A cyberpunk/hacker-oriented newsgroup, but with a focus on new technology and hardware. Useful inside information on the latest in cutting edge computer technology, communications, voice recognition and keyboards. A great place to discuss new technology and, as a bonus, get a first look at technology from major manufacturers that's not yet on the market.

Sample Subjects:
Voice recognition/Keyboards/Best ways to process e-mail/Update: Sega interface available!

Video Production
rec.video.production **M**

A valuable resource for both amateur and professional video producers, this group features extensive practical advice on video recording and sound equipment, studio and editing gear, equipment troubleshooting, editing techniques, and discussions about the emerging computer/digital video recording field.

Video: Cable TV Talk
rec.video.cable **M**

Net participants endlessly complain about big cable TV companies, the ethics of cable TV, piracy and other cable TV-related issues.

Laserdisc Players
alt.video.laserdisc **M**

Everybody's got VCRs these days, but if you're a true TV obsessive you also own a laserdisc player. If so, this active newsgroup can provide you with useful information about laserdiscs: new movie titles, comments on various laserdisc systems, movies currently on the market and discounted-price sources of laserdisc movies.

Sample Subjects:
Digital sound versus analog sound/Laserdisc release/ Bram Stoker's Dracula

New Movies on Video & Laserdisc
rec.video.releases **M**

Hard-core video enthusiasts discuss the technical aspects of the latest high-end movies released on video and laserdisc. Also includes video and laserdisc equipment wanted-to-buy/for sale.

Satellite TV Dish Owners
rec.video.satellite **M**

High-end satellite dish users' group for in-depth discussions of the latest satellite TV gear, signal-grabbing, programming and SAT TV technical advice.

FAQ ▶ The following FAQs are available via FTP from RTFM.MIT.EDU in the directory:
pub/usenet/rec.video.satellite:
rec.video.satellite:_Pointer_to_the_South_Scanner_Satellite_____Services_Chart
Satellite_TV_Frequently_Asked_Questions_List

▲ *ENIAC computer, downloaded from Smithsonian photo archives at* **sunsite.unc.edu**

Acoustics & Sound Engineering Resource Group
alt.sci.physics.acoustics **L**

A small and technical-oriented discussion group devoted to theoretical and applied concepts of acoustical and sonic engineering, including recent discussions on active noise control technology, homemade diffusers, Doppler effects and underwater radio wave propagation. This would be a good place to go for solid advice and referrals on any technical question related to the use of electronics in sonic engineering, or a general question on acoustics, as there are a number of good technical experts in this field who access this group on a regular basis.

Vintage Personal Computer Collector's Group
alt.technology.obsolete **L**

If you've been around personal computers long enough to remember the TI99/4 or the Exidy Sorcerer, have we got a newsgroup for you! Obsolete computer enthusiasts reminisce about the old personal computers they have known and loved. Also includes talk about other forms of obsolete technology such as radios, hi-fi, vacuum tubed-based electronics, finding parts, etc.

Sample Subjects:
Computer orphans/Obsolete technology sources

High-Tech Toys Talk Group
alt.toys.hi-tech **M**

Want to know where to find the latest in

cutting-edge electronics for consumers? Participants swap info on where to find—and what are the best—high-tech doodads of all kinds: cordless phones, VCR and video gear, neat tools, radar detectors and stuff from the Sharper Image catalog.

Cars & Driving

Cars: Driving, Racing, Restorations & Repairs

Knowledgeable car buffs are always available on the Net to answer most any car-related question, solve mechanical problems and dish the dirt on most any car-related topic. It also helps that participants in these newsgroups are enthusiastic car buffs and competent shade-tree mechanics who can provide you with solid information and advice on most anything related to autos. It's the online equivalent of the "around the water cooler" car buff bull session.

▲ *Acura NSX sports car, downloaded via Internet FTP from* **grind.isca.uiowa.edu**

How to Restore Your Antique or Collectible Car

alt.autos.antique **L**

Fun and informative place to trade information and tips on the old car restoration hobby. Includes car buy/sell postings, questions and answers on restoration tips, and many car-specific restoration tips and techniques.

Sample Subjects:
Leaded gas vs. lead additives/1951 Willys Overland suspension advice/Help needed on Lucas electrics for Triumph Spitfire/Stainless polishing tips

Best Auto Hot Rod Talk Group

alt.hotrod **M**

An active, excellent talk and information exchange group for enthusiastic performance car builders, shadetree car and motorcycle mechanics or anyone interested in automotive performance improvement. Net car buffs exchange information on all aspects of high-performance engine building, intakes, exhausts, carburetion, suspensions and more, backing up their statements with well-written, factual documentation.

If you're into auto engine performance building, don't let this newsgroup pass you by! Also features a large number of hands-on information postings on do-it-yourself auto mechanics and auto body restoration, plus buy/sell listings for high-performance cars, parts and accessories.

Sample Subjects:
Holley carburetor/Exhaust system tuning/Corvette for sale/Fuel injecting an old car/Sandblasting

Hot Rods & Custom Cars: How-To Tips

alt.autos.rod-n-custom **L**

Discussions of high-performance autos, modifications and customizing, including questions and answers about specific car performance, nostalgia cars and buy/sell listings.

Sample Subjects:
1963 Corvette wanted/Buick Grand National talk and tips/1988 350 block and roller lifters

Car Talk

rec.autos **HI**

General-interest discussion group for any auto-related topic or question. Model-specific car problems, mechanical glitches, speeding tickets, car news, advice on what type of car to buy, car care tips, etc.

Antique Auto Restoration

rec.autos.antique **M**

A must if you're into old car restorations. Features plenty of good, do-it-yourself auto restoration tips related both to specific old car models and to old cars in general. Everything from refinishing stainless steel trim to restoring old license plates to convertible top replacements and cars for sale.

▲ *1950 Volkswagen Beetle, downloaded via Internet FTP from* **wuarchive.wustl.edu** ▶ *Four-valve cylinder head photo, downloaded via Internet FTP from* **grind.isca.uiowa.edu** ▶ *Formula I race car, downloaded from* **wuarchive.wustl.edu**

Driving Tips

rec.autos.driving **M**

General-interest newsgroup with information on good driving tips, traffic laws in various states and car buying advice.

Street Rods

rec.autos.rod-n-custom **M**

For builders of street rods, this newsgroup features good information on engine swaps, chassis fitting and other good Q&A stuff for car builders.

Auto Racing

rec.autos.sport **HI**

Good inside dope, from all around the world, for hard-core racing fans. Covers the entire world of motor racing, from Formula One to Indy, as well as amateur action at local tracks across the U.S.

Motorcycle Owner's Talk & Info Group

rec.motorcycles **HI**

Motorcycle owners (mostly road bikes) trade information on good bike maintenance and repair techniques, new accessories on the market and recent crashes. More information for motorcyclists can be found in some of the more specialized bike-related groups, such as **rec.motorcycles.dirt**.

FAQ ▶ The following FAQs are available via FTP from RTFM.MIT.EDU in the directory:
pub/usenet/rec.motorcycles:
Beginner_Motorcycle_Info:_Periodic_Post

FAQ_-_What_is_the_DoD?
rec.motorcycles_FAQ_of_93.09.01____(Part_1_of_6)
rec.motorcycles_FAQ_of_93.09.01____(Part_3_of_6)
rec.motorcycles_FAQ_of_93.09.01____(Part_4_of_6)
rec.motorcycles_FAQ_of_93.09.01____(Part_5_of_6)
rec.motorcycles_FAQ_of_93.09.01____(Part_6_of_6)
What_is_the_DoD?_-_Weekly_Micro-FAQ

Do-It-Yourself Auto Repair & Maintenance

rec.autos.tech **HI**

Good advice available from thousands of fellow car enthusiasts on most any auto-related do-it-yourself problem (mostly for late-model cars). Topics range from minor mechanical problems and routine maintenance to accessories, specific car model problems/fixes and cosmetic car care.

Snowmobile Talk Group

alt.snowmobiles **M**

Snowmobilers from northern parts of the U.S., Finland and Europe trade info on snowmobile care and performance (they're called "sleds," by the way), good snowmobiling trails and used snowmobile prices.

Volkswagen Car Repairs

rec.autos.vw **HI**

Popular newsgroup for both late-model and

▲ *Sailboat, photo image downloaded from* **wuarchive.wustl.edu** ▲ *Goldfinch, downloaded via Internet FTP from* **grind.isca.uiowa.edu**

classic VWs including, of course, the venerable Beetle. Model-specific do-it-yourself technical tips, parts availability and specific advice for keeping any Rabbit, Golf, Bug or other VW alive.

Boats & Sailing

Sailboats, Kayaks & Canoes

Two newsgroups devoted to everything and anything related to (mostly) wind-powered or paddle-powered boating.

Sailing Tips & Talk

rec.boats **HI**

Newsgroup devoted to sailing enthusiasts including info on boats, gear, places to sail, clubs, repairs and racing.

Kayaks, Canoes & Whitewater Rafting

rec.boats.paddle **HI**

This newsgroup takes care of the "arm-powered" side of boating. Comments on participant's experiences with white-water rafting trips and kayaking around the U.S. and Surf Ski enthusiasts' talk.

FAQ▶ The following FAQs are available via FTP from RTFM.MIT.EDU in the directory:
pub/usenet/rec.boats.paddle:
rec.boats.paddle_frequently_asked_questions_and_answers
Whitewater_outfitter_dealer_address_list

Pet Care & Talk

Tips & Talk for Aquarium Owners & Buyers

alt.aquaria **M**

Discussion group for aquarium owners—use it to post your own questions and get answers on your own aquarium and fish-related problems. Also features product recommendations and tips on suppliers of a wide variety of aquarium-related products and merchandise, including buy-and-sell listings of aquarium stuff.

Sample Subjects:
Aquaria & equipment for sale/Request for advice on ozonizers/Oscar questions/Aquariums and apartments/Homebuilt filter systems/How to cool a tank aquarium

FAQ▶ The following FAQs are available via FTP from RTFM.MIT.EDU in the directory:
pub/usenet/alt.aquaria:
FAQ:_Beginner_topics_and_books
FAQ:_Filters
FAQ:_Magazines_and_mail_order
FAQ:_Plants
FAQ:_Water_quality

Pets: General Interest

rec.pets **M**

Generally serves as a catch-all newsgroup for owners of small, unusual pets such as ferrets, prairie dogs, pot-bellied pigs, hamsters and even Jamaican River Rats! Feeding tips, care and stories relating to these unusual small pets.

FAQ▶ The following FAQ is available via FTP from RTFM.MIT.EDU in the directory:
pub/usenet/rec.pets:
Fleas,_Ticks,_and_Your_Pet:_FAQ

Pet Bird Owners Group

rec.pets.birds **M**

Care and feeding of pet birds of all kinds, from keets to cockatiels and exotic parrots. Good bird care advice, mail order supplier info, bird care stories and bird care problem-solving.

FAQ ▶ The following FAQs are available via FTP from RTFM.MIT.EDU in the directory: **pub/usenet/rec.pets.birds:**
rec.pets.birds_FAQ:_Monthly_Posting_(1_3)
rec.pets.birds_FAQ:_Monthly_Posting_(2_3)
rec.pets.birds_FAQ:_Monthly_Posting_(3_3)

Pets: Snakes & Lizards

rec.pets.herp **M**

What do you do when your iguana's constipated? How do you prepare gerbils as a meal for your pet boa constrictor? Offbeat discussion group for fanatical owners of big snakes, strange and exotic lizards, turtles and other unusual critters.

Bird Watching Group

rec.birds **HI**

Whether you're an enthusiastic bird watcher (OK—we're sorry—we know you'd like to be called Birders) or just want to know how to attract more interesting and colorful birds to your backyard, here's a good spot to learn more. Enthusiasts share their latest bird sighting lists, info on specific bird species and neat ideas on homemade birdfeeders. A sweet, good-natured discussion group that is also quite (unexpectedly) interesting, too!

Sample Subjects:
Hummingbird food/Quaker Parakeets/Backyard birds

▲ *"Boots," downloaded from* **access.digex.net**

Cat Lovers Group

rec.pets.cats **HI**

Cat lovers (millions of them) have always been a very close-knit group, and now there's a place for them on the Net. Useful info from experienced cat owners on all different kinds of cat care and health topics: spaying, cat health symptoms, problems and owners' favorite cat stories, including informal insights into cat psychology

▲ *Terrier and wolf photo images, downloaded via Internet FTP from* **grind.isca.uiowa.edu**

and behavior, often from a humorous point of view.

Sample Subjects:
Kitty with discolored tongue/Amoxicillin/New toy for Gracie

FAQ ▶ The following FAQs are available via FTP from RTFM.MIT.EDU in the directory: **pub/usenet/rec.pets.cats:**
rec.pets.cats_FAQ_(part_1_4)
rec.pets.cats_FAQ_(part_2_4)
rec.pets.cats_FAQ_(part_3_4)
rec.pets.cats_FAQ_(part_4_4)

Dogs: Pets & Care

rec.pets.dogs **HI**

Good dog care advice, focusing on dog training, discipline and behavior. Includes exchange of dog care advice for specific breeds from knowledgeable breed owners, plus many humorous dog pet stories.

Sample Subjects:
Looking for a non-shedding dog/Renaming a dog/My Rottweiler bit me

FAQ ▶ The following FAQs are available via FTP from RTFM.MIT.EDU in the directory: **pub/usenet/rec.pets.dogs:**
Complete_List_of_rec.pets.dogs_FAQ_s
rec.pets.dogs:_Breed_Rescue_Organizations_FAQ_Part_1_2
rec.pets.dogs:_Breed_Rescue_Organizations_FAQ_Part_2_2
rec.pets.dogs:__American_Kennel_Club_FAQ
rec.pets.dogs:__Assorted_Topics_[Part_1]_FAQ
rec.pets.dogs:__Assorted_Topics_[Part_II]_FAQ
rec.pets.dogs:__Behavior:_Understanding_and_Modifying_FAQ
rec.pets.dogs:__Border_Collies__Breed-FAQ
rec.pets.dogs:__Breeding_Your_Dog_FAQ
rec.pets.dogs:__Canine_Medical_Information_FAQ
rec.pets.dogs:__Getting_A_Dog_FAQ
rec.pets.dogs:__Introduction_FAQ
rec.pets.dogs:__Publications_FAQ
rec.pets.dogs:__Resources_FAQ
rec.pets.dogs:__Saint_Bernards__Breed-FAQ
rec.pets.dogs:__Service_Dogs_FAQ
rec.pets.dogs:__Training_Your_Dog_FAQ
rec.pets.dogs:__Working_Dogs_FAQ
rec.pets.dogs:__Your_New_Dog_FAQ
rec.pets.dogs:__Your_New_Puppy_FAQ

Wolves as Pets?

alt.wolves [L]

No, this group isn't about werewolves—it's an honest-to-gosh group for people (mostly on farms) who keep wolves as pets! If you ever wanted to raise a wolf as a pet, you would probably want to know how to stop it from howling, and you would find the answer here!

Amateur Radio

Radio: Ham, CB, Packet, Amateur & Commercial

Ham radio enthusiasts have always been notorious early technology adopters, so it's no surprise they started some of the very first newsgroups on the Net many years ago. rec.radio newsgroups cover the entire spectrum of the amateur radio hobby with popular discussion groups featuring plenty of the usual radio tech tips, gear setups, signal-grabbing info, equipment wanted-to-buy/swap/sell and more.

Get the Most from Your Scanner Radio

alt.radio.scanner [HI]

The busy, comprehensive clearinghouse for everything about radio scanners and related equipment—from police, fire, air, government and Air Force One radio frequencies to new equipment, scanner radios for sale and modifications for increased reception. Plenty of information here for people who are heavily involved in scanner radio listening, as well as people who are just starting out in this interesting and informative hobby.

Sample Subjects:
Air traffic control/Scanner antenna/Scanner for sale/Air Force One frequencies

[FAQ] ▶ The following FAQs are available via FTP from RTFM.MIT.EDU in the directory:
pub/usenet/alt.radio.scanner:
FCC_License_Data_Source
Welcome_to_rec.radio.info!

Ham Radio: General Info

rec.radio.info [M]

Useful general-interest category containing many FAQs, info files and daily solar/ionospheric data report summaries of interest to amateur broadcasters.

[FAQ] ▶ The following FAQs are available via FTP from RTFM.MIT.EDU in the directory:
pub/usenet/rec.radio.info:
(PKT):_Daily_Solar_Geophysical_Data_Broadcast_for_01_October
(PKT):_Daily_Solar_Geophysical_Data_Broadcast_for_02_October
(PKT):_Daily_Summary_of_Ionospheric_Data_(1_2)_for_02_October
(PKT):_Daily_Summary_of_Ionospheric_Data_(1_2)_for_06_October
(PKT):_Weekly_Solar_Terrestrial_Forecast_(1_2)_for_01_October
(PKT):_Weekly_Solar_Terrestrial_Forecast_(1_2)_for_08_October
A_Guide_to_Buying_and_Selling_on_Usenet
Daily_Summary_of_Ionospheric_Data_for_01_October
Daily_Summary_of_Ionospheric_Data_for_02_October
Daily_Summary_of_Ionospheric_Data_for_03_October
Daily_Summary_of_Solar_Geophysical_Activity_for_01_October
Daily_Summary_of_Solar_Geophysical_Activity_for_02_October
Daily_Summary_of_Solar_Geophysical_Activity_for_03_October
nic.funet.fi:__pub_dx_new_files_[week_36]
nic.funet.fi:__pub_dx_new_files_[week_37]
rec.radio.info_Submission_Guidelines
US_License_Examinations_Scheduled_10_01_93_to_1_03_94
Welcome_to_rec.radio.info!
Welcome_to_rec.radio.shortwave
Welcome_to_rec.radio.shortwave_(AM_FM_DXing)
Welcome_to_rec.radio.shortwave_(Scanning)
Welcome_to_rec.radio.shortwave_(Shortwave)

Ham Radio

rec.radio.amateur.misc [HI]

Catch-all newsgroup where ham radio enthusiasts trade comments on new gear, radio access, hassles with the FCC and other ham radio war stories.

[FAQ] ▶ The following FAQs are available via FTP from RTFM.MIT.EDU in the directory:
pub/usenet/rec.radio.amateur.misc:
Amateur_Radio_Elmers_List_Info_and_Administrivia
Amateur_Radio_Elmers_Resource_Directory
Changes_to_Amateur_Radio_Elmers_Resource_Directory
Examination_Opportunities_Scheduled_10_01_93_to_1_03_94
Examination_Opportunities_Scheduled_9_17_93_to_12_27_93
Examination_Opportunities_Scheduled_9_2_93_to_12_6_93
How_to_find_the_answers_to_frequently-asked_questions_about_Ham_Radio
Index_to_the_rec.radio.amateur.*_Supplemental_Archives
Radio_Amateurs_on_USENET_List__Sep_1993__Part_1_of_6
Radio_Amateurs_on_USENET_List__Sep_1993__Part_2_of_6
Radio_Amateurs_on_USENET_List__Sep_1993__Part_3_of_6
Radio_Amateurs_on_USENET_List__Sep_1993__Part_4_of_6
Radio_Amateurs_on_USENET_List__Sep_1993__Part_5_of_6
Radio_Amateurs_on_USENET_List__Sep_1993__Part_6_of_6
Readership_Report_for_the_Radio-Related_Usenet_Newsgroups
rec.radio.amateur.misc_Frequently_Asked_Questions_(Part_1_of_3)
rec.radio.amateur.misc_Frequently_Asked_Questions_(Part_2_of_3)
rec.radio.amateur.misc_Frequently_Asked_Questions_(Part_3_of_3)
US_License_Examinations_Scheduled_10_01_93_to_1_03_94
US_License_Examinations_Scheduled_9_17_93_to_12_27_93

Packet Radio

rec.radio.amateur.packet [L]

Frequency info, equipment tips and software programming advice for computer-based, digital packet radio broadcasters.

Ham Radio Licensing Policy Discussions

rec.radio.amateur.policy [HI]

Ham radio enthusiasts discuss the ins and outs of radio license tests and complain about FCC policies and testing procedures.

Radio: College & Commercial Broadcasting

rec.radio.broadcasting [M]

Enthusiastic participants provide interesting information on setting up college radio stations, low-power FM broadcast stations, related electronics gear, nationwide

FM commercial station lists, programming availability and commercial broadcasting news of the day.

FAQ ▶ The following FAQ is available via FTP from RTFM.MIT.EDU in the directory:
pub/usenet/rec.radio.broadcasting:
Introduction_to_rec.radio.broadcasting_(7-29-93)

CB Radio
rec.radio.cb **M**

Info of interest to citizens' band radio enthusiasts around the world, including other forms of unlicensed or minimally licensed amateur radio broadcasting.

FAQ ▶ The following FAQs are available via FTP from RTFM.MIT.EDU in the directory:
pub/usenet/rec.radio.cb:
rec.radio.cb_Frequently_Asked_Questions_(Part_1_of_4)
rec.radio.cb_Frequently_Asked_Questions_(Part_2_of_4)
rec.radio.cb_Frequently_Asked_Questions_(Part_3_of_4)
rec.radio.cb_Frequently_Asked_Questions_(Part_4_of_4)

Shortwave Radio
rec.radio.shortwave **HI**

Shortwave radio listeners post info on stations heard, questions and answers on SW equipment and new shortwave programming.

FAQ ▶ The following FAQs are available via FTP from RTFM.MIT.EDU in the directory:
pub/usenet/rec.radio.shortwave:
Handy_Shortwave_Chart
Phone_line_as_SW_antenna

Ham Radio Swap Meet
rec.radio.swap **HI**

Amateur radio enthusiast's marketplace for buying/selling/swapping radio equipment and accessories of all types. Includes requests for information and answers on specific radio models.

Travel & Tourism

Appalachian Travel Tips
alt.appalachian **M**

Comments, observations, tourist tips and miscellany concerning the Appalachian region of the U.S. Includes questions and answers about history surrounding the Appalachian region, recommended towns and other places of interest.

Sample Subjects:
Appalachian summer/Chief Cornstalk/Blue Ridge Mountains/West Virginia vs. Appalachia/Emancipation celebration Gallia Appalachian

Disney World & Disneyland Travel Tips
rec.arts.disney **HI**

Planning to take the family to Disneyland or Disneyworld soon? If so, participants on this active newsgroup give you good insider tips on Disney attractions, accommodations and other aspects of visiting Disney theme parks.

Sample Subjects:
Hotel suites just outside Disneyworld/Travel packages and Disneyland tips/Swimming pools at Walt Disney World

FAQ ▶ The following FAQs are available via FTP from RTFM.MIT.EDU in the directory:
pub/usenet/rec.arts.disney:
Disneyland_FAQ
rec.arts.disney_FAQ,_part_1a
rec.arts.disney_FAQ,_part_1b
rec.arts.disney_FAQ,_part_1c
rec.arts.disney_FAQ,_part_2

Theme Park Talk
rec.parks.theme **L**

Netters provide helpful advice on attractions and things to see at various theme parks around the world. Also features many comments from roller coaster fanatics on the Net.

Hawaii: Local Life and Talk
alt.culture.hawaii **M**

Group discussions for Hawaiian residents covering local news items, local political issues, employment and local attractions. Despite its use as a local resident's discussion forum, participants are happy to provide useful advice on moving to or living in Hawaii, travel and sightseeing tips and cost of living issues. A posting of your questions to this group a week or so before a Hawaiian vacation could give you some good down-to-earth advice on things to do and places to see.

Travel & Vacations
rec.travel **HI**

An invaluable service for any business or vacation traveller, **rec.travel** is a must for insider advice on any travel location or vacation spot you have in mind. Net participants are eager to provide you with solid advice on out-of-the-way places to visit, low-cost accommodations and other travel/vacation tips. Covers the widest possible range of travel and vacation spots around the world, from sailing vacations in the Baltics to European country biking tours, South American adventure excursions and much more. You'll find consistently good and solid advice from well-travelled Net participants who can make your next vacation a more memorable experi-

▲ *Mount Rushmore "Dune" fantasy graphic by Dion Kraft, downloaded from* **wuarchive.wustl.edu**

ence. Check this newsgroup for its excellent FAQ (Frequently Asked Question) files containing volumes of excellent travel, airfare, tourism and accommodation advice for many travel locations across the world.

Sample Subjects:
London—where to stay?/Hong Kong cheap hotels/House for rent in Ireland/Weather in Siberia

FAQ ▶ The following FAQs are available via FTP from RTFM.MIT.EDU in the directory:
pub/usenet/rec.travel:
Directory_of_tourist_information_offices_worldwide
Directory_of_travel_information_available_via_internet
Index_to_rec.travel_ftp_archive
Simple_suggestions_for_travel_(net_reminders_really)

Travel & Tourism Tips
bit.listserv.travel-l **M**
Jet-set Netters trade interesting travel tips for visits to exotic locales around the world, from travel to Iran to setting up a fax machine in Russia.

Oregon Travel, Tourism, & Tips for New Residents
alt.culture.oregon **M**
Get the latest info on what's happening in Oregon: jobs, housing, taxes and local events. Quite useful if you're visiting or thinking about relocating to Oregon.

Sample Subjects:
Job market—how's it doing?/Moving to Eugene—advice/ Oregon taxes/Oregon brewers festival

Upstate New York Travel & Places to See
alt.culture.ny-upstate **M**
A quirky and offbeat discussion on upstate NY tourist attractions, land-marks, bars and out-of-the-way places. Also includes advice if you are inter-ested in moving or working there.

Sample Subjects:
Mid-Hudson Valley/Victorian architecture/Anchor steam bar and restaurant

Air Travel Bargains
rec.travel.air **HI**
Another travel-oriented newsgroup with many excellent comments from seasoned Net air travellers.
rec.travel.air has also become an active and popular clearinghouse for ex-change, sale or barter of major airline Frequent Flyer discount miles. Fea-tures useful airline advice and personal flight experiences, international air travel tips and worst airline experiences.

Sample Subjects:
Denver's new airport/Singapore stopover/UA travel certificate needed/Two thousand bonus miles

FAQ ▶ The following FAQs are available via FTP from RTFM.MIT.EDU in the directory:
pub/usenet/rec.travel.air:
FAQ:_How_to_Get_Cheap_Airtickets_1_2_[Monthly_posting]
FAQ:_How_to_Get_Cheap_Airtickets_2_2_[Monthly_posting]

Travel & Vacation Marketplace
rec.travel.marketplace **M**
We highly recommend this group if you're looking to buy or sell plane tickets, vacation packages, frequent flyer miles, vacation rentals or other accommodations. Also features great last-minute plane ticket bargains posted by people desperate to sell.

Sample Subjects:
Two tickets RT SF to London/Fly to Florida only $75/For Sale: Cheap tickets/Lake Tahoe with a great view

Theatre Arts Group
rec.arts.theatre **M**
Theatregoers discuss their favorite plays. Also includes behind-the-scenes talk by actors, actresses and others involved in college, amateur and Off-Broadway produc-tions.

FAQ ▶ The following FAQs are available via FTP from RTFM.MIT.EDU in the directory:
pub/usenet/rec.arts.theatre:
rec.arts.theatre_Frequently_Asked_Questions_(FAQ):_part_1_2
rec.arts.theatre_Frequently_Asked_Questions_(FAQ):_part_2_2

Miscellaneous Hobbies

Genealogy Discussion & Information Exchange
soc.roots **HI**

There are literally millions of active and highly enthusiastic genealogy enthusiasts tracing their families' roots and thousands of them have discovered the Net! This group is a must for any amateur or professional genealogist. Netters post their requests for the historical genealogy information they require (such as information on lost distant relatives in specific cities, voting, census and old municipal records, maps, etc.), and get solid answers from other Net genealogists. Participants also discuss research techniques, older customs and traditions affecting genealogical searches, software and computer databases. Whether you're just curious about starting a family search or you've been involved in one for some time, this group should be an important part of your genealogical brain trust.

FAQ ▶ The following FAQ is available via FTP from RTFM.MIT.EDU in the directory:
pub/usenet/soc.roots:
Index_of_soc.roots_ROOTS-L_FAQ_files

Gambling & Games of Chance
rec.gambling **HI**

Very popular and active discussion group for serious and (sometimes) successful gamblers. Covers all games of chance—from winning blackjack card-counting strategies to sports handicapping, poker, etc. Net participants also share their experiences at various gambling meccas and give you their opinions on the best casinos, games, and hotel accommodations available there.

Sample Subjects:
Sports betting/Poker tournament partners/Blackjack counting advice needed/Reno developments

FAQ ▶ The following FAQs are available via FTP from RTFM.MIT.EDU in the directory:
pub/usenet/rec.gambling:
rec.gambling_Changes_to_Frequently_Asked_Questions
rec.gambling_Frequently_Asked_Questions

Medieval Re-Enactments
rec.org.sca **HI**

For modern-day groups like the SCA (Society For Creative Anachronism) involved in holding medieval festivals and combat reenactments. Info on armor, weaving, chivalric justice and other topics of interest to modern-day knights and damsels.

FAQ ▶ The following FAQs are available via FTP from RTFM.MIT.EDU in the directory:
pub/usenet/rec.org.sca:
Monthly_Posting_-_Consultant_List
rec.org.sca___Rialto_Frequently_Asked_Questions_-_part01_04
rec.org.sca___Rialto_Frequently_Asked_Questions_-_part02_04
rec.org.sca___Rialto_Frequently_Asked_Questions_-_part03_04
rec.org.sca___Rialto_Frequently_Asked_Questions_-_part04_04

Roller Coasters
rec.roller coaster **M**

Roller coaster fanatics discuss their favorite roller coasters, upcoming coaster rides, morbid details on roller coaster accidents and other (happier) roller coaster news.

Marching Bands & Drum Corps
rec.arts.marching **L**

Includes two active newsgroups for students involved in marching bands and drum corps. **rec.arts.marching.drumcorps** and **rec.arts.marching.misc** feature discussion on different college marching bands, contests, auditions and news.

Therapeutic Massage Advice
alt.backrubs **M**

A group that won't rub you the wrong way. Detailed discussions of various (non-sexual) massage techniques, advice and products, proving once again that there's room for all kinds on the Net.

Sample Subjects:
Massage oil suggestions/Oil removal/Advice on massage books/Soothing baths massage

Astrology Talk & Readings Advice
alt.astrology **HI**

If you're interested in astrology, this group's for you! Complex, wide-ranging discussions of astrological reading techniques, opinions and topics for those whose interests in astrology go beyond reading their daily horoscope. Who knows, you might even get a free astrological reading online here if you ask for one!

Sample Subjects:
World's most accurate astrology/Vedic astrology/Using progressions/Readings wanted/ The end of the world

FAQ ▶ The following FAQs are available via FTP from RTFM.MIT.EDU in the directory:
pub/usenet/alt.astrology:
_NEWCOMERS_READ_THIS:_FREQUENTLY_ASKED_QUESTIONS_
ALT.ASTROLOGY_NEWCOMERS_READ_THIS:_FREQUENTLY_ASKED_QUESTIONS

Lego Toy Talk
alt.toys.lego **M**

An unbelievably popular interest group devoted specifically to fans and builders of Lego building block models. Everything for Lego builders, including info on old Lego toys, parts, kits and Lego in the news.

Chapter 7: Headline News

Would you like to create your own personal electronic newspaper? ClariNet News Services are available on the Internet in Usenet newsgroup format, providing AP and Reuters news wire feeds for national, local and metro area news items, business/ technical features, and international news.

Your Personal "Electronic Newspaper"

by Brad Templeton (reprinted with permission)

ClariNet provides an "electronic newspaper" and more, in formats used by popular electronic conferencing systems. You can read and access a full range of electronic news on your own computer, with your own software, at your own pace.

ClariNet news services are available through many commercial Internet access providers. You can get subscription information on ClariNet by sending Internet electronic mail to **info@clarinet.com** or by phoning 1 (800) USE-NETS or 1 (408) 296-0366.

The primary format for ClariNet news is the Usenet newsgroup message interchange format, which makes ClariNet look a lot like the other newsgroups featured in ***What's on the Internet***.

You can think of many ClariNet newsgroups as vaguely analogous to pages in a newspaper. Our baseball group, for example, has all the information that you will find on the baseball pages of a newspaper.

How to Read ClariNet News Features

Those familiar with Usenet should be able to ease right into reading ClariNet news. All ClariNet newsgroups begin with the prefix "**clari.**" and fall into one of a small number of product hierarchies. You subscribe to and read these groups in the same manner as Usenet groups.

There are some fundamental differences, however, that you will want to consider:

■ ClariNet articles have a meaningful headline prepared by a professional journalist. You can scan the headlines quickly to see what you wish to read.

■ ClariNet articles are keyworded using the topics the article covers.

■ ClariNet articles aren't discussions, they are news. There are no follow-ups, though reference chains exist.

■ ClariNet articles come with a wide variety of extra headers providing useful classifying information about the article.

■ ClariNet articles come fast, and network links are designed to propagate them quickly. They also become stale more quickly, turning into "yesterday's news."

■ ClariNet articles on big stories are updated frequently. Each update cancels the previous article and adds a new one with the latest details. You will thus find lots of gaps in ClariNet newsgroups where canceled articles used to be.

■ As a consequence of the above, ClariNet feeds generate hundreds of cancel messages every day.

■ ClariNet articles are all copyrighted, and may not be distributed without permission. See the license terms.

■ Most ClariNet articles are cross-posted to 2-4 groups, if their subject matter falls in multiple categories.

■ You can't reply to, or follow-up ClariNet articles. They are publications, not discussions. Some groups exist for the discussion of ClariNet and articles within it. Most ClariNet groups are marked as "moderated," but you may not submit to them, even by mail.

At first glance, your reactions to ClariNet may well be that there are a lot of newsgroups, a lot of stories in these groups, and that stories seem to repeat annoyingly. How does one deal with this?

With over a megabyte a day of information, nobody can read all of ClariNet. It is divided into many newsgroups so that you can select just the news you want. It is further categorized so that you can use tools such as kill files and Newsclip to greatly refine your reading.

Beyond the groups for top news, you will want to pick a small to medium number of groups that cover your specific interests. Naturally, the group clari.tw.computers is very popular. Many people used to scan their newspapers for computer related stories before ClariNet came along. Now you can find those stories all in one place. The TechWire (clari.tw.*) groups are all very popular in the computer community—no surprise there.

There are groups for specific interests. For example, there are groups like clari.news.jews and clari.news.women where issues related to these groups like Israel and abortion (respectively!) are covered.

Read the specific group descriptions to decide which groups are of interest to you. Or better still, subscribe to several groups to start, and unsubscribe to those that don't match your interests or reading patterns.

Soon you will settle down to reading the top newsgroups and the few of particular interest to yourself. You may also have a filter program scan groups of lesser interest for stories that contain keywords you are tracking. NewsClip can do this for you.

(NewsClip is the news filtering language supplied free to all ClariNet subscribers. It has its own manual.)

Urgent ClariNet News Features

In general, you'll always want to read the groups that present the very biggest news—**clari.news.urgent** and **clari.biz.urgent**.

Then you'll want to read the groups for top news in the categories of interest to you. **clari.news.top** covers top U.S.A.-related news, while the very popular **clari.world.top** covers top international stories. General sports fans enjoy clari.sports.top and business readers subscribe to **clari.biz.top**.

As a substitute, you can also read **clari.news.briefs**. This offers a regularly updated short summary of the current top news, and is joined by **clari.world.briefs** (an international brief) and **clari.biz.briefs** (a business brief). If you see a story you are interested in, you can temporarily subscribe to the appropriate topic group for the story to get the full details.

You may decide not to read any groups for major news at all. Many still prefer to get this sort of news from television or newspapers. ClariNet can still serve you by presenting you with the more obscure stories on topics of interest to you that never reach those media.

News Talk Newsgroups

Headline News Discussions
misc.headlines **M**

This is the place to go if you want to share your views on current major news items or the latest inside dope from other Netters who provide interesting source material, references or other information relating to major national and international headline news stories. Although some of the postings contain heavy conspiratorial undertones, dig deep enough and you will be able to extract things you didn't know before. A good resource for getting solid, factual information on rumors you've heard or in-depth details on recent stories you may have missed due to shallow coverage by network TV or mass print media.

Medical News
bit.listserv.mednews **L**

A comprehensive, interesting and informative daily news digest, HICNet Medical News Digest is an extensive daily news file containing (on average) a half-dozen or more informative data files reprinted from FDA Medical Bulletins, The American Cancer Society, and other medical organizations. Recent news items have included topics such as cancer information resources, ranges of emotions for the infertile couple, AIDS and cholesterol screening.

Clinton White House News & Announcements
alt.news-media **M**

An online repository of daily official transcriptions, briefings, remarks, backgrounders and other official information from the Clinton White House. A useful online resource for members of the media, students or others interested in getting access to official White House news release documents, posted and updated daily.

Sample Subjects:
Background briefing on gays in the military/Press briefing by Dee Dee Myers/Press briefing on base closings

Balkans News & Discussion Group
alt.news.macedonia **L**

As the crisis and conflict in the Balkans continues to make headlines, this discussion group on the Balkan country of Macedonia continues to be very active. Includes discussion, debate, news and information on the country of Macedonia from Macedonian and Greek nationals concerning this country's potential involvement in the Balkan crisis. Also features interesting official news releases from on-site local news agencies such as the Balkan Information Pool and the Macedonian Information Liaison Service

LILS, both providing live reporting from the area. Very useful if you are following events in this area and want your information straight from the source.

Sample Subjects:
Macedonia census/Disasters in Bitola

Russian & Eastern European News
misc.news.east-europe.rferl **L**

A daily digest of late-breaking news from Russia, Caucasia, Central Asia and Eastern Europe from Radio Free Europe and Radio Liberty.

South Asian News
misc.news.southasia **L**

Postings of news articles written by Net participants or excerpted from publications relating to news from countries in South Asia: Afghanistan, Bangladesh, Bhutan, India, Nepal, Pakistan and Sri Lanka. Features both headline news summaries and in-depth news accounts from the area.

Supreme Court Decisions Online
courts.usa.federal. **L**

Daily U.S. Supreme Court orders posted online, courtesy of Case Western Reserve University, Cleveland, Ohio.

ClariNet News Services

Ultra-Important Once-A-Year News Flashes
clari.news.flash

Daily Almanac—Quotes, "This Date in History" Etc.
clari.news.almanac

Newsbytes Top Stories (Cross-posted)
clari.nb.top

Stage, Drama & Other Fine Arts
clari.news.arts

Aviation Industry & Mishaps
clari.news.aviation

Books & Publishing
clari.news.books

Regular News Summaries
clari.news.briefs

Major Breaking Stories of the Week
clari.news.bulletin

News Related to Canada
clari.news.canada

Regular U.S. News Summary
clari.news.cast

Stories Related to Children & Parenting
clari.news.children

Consumer News, Car Reviews, Etc.
clari.news.consumer

Demonstrations around the World
clari.news.demonstration

Major Problems, Accidents & Natural Disasters
clari.news.disaster

General Economic News
clari.news.economy

News Regarding Both U.S. & International Elections
clari.news.election

Entertainment Industry News & Features
clari.news.entertain

News Related to Europe
clari.news.europe

Unclassified Feature Stories
clari.news.features

Clashes around the World
clari.news.fighting

Stories of Success & Survival
clari.news.goodnews

General Government Related Stories
clari.news.gov

Government Agencies, FBI, Etc.
clari.news.gov.agency

Budgets at All Levels
clari.news.gov.budget

Government Corruption, Kickbacks, Etc.
clari.news.gov.corrupt

International Government-Related Stories
clari.news.gov.international

Government Officials & Their Problems
clari.news.gov.officials

State Government Stories of National Importance
clari.news.gov.state

Tax Laws, Trials, Etc.
clari.news.gov.taxes

U.S. Federal Government News (High Volume)
clari.news.gov.usa

Special Interest Groups Not Covered Elsewhere
clari.news.group

News of Interest to Black People
clari.news.group.blacks

Homosexuality & Gay Rights
clari.news.group.gays

Jews & Jewish Interests
clari.news.group.jews

Women's Issues & Abortion
clari.news.group.women

Hourly List of the Top U.S./World Headlines
clari.news.headlines

News from Eastern Europe
clari.news.hot.east_europe

News from Somalia
clari.news.hot.somalia

News from the Soviet Union
clari.news.hot.ussr

Human Interest Stories
clari.news.interest

Animals in the News
clari.news.interest.animals

Human Interest Stories & History in the Making
clari.news.interest.history

Famous People in the News
clari.news.interest.people

Daily "People" Column—Tidbits on Celebs
clari.news.interest.people.column

Unusual or Funny News Stories
clari.news.interest.quirks

Stories on Major Issues Not Covered in Their Own Groups
clari.news.issues

Freedom, Racism, Civil Rights Issues
clari.news.issues.civil_rights

Conflict Between Groups around the World
clari.news.issues.conflict

Family, Child Abuse, Etc.
clari.news.issues.family

Unions, Strikes
clari.news.labor

Strikes
clari.news.labor.strike

General Group for Law-Related Issues
clari.news.law

Civil Trials & Litigation
clari.news.law.civil

Major Crimes
clari.news.law.crime

Sex Crimes & Trials
clari.news.law.crime.sex

Trials for Criminal Actions
clari.news.law.crime.trial

Violent Crime & Criminals
clari.news.law.crime.violent

Drug-Related Crimes & Drug Stories
clari.news.law.drugs

Investigation of Crimes
clari.news.law.investigation

Police & Law Enforcement
clari.news.law.police

Prisons, Prisoners & Escapes
clari.news.law.prison

Lawyers, Judges, Etc.
clari.news.law.profession

U.S. Supreme Court Rulings & News
clari.news.law.supreme

Fashion, Leisure, Etc.
clari.news.lifestyle

Military Equipment, People & Issues
clari.news.military

Reviews, News & Stories on Movie Stars
clari.news.movies

Reviews & Issues Concerning Music & Musicians
clari.news.music

Politicians & Politics
clari.news.politics

Politicians & Political Personalities
clari.news.politics.people

Religion, Religious Leaders & Televangelists
clari.news.religion

Sexual Issues & Sex-Related Political Stories
clari.news.sex

Terrorist Actions & Related News Around the World
clari.news.terrorism

Top U.S. News Stories
clari.news.top

Top International News Stories
clari.news.top.world

Surveys & Trends
clari.news.trends

Less-Major Accidents, Problems & Mishaps
clari.news.trouble

TV News, Reviews & Stars
clari.news.tv

Major Breaking Stories of the Day
clari.news.urgent

Weather & Temperature Reports
clari.news.weather

The first full-feature movie ever "shown" on the Internet was transmitted on May 22, 1993. The cult film "Wax: Or the Discovery of Television Among the Bees" had to be shown in black and white (because color images take up far more disk space), but its transmission by David Blair was an historic first step in digital video broadcasting.

John Markoff, "Cult Film Is a First on Internet," *New York Times* (5/24/93)

Chapter 8: Entertainment & the Media

Entertainment-and media-related newsgroups on the Internet are rapidly evolving from their computer geek origins of just one year ago. Nowadays, there are fan newsgroups on the Net for nearly every musical recording artist, author, prime-time television show and movie.

Fan's Groups on the Net

Scores of extremely active fan groups on the Net represent a place in cyberspace where devoted followers of, say, David Letterman can go to chat about Dave's monologue from last night's show with thousands of other *Late Show* watchers. You can apply this sense of shared interest and enthusiasm, immediacy and individual participation to literally hundreds of fan and entertainment-oriented newsgroups on the Net: Music fans share the latest info on new album releases for their favorite pop music groups, soap opera fans speculate on their favorite character's romantic liaisons and book lovers track character development in their favorite author's works. All of this occurs millions of times a day, in hundreds of online fan clubs on the Net.

Games and Jokes

There are newsgroups devoted to games of all kinds—conventional board games, computer/video games and the highly popular multi-user role-playing games taking place among thousands of online Internet users every night—providing enthusiasts with how-to playing tips, advice, news of the game and chitchat.

Netters also trade their favorite jokes and funny stories on several Net newsgroups covered in this Chapter. For a look at some truly off-the-edge and tasteless-but-funny jokes, check out some of the newsgroups in Chapter 13, "Off the Wall, Singles & Adult."

Music Making, Movies, Radio, TV and Electronics

There are also a large number of nuts-and-bolts-oriented groups of interest to you if you're a musician or electronic music maker. This hands-on approach can also be found when it comes to media-oriented crafts, such as moviemaking, sound, and video production. These are the groups where you can find out how to produce a low-budget film or set up a professional sound system in your basement, among many other things.

Books & Language

Book Reviews & Book Talk

alt.books.reviews **M**

Contains book reviews on a wide variety of topics—from history of feminism to high-performance computers and current fiction. Also contains requests for information about new and old books.

Sample Subjects:
Reviews of new fiction/Book review requests

FAQ ▶ The following FAQs are available via FTP from RTFM.MIT.EDU in the directory:
pub/usenet/alt.books.reviews:
FAQ_for_alt.books.reviews

Technical Books Info

biz.books.technical **M**

Reviews of technical books under the subjects of computer software and electrical engineering posted by Net participants, books wanted to buy/sell, and technical book recommendations by readers.

▲ *Typography graphic, downloaded via Internet FTP from* **wuarchive.wustl.edu**

Dave Barry Fan Club

alt.fan.dave_barry **M**

Online fan club for readers of Dave Barry's popular books and syndicated column. Includes all you'd want to know about the doings of this popular author and information for online access to Dave Barry columns accessible on the Internet.

FAQ ▶ The following FAQ is available via FTP from RTFM.MIT.EDU in the directory:
pub/usenet/alt.fan.dave_barry:
alt.fan.dave_barry_Frequently_Asked_Questions

Hitchhiker's Guide to the Galaxy Fan Club

alt.fan.douglas-adams **HI**

The official online fan group for Douglas Adams, best known as the author of *The Hitchhiker's Guide to the Galaxy* and other humorous science fiction books. Includes talk on the popular BBC radio series based on the book, and the PBS TV shows that followed.

Sample Subjects:
Help! ooking for oolankaloot/Hitchhiker's Guide paraphernalia/Douglas Adams frequently asked questions

FAQ ▶ The following FAQ is available via FTP from RTFM.MIT.EDU in the directory:
pub/usenet/alt.fan.douglas-adams:
alt.fan.douglas-adams_FAQ

Anne Rice Books Talk Group

alt.books.anne-rice **M**

A fan group for enthusiastic readers of the erotic vampire horror books by Anne Rice. Participants discuss recent Anne Rice interviews, book signings and appearances and speculate on characters and plot meanings in various Rice books. In typical Net fashion, discussion meanders off to speculations on vampire physiology and capability.

Sci-Fi Fantasy Talk

alt.fan.eddings **M**

Discussion group for readers/fans of science fiction fantasy books.

Sherlock Holmes Fan Club

alt.fan.holmes **M**

Sherlock Holmes fans unite! Online fan group for that favorite turn-of-the-century sleuth. Includes discussions of recent Holmes-related radio and TV shows and comments on favorite Sherlock Holmes mysteries. Also featured are extensive Sherlock Holmes book and article reference listings.

Sample Subjects:
Sherlock Holmes/Unresolved Doyle comments/Sherlock Holmes on BBC shortwave

FAQ ▶ The following FAQs are available via FTP from RTFM.MIT.EDU in the directory:
pub/usenet/alt.fan.holmes:
Changes_to_Holmes_Booklist_(rec.arts.books)
Holmes_Booklist_(rec.arts.books)
LIST:_Sherlock_Holmes_Illustrated

Self-Published Short Stories Online

alt.prose **M**

A small but very intense newsgroup containing online posted works of fiction and short stories written by Net participants. Most works are in the science fiction and fantasy vein. Other works include intriguing novels and short stories written interactively by several Net participants.

Snappy Quotes & "Who Said That?"

alt.quotations **M**

Are you a lover of quotes and snappy epigrams? Think of **alt.quotations** as a trading post for vast numbers of funny, interesting and thought-provoking quotations from famous authors, personalities and raconteurs. A good place to find out who said what. Posters on this newsgroup also place files containing multiple quotations, subject-oriented quotes and comments relating to famous sayings throughout history and literature.

Sample Subjects:
Wanted-computer quotes/ Question on a quote/ Confucius wanted/Query: Bertrand Russell quote

FAQ▶ The following FAQs are available via FTP from RTFM.MIT.EDU in the directory:
pub/usenet/alt.quotations:
Quotations_monthly_FAQ_v1.00_04-13-93
Quotations_monthly_FAQ_v1.01_08-02-93

▲ ▶ *Illustrations from the science fiction classic "Dune," downloaded via Internet FTP from science fiction photo archives at* **grind.isca.uiowa.edu**

The King's English

alt.usage.english **HI**

Lovers of the English language will find many kindred spirits in this Net newsgroup. A home for English professors, English language enthusiasts, writers and those who are simply interested in word usage and meaning. Comment topics cover pet peeves in English usage, word meanings, word usage, dictionary definitions and other esoterica related to the King's English.

Sample Subjects:
An interesting redundancy/My list of pet peeves/*OED* Second Edition

Dune Talk Group
alt.fan.dune **M**

Group for enthusiastic readers of Frank Herbert's *Dune* series, a science fiction classic. Also covers the *Dune* movie, various computer games and Dune-related books.

FAQ▶ The following FAQ is available via FTP from RTFM.MIT.EDU in the directory:
pub/usenet/alt.fan.dune:
alt.fan.dune_Introduction_and_FAQ

Tolkien Books
rec.arts.books.tolkien **M**

Popular discussion group for enthusiastic readers of J.R.R. Tolkien's *The Hobbit, Lord of the Rings* and *Silmarillion* fantasy novels. Features in-depth discussion and speculations on characters, stories and miscellany concerning characters from these books.

Sample Subjects:
A Middle Earth riddle/Gandalf on abortion/Ramblings of a Tolkien fan/Ents, trees and all that

Deryni Fantasy Books Talk Group
alt.books.deryni **L**

Fantasy discussion group relating to Deryni and hortic power.

Sample Subjects:
Morality of Deryni/The hortic power possibility/ Aristocracy and kk

Pern Books Fan Club
alt.fan.pern **M**

For fans of the Pern dragon stories and science fiction fantasy books.

FAQ▶ The following FAQs are available via FTP from RTFM.MIT.EDU in the directory:
pub/usenet/alt.fan.pern:
Welcome_to_alt.fan.pern_(Semi-monthly_posting)_(Part_1_of_2)
Welcome_to_alt.fan.pern_(Semi-monthly_posting)_(Part_2_of_2)

Piers Anthony Talk Group
alt.fan.pier-anthony **M**

Fans group for science fiction author Piers Anthony, writer of the short story that eventually became the hit movie *Total Recall.*

Terry Pratchett Fan Group
alt.fan.Pratchett **M**

Talk group for devoted readers of English fantasy science fiction writer Terry Pratchett.

FAQ▶ The following FAQs are available via FTP from RTFM.MIT.EDU in the directory:
pub/usenet/alt.fan.pratchett:
alt.fan.pratchett_FAQ
Terry_Pratchett_Bibliography
Welcome_to_alt.fan.pratchett!_(mini-FAQ,_please_read)

Isaac Asimov Books Chat Group
alt.books.isaac.asimov **L**

Discussion group for readers and enthusiasts of books, short stories and other collected writings of sci-fi author Isaac Asimov.

Entertainment & Media

▲ *Marvel Comics characters Spiderman, Silver Surfer and X-Men, downloaded from comics image archives via Internet FTP from* **wuarchive.wustl.edu**

Interactive Fiction

rec.arts.int-fiction **M**

A cutting-edge newsgroup dealing with the craft of writing computer-based interactive fiction where you as a reader of a story can become a character in the story. These include adventure games and other interactive computer-based fantasy games. Oriented mainly toward providing information about technical software utilities used for writing interactive adventure-style story games.

FAQ ▶ The following FAQ is available via FTP from RTFM.MIT.EDU in the directory:
pub/usenet/rec.arts.int-fiction:
Adventure_Authoring_Systems_FAQ

Japanese Storytelling Art

rec.arts.manga **M**

Newsgroup for fans of manga, a Japanese storytelling art form used in Japanese comics, graphic novels and stories.

FAQ ▶ The following FAQs are available via FTP from RTFM.MIT.EDU in the directory:
pub/usenet/rec.arts.manga:
rec.arts.manga:_FAQ_Availability_Info
rec.arts.manga:_Frequently_Asked_Questions
rec.arts.manga:_Manga_Guide_Part_1_2
rec.arts.manga:_Manga_Guide_Part_2_2
rec.arts.manga:_Manga_Resources
rec.arts.manga:_Welcome_to_rec.arts.manga

Amateur Poet's Society

rec.arts.poems **HI**

Online equivalent of amateur poet's night at a Beat coffeehouse. In this popular group, online poets post their writings and get immediate response from other readers on the Net. If you're an aspiring poet, this is the quickest and best place to publish your own poems to get immediate feedback from other readers.

Sample Subjects:
I saw your brother today/Amaranths/A feline sonnet

Comics & Graphic Novels

Superheroes, Comics & Graphic Novels

Comics-related newsgroups on the Net cover the whole spectrum of the comics world: From the comic books and superheroes you grew up with as a kid (you remember—those old comic books your mother made you throw out, some of which are now worth a small fortune), to daily newspaper comic strips, racier underground strips, upscale epic graphic novels and the more exotic imported animated books. Participants in comics newsgroups discuss and debate the actions and recent storylines involving their favorite comic characters, old and new comic editions and published editions and talk about favorite cartoon artists, writers, publishers and technical story points.

Create Your Own Comic Book

alt.comics.lnh **M**

Ever wanted to write you own comic book? On **alt.comics.lnh** (lnh by the way, stands for Legion of Net Heroes) you, too, can participate in your very own interactive comic book storyline. Create your own character and enter it into this fantasy comic book world and interact with other comic fanatics in the plot.

Superman Fan Club

alt.comics.superman **M**

Superman fans gather here to discuss every aspect of

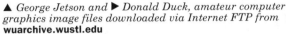

▲ *George Jetson and* ▶ *Donald Duck, amateur computer graphics image files downloaded via Internet FTP from* **wuarchive.wustl.edu**

America's favorite action superhero. Lots of enthusiatic discussion and extremely detailed comments on Superman characters, recent issues and story lines.

Sample Subjects:
Real Superman/Superman in armor/History of Supergirl

Comics Info

rec.arts.comics.info **L**

Moderated discussion group for high-quality informational postings, FAQs, and detailed reviews of comics.

FAQ ▶ The following FAQs are available via FTP from RTFM.MIT.EDU in the directory:
pub/usenet/rec.arts.comics.info:
WELCOME_TO_REC.ARTS.COMICS_(parts_2-3_of_6:_the_r.a.c_FAQ)
WELCOME_TO_REC.ARTS.COMICS_(parts_5-6_of_6:_other_net_sources)
WELCOME_TO_REC.ARTS.COMICS_(part_1_of_6:_introduction)
WELCOME_TO_REC.ARTS.COMICS_(part_4_of_6:_netiquette)

Comic Strips

rec.arts.comics.strips **M**

Discussion group for newspaper comic strips, editorial cartoons, comic strip authors, creators and spinoffs (TV, movies, merchandise).

Marvel Comics

rec.arts.comics.xbooks **M**

Discussion group for fans of Marvel comics and mutant superhero characters: X-Men, X-Force and their respective superhero characters.

Comics: Buy & Sell

rec.arts.comics.marketplace **HI**

An active buy/sell/wanted group for collectible and new comics for sale, for trade and wanted-to-buy.

Comics Talk

rec.arts.comics.misc **HI**

An informal discussion group for eclectic chatter about comics, comic book characters and superheroes.

Animation

Animation, Fantasy & Cartoons

A number of discussion groups dedicated to fans of animation of all kinds and from all over the world. Animation-related features range from animation to the cartoons that everybody knows and loves (such as *Tom and Jerry, George of the Jungle, Looney Toons,* etc.) to modern-day cartoons such as the *Tiny Toons* series and cable offerings such as *Beavis and Butt-Head.* There are also newsgroups that have in-depth discussions on more exotic types of cartoons and animation, with extensive discussions of Japanese animation features called "anime"—wildly futuristic (and sometimes graphically violent) fantasy stories. Whether your favorite cartoon tastes run to *Bugs Bunny* or to exotic Japanese imports, there are a remarkably large number of fellow fans who will share your interests. Typically, newsgroups feature discussion and comments on various cartoon/animated feature episodes, story summaries and info on where to buy episodes on video or CD.

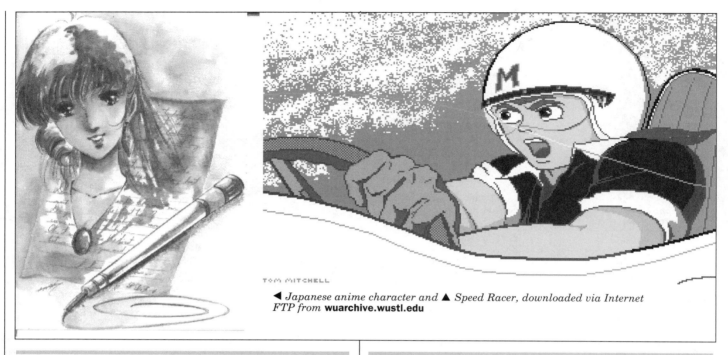

◀ *Japanese anime character and* ▲ *Speed Racer, downloaded via Internet FTP from* **wuarchive.wustl.edu**

General Cartoons & Animation
rec.arts.animation **M**

General discussions of cartoon/animated feature episodes of all types (except the exotic Japanese and international offerings).

FAQ ▶ The following FAQ is available via FTP from RTFM.MIT.EDU in the directory:
pub/usenet/rec.arts.animation:
[rec.arts.animation]_Frequently_Asked_Questions_v._1.24

Japanese Animated Features
rec.arts.anime **HI**

Active newsgroup for fans of Japanese fantasy-action animated features called anime.

FAQ ▶ The following FAQs are available via FTP from RTFM.MIT.EDU in the directory:
pub/usenet/rec.arts.anime:
rec.arts.anime:_Anime_Primer
rec.arts.anime:_Anime_Resources_List
rec.arts.anime:_FAQ_Availability_Info
rec.arts.anime:_Frequently_Asked_Questions
rec.arts.anime:_Welcome_to_rec.arts.anime!

Japanese Animated Features: Info
rec.arts.anime.info **M**

Story summaries and Frequently Asked Question (FAQ) files relating to Japanese anime features.

FAQ ▶ The following FAQs are available via FTP from RTFM.MIT.EDU in the directory:
pub/usenet/rec.arts.anime.info:
Anime_Manga_Convention_List
National_Anime_BBS_Watch
rec.arts.anime:_Anime_Primer
rec.arts.anime:_Anime_Resources_List
rec.arts.anime:_Frequently_Asked_Questions
rec.arts.anime:_Welcome_to_rec.arts.anime!

Japanese Animated Features: Buy & Sell
rec.arts.anime.marketplace **M**

Buy/sell group for videos, toys, models, cel books and other collectibles related to Japanese anime animated features.

Japanese Animated Features: Story Lines
rec.arts.anime.stories **L**

Story summaries of Japanese anime features, plus self-published anime stories authored by Net participants.

Games

Sega Genesis Game Players Group
alt.sega.genesis **M**

Fans of the Sega Genesis TV game system will find lots to talk about here, including tips on popular Genesis games, equipment for sale or trade and other comments on Sega video game systems.

Sample Subjects:
Shining Force/Sega Genesis games for sale/Help Genesis hockey '93

Games: Computer, Arcade & Video
rec.games.video.arcade **HI**

Players of any PC-based or MAC-based video game, arcade or arcade-style game or popular home-based video game (like Nintendo) will find many fun and useful game-playing tips, buy/sell game postings, news of new games, inside info and friendly discussions on a wide variety of computer and video gaming interests. Related newsgroups on the Net: **rec.games.video.arcade** (for old and new public arcade game players), **rec.games.video.classic** (discussions for fans of older PC-based video games), **rec.games.video.marketplace**, **rec.games.video.misc**, **rec.games.video.nintendo**, **rec.games.video.sega**, **rec.games.mecha** (for fans of Japanese-cartoon-based futuristic space fighter/robot games) and **rec.games.video.pinball**.

FAQ ▶ The following FAQs are available via FTP from RTFM.MIT.EDU in the directory:
pub/usenet/rec.games.video.arcade:
rec.games.video.arcade_Frequently_Asked_Questions
rec.games.video.arcade_Mailserver_and_FTP_information

Games: General
bit.listserv.games-l **M**

A popular discussion group whose participants comment on all different kinds of games—video, computer, TV and strategy. A smaller newsgroup combining elements from all other game categories.

Toy Soldiers & Miniatures
rec.games.miniatures **M**

Fun group for miniatures game players (the rest of us call these "toy soldiers") containing comments on popular board games and casting techniques for miniatures used in these games.

Play by Mail Games: General Info
rec.games.pbm **M**

Talk group for the predecessor to role-playing games, Play-By-Mail (PBM) games allow players to participate in games either through regular postal mail or electronic mail on the Internet.

FAQ ▶ The following FAQ is available via FTP from RTFM.MIT.EDU in the directory:
pub/usenet/rec.games.pbm:
FAQ:_rec.games.pbm_Frequently_Asked_Questions

Game Programmer's How-To
rec.games.programmer **HI**

A useful technical resource for question-and-answer info for game software developers, designers and programmers.

Board & Strategy Games
Board Games, War & Strategy Games
The Net features a number of interest groups for players of board games, card games and strategy/war/fantasy games.

▲ *Fantasy woman slays dragon, image file downloaded from* **grind.isca.uiowa.edu**

Backgammon
rec.games.backgammon **M**

Tips and strategies for backgammon players.

Fantasy/Strategic Board Games
rec.games.board **HI**

For players of various strategic war and, fantasy board games and other non-computer-related, commercially available board and strategy games.

FAQ ▶ The following FAQs are available via FTP from RTFM.MIT.EDU in the directory:
pub/usenet/rec.games.board:
rec.games.board_FAQ_and_intro
Scrabble_FAQ_-_Club_and_Tournament_Supplement
Scrabble_FAQ_-_General_Information
Talisman_boardgame_FAQ_(Frequently_Asked_Questions)

Bridge
rec.games.bridge **M**

Skilled bridge players discuss their opening strategies and other tricks.

FAQ ▶ The following FAQ is available via FTP from RTFM.MIT.EDU in the directory:
pub/usenet/rec.games.bridge:
rec.games.bridge_style_guide

Chess
rec.games.chess **HI**

Serious chess players discuss playing tactics and strategies. Also includes discussions on organized computer chess-playing events and chess software.

FAQ ▶ The following FAQs are available via FTP from RTFM.MIT.EDU in the directory:
pub/usenet/rec.games.chess:
rec.games.chess_Answers_to_Frequently_Asked_Questions_[1_2]
rec.games.chess_Answers_to_Frequently_Asked_Questions_[1_2]_93_07_01
rec.games.chess_Answers_to_Frequently_Asked_Questions_[2_2]
rec.games.chess_Answers_to_Frequently_Asked_Questions_[2_2]_93_07_01

▲ *Fantasy painting image files downloaded via Internet FTP from* **grind.isca.uiowa.edu**

Trivia Games
rec.games.trivia **M**

Discussion group for lovers of all types of trivia games such as *Jeopardy!*, popular trivia board games, trivia-related TV shows and computer trivia games.

Multi-Player Games

Play by Mail Games: Diplomacy
rec.games.diplomacy **M**

For players of the intellectual, statecraft-oriented play-by-mail game "Diplomacy."

FAQ ▶ The following FAQ is available via FTP from RTFM.MIT.EDU in the directory:
pub/usenet/rec.games.diplomacy:
rec.games.diplomacy_FAQ

Furry Fantasy Game Role Players
alt.fan.furry **M**

For players of Dungeons and Dragons-style role playing games involving furry creatures.

Sample Subjects:
Humanoid bird morphs/Atlanta dragoncon freeze

Bolo: Multi-Player Action Game on the Net
alt.netgames.bolo **HI**

Discussion area for a unique and interesting multi-player, online game called Bolo, where widely dispersed players use tanks, cyborg brains and mines against each other's pillboxes, with help from other player-allies on the Net. Discussion group features tips on playing Bolo, ideas for Bolo game improve-

ments and graphic player's maps that can be downloaded to your PC.

Sample Subjects:
Game time/Favorite maps/Bolo map arena

FAQ ▶ The following FAQ is available via FTP from RTFM.MIT.EDU in the directory:
pub/usenet/alt.netgames.bolo:
FAQ:_alt.netgames.bolo

Multi-Player Medieval Fantasy Game
alt.pub.dragons-inn **M**

A very popular adventure-style interactive game/story where you create a medieval character that interacts with other player-created characters on the Net.

FAQ ▶ The following FAQs are available via FTP from RTFM.MIT.EDU in the directory:
pub/usenet/alt.pub.dragons-inn:
ADMIN:_Atlas_of_the_Known_Lands
ADMIN:_Bestiary_of_the_Known_Lands
ADMIN:_Bulletin_Board
ADMIN:_Character_Summaries_List_Part_1_(A-E)
ADMIN:_Character_Summaries_List_Part_1_(A-G)
ADMIN:_Character_Summaries_List_Part_2_(F-L)
ADMIN:_Character_Summaries_List_Part_2_(H-L)
ADMIN:_Character_Summaries_List_Part_3_(M-Z)
ADMIN:_Directory_of_Generica_(930820)
ADMIN:_Frequently_Asked_Questions
ADMIN:_History_of_Nexus
ADMIN:_MiniFAQ_:_New_users_please_read
ADMIN:_Synopses
ADMIN:_The_Directory_of_Generica
ADMIN:_Tourist_s_Guide

Futuristic, Interactive Hyperspace Game
alt.pub.havens-rest **L**

An interactive text fantasy game set in a futuristic hyperspace world, based on a man-made planet called Serendipity.

Multi-User Role-Playing Internet-Based Games

rec.games.mud.misc **HI**

A miniature world has sprung up on the Net for players of various Multiple User Dialogues (called MUDs) featuring thousands of enthusiastic players who explore imaginary group-created worlds and interact with other users on the Net with their own created characters. Players on these network games chat, meet each other, make friends, joke and form alliances to kill monsters and solve various puzzles, with the final object of the game being to become a wizard. Games change and new ones start up every Friday of the week, with players participating from around the world. Information for start-ups and new MUDs can be found in the newsgroup **rec.games.mud.announce**. Other MUD-related game newsgroups on the Net include: **rec.games.mud.admin**, **rec.games.mud.diku**, **rec.games.mud.lp**, **rec.games.mud.misc**, **rec.games.mud.tiny**. To get started playing multi-user games on the Net, access the FAQ files posted under **rec.games.mud.announce**. Another Internet multi-user game called Xtank is a war-based tank-robot game where you create and program your own tank and join up with other tank drivers in a team to run mazes and kill other tank teams. These extensive newsgroups will provide you with all the information you need to get started in multi-user gaming on the Net.

▲ *Fantasy painting image file downloaded via Internet FTP from sci-fi images archive at* **grind.isca.uiowa.edu**

Fantasy Games

Fantasy Role-Playing Games

The Net features many newsgroups of interest to players of computer-based role-playing games from the most popular and well-known games like Dungeons and Dragons to the lesser-known fantasy games taking place in faraway worlds and time dimensions. Players discuss the ins and outs of various games, character development, capabilities and strategy. Fantasy role-playing newsgroups also feature related items wanted-to-buy/sell, announcements of upcoming game conventions and new games. Most fantasy role-playing newsgroups on the Net are identified by the frp. designation (which stands for "fantasy role-playing").

Medieval Fantasy Role-Playing Game Group

alt.pub.cloven-shield **L**

An interactive adventure-style gaming newsgroup set in the Dark Ages, where you create your own character who interacts with others in this medieval fantasy environment. The game works like an interactive story where game participants take turns writing the story.

Fantasy Role-Playing Games: General Info

rec.games.frp.misc **HI**

Informal discussions on the ins and outs of various fantasy-type role-playing science fiction games.

Fantasy Role-Playing Games: New Games

rec.games.frp.advocacy **M**

Announcements of new role-playing games, comments on new games, etc.

Fantasy Role-Playing Games: Buy & Sell

rec.games.frp.marketplace **M**

Fantasy role-playing games and related paraphernalia for sale/wanted.

Fantasy Role-Playing Games: Info

rec.games.frp.moria **L**

For players of the well-known Dungeons & Dragons fantasy role-playing games.

Fantasy Role-Playing Games: Cyberpunk Fantasies

rec.games.frp.cyber **M**

Group for talk about futuristic, nihilistic, cyberpunk role-playing games.

▲ *The Three Stooges, downloaded from* **wuarchive.wustl.edu**

Humor & Jokes

Humor & Jokes

There are a variety of humor categories on the Net for posting the great joke you've just overheard, getting new jokes to tell or just stopping by for a few laughs.

Firesign Theater Talk Group

alt.comedy.firesigntheater **M**

A fan group for the Firesign Theater radio program.

Newsgroup Humor

alt.humor.best-of-usenet **L**

Contains excerpts of (sometimes) funny messages posted from all other newsgroups on the Net.

Blonde Jokes

rec.humor **HI**

Features a wide variety of jokes that follow the usual classifications (blonde jokes, ethnic jokes, etc.) plus homemade jokes reflecting current events and jokes heard-'round-the-office.

Jokes Discussion Group

rec.humor.d **M**

The place for humorous back-and-forth discussions and requests for jokes on any subject.

Story Jokes

rec.humor.funny **L**

More jokes but (mostly) in narrative/story format.

FAQ ▶ The following FAQs are available via FTP from RTFM.MIT.EDU in the directory:
pub/usenet/rec.humor.funny:
Editorial_Policy_on_Offensive_Jokes_—_Monthly_Posting
Guidelines_for_Submissions_—_Monthly_Posting
Introduction_to_REC.HUMOR.FUNNY_—_Monthly_Posting

Bad Jokes

rec.humor.oracle **L**

Over-long, smirky, sophomoric and not-very-funny files posted by self-appointed oracles on the Net.

FAQ ▶ The following FAQ is available via FTP from RTFM.MIT.EDU in the directory:
pub/usenet/rec.humor.oracle:
[rec.humor.oracle]_Intro_to_the_Usenet_Oracle_(Monthly_Posting)

More Bad Jokes

rec.humor.oracle.d **L**

Discussions relating to the sophomoric "oracle" newsgroup.

ClariNet News—Humor

Columns of Humorist Dave Barry
clari.feature.dave_barry

Judith Martin's Humorous Etiquette Advice
clari.feature.miss_manners

Chicago Opinion Columnist Mike Royko
clari.feature.mike_royko

▲ *The Beatles, from the "Beatles For Sale" album cover, downloaded from* **ftp.uwp.edu** ▶*(Top) Madonna, and* ▶ *Jerry Garcia of The Grateful Dead, both downloaded from* **wuarchive.wustl.edu**

Music: Rock & Roll

Music: Recording Artists' Fan Groups on the Net

The Net features a large number of wildly popular fan groups covering most any imaginable musical taste, reflecting both the youthful, cutting-edge nature and the eclectic musical interests of Net participants. Fan music groups typically feature (for each specific newsgroup) enthusiastic chatter about the particular recording artist or group in question, talk about their latest releases, albums or—as with older or disbanded groups—retrospective collections, conversations and comments on favorite songs, trivia, concert news and concert dates, rumors and other speculations about artists/groups covered by the particular newsgroup. What is striking about fan music newsgroups on the Net is the keen attention to detail shown by key newsgroup discussion participants, who not only do a great job keeping the flow of online conversation going with respect to individual music newsgroups, but can also answer just about any obscure question you might ever ask about your favorite type of music, artist or group.

Beatles Fan Group

rec.music.beatles **HI**

Popular group covering any item of interest relating to the Fab Four, including discussions of new CD collections and lesser-known Beatles tunes.

Bob Dylan

rec.music.dylan **HI**

Everything of interest for Bob Dylan fans: bootleg tape exchange, new releases, trivia, sightings, concert dates and general Dylan adoration.

FAQ ▶ The following FAQs are available via FTP from RTFM.MIT.EDU in the directory: **pub/usenet/rec.music.dylan:**
Guide_to_Frequently_Asked_Questions_(1_of_2)
Guide_to_Frequently_Asked_Questions_(2_of_2)
REC.MUSIC.INFO_[Monthly__pointer_]

Jimmy Buffett Fans Group

alt.fan.Jimmy-Buffett **M**

Fans of popular singer/songwriter/author Jimmy Buffett (who call themselves "Parrotheads") swap stories on favorite Jimmy Buffet concerts, songs and albums, news items and personal stories involving Jimmy Buffett songs.

Frank Zappa Talk Group

alt.fan.frank-zappa **M**

The place where devoted Frank Zappa fans go to chat about the late Frank Zappa's music, his previous groups, more recent albums, songs, CD collections and television appearances.

Sample Subjects:
Frank Zappa and Saturday Night Live/Prague 1991/*200 Motels* on TV

Grateful Deadheads Group

rec.music.gdead **HI**

For followers of the Grateful Dead and its

◀ *Eric Clapton and* ▲ *Prince, photo image files downloaded via Internet FTP from* **wuarchive.wustl.edu**

extensive, obsessed, fan subculture. Concert/tour info, personal messages and everything of interest to Deadheads.

Madonna Fan Group

alt.fan.madonna **M**

An active, obsessive and popular newsgroup for Madonna fans (mostly) and a handful of detractors. Netters talk about recent Madonna concert appearances, live-concert TV shows, favorite shows, albums, etc. The idol worship that goes on in this group can be a little hard to take, but if you're a Madonna fan we guess you won't mind.

Sample Subjects:
Madonna in Montreal/HBO Concert/Madonna banned from Mexico

Spinal Tap Fan Group

alt.fan.spinal-tap **L**

For Net fans of the satirical heavy metal rock group Spinal Tap, subject of the humorous rock documentary parody film.

More Rock & Roll Fan Groups...

(various newsgroups)

Pop culture newsgroups are very big on the Net and when it comes to rock-n-roll music, there's a wide variety of discussion to meet almost any rock music interest: **alt.rock'n'roll** is a big, general-interest newsgroup that covers the entire category—everything from Jimi Hendrix and the Stones to the latest

groups; **alt.rock-n-roll.classic** is for fans of the groups of the 1950s, 1960s and 1970s and includes talk about new releases of old or obscure recordings, playlists of classic rock groups and more; **alt.rock- n-roll.hard**, **alt.rock-n-roll.metal**, and **alt.rock-n-roll.heavy** feature more talk on that hard-driving genre, such as concert dates for favorite groups, availability of bootleg tapes and records/CDs/tapes wanted or for sale; rock'n'roll discussion groups on the Net like **alt.rock-n-roll.ACDC**, **alt.rock-n-roll.metal.ironmaiden**, **alt.rock-n-roll.metallica**, **alt.rock-n-roll.stones**, are all very active newsgroups with plenty of fan-oriented talk and comments specifically related to these performers and their songs.

Rock Talk: General

alt.rock-n-roll

FAQ ▶ The following FAQ is available via FTP from RTFM.MIT.EDU in the directory:
pub/usenet/alt.rock-n-roll:
RELEASE:_Recent_and_Upcoming_Album_Releases:_93-41

Classic Rock Fan Talk Group

alt.rock-n-roll.classic

Hard Rocker's Talk Group

alt.rock-n-roll.hard

Heavy Metal Fan Talk Group

alt.rock-n-roll.metal

ACDC Rock Fan Talk Group

alt.rock-n-roll.acdc

Metallica Fan Rock Talk Group

alt.rock-n-roll.metallica

Rolling Stones Fan Talk Group

alt.rock-n-roll.stones

FAQ ▶ The following FAQs are available via FTP from RTFM.MIT.EDU in the directory:
pub/usenet/alt.rock-n-roll.stones:
Rolling_Stones_FAQ_[1_4]
Rolling_Stones_FAQ_[2_4]
Rolling_Stones_FAQ_[3_4]
Rolling_Stones_FAQ_[4_4]

Ironmaiden Rock Fan's Talk Group

alt.rock-n-roll.metal.ironmaiden

Urban & Jazz Music

Rap Music Rap
alt.rap **HI**

A very busy place for rap fanatics and devoted followers of all rap music groups. Talk on new rap performers, albums, concerts and other aspects of rap.

Sample Subjects:
Best samplers out there/Marky Mark and the Funky Bunch/Van full of Pakistans

Afro-Latin Music
rec.music.afro-latin **L**

For fans interested in Latin jazz, Salsa and other hot Latin music variations.

Funk Music
rec.music.funky **M**

Popular funk groups from the '70s live on. George Clinton, Ohio Players, Funkadelic, etc.

FAQ ▶ The following FAQ is available via FTP from RTFM.MIT.EDU in the directory:
pub/usenet/rec.music.funky:
CHART:_Dutch_Dance

Reggae Music Fans
rec.music.reggae **M**

Focusing mostly on modern-day reggae performers and groups, concerts and reggae lifestyle.

Blue Note Jazz Artists
rec.music.bluenote **HI**

For fans of the popular Blue Note jazz recording label that featured many of the best jazz recording artists and groups of all time. Discussions of favorite Blue Note recording artists of the past and future jazz directions.

FAQ ▶ The following FAQs are available via FTP from RTFM.MIT.EDU in the directory:
pub/usenet/rec.music.bluenote:
FAQ:_Rec.music.bluenote:_Frequently_Asked_Questions_(FAQs)
FAQ:_Rec.music.bluenote:_Further_sources_of_information
FAQ:_Rec.music.bluenote:_Welcome_to_rec.music.bluenote!
Listing_of_open_musical_jam_sessions

Classical/Opera

Classical & Opera Music
rec.music.classical **HI**

Enthusiastic, extensive newsgroup for classical music lovers. News about orchestral performances, classical composers, new recordings and opera. Features many thoughtful and intelligent reviews, comments and critiques from Net participants.

FAQ ▶ The following FAQ is available via FTP from RTFM.MIT.EDU in the directory:

▲ *Stradivarius violins, downloaded from Smithsonian FTP archives at* **sunsite.unc.edu**

pub/usenet/rec.music.classical:
rec.music.classical_FAQ

Early Classical Music
rec.music.early **M**

Focuses on early classical composers and music types such as Baroque, Harpsichord and recorder music, etc.

Folk & Country Music

Folk, Protest & Revolution Music
rec.music.folk **HI**

Active discussion group for politically motivated music fans covering all types of protest, revolution and union-oriented folk singers, groups and songs, including current performers and well-known artists from the 1950s and 1960s.

Country & Western Music
rec.music.country.western **M**

Net participants join in down-home discussions of today's top country & western recording stars.

Kate Bush Fan Group
rec.music.gaffa **HI**

For fans of English recording artist Kate Bush.

FAQ ▶ The following FAQ is available via FTP from RTFM.MIT.EDU in the directory:
pub/usenet/rec.music.gaffa:
REC.MUSIC.INFO_[Monthly__pointer_]

▲ *Early 45 rpm phonograph, downloaded via Internet FTP from Smithsonian photo archives at* **sunsite.unc.edu**

Indian Classical Music

rec.music.indian.classical **HI**

Items of interest for lovers of Indian classical music. Amjad Ali Khan, Maru Bihag, etc.

Indian Pop Music & Culture

rec.music.indian.misc **HI**

Fan group for Indian pop/modern music, films and culture.

Alternative Music

Industrial Music Fan Group

rec.music.industrial **HI**

For fans of industrial, EuroPop and other high-tech music.

FAQ ▶ The following FAQs are available via FTP from RTFM.MIT.EDU in the directory:
pub/usenet/rec.music.industrial:
FAQ:_rec.music.industrial_Part_1_2_—_Questions_and_History
FAQ:_rec.music.industrial_Part_2_2_—_Mailorder_Sources_and__Zines
rec.music.industrial_FAQ_Part_1_2_—_Questions_and_History
rec.music.industrial_FAQ_Part_2_2_—_Mailorder_Sources_and__Zines

Music Chat Group

bit.listserv.allmusic **M**

An oddball, anything-goes newsgroup with ramblings on artists, groups and albums of all kinds, with a sizable amount of talk on alternative and offbeat music and performances.

New Age Music

rec.music.newage **HI**

Net participants chat about New Age music. Enthusiastic comments, discussions and searches for meanings in songs.

Phish Phans

rec.music.phish **HI**

Cult-like group for irrepressible fans of a Frank Zappa-like band called Phish.

Demented Music

rec.music.dementia **M**

Satirical, weird and off-the-wall music fan group. Dr. Demento, Weird Al Yankovic, Tom Lehrer, etc.

Ska Music

alt.music.ska **M**

A fan group for lovers of Ska music, a blend of rock 'n' roll, reggae and Latin music types. Discussions of new Ska groups, club dates and albums.

Sample Subjects:
Ska in Chicago/Ska flames and Laurel Aitken/Skalapalooza

FAQ ▶ The following FAQ is available via FTP from RTFM.MIT.EDU in the directory:
pub/usenet/alt.music.ska:
FAQ:_Ska_(alt.music.ska)_Frequently_Asked_Questions

They Might Be Giants Fan Group

alt.music.tmbg **M**

Fan group for lovers of the pop music group They Might Be Giants. Latest concert dates, locations, current albums, etc.

Sample Subjects:
Central Park performance/Concert info. wanted

FAQ ▶ The following FAQ is available via FTP from RTFM.MIT.EDU in the directory:
pub/usenet/alt.music.tmbg:
alt.music.tmbg_FAQ
REC.MUSIC.INFO_[Monthly__pointer_]

Christian Pop Music

rec.music.christian **HI**

Covers a wide range of Christian pop music: rock, Christian rap and other Christian-oriented variations of pop music.

Enya Fan Club

alt.fan.enya **L**

Category for discussions among fans of the Irish female recording artist Enya.

▲ *MTV logo graphic, downloaded via Internet FTP*
from **wuarchive.wustl.edu**

Music Talk & Reviews

Music: Pop & General Interest

The Net features a large number of special-interest newsgroups for all music lovers and for many other interests related to music, songs, and the recording arts.

Pop Music Top Ten Lists & News

rec.music.info **M**

An extensive newsgroup that contains many comprehensive FAQ (Frequently Asked Question) files, Top Ten lists from around the world and many other large information files posted by Net users related to specific recording artists.

FAQ ▶ The following FAQs are available via FTP from RTFM.MIT.EDU in the directory:
pub/usenet/rec.music.info:
C:_V_B_C:_02_S_93_[R]
CHART:_Austrian_Top_20_Singles
CHART:_Bavarian_Top_15_(singles),_09_17_93
CHART:_Bavarian_Top_15_(singles),_09_24_93
CHART:_Bavarian_Top_15_(singles),_10_01_93
CHART:_Bavarian_Top_15_(singles),_10_08_93
CHART:_Bavarian_Top_15_(singles),_10_09_93
CHART:_Dutch_Albums
CHART:_Dutch_Dance
CHART:_Dutch_Singles
CHART:_European_Top_20
CHART:_German_Top_10_(singles),_fourtieth_week
CHART:_German_Top_10_(singles),_thirty-eighth_week
CHART:_German_Top_10_(singles),_thirty-ninth_week
CHART:_German_Top_10_(singles),_thirty-seventh_week
CHART:_Vancouver_BC_Canada:_16_Sep_93
CHART:_Vancouver_BC_Canada:_23_Sep_93
REC.MUSIC.INFO:_List_of_Internet_Musical_FTP_Sites
REC.MUSIC.INFO:_List_of_Internet_Musical_Resources
REC.MUSIC.INFO:_List_of_Musical_Mailing_Lists_(MLoL)
REC.MUSIC.INFO:_List_of_Usenet_Musical_Newsgroups
REC.MUSIC.INFO:_no_requests_for_info,_*please*_[bi-weekly_reminder]
REC.MUSIC.INFO:_Submission_Guidelines_for_rec.music.info
REC.MUSIC.INFO:_Welcome_to_rec.music.info!
RELEASE:_Recent_and_Upcoming_Album_Releases:_93-38
RELEASE:_Recent_and_Upcoming_Album_Releases:_93-39
RELEASE:_Recent_and_Upcoming_Album_Releases:_93-40

Album Reviews

rec.music.reviews **L**

Amateur critics post their own music album reviews. Mainly covers alternative and cutting-edge groups, but does contain some coverage of more popular recording artists.

CDs, Tapes & Records Marketplace

rec.music.marketplace **HI**

Buy/sell group for used CDs, records and electronic musical instruments, including many interesting music-related collectible items.

Pop Music Q&A

rec.music.misc **HI**

Catch-all group featuring Top Ten lists, radio station playlists, some buy/sell postings, but mainly used for posting questions about specific music groups, songs, concert dates and albums.

FAQ ▶ The following FAQs are available via FTP from RTFM.MIT.EDU in the directory:
pub/usenet/rec.music.misc:
C:_A_T_20_S_[R]
CHART:_Dutch_Albums
CHART:_Dutch_Dance
CHART:_Dutch_Singles

Music Videos, MTV

rec.music.video **M**

Avid viewers discuss music videos and other programs seen recently on MTV. Good place to get a sampling of the latest pop culture trends.

Cyberpunk

Rave Party News

alt.rave **HI**

One of the latest pop culture crazes these days are raves—floating, free-form dance clubs held in deserted buildings or other out-of-the-way spaces that attract thousands of people. **alt.rave** is an active messaging center for information on raves held in the U.S. and in Europe. Participants talk about various kinds of rave music and local color relating to the rave craze.

Sample Subjects:
Music stores in San Francisco/Looking for a song/Psychedelic video wanted

▲ *Atomic Cafe BBS promotional computer graphic, downloaded from* **wuarchive.wustl.edu**

lifestyles and a distinctive philosophical outlook. Participants comment on cyberpunk authors, news articles, stories, etc.

Wired Magazine Talk Group

alt.wired **M**

A reader's Internet-based talk group for *Wired*, an exciting new magazine focusing on information, media and communications technology, lifestyles, hardware and personalities. Netters discuss recent issues, features and trivia from the magazine, focusing on references to the Internet from *Wired*. Who knows, maybe one day many more magazine publishers will be smart enough to start their own parallel discussion groups on the Internet!

Conversations in Cyberspace

alt.cyberspace **M**

Cyberspace is a philosophical term used to describe the environment of computer networking and technology. It is often linked with the concept of virtual reality that has gotten a lot of press in the past few years. In the context of the Net, cyberspace is often used to describe aspects of detached, text-based exchange of information and communications using computer technology. This newsgroup covers all cyberspace/VR issues, controversies and related products and news concerning virtual reality systems, personal computing, network communications, and other hardware associated with Virtual Reality. Online discussions feature interesting and intriguing comments on virtual reality, artificially designed environments and three-dimensional representations of graphic displays. Also includes discussions on virtual reality and its impact on architecture, military technology and current events. All in all, a good place to go on the Net if you like to talk about technology or want to find interesting insights into where high tech is headed.

Sample Subjects:
Rumors about Macs/The freeway metaphor/Society/VR in the military/Using cyberspace to represent data

Cyberpunk Advocacy

alt.cyberpunk.movement **L**

Members of Generation X argue about the true meaning of the cyberpunk movement, inspired by sci-fi author William Gibson and others, which combines elements of high tech, new musical forms, alternative

Musician's Groups

Musician's Groups on the Net

Musicians have always had a special bond all their own, and on the Net you'll see nine well-travelled newsgroups that are a must if you're a rock or electronic musician.

Musician's General-Interest Group

rec.music.makers **HI**

General tips and info of interest to any musician and band member. Focus is on electronic keyboards, synthesizers and other high-tech music gear, with additional info on songwriting, instruments to buy/sell and homemade music recording techniques.

FAQ ▶ The following FAQ is available via FTP from RTFM.MIT.EDU in the directory:
pub/usenet/rec.music.makers:
Music_Equipment_Mail_Phone_List

Bass Players Group

rec.music.makers.bass **M**

Resource group primarily for electronic bass players. Instruments to buy/sell, tips on bass refinishing and advanced rock bass playing techniques.

Rock Vintage Guitar Player Group

rec.music.makers.guitar **HI**

For rock and vintage guitar players. Lots of useful information on playing techniques, equipment for sale, guitar playing question and answers and homemade guitar electronics. Everything from where to buy a 1958 Les Paul guitar to ultimate rock guitar setups.

Rock Guitar Chords

rec.music.makers.guitar.tablature

HI

Rock guitarists exchange chord notations for all kinds of modern and classic rock tunes. Also features playing techniques for both beginners and advanced guitar players.

Drummer's Group

rec.music.makers.percussion

M

The ultimate information source for drummers. Tips on the best and latest drumming gear, advanced techniques, extensive equipment information files and friendly camaraderie among fellow drummers.

Electronic Musician's Group

rec.music.makers.synth **HI**

Covers the entire range of topics of interest to enthusiasts of electronic keyboards, MIDI gear, instruments and computer-based music-making and recording techniques for Macs and IBM PCs.

FAQ ▶ The following FAQ is available via FTP from RTFM.MIT.EDU in the directory:
pub/usenet/rec.music.makers.synth:
FAQ:_Gravis_Ultrasound_(_GUS_)_FAQ_v1.30

Electronic Music: High Tech

bit.listserv.emusic-l **M**

Complex, technical discussion group for enthusiasts of computer-and MIDI-generated music for both PCs and Macintosh computers.

FAQ ▶ The following FAQ is available via FTP from RTFM.MIT.EDU in the directory:
pub/usenet/bit.listserv.emusic-l:
Computer_Music_bibliography

Electronic & MIDI Music

alt.emusic **M**

A discussion group devoted to high-tech musicians and players of electronic/MIDI musical instruments.

FAQ ▶ The following FAQs are available via FTP from RTFM.MIT.EDU in the directory:
pub/usenet/alt.emusic:
REC.MUSIC.INFO_[Monthly__pointer_]

Music Synthesizers: General

rec.music.synth **L**

Small newsgroup containing buy/sell postings for keyboards and other electronic music equipment.

FAQ ▶ The following FAQ is available via FTP from RTFM.MIT.EDU in the directory:
pub/usenet/rec.music.synth:
FAQ:_Gravis_Ultrasound_(_GUS_)_FAQ_v1.28

▲ *1969 Rickenbacker electric guitar, downloaded via Internet FTP from* **grind.isca.uiowa.edu**

Audio Electronics

Audio: From Mild to Wild

If you're seriously into high-end home, car or professional audio equipment, or you just want to know what speakers to buy or have a technical question, there are thousands of audiophiles on the Net who can help you—from knowledgeable amateurs with big ticket or home-built audio gear to professional audio engineers. In addition to the large volume of solid what-to-buy questions and advice, these audio newsgroups are also a fantastic marketplace for buying and selling new and used audio gear components, accessories and parts.

The buzz on these newsgroups is that they are just about the fastest way to buy or sell any audio paraphernalia.

Audio General Discussion

rec.audio **HI**

A general category for home audio, from mid-range to high-end. Includes troubleshooting, feedback on new audio products (speakers, receivers, CD players, etc.), and a good deal of troubleshooting advice on home audio setups, sound dynamics, acoustics and audio electronics.

FAQ ▶ The following FAQs are available via FTP from RTFM.MIT.EDU in the directory:
pub/usenet/rec.audio:
FAQ:_rec.audio_(part_1_of_4)
FAQ:_rec.audio_(part_2_of_4)
FAQ:_rec.audio_(part_3_of_4)
FAQ:_rec.audio_(part_4_of_4)
LIST_OF_LOW_FREQUENCY_LOUDSPEAKER_DRIVERS
rec.audio_FAQ_(part_1_of_4)
rec.audio_FAQ_(part_2_of_4)
rec.audio_FAQ_(part_3_of_4)
rec.audio_FAQ_(part_4_of_4)

Car Audio

rec.audio.car **M**

Car audio enthusiasts trade useful technical tips, info and reviews on good car audio equipment and do-it-yourself installations.

FAQ ▶ The following FAQs are available via FTP from RTFM.MIT.EDU in the directory:
pub/usenet/rec.audio.car:
rec.audio.car_FAQ_(part_1_3)
rec.audio.car_FAQ_(part_2_3)
rec.audio.car_FAQ_(part_3_3)

Audiophile Talk

rec.audio.high-end **M**

The place to go if you're a serious audiophile. Equipment tips, question-and-answer info on audio bugs and component/parts advice. Everything from where to buy vacuum tubes and top-end receivers to how to build homemade homebrew cables and speakers.

Professional Audio Group

rec.audio.pro **M**

Top-notch product and tech info for home/basement sound studios and high-end remote recording. A must for any audiophile interested in achieving optimized live recording performance. Information on acoustics, recording techniques and components to buy/sell, and professional grade equipment reviews and comments.

CD Music Talk

rec.music.cd **M**

A wide variety of interesting information all about compact discs. Everything from how to record your own songs on CDs to the latest CD players, technical tips and buy/sell info. Includes discussions on the latest major CD collections released by recording artists.

FAQ ▶ The following FAQ is available via FTP from RTFM.MIT.EDU in the directory:
pub/usenet/rec.music.cd:
INFO:_Wanted_Disc_List,_9_10_93_[Repost]

Movies & Moviemaking

All About Moviemaking

rec.arts.cinema **L**

Excellent, must-read newsgroup for film students, filmmakers and do-it-yourself cinematographers, **rec.arts.cinema** is packed with great info on the art and craft of filmmaking. Everything from discussions of Godard and Cuban cinema to useful tips on low-cost camera equipment (Super 8, 16mm and 70mm) and editing equipment. Also features many good pointers on the technical side of movie-making, post-production and editing.

Sample Subjects:
Film and equipment/70mm film format/Russian 16mm camera/Small film production companies

All About Horror Movies

alt.horror **M**

Fans of modern-day and classic horror films, books, novels and short stories gather here for extremely active discussions and exchange of facts and trivia. Includes discussions on modern films and books (like *Night of the Living Dead* and Stephen King novels)

▲ *Freddy Krueger, graphics image file downloaded via Internet FTP from* **wuarchive.wustl.edu**

and many far more obscure movies, short stories, books and anthologies. Good fellowship and enthusiasm exchanged among horror fans in this popular group.

Sample Subjects:
Worst movies!/Drive-in reviews/Net Halloween greeting/ Cemetery of the living dead

Movie Chat Group

rec.arts.movies **HI**

This is the free-for-all group for questions, comments and other chat mostly about the latest movies. Good place to get answers to questions you might have about a specific movie or to contribute your two cents' worth on the movie of your choice.

Sample Subjects:
Songs in movies/Most beautiful actresses/Review: *Rising Sun*/Review: *Heart and Soul*

FAQ ▶ The following FAQs are available via FTP from RTFM.MIT.EDU in the directory:
pub/usenet/rec.arts.movies:
BLADE_RUNNER_Frequently_Asked_Questions_(FAQ)
rec.arts.movies_Frequently_Asked_Questions

Movie Chat Group II

bit.listserv.cinema-l **M**

Students and academics engage in informal chats about their favorite films, actors and actresses, directors, etc. Discussions on movies are wide-ranging and highly opinionated, but also very civilized. Includes impromptu movie reviews contributed by Netters on new box office films.

Sample Subjects:
***Boxing Helena*/Branagh in Britain/Kathleen Turner Fan Club**

▲ *Sharon Stone,* ▲ *Humphrey Bogart,* ▲ *Clint Eastwood and* ▲ *Clark Gable and Vivian Leigh, all from* **wuarchive.wustl.edu**; ▶ *Sean Connery as James Bond in "Never Say Never Again," from* **grind.isca.uiowa.edu**

Amateur Movie Reviews

rec.arts.movies.reviews **L**

In **rec.arts.movies.reviews**, you'll find passable-to-fairly good reviews of current movies, all written by enthusiastic moviegoers. You have to respect the sincerity and effort put forth by this newsgroup's amateur critics who give their "regular guy" perspective on Hollywood's latest releases.

James Bond 007 Talk & Trivia

alt.fan.james-bond **M**

The group for fans of Ian Fleming's famous secret agent novels and the (even more famous) blockbuster movies of the 1960s featuring Sean Connery's Bond. Lots of trivia related to Bond movies (mainly) and also talk/speculation on upcoming James Bond 007 movies and other events.

Sample Subjects:
List of weapons in 007 novels/*Casino Royale*/Bond gadgets

The World of Cult Movies

alt.cult-movies **HI**

Do you like cult films? Discuss your favorite cult movie with many other fans. Comments on many, many cult films, broadcast/exhibition dates and videocassette availability. Covers horror, science fiction movies and a wide variety of other films you probably never even heard of! Includes a great many offbeat and unusual movie descriptions.

Sample Subjects:
Cult movie night/Andy Warhol movies/*Rocky Horror Picture Show*/*Godzilla*

FAQ ▶ The following FAQs are available via FTP from RTFM.MIT.EDU in the directory:
pub/usenet/alt.cult-movies:
LIST:_Crazy_Movie_Credits
LIST:_MOVIE_TRIVIA:_in-jokes,_cameos,_signatures
Rocky_Horror_Theater_List

Rocky Horror Fan Club

alt.cult-movies.rocky-horror **M**

For fans of the 1974 film *Rocky Horror Picture Show*.

Radio Talk

Greaseman Fan Club on the Net

alt.fan.greaseman **L**

If you can appreciate the humor of radio's shock jock, the Greaseman, you will find good fellowship among other fans on this online discussion group. Plenty of chitchat on favorite Greaseman bits, definition of Greaseman inside jokes and more. There is even access to an online repository of computer-stored Greaseman bits you can download for use with any PC soundboard.

Sample Subjects:
Grease words/List of markets/The Grease tapes

Howard Stern Fan Club

alt.fan.howard-stern **HI**

An active fan group for listeners of radio shock jock Howard Stern. Includes detailed discussions of every little Howard Stern radio bit, latest Howard Stern stories, show availability on local radio stations, and chitchat about Howard Stern's most recent controversies.

Sample Subjects:
Howard Stern monthly radio listing/Stern in new markets/Best of Stern

FAQ ▶ The following FAQ is available via FTP from RTFM.MIT.EDU in the directory:
pub/usenet/alt.fan.howard-stern:
[alt.fan.howard-stern]_FAQ:_Frequently_Asked_Questions_about_Howard_Stern,_Monthly_Posting

Lake Wobegon Lore

rec.arts.wobegon **M**

For fans of the popular radio shows and books by humorist Garrison Keillor. Includes radio show schedules, local availability and talk about the past and current radio shows, *A Prairie Home Companion* and *American Radio Company*.

Prime-Time & Cult TV Talk

Prime-Time TV Talk Groups on the Net

A look at the large number of very active TV-related newsgroups on the Net will tell you that Net users seem to watch as much TV as the general population. That fact, combined with their usual high enthusiasm (some might say obsession) with arcane facts mean there's lots here to talk about when it comes to tube talk. In the alt. category, there are TV-related newsgroups covering many past or present television shows from obscure episodes of *The Prisoner* to *Beverly Hills 90210* and *Seinfeld*. Newsgroups on old television shows from the 1960s and 1970s typically feature information on availability of episodes on video, show trivia (usually more than you'd ever want to know), comments by fans on their favorite shows, info on fan clubs and more. Discussion groups on current shows have the usual banter about cast characters ("who's my favorite," "did you see what Kramer did on *Seinfeld* last night?" etc.) and speculation on future plots, storylines, characters, etc. If you're a serious fan of any of the following TV shows, you'll think you found Heaven when you've logged on to these newsgroups.

▲ *Herman Munster, downloaded via Internet FTP from* **wuarchive.wustl.edu**

Babylon 5

alt.tv.babylon-5 **HI**

Plenty of talk about the current syndicated sci-fi series

Beverly Hills 90210

alt.tv.bh90210 **M**

The latest on Dylan, Kelly, Brandon and the rest of America's oldest 18 year-olds.

Dinosaur & *Barney* Hate Group

alt.tv.dinosaur.barney.die.die.die **M**

Yep, you guessed it—our big purple friend isn't too popular on this group and some of the things Net folks want to do to Barney can't be talked about here.

Dinosaurs TV Show

alt.tv.dinosaurs **M**

Group for fans of the ABC-TV prime-time series.

Infomercials Talk Group

alt.tv.infomercials **M**

Do you know what a FlowBee is? Where's Tom Vu? If you want to know if products advertised on TV infomercials are any good, ask your question here.

LA Law Talk

alt.tv.la-law **M**

Group for fans of the popular NBC series.

David Letterman Fans Talk Group

alt.fan.letterman **M**

An indispensable Net chat group for Dave fans. Netters talk about their favorite bits from last night's show, guest appearances and recent news items. Current talk has included argument over the quality of Dave's current CBS show versus the old NBC show, quality of stand-up comics on the show, and more show trivia than can be read at one sitting. The high volume of postings by Letterman fans and their immediacy gives you instant feedback on every aspect of Dave's show.

Sample Subjects:
Scripted Letterman act versus Ted Kennedy/The miracle of the Top Ten List/Wednesday's Letterman

FAQ ▶ The following FAQs are available via FTP from RTFM.MIT.EDU in the directory:
pub/usenet/alt.fan.letterman:
alt.fan.letterman_Official_David_Letterman_Song_Book_changes_since_last_posting
FAQ:_alt.fan.letterman_FAQ_changes_since_last_posting
FAQ:_alt.fan.letterman_Frequently_Asked_Questions_(read_before_posting)
The_alt.fan.letterman_Official_David_Letterman_Song_Book

Beavis and Butt-Head

alt.tv.liquid-tv **L**

Fan group for America's favorite teenage cartoon burnouts. If you don't know who Beavis and Butt-head are by now, you won't care. If you do, then many kindred souls are waiting to hear from you!

▲ *(Top) David Letterman,* ▲ *The cast of "Seinfeld," and* ▶ *Beavis and Butt-head, all downloaded via Internet FTP from* **wuarchive.wustl.edu**

M*A*S*H

alt.tv.mash **M**

Hawkeye, Trapper and Hotlips live on forever in re-runs, and also here on the Net in this active group.

Melrose Place

alt.tv.melrose-place **M**

Will Billy get back together with Alison? Is Amanda really pregnant? All this and more is discussed on this group for fans of Fox-TV's *90210* spinoff.

Monty Python Fan Talk

alt.fan.Monty-Python **HI**

Disjointed talk group where Netters trade their inside jokes on old Monty Python bits and characters. Monopolized by a small handful of Net people using this newsgroup as an excuse to trade insults.

Mystery Science Theater 3000

alt.tv.mst3K **HI**

For fans of the camp cable sci-fi show *Mystery Science Theater 3000.*

FAQ ▶ The following FAQs are available via FTP from RTFM.MIT.EDU in the directory:
pub/usenet/alt.tv.mst3k:
Mystery_Science_Theater_3000_Episode_Guide
Mystery_Science_Theater_3000_FAQ
Mystery_Science_Theater_3000_Songs

Muppets

alt.tv.muppets **M**

Talk group for fans of Kermit, Miss Piggy, and

▲ *Ren & Stimpy, video capture image file, downloaded via Internet FTP from* **wuarchive.wustl.edu**

the rest of the late Jim Henson's marvelous characters.

Married With Children

alt.tv.mwc **M**

Dish the dirt on Al Bundy and his family on *Married With Children*.

FAQ▶ The following FAQs are available via FTP from RTFM.MIT.EDU in the directory:
pub/usenet/alt.tv.mwc:
MARRIED_WITH_CHILDREN_PROGRAM_GUIDE__(Part_1_5)
MARRIED_WITH_CHILDREN_PROGRAM_GUIDE__(Part_2_5)
MARRIED_WITH_CHILDREN_PROGRAM_GUIDE__(Part_3_5)
MARRIED_WITH_CHILDREN_PROGRAM_GUIDE__(Part_4_5)
MARRIED_WITH_CHILDREN_PROGRAM_GUIDE__(Part_5_5)

Northern Exposure

alt.tv.northern-exp **M**

What's the latest from Cicely? If you like *Northern Exposure*, join up with this very popular newsgroup on the Net and find out for yourself.

FAQ▶ The following FAQs are available via FTP from RTFM.MIT.EDU in the directory:
pub/usenet/alt.tv.northern-exp:
alt.tv.northern-exp_FAQ_reminder
alt.tv.northern-exp_Frequently_Asked_Questions

The Prisoner

alt.tv.prisoner **M**

All you'd ever want to know about the 1960s cult TV classic *The Prisoner* starring Patrick (*Secret Agent*) McGoohan, immortalized here as "Number 6."

FAQ▶ The following FAQs are available via FTP from RTFM.MIT.EDU in the directory:
pub/usenet/alt.tv.prisoner:
THE_PRISONER_FAQ_Part_I_(no_spoilers)
THE_PRISONER_FAQ_Volume_I_(no_spoilers)

Red Dwarf

alt.tv.red-dwarf **M**

Talk group for fans of the *Red Dwarf* British sci-fi series.

FAQ▶ The following FAQ is available via FTP from RTFM.MIT.EDU in the directory:
pub/usenet/alt.tv.red-dwarf:
Red_Dwarf_FAQ,_version_3.5

Ren & Stimpy

alt.tv.ren-n-stimpy **M**

They're gross! They're disgusting! Plenty of talk here about this animated cable cartoon show.

Rockford Files

alt.tv.rockford-files **L**

Fans of James Garner's character in the popular 1970s series *The Rockford Files* discuss various characters and favorite episodes.

Saved by the Bell

alt.tv.saved-bell **L**

For fans of the NBC-TV series *Saved By The Bell*.

Seinfeld

alt.tv.seinfeld **M**

A very active and popular newsgroup for *Seinfeld* watchers, including news of upcoming episodes, comments, Kramer one-liners, etc.

FAQ▶ The following FAQs are available via FTP from RTFM.MIT.EDU in the directory:
pub/usenet/alt.tv.seinfeld:
alt.tv.seinfeld_FAQ_List_and_Info_File_(part_01_03)
alt.tv.seinfeld_FAQ_List_and_Info_File_(part_02_03)
alt.tv.seinfeld_FAQ_List_and_Info_File_(part_03_03)

The Simpsons

alt.tv.simpsons **HI**

Fans of the Bart-dude discuss their favorite episodes and scene details of the hit cartoon series.

FAQ▶ The following FAQ is available via FTP from RTFM.MIT.EDU in the directory:
pub/usenet/alt.tv.simpsons:
alt.tv.simpsons_Frequently_Asked_Questions

Tiny Toon Adventures

alt.tv.tiny-toon **M**

A popular chat group for fans of the Steven Speilberg-produced *Tiny Toon Adventure* cartoon series.

FAQ▶ The following FAQ is available via FTP from RTFM.MIT.EDU in the directory:
pub/usenet/alt.tv.tiny-toon:
alt.tv.tiny-toon_Frequently_Asked_Questions

Twin Peaks

alt.tv.twin-peaks **M**

Even though *Twin Peaks* hasn't been seen on TV in a couple of years, its large cult following continues on the

Net, with a massive Net volume of back-and-forth on *Twin Peaks* characters, plot, and trivia.

TV Soaps

rec.arts.tv.soaps **HI**

Catch up with your favorite daytime soaps in this very popular newsgroup. Includes recent episode story summaries, chitchat and comments on all the daytime soap characters.

FAQ ▶ The following FAQs are available via FTP from RTFM.MIT.EDU in the directory:
pub/usenet/rec.arts.tv.soaps:
_REC.ARTS.TV.SOAPS_POSTING_GUIDELINES_
ALL:_rec.arts.tv.soaps_Monthly_FAQ_(Frequently_Asked_Questions)

Disney TV Cartoon Talk

alt.fan.disney.afternoon **L**

Fans group for talk about Disney afternoon TV cartoons and related Disneyana.

TV Trivia Talk

rec.arts.tv **HI**

Trivia questions and answers including plenty of discussion on obscure old TV shows as well as present prime-time and new fall season offerings.

FAQ ▶ The following FAQs are available via FTP from RTFM.MIT.EDU in the directory:
pub/usenet/rec.arts.tv:
_REC.ARTS.TV_POSTING_GUIDELINES_
_FLYING_BLIND__PROGRAM_GUIDE
_HERMAN_S_HEAD__PROGRAM_GUIDE
_SHAKY_GROUND__PROGRAM_GUIDE

British Comedy: Film & TV

alt.comedy.british **M**

This discussion group is specifically for fans of various British comedies seen on PBS in the United States. Lots of chat about *Monty Python*, *Are You Being Serv*ed?, *Fawlty Towers*, *Black Adder*, and other comedies from the BBC. And, because it's on the Internet, you'll get feedback from people in British Commonwealth countries like New Zealand, Australia and Great Britain on these comedy shows, all of which adds an interesting element to the discussions (such as why certain jokes on certain shows are actually funny). Also features discussions on new episodes of shows that will soon appear in the US.

Sample Subjects:
Monty Python on video/**Waiting for God**/**Are You Being Served?** not funny

British Prime-Time TV

rec.arts.tv.uk **M**

Brit fans of current U.K. prime-time TV shows discuss current shows and TV actors in the U.K., from a hometown point of view.

Science Fiction

Science Fiction Fan Groups on the Net

Given the fact that many hard-core computer users are also science fiction fans, there are a good number of big and very busy newsgroups relating to just about any science fiction topic. Whether you're a reader of contemporary science fiction books, a devoted *Star Wars* fan or a devotee of old cult sci-fi TV shows of the 1960s or the present, there are many, many other equally enthusiastic people who share your enthusiasms on the Net.

Sci-Fi Conventions

rec.arts.sf.announce **L**

Announcements and other info on local sci-fi conventions.

FAQ ▶ The following FAQ is available via FTP from RTFM.MIT.EDU in the directory:
pub/usenet/rec.arts.sf.announce:
Rec.arts.sf_groups,_an_introduction

Science Fiction Conventions-Talk

alt.fandom.cons **M**

Science fiction fanatics discuss their adventures and experiences at local science fiction conventions.

Sci-Fi Collectibles: Buy & Sell

rec.arts.sf.marketplace **M**

Interested in buying/selling sci-fi toys or other collectibles? Post them here on this very active newsgroup.

Sci-Fi Talk & Speculations

rec.arts.sf.misc **HI**

A catch-all conversational group having many (mostly sci-fi speculation) discussions occurring simultaneously. Post your questions or queries having to do with anything sci-fi-related.

FAQ ▶ The following FAQs are available via FTP from RTFM.MIT.EDU in the directory:
pub/usenet/rec.arts.sf.misc:
rec.arts.sf.written_FAQ
SF-references-in-music_List

Sci-Fi Technical Talk

rec.arts.sf.science **M**

Definitely the best and most intellectually challenging of all the sci-fi newsgroups. Participants discuss the SCIENCE of science fiction, debating many hypothetical assumptions made in science fiction books, TV shows and movies (can you hear noises in explosions in *Star Wars* battles? Is faster-than-light travel really possible? How would you make solar sails work for interstellar space travel?)

▲ *Yoda, downloaded from* **wuarchive.wustl.edu**

Star Wars

rec.arts.sf.starwars **HI**

Fans of the *Star Wars* trilogy chat about The Empire, Luke, Darth, Han, Obi-Wan, and the rest of the *Star Wars* world.

Sci-Fi TV Shows

rec.arts.sf.tv **HI**

Tube-watchers talk about their favorite sci-fi TV shows of past and present, such as *Star Trek, Quantum Leap*, and the obscure shows you watched as a kid in the 1950s and 1960s, like *Thunderbirds* and *The Invaders*.

FAQ ▶ The following FAQ is available via FTP from RTFM.MIT.EDU in the directory:
pub/usenet/rec.arts.sf.tv:
TV_Discussion_Groups,_Etc._(monthly_posting)

Dr. Who

rec.arts.drwho **HI**

Cult discussion group for the BBC sci-fi TV series *Dr. Who*. Fans discuss their favorite *Dr. Who* characters, episodes and submit their own story ideas.

Sample Subjects:
The Dr. without companions/New companion/Five Dr.'s questions

Sci-Fi Books

rec.arts.sf.written **HI**

Sci-fi readers review and discuss current works of science fiction and authors.

FAQ ▶ The following FAQs are available via FTP from RTFM.MIT.EDU in the directory:
pub/usenet/rec.arts.sf.written:
B_i_N_N_A_C_(r.a.b)
index

▲ *Starship USS Enterprise, downloaded via Internet FTP from* **wuarchive.wustl.edu**

Star Trek

Star Trek Newsgroups

If you're a *Star Trek* fan, you can select from a number of newsgroups for both the original 1960s series and *Star Trek: The Next Generation, Deep Space Nine,* and the seven blockbuster *Star Trek* movies. In general, newsgroups accommodate a wide range of participants' interest levels relating to *Star Trek*—from the mildly interested to the truly obsessive-compulsive—so there's always a lot of interesting information and answered questions if you'd like to know about anything that's Trek-related.

Star Trek Talk

rec.arts.startrek **L**

Catch-all category for questions, comments or observations about the original *Star Trek* series (called TOS—"The Old Show"—on the Net), *Star Trek: The Next Generation* (called STTNG) and its spinoff, *Star Trek: Deep Space Nine* (called DS9).

▲ *"Locutus of Borg" (Captain Jean-Luc Picard) and* ▲ *Spock, photo image files downloaded via Internet FTP from* **wuarchive.wustl.edu**

Star Trek: *The Next Generation*
rec.arts.startrek.current [HI]

Fans of *Star Trek: The Next Generation* chat about recent episodes, characters and ideas for future episodes.

FAQ ▶ The following FAQs are available via FTP from RTFM.MIT.EDU in the directory:
pub/usenet/rec.arts.startrek.current:
DSN_Promos_for:_INVASIVE_PROCEDURES_(#424)
DSN_Promos_for:_THE_CIRCLE_(#422)
DSN_Promos_for:_THE_HOMEC
DSN_Promos_for:_THE_HOMECOMING_(#421)
DSN_Promos_for:_THE_SIEGE_(#423)
FAQL:_diff_listing_(changes_since_last_posting_of_rasc_FAQL)
FAQL:_FREQUENTLY_ASKED_QUESTIONS_LIST_for_rec.arts.startrek.current
R.A.S.*_NETIQUETTE_LIST_(10_1_93_version)
R.A.S.*_NETIQUETTE_LIST_(8_15_93_version)
R.A.S.*_SPOILER_LIST_(8_15_93_version)
Star_Trek_DSN_List_of_Lists_(July,_1993)
TNG_Promos_for:_GAMBIT,_Part_II_(#257)
TNG_Promos_for:_INTERFACE_(#255)
TNG_Promos_for:_LIAIS
TNG_Promos_for:_LIAISONS
TNG_Promos_for:_LIAISONS_(#254)

Star Trek *Conventions*
rec.arts.startrek.fandom [M]

Hard-core Trekkers swap news about *Star Trek* conventions held in various cities.

Star Trek *Conventions Schedule*
rec.arts.startrek.info [L]

A small newsgroup featuring postings of lists of upcoming *Star Trek* conventions and *Star Trek* attractions in various other locations.

FAQ ▶ The following FAQs are available via FTP from RTFM.MIT.EDU in the directory:
pub/usenet/rec.arts.startrek.info:

Guidelines_For_Submitting_Articles
Introduction_to_rec.arts.startrek.info
List_of_Upcoming_Conventions

Star Trek: *More Talk*
rec.arts.startrek.misc [HI]

Catch-all discussion group for any comment, question or speculation involving *Star Trek*.

FAQ ▶ The following FAQs are available via FTP from RTFM.MIT.EDU in the directory:
pub/usenet/rec.arts.startrek.misc:
FAQ:_Star_Trek_Spelling_List_v5.0_[1_2]
FAQ:_Star_Trek_Spelling_List_v5.0_[2_2]
FAQ:_Star_Trek_Spelling_List_v6.0_[1_2]
FAQ:_Star_Trek_Spelling_List_v6.0_[2_2]
FAQL:_ACRONYMS_USED_IN_THE_REC.ARTS.STARTREK.*_NEWSGROUPS
FAQL:_diff_listing_(changes_since_last_posting_of_rasm_FAQL)
FAQL:_FREQUENTLY_ASKED_QUESTIONS_LIST_for_rec.arts.startrek.misc
FAQL:_FTP_SITES_WITH_TREK-RELATED_FILES
FAQL:_HOW_TO_SUBMIT_CREATIVE_MATERIAL
FAQL:_LIST_OF_PERIODIC_POSTINGS_TO_r.a.s.*_NEWSGROUPS
FAQL:_NAMES,_RANKS,_AND_SERIAL_NUMBERS_(AND_CREW_DATA)
FAQL:_PILOT_EPISODES_AND_UNAIRED_EPISODES
FAQL:_SNAFUs
FAQL:_STAR_TREK_ABROAD
FAQL:_STAR_TREK_MUSIC
FAQL:_TIME_LOOPS,_YESTERDAY_S_ENTERPRISE,_AND_TASHA_YAR_EXPLAINED
Star_Trek_Actors__Other_Roles_FAQ_[02_07]
Star_Trek_Actors__Other_Roles_FAQ_[03_07]
Star_Trek_Actors__Other_Roles_FAQ_[04_07]
Star_Trek_Actors__Other_Roles_FAQ_[05_07]
Star_Trek_Actors__Other_Roles_FAQ_[06_07]
Star_Trek_Actors__Other_Roles_FAQ_[07_07]
Star_Trek_Actors__Other_Roles_FAQ_[INTRO]_[01_07]
Star_Trek_Books-On-Tape
Star_Trek_Comics_Checklist,_Part_1_2
Star_Trek_Comics_Checklist,_Part_2_2
Star_Trek_Comics_Checklist,_README
STAR_TREK_LOCATIONS_[Updated:_Aug_17,_1993]
STAR_TREK_LOCATIONS_[Updated:_Oct_14,_1993]
STAR_TREK_SHIPS_[Updated:_Aug_17,_1993]
STAR_TREK_SHIPS_[Updated:_Oct_14,_1993]
Star_Trek_Spelling_List_v5.0_[2_2]
Star_Trek_TOS_TAS_List_of_Lists_(April,_1993)
TNG_Novels_Compendium_[Changes_since_last_release]

▲ *"Star Trek" cast photo and* ▲ *Kirk and Spock from "Star Trek VI: The Undiscovered Country," downloaded via Internet FTP from* **wuarchive.wustl.edu**

TNG_Novels_Compendium_[Update]
TOS_Novels_Compendium_[Changes_since_last_release]
TOS_Novels_Compendium_[Update]
TREK_RATE_ballot
TREK_RATE_results_(BOOKS)
TREK_RATE_results_(DS9)
TREK_RATE_results_(MOVIES)
TREK_RATE_results_(TAS)
TREK_RATE_results_(TNG)
TREK_RATE_results_(TOS)
_Star_Trek__Quotes_Part_01:__ST:TOS_
_Star_Trek__Quotes_Part_02:__ST:TMP_
_Star_Trek__Quotes_Part_03:__STII:TWOK_
_Star_Trek__Quotes_Part_04:__STIII:TSFS_
_Star_Trek__Quotes_Part_05:__STIV:TVH_
_Star_Trek__Quotes_Part_06:__STV:TFF_
_Star_Trek__Quotes_Part_07:__STVI:TUC_
_Star_Trek__Quotes_Part_08:__ST:TNG__Season_One
_Star_Trek__Quotes_Part_09:__ST:TNG__Season_Two
_Star_Trek__Quotes_Part_10:__ST:TNG__Season_Three
_Star_Trek__Quotes_Part_11:__ST:TNG__Season_Four
_Star_Trek__Quotes_Part_12:__ST:TNG__Season_Five
_Star_Trek__Quotes_Part_13:__ST:TNG__Season_Six
_Star_Trek__Quotes_Part_15:__ST:DS9__Season_One

Technology of *Star Trek*

rec.arts.startrek.tech **M**

A must-read newsgroup in the *Star Trek* category featuring detailed information on and about the futuristic and speculative technology used in *Star Trek*. Everything from Warp Drive to Romulan weapons systems, plus many other good questions and answers.

FAQ ▶ The following FAQs are available via FTP from RTFM.MIT.EDU in the directory:
pub/usenet/rec.arts.startrek.tech:
FAQL:_FREQUENTLY_ASKED_QUESTIONS_LIST_for_rec.arts.startrek.tech
Holodeck_Mini-FAQ
Not_the_Technical_Manual
Relativity_and_FTL_Travel

Star Trek Tales: Self-Published Online Stories

alt.startrek.creative **M**

Are you a devoted Trekkie? Have you ever wanted to write your own *Star Trek* episode? This newsgroup is a publish-it-yourself place to post your own *Star Trek* stories and read stories posted by other talented Net amateur writers. Contains several different stories featuring characters from both the original *Star Trek*, as well as *Star Trek: The Next Generation*. Also features numerous comments on present and future *Star Trek* shows and movies.

FAQ ▶ The following FAQs are available via FTP from RTFM.MIT.EDU in the directory:
pub/usenet/alt.startrek.creative:
Star_Trek_story_archive_(weekly_FAQ_—_automated_posting)
What_is_alt.startrek.creative?_(FAQ)

Star Trek Weird Spoofs

alt.ensign.wesley.die.die.die **M**

This online discussion group is devoted to *Star Trek* fans who hate Ensign Wesley Crusher, a character on *Star Trek: The Next Generation*. Suggestions on ways for torturing and eliminating the young ensign, plus discussions of various other *Star Trek* and *Deep Space Nine* characters.

Chapter 9: Science, Technology & Education

Connecting our schools, colleges and companies to the Information Superhighway may be the single most important thing we do this decade to maintain this country's economic vitality.

Why should schools and educators hook into the Internet?

Education on the Net

No one is pleased with schools in America today. The Internet can help. Good teachers struggle in isolation, with limited resources trying desperately to get kids excited about learning. Companies find high school (and, in many cases, college) graduates they hire don't have the basic skills needed to perform today's high-tech jobs. The end result is that American companies have to spend significant funds training workers, or worse—export those jobs overseas to remain competitive in today's global market.

By introducing the Internet into their schools, educators can significantly expand the resources available to teachers and students. *The CIA Fact Book*, available online, may be more relevant than a five-year-old geography text. A high school government class debating the merits of a bill before Congress can get immediate access to the proposed legislation. Or a junior high school student doing a science project can download NASA moon pictures for inclusion in his or her report. The Internet can ease teachers' isolation by allowing them to connect with other colleagues and experts.

Databases of text and graphics available on the Net are impressive, but probably the most valuable aspect of the Net is the way it can provide access to other people—teachers, students, scientists and experts throughout the country and the world. A lesson plan developed in Ohio can be shared with a teacher in Texas. Students can conduct shared experiments like tracking the population density of the monarch

MIT researchers Amy Bruckman and Mitchel Resnick have developed a new application of computer networking that may allow scientists to collaborate without leaving their workplaces. Researchers connecting to the system through Internet can gather in a simulated auditorium to conduct the kind of business that normally occurs at a professional seminar. The MIT system's programming language does not require users to have much specialized knowledge before they can communicate and move among the simulated environment of imaginary rooms. Users say that the system has been helpful and that the "playful atmosphere" developed encourages informal discussions resembling real talk.

Wade Roush, "Have Computer, Won't Travel," *Technology Review,* (7/93)

Electronic networks are sparking the kind of excitement not seen in U.S. classrooms since the space race. In scores of programs and pilot projects, networks are changing the way teachers teach and students learn. For example, students in Minnesota recently exchanged electronic mail with their peers on the Kamchatka Peninsula in eastern Siberia, rather than merely reading about life in Russia from outdated books. By tapping into the nets, kids discover ways of working and communicating that will powerfully enhance their prospects when they join the workforce of the 21st century. The networks may also play a key role in helping U.S. schools overcome their notorious weakness in teaching math, science and geography.

Elizabeth Corcoran, "Why Kids Love Computer Nets," *Fortune* (9/20/93)

butterfly throughout the United States, or replicating the Eratosthenes experiment in an international project.

Students learn by doing—by interacting with their environment—not by sitting passively and listening to a teacher lecture them on the principles of electricity.

Science on the Net

Technology and related information are now advancing at breakneck speed. Scientists, engineers and businesspeople affected by technology have to devote a significant amount of time to gathering and processing information, or they will quickly fall behind. In today's competitive environment, learning must be a continuous process.

The science groups on the Net are a great way to stay abreast of developments, not only in your field, but in related fields as well. When a problem comes up outside of your specialty, you'll probably be able to find an expert quickly by posting a query to a relevant newsgroup. And when you do find them, they tend to be extremely helpful.

Bioscience and Bionet: Hard Science

No branch of science is moving any faster than bioscience. The rate of scientific discovery is so fast that traditional hard-copy journals may become obsolete. These are the groups to observe if you want to see how real science is done—patents being filed daily and discoveries corroborated overnight. On most of the other Internet newsgroups we actively encourage your participation. In these groups, unless you have a degree in biology, we recommend you don't post questions—just let the scientists work.

Science & Technology

Architecture Discussions
alt.architecture **M**

This group is mostly populated by amateur architects designing their dream homes. The pros and cons of various CAD software packages are debated and an occasional professional architect or student will lend some advice.

Sample Subjects:
Info on passive solar systems/Building with straw/Costs of a complete CAD system

Technical Books
alt.books.technical **L**

Looking for an obscure book on FETs or the definitive work on AIX? This is a good group to check. Participants also help each other find the best "online bookstores."

Sample Subjects:
New adaptive technology book/Books on tsch/Any bookstores online?

FAQ ▶ The following FAQ is available via FTP from RTFM.MIT.EDU in the directory:
pub/usenet/alt.books.technical:
[misc.books.technical]_A_Concise_Guide_to_UNIX_Books

Fractals
alt.fractals **L**

A lightly populated fractals discussion group. **sci.fractals** is much more active.

Physics: New Theories
alt.sci.physics.new-theories **M**

Catch the great theories before you read them in the scientific journals (if ever). For example, there's biofusion, whereby living organisms can transmute elements. We're not talking about the mundane stuff like microbes eating toxic waste. We're talking about chickens converting calcium to lead. And, of course, there's the car that burns water (supposedly it's been sighted in Sacramento!).

Sample Subjects:
The speed of light/Time and gravity/The quantum watched pot

FAQ ▶ The following FAQs are available via FTP from RTFM.MIT.EDU in the directory:
pub/usenet/alt.sci.physics.new-theories:
Sci.physics_Frequently_Asked_Questions_-_October_1993__-_Part_1_2
Sci.physics_Frequently_Asked_Questions_-_October_1993__-_Part_2_2
Sci.physics_Frequently_Asked_Questions_-_September_1993__-_Part_1_2
Sci.physics_Frequently_Asked_Questions_-_September_1993__-_Part_2_2

Biosphere Discussion Group
bit.listserv.biosph-l **L**

Forum for those interested in environmental issues.

Participants trade information about environmental alerts and seminars.

Sample Subjects:
EPA/DOE greenhouse gases meeting/Biodiversity list/Green cleaners

Technology Transfer & International Development
bit.listserv.devel-l **L**

Renewable energy, sustainable agriculture and telecommunications are some of the topics discussed here.

Fractals Discussion Group
bit.listserv.frac-l **L**

Forum for those interested in Chaos Theory and the Mandelbrot Set.

▲ Mandelbrot fractal computer-generated image, downloaded via Internet FTP from **wuarchive.wustl.edu**

Geodesic Domes
bit.listserv.geodesic **L**

Followers of Buckminster Fuller still believe geodesic domes can solve the world's housing shortage. In the meantime, participants help each other with more mundane issues—such as getting your geodesic dome past the local zoning board.

Medical Libraries
bit.listserv.medlib-l **M**

Information specialists from medical libraries around the world share referrals on hard-to-find resources.

Sample Subjects:
So what's with Clinical Practice Guidelines?/CD-ROM Compendium/Hospital strategy report

Technical Books
misc.books.technical **M**

Looking for that hard-to-find technical book? Post your queries to this group. You might even find a used copy at a bargain price. This is also a good group to check for references to online bookstores.

FAQ ▶ The following FAQ is available via FTP from RTFM.MIT.EDU in the directory:
pub/usenet/misc.books.technical:
misc.books.technical_FREQUENTLY_ASKED_QUESTIONS_(Periodic_post)

Aeronautics
sci.aeronautics **M**

Engineers from universities, companies and NASA help each other online. When one participant wanted to know how to build a homemade wind tunnel, the answers he received ranged from "Impossible!" (MIT engineer), "Difficult and $10 million dollars" (NASA engineer), to "Hey guy, just put the damned model aircraft on the roof of your car...that's the way Burt Rutan [kit plane designer] tested it" (shade-tree plane builder).

Sample Subjects:
Rules of thumb on a hovercraft/Need advice on good grad programs/Aircraft with winglets

Airliners & Aviation Talk Group
sci.aeronautics.airliners **M**

Airplane buffs trade information and stories about old and new birds. Occasionally, an engineer from Boeing or Lockheed will join the discussion to resolve questions and offer interesting tidbits. For example, the reason some 747s have winglets is that it enables the wing to be shortened (the winglets compensate by providing more lift), thereby allowing 747s to enter smaller gate areas.

Sample Subjects:
Landing gear design/ABS braking systems for airplanes/ New airliner in service

Anthropology
sci.anthropology **HI**

Can you prove mathematically that humans evolved from one common ancestor (the "Eve Hypothesis")? Folks in this group debate this issue in a lively fashion. Another hot debate is the origin of the term "Black Irish" and, after having defined the term with sufficient rigor, the Netters go on to find its origin (Hint: The general consensus is that it has something to do with the Spanish Armada).

Sample Subjects:
Evolution and jobs/French speakers in Missouri/Ancient Egyptians

FAQ ▶ The following FAQ is available via FTP from RTFM.MIT.EDU in the directory:
pub/usenet/sci.anthropology:
Shamanism-General_Overview-Frequently_Asked_Questions_(FAQ)

Aquaria
sci.aquaria **M**

We never thought there was so much to know about keeping an aquarium. Participants trade information on topics ranging from environmental damage caused by the pursuit of their hobby, to the correct pH factors for various fish. There's even a computer-based archive set up just for information on reefkeeping.

Sample Subjects:
Reef depletion/Cardinal tetras/Blue green algae takeover

FAQ ▶ The following FAQ is available via FTP from RTFM.MIT.EDU in the directory:
pub/usenet/sci.aquaria:
FAQ:_Beginner_topics_and

Archaeology
sci.archaeology **HI**

Professional archaeologists and enthusiasts trade information on subjects as diverse as the origin of writing, the oldest cloth and subtle differences between pots and baskets.

Sample Subjects:
Digital models of the pyramids/The inland ocean (Kansas)/ Etruscans from Lydia

Astronomy
sci.astro **HI**

Where else can a layman post a question entitled "Ignorant questions about black holes" and get the question answered—in detail—a few days later from a professor at the Institute for Geophysics and Planetary Physics? Participants trade information on meteor showers, telescope tips and debate on such topics as the Earth's axial tilt.

Sample Subjects:
Rotating black holes/Time has Inertia/Names of Neptune's moons

FAQ ▶ The following FAQs are available via FTP from RTFM.MIT.EDU in the directory:
pub/usenet/sci.astro:
Astro_Space_Frequently_Seen_Acronyms
Daily_Solar_Geophysical_Data_Broadcast_for_27_August
Diffs_to_sci.space_sci.astro_Frequently_Asked_Questions
Earth_and_Sky_-_Week_of_August_30-September_3,_1993
Earth_and_Sky_-_Week_of_October_11-15,_1993
Earth_and_Sky_-_Week_of_October_18-22,_1993
Earth_and_Sky_-_Week_of_October_25-29,_1993
Electronic_Journal_of_the_ASA_(EJASA)_-_October_1993
NRAO_RAP_unRAPsheet_#93-19,_17_September_1993
NRAO_RAP_unRAPsheet_#93-21,_15_October_93
Purchasing_Amateur_Telescopes_FAQ_(part_1_2)
Purchasing_Amateur_Telescopes_FAQ_(part_2_2)
Sky_&_Telescope_Weekly_News_Bulletin:_02_Oct_93
Sky_&_Telescope_Weekly_News_Bulletin:_04Sep93
Sky_&_Telescope_Weekly_News_Bulletin:_09Oct93
Sky_&_Telescope_Weekly_News_Bulletin:_25_Sep_93
Space_FAQ_01_13_-_Introduction
Space_FAQ_02_13_-_Network_Resources
Space_FAQ_03_13_-_Data_Sources
Space_FAQ_04_13_-_Calculations
Space_FAQ_05_13_-_References
Weekly_reminder_for_Frequently_Asked_Questions_list

Biology
sci.bio **HI**

Although serious science is covered in this group, discussions tend to be more speculative than the ones you see elsewhere on the Net. Researchers and interested laymen from around the world debate such issues as whether life can be recreated from fossilized DNA, as seen in *Jurassic Park*.

▲ *Milky Way Galaxy, downloaded via Internet FTP from* **wuarchive.wustl.edu**

Sample Subjects:
Why don't plants fix nitrogen?/How old is fossil DNA?/ Phylogeny software

FAQ▶ The following FAQs are available via FTP from RTFM.MIT.EDU in the directory:
pub/usenet/sci.bio:
A_Biologist_s_Guide_to_Internet_Resources_(1_of_6)
A_Biologist_s_Guide_to_Internet_Resources_(2_of_6)
A_Biologist_s_Guide_to_Internet_Resources_(3_of_6)
A_Biologist_s_Guide_to_Internet_Resources_(4_of_6)
A_Biologist_s_Guide_to_Internet_Resources_(5_of_6)
A_Biologist_s_Guide_to_Internet_Resources_(6_of_6)

Biotechnology
sci.bio.technology **M**

This group is all about *doing* bioscience. Researchers help each other locate software, lab equipment and resources to get projects done. A Berkeley-based grad student posts a query on behalf of a Japan-based colleague looking for software to compute the surface area of irregular shapes for a brain research project. A consortium of Israeli companies doing feasibility studies on biotech projects posts a query looking for experts on biosensors.

Sample Subjects:
Hydrogen bond calculator/Enzyme kinetics/Phylogenetic analysis of sequence data

Chemistry Resources
sci.chem **HI**

Chemists from companies, government labs and universities help each other locate the resources to keep their research going. A chemist from Pretoria looks for a database of chemical suppliers. A graduate student from Carnegie-Mellon posts a query on fuel cells and gets flooded with replies. A chemist who posts his secret for "Making pretzels look right" starts a raging and sometimes humorous debate

about the wisdom of using potentially poisonous compounds in food processing.

Sample Subjects:
Molecular visions darling models/Proton affiliates/Rodenticide longevity

Classic Literature Discussion Group
sci.classics **M**

The classics—as in *The Iliad, Beowulf,* and *The Aeneid* are discussed here. This group seems a little misplaced deep in the heart of the physical sciences area. Scholars ask for and get advice on the best original language and computer versions of the classics.

Sample Subjects:
Greek text recommended/Source for the Loeb Library/Lists of gods

FAQ▶ The following FAQ is available via FTP from RTFM.MIT.EDU in the directory:
pub/usenet/sci.classics:
sci.classics_FAQ

Cognitive Sciences
sci.cognitive **M**

This group discusses the human brain—what we know and what we don't know. Most of the recent discussion centers around Freeman Nets, a theory proposed by Walter Freeman in his book *How the Brain Makes Chaos in Order to Make Sense of the World.*

Sample Subjects:
Prenatal stress on cognition/Word frequency effects on recognition/Autism

Cryonics Discussion Group
sci.cryonics **L**

If you are interested in suspended animation, this is the group for you. Find out about the latest experiments in deep-freeze technology.

FAQ▶ The following FAQs are available via FTP from RTFM.MIT.EDU in the directory:
pub/usenet/sci.cryonics:
Cryonics_FAQ_1:_Index
Cryonics_FAQ_2:_Science_Technology
Cryonics_FAQ_3:_Philosophy_Religion
Cryonics_FAQ_4:_Controversy_surrounding_Cryonics
Cryonics_FAQ_5:_Neurosuspension
Cryonics_FAQ_6:_Suspension_Arrangements
Cryonics_FAQ_7:_Cost_of_Cryonics
Cryonics_FAQ_8:_Communications
Cryonics_FAQ_9:_Glossary

Cryptology
sci.crypt **HI**

Cryptology is the science and art of encrypting messages and databases. Hot topics in this group cover encryption methods such as PGP (pretty good privacy) and the Clipper chip (the government's answer to privacy). Although the discussions are technical in nature, even the beginner can get pointers to reference works that explain the field in greater detail.

Sample Subjects:
Block ciphers with CBC/Unix security/ Forging hash functions

FAQ ▶ The following FAQs are available via FTP from RTFM.MIT.EDU in the directory:
pub/usenet/sci.crypt:
Cryptography_FAQ_(01_10:_Overview;_last_mod_19930504)
Cryptography_FAQ_(02_10:_Net_Etiquette;_last_mod_19930504)
Cryptography_FAQ_(03_10:_Basic_Cryptology;_last_mod_19930504)
Cryptography_FAQ_(04_10:_Mathematical_Cryptology;_last_mod_19930504)
Cryptography_FAQ_(05_10:_Product_Ciphers;_last_mod_19930504)
Cryptography_FAQ_(06_10:_Public_Key_Cryptography;_last_mod_19930504)
Cryptography_FAQ_(07_10:_Digital_Signatures;_last_mod_19930504)
Cryptography_FAQ_(08_10:_Technical_Miscellany;_last_mod_19930504)
Cryptography_FAQ_(09_10:_Other_Miscellany;_last_mod_19930504)
Cryptography_FAQ_(10_10:_References;_last_mod_19930504)

Economics Discussion Group

sci.econ **HI**

Economics has been called "the dismal science," so you can make an argument for placing it with the other science subjects. Interspersed between the polite debate of academic economists about the merits of Burma's new exchange-rate policy, you'll find heated discussions about the wisdom of Clinton's economic policies. Occasionally, you'll find a posting from an unemployed economics major that makes for interesting reading.

Sample Subjects:
Why Russia's inflation is so high/Workmens comp system in the U.S./Privatization

FAQ ▶ The following FAQ is available via FTP from RTFM.MIT.EDU in the directory:
pub/usenet/sci.econ:
Economists__Resources_on_the_Internet

Electronics Tech Discussion Group

sci.electronics **HI**

A high-volume group where nerds look for nerdy stuff. They discuss such issues as making photoresist PCBs, trying to catch lightning bolts with CO2 lasers, and how to make a home-style laser. You should sign on to this group just to check and see whether any of these mad scientists live in your neigborhood. If they do...*move*!!!

Sample Subjects:
Video switching/Depth sounder/Single crystal indium phosphide

Energy Technology Discussions

sci.energy **HI**

The new miracle engines, windpower generation performance, and fuel cells. It's all here and more. In an interesting discussion, an engineer from Bellcore and a professor from Purdue reach the conclusion that it would cost $50,000 to outfit a house with enough solar panels to generate the average daily

▲ *Historic Apollo 11 moon landing photo, downloaded from* **wuarchive.wustl.edu**

household requirements for electricity (sounds like solar panels need a little more work!).

Sample Subjects:
Stirling engine update/Who has flue gas-scrubbers?/ Summary of efficiency software

Hydrogen & Solar Energy Discussion Group

sci.energy.hydrogen
M

Spirited, interesting and informative discussions on the latest in hydrogen and solar energy-producing technology. Discussions cover a wide range of new technologies, including new materials for development of hydrogen-based energy sources, solar energy collectors, sun-to-electricity technology, references to the latest news in scientific journals, and other discussions both practical and theoretical.

Engineering: General

sci.engr **HI**

Engineering covers a broad area. Questions posted to this group include everything from advice on the availability of plastic molding material for a home-based workshop to finite element/thermal analysis. Considering the broad range of questions, it's amazing that questions get answered here, but they do.

Sample Subjects:
Putting solvent into polyisobutylene/Electric vehicle mailing list/Starting salary

Engineering: Biomedical

sci.engr.biomed **M**

Engineers in companies and universities help each other out with information and pointers. A medical engineer in Boston who has developed an "eye tracker" tries to determine whether there is a market for the device. A researcher in Portugal wants reference information on the use of impedance to measure fat. As with most of the science groups, an occasional job offered/job wanted message floats by.

Sample Subjects:
Ranking of biomedical engineering schools/Ultrasound tutorial/ECG signal compression

Engineering: Chemical

sci.engr.chem **M**

Engineers help each other online. A researcher at Brown University wants to know the state of the art regarding the use of absorbents to store natural gas in low-pressure natural gas vehicles. Another researcher wants to know the rate oxygen dissolves in water. Both queries were answered quickly and succinctly.

Sample Subjects:
Looking for chemical equilibrium/ Metal matrix composites/The science of polymers

Engineering: Civil

sci.engr.civil [M]

Why did some levees break and some hold in the recent Mississippi flood? Civil engineers debate the merits of various levee designs. Here, as in other newsgroups, when a user receives a large volume of answers to a query, he usually posts a brief summary of the responses. These summaries provide valuable resources on topical issues.

Sample Subjects:
Standards available online/ Summary of efficiency software/ Artificial intelligence and fuzzy logic

Engineering: Control

sci.engr.control [M]

Feedback loops, fuzzy control and fuzzy logic controllers—these and other control-related topics are discussed here. When a self-described "Newbie" on the Net posts a query about whether neural nets have been applied to control problems, a professor from Rutgers shows him where he can download two of his recently completed papers on the subject.

Sample Subjects:
Generalized Eigenvectors/Overcompensating program/ Robust stability

Engineering: Mechanical

sci.engr.mech [HI]

Heat pipes for electronics cooling, the scuttlebutt on companies writing software for mechanical engineering applications and more. When an engineer posts a note about an upcoming software release from Company "X," a software programmer recently laid off from Company "X" tells him "not to hold his breath."

Sample Subjects:
Advice on FE software/Material properties of fibre-comps/Public domain pre-processor

Environment Discussion Group

sci.environment [HI]

Everyone's interested in the environment—probably too interested. The topics in this newsgroup sound

▲ *Albert Einstein, photo image file downloaded from* **ftp.sunet.se**

interesting: biodiversity, nuclear energy and global warming, natural gas and nuclear accidents. The problem is that here Greens and anti-Greens spend so much time taking potshots at one another, scientists have very little chance to add an occasional fact to the dialogue.

Sample Subjects:
ISO ozone depletion/Let's quantify the risks/Organochlorine misinformation

[FAQ] ▶ The following FAQs are available via FTP from RTFM.MIT.EDU in the directory:
pub/usenet/sci.environment:
Electronic_Journal_of_the_ASA_(EJASA)-_August_1993_*_FOURTH_YEAR!
Ozone_Depletion_FAQ_Part_I:_Introduction_to_the_Ozone_Layer
Ozone_Depletion_FAQ_Part_II:_Stratospheric_Chlorine_and_Bromine
Ozone_Depletion_FAQ_Part_III:_The_Antarctic_Ozone_Hole
Ozone_Depletion_FAQ_Part_IV:_UV_Radiation_and_its_Effects
Sea_Level,_Ice,_and_Greenhouses_—_FAQ

Fractals Discussion Group

sci.fractals [M]

If you know what the Mandelbrot Set and Feigenbaum's Constant are, then you might be interested in this group. If you're not a programmer and not mathematically inclined, then the only thing you need to know about fractals is that, if you run a software company, your software development projects will grind to a halt when your programmers start playing with fractals.

Sample Subjects:
Fractal programs for SGI/SPANKY fractal database/Percolation & D

[FAQ] ▶ The following FAQs are available via FTP from RTFM.MIT.EDU in the directory:
pub/usenet/sci.fractals:
Fractal_FAQ
Fractal_Questions_and_Answers

Fluid Dynamics

sci.geo.fluids [M]

All about fluid dynamics, like airflow over the surface of a wing, an esoteric and relatively low-volume newsgroup. Even in the slowest areas of the Net you can find something interesting, like a posting calling for a vote on the scientific competence of Carl Sagan.

Sample Subjects:
Airflow modeling code/Info on flood modeling software/Looking for Modflo

Geology Discussions

sci.geo.geology [HI]

You thought geology was about rocks? Well it is—mostly. But while some scientists get some work done on topics like filtering of geo[physi]cal surfaces and discussing the salinity of seawater, the more politically inclined Netters turn the issue of fossil-hunting and the Mississippi floods into a raging debate.

Sample Subjects:
Afghanistan geological map/Hawaiian volcano/Geostatistical toolbox primer

Meteorology Forum
sci.geo.meteorology **HI**

Meteorologists trade information on weather-pattern data sets and the latest modeling software. As you would expect, lots of laypeople wander into this newsgroup and offer their own theories for floods and hurricanes. Occasionally, meteorologists are asked to defend their poor prediction records.

FAQ ▶ The following FAQs are available via FTP from RTFM.MIT.EDU in the directory:
pub/usenet/sci.geo.meteorology:
Sources_of_Meterological_Data_FAQ
Tropical_Cyclone_Weekly_Summary_#110_(September_5_-_12,_1993)
Tropical_Cyclone_Weekly_Summary_#111_(September_12_-_19,_1993)
Tropical_Cyclone_Weekly_Summary_#112_(September_19_-_26,_1993)
Tropical_Cyclone_Weekly_Summary_#113_(September_26_-_October_3,_1993)
Tropical_Cyclone_Weekly_Summary_#114_(October_3_-_10,_1993)

Image Processing
sci.image.processing **HI**

This is a high-volume group without a lot of banter. Image processing is used in medicine, meteorology, geology, space exploration and many other fields. It's no surprise to see the queries posted from around the world. Questions range from the availability of public domain image-conversion software, to the use of fractals to re-create scenic backgrounds.

Sample Subjects:
NIH image macro/Slides from monitor images/Image processing and parallel architecture

Languages Conference
sci.lang **HI**

This group is all about spoken and written natural languages. Languages are compared and new alphabets are analyzed here.

Sample Subjects:
Gothic words still spoken/Spatial relationships in natural languages/European languages similarities

FAQ ▶ The following FAQ is available via FTP from RTFM.MIT.EDU in the directory:
pub/usenet/sci.lang:
sci.lang_FAQ_(Frequently_Asked_Questions)

Languages: Japan
sci.lang.japan **HI**

There is very little linguistics in this group. It's

▲ *Einstein, downloaded from* **ftp.sunet.se**

mostly posts from people asking advice on sushi, requests for Japanese novels and advice on Japanese computer printers.

Sample Subjects:
Looking for Japanese LaTeX for IBM, Ways to find Kanji/Wordperfect 2.1.3

Logic Discussion Group
sci.logic **HI**

This is a lightly traveled newsgroup covering such topics as linear logic, propositional temporal logic and coherent spaces. As you can see, these dense topic areas keep the riff-raff out.

Sample Subjects:
Does Tweety fly?/Second-order logics/Uncertainty theory

Materials Engineering
sci.materials **M**

"Materials" covers a wide number of disciplines. Smart materials, those that sense and respond to their environment, are a hot topic of discussion. Will they ever become commercially feasible? Also, a researcher in the U.K. is trying to find alternative uses for straw, since recent legislation in that country forbids farmers from burning it.

Sample Subjects:
Recipes for anodic oxidation/Metallurgy of Ni-Ti shape memory/Bursting films

Mathematician's Discussion Group
sci.math **HI**

Professional and amateur mathematicians challenge each other with mathematical puzzles, debate theories and prove theorems. Discussions are generally polite, but an occasional brawl breaks out when someone feels their proof has been attacked.

Sample Subjects:
Picard's theorem/Functions vs. equations/Calling algebra gurus

FAQ ▶ The following FAQ is available via FTP from RTFM.MIT.EDU in the directory:
pub/usenet/sci.math:
sci.math:_Frequently_Asked_Questions

Numerical Analysis
sci.math.num-analysis **HI**

A high-volume group for the discussion of numerical analysis. Participants discuss such issues as representations of splines, queueing analysis, and n-dimensional real FFT.

Sample Subjects:
Geodesic dome/Finite element/Thermal analysis/Needed— awesome random number generator

FAQ ▶ The following FAQ is available via FTP from RTFM.MIT.EDU in the directory:
pub/usenet/sci.math.num-analysis:
Linear_Programming_FAQ

Mathematics Research

sci.math.research **M**

Cutting-edge discussions, such as using fractal analysis for visualizing DNA sequences. Interesting to see a science reporter from *The Wall Street Journal* drop by and post a query about math research that can be applied to industry.

Sample Subjects:
Energy of knots/Optimization and Brownian Motion/Langlands Yale notes

Mathematics Statistics

sci.math.stat **L**

Statistics are the lingua franca of scientific research. Participants of this group help each other apply statistics to real research problems and discuss a wide variety of commercial and public domain statistical software packages.

Sample Subjects:
A little SAS question/Stochastic process control/Geostatistical toolbox primer

Mathematics: Symbolic Software

sci.math.symbolic **HI**

Discussions about the breakthrough software package Mathematica.

Sample Subjects:
Memory problem with xmaple/Plotting numeric integral/Maple and spherical harmonic

Medicine Talk Group

sci.med **HI**

Too many people posting symptoms in search of free medical advice and a quick cure. Not too many medical professionals show up on this group. Small wonder! Most of the discussions are about bad doctors, poor hospitals and usurious insurance carriers. Oh well! Sometimes the democracy of the Net gets in the way of information flow.

Sample Subjects:
Myelodysplasia/Smoking in public places/Water and kidneys

Medicine: AIDS

sci.med.aids **HI**

This is a good way to stay up on the current research and treatment of AIDS. Information from the Center for Disease Control is frequently posted. Considering

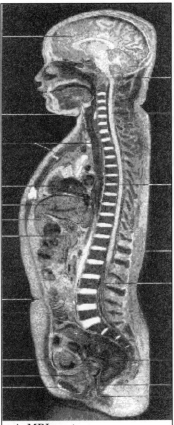

▲ *MRI anatomy scan, image file downloaded via Internet FTP from* **grind.isca.uiowa.edu**

the nature of the subject, this newsgroup has not become too politicized.

Sample Subjects:
AIDS treatment #179/Korean AIDS treatment/New HIV infections per day

Nutrition

sci.med.nutrition **HI**

Not much science here, unfortunately. Participants debate the wisdom of using Nutrasweet, giving up sugar and the symptoms of protein deficiency. Very few of the participants appear or claim to have any credentials as nutritionists—so take their advice with a grain of salt.

Sample Subjects:
Ultraslimfast query/Stop the FDA, support S784/Vegetarian needing weight gain

Medical Physics

sci.med.physics **L**

Ultrasound, impedance measurement and the danger of UV radiation are topics discussed in this group. An interesting discussion on comparative risk analysis—are you more likely to die from carcinogenic water or by being hit by a drunk motorist?

Sample Subjects:
Simulation of blood flow/ Impedence imaging/Biofeedback project

Military Technology

sci.military **HI**

Tom Clancy would feel right at home with this group. Participants discuss such issues as new uses for military submarines and how Iowa-Class battleships would fare in a missile attack. The group also looks at old military technology like comparing Yamato vs. Iowa-Class ships.

Sample Subjects:
The mathematics of warfare/Traditional ship names/Yamato's AA battery

Miscellaneous Science Discussions

sci.misc **HI**

Truly a scientific catch-all. Questions posed from many different disciplines receive thoughtful and sometimes humorous replies.

▲ *Submarine computer graphics image, downloaded via Internet FTP from* **wuarchive.wustl.edu**

A simple question on how scales work receives six replies in a couple of days, a university researcher proposes a new way to achieve virtual reality, and much more.

Sample Subjects:
Nanotechnology conference/Energy efficiency of a plant/ Fellowships in physics

Nanotechnology

sci.nanotech **L**

The technology of very little things (very, very, very, little). Pumps and valves measured in microns. Computer circuits functioning at the molecular level. This field was popularized (if not founded) by Eric Drexler when he wrote the book *Engines of Creation* as an MIT graduate student. Although the predictions you see in this group seem a little far-fetched, you'll see postings from people at Xerox's Palo Alto Research Campus (PARC), Berkeley's Lawrence Livermore Labs, and Japan's prestigious ATR Human Information Processing Research Labs.

Sample Subjects:
Workshop on micromachining/Nanotech and its implications/LBL deep etch lithography workshop

Optics

sci.optics **M**

Lasers, lenses and liquid fiber optics dominate the discussions. A U.K. researcher asks for help finding fiber optic cables that function in a vacuum. It appears that most current cables have organic cladding that gases in a vacuum. Another participant who has recently formed a fiber optics consulting firm is looking for consultants to join him.

Sample Subjects:
Phosphorescence mystery elucidated/Notch filters for HeNe laser/Thyratrons for excimers

Philosophy: Meta Discussions

sci.philosophy.meta **HI**

Anti-realism, the concept of God, and ball lightning are debated in a lively fashion. This group has a strong core of participants who contribute heavily and write well. It's fun to read even if you don't agree with their positions.

Sample Subjects:
Hegel and Christ/Philosophic challenge/Justification for abortion

Philosophy: Technology

sci.philosophy.tech **HI**

A physics enthusiast posts what could well be the final exam questions for a course entitled "Physics and Philosophy." A professor from York University announces a mailing list service for "pre-prints" so philosophers can exchange drafts of unpublished papers over the Net for comment by their peers.

Sample Subjects:
Indeterminacy—a challenge/Neutral models in Biology— book review/The future of RAND

Physics: General Discussion

sci.physics **HI**

Transcendental universe, the Red Shift and the possibility of travelling faster than light are discussed by academics and enthusiastic laymen here. There is a large volume of posts from a diverse audience in this group. Even "silly" questions, if couched appropriately, receive thoughtful responses.

Sample Subjects:
Polarization/The Klein bottle/Time has inertia/Survey of ZPE terminology

Physics: Fusion

sci.physics.fusion **HI**

And you thought cold fusion was dead: The issue is hotly debated in this group. Researchers post results of experiments and question each other on the calibration of their equipment. One researcher even threatens to sue another for slander. Who says science is boring?

Sample Subjects:
Vigier theory leads to what?/In defense of Dick Blue/Steve Jone's detector background

Psychology: Clinical Discussions

sci.psychology **HI**

Participants debate issues such as the genetic and/or chemical basis of depression, announce support groups for syndromes such as Obsessive Compulsive Behavior (OCB) and discuss whether computer use is addictive. The group is dominated by interested laypeople, although an occasional researcher/practitioner will post a response.

Sample Subjects:
Help re therapist/Multiple personalities/Social contagion and pheromones

Research Grants
sci.research **M**

Mostly about how to get that grant money from NSF and NIH. An occasional humorous post lightens up the group.

Sample Subjects:
Nobel prize/Should researchers be marketers?/NSF grants and such

Research Careers
sci.research.careers **M**

Tough times in the physical sciences. Many postings from unemployed Ph.Ds, requests for information on how to obtain those research positions and master's students wondering whether they should attempt to get Ph.Ds. Quite a bit of good advice from existing researchers to the wannabes regarding career tracks and balancing their family life with research careers.

Sample Subjects:
NSF grants/The poor prospects for scientific employment/Directory of research

The Skeptical Scientist
sci.skeptic **HI**

This group is for those who like to poke fun at pseudo-science. Discussions range from spontaneous human combustion to "Sociobiology."

Sample Subjects:
Challenger disaster/Bumblebees can't fly/Psychic networks

FAQ ▶ The following FAQ is available via FTP from RTFM.MIT.EDU in the directory:
pub/usenet/sci.skeptic:
sci.skeptic_FAQ:_The_Frequently_Questioned_Answers

Virtual Worlds
sci.virtual-worlds **M**

Fascinating discussion group about all aspects of virtual reality. Put on special goggles and fight with imaginary monsters—good clean fun and nobody gets hurt. But have you heard about tele-operations? Sit in the comfort of your home and control a vehicle 100 miles away with your home computer. A group of hobbyists in California (where else?) have done just that. Granted, it's only a model of the lunar rover, but the concept is fascinating. Think of the possibilities! Why have those expensive manned missions in space when you can control the mission remotely? Better yet, why spend your time driving the kids all over town? Just pop them in your RPV (looks a lot like a Honda Civic but has no steering wheel) and drive them to the mall while you play Flight Simulator on the other half of the computer screen!

Sample Subjects:
Tech seeking info on optical tracking/Toshiba 3D glasses/Using virtual reality to treat Parkinson's disease

Biology

Bionet Newsgroups
The Bionet and its related newsgroups represent the best example of how the Internet is being used to accelerate the pace of scientific research. These Bionet newsgroups are highly technical, no-nonsense forums where biologists trade information about the latest discoveries and methodologies. For example, when you're working with other scientists around the world mapping the Human Genome, you can't wait for scientific journals to announce the most recent discoveries. Now it all occurs on the Net. Even patents for recently discovered genes are filed with the U.S. Patent Office via the Net.

Announcements
bionet.announce
FAQ ▶ The following FAQ is available via FTP from RTFM.MIT.EDU in the directory:
pub/usenet/bionet.announce:
BIOSCI_bionet_Frequently_Asked_Questions

General News
bionet.general
FAQ ▶ The following FAQ is available via FTP from RTFM.MIT.EDU in the directory:
pub/usenet/bionet.general:
A_Biologist_s_Guide_to_Internet_Resources

Information Theory
bionet.info-theory
FAQ ▶ The following FAQ is available via FTP from RTFM.MIT.EDU in the directory:
pub/usenet/bionet.info-theory:
Biological_Information_Theory_and_Chowder_Society_FAQ

Jobs in Biology
bionet.jobs

Biology Journal Contents
bionet.genome.arabidopsis

Biology Journal Contents
bionet.journals.contents

Evolution
bionet.molbio.evolution

Genebank Info
bionet.molbio.genbank

Genebank News
bionet.molbio.genbank.updates

Molecular Biology Methods
bionet.molbio.methds-reagnts

Proteins
bionet.molbio.proteins

Neuroscience
bionet.neuroscience

Plants
bionet.plants

Science Resources
bionet.sci-resources

Software for Biology
bionet.software

People in Biology
bionet.users.addresses

Space

Planetary Exploration
alt.sci.planetary **L**

For those interested in deep space exploration. Will Jupiter collide with a comet and what will the ramifications be for the solar system? (Don't worry, it's not scheduled until 2043.)

Sample Subjects:
Looking for images of probes/Electroglow/James Maxwell's higher dimensional equations

FAQ ▶ The following FAQs are available via FTP from RTFM.MIT.EDU in the directory:
pub/usenet/alt.sci.planetary:
Electronic_Journal_of_the_ASA_(EJASA)_-_September_1993
Space_Calendar_-_08_28_93

Students for Exploration & Development of Space
bit.listserv.seds-l **L**

These students feel strongly that space should be explored, no matter what it costs. A good group to review for local space educational events.

Sample Subjects:
GA Tech SEDS on Pluto/SEDS sets up a new FTP site/ Mars observer and NOAA-13 died on same day

Space Topics Discussion Group
sci.space **HI**

Anything and everything relating to space, from the

▲ *View from Space Shuttle cargo bay, downloaded via Internet FTP from Smithsonian photo archives at* **sunsite.unc.edu**

serious (information on the calculation of the local hour angle) to the more lighthearted (given their current chaotic state, should anyone accept a recent offer from the Russian space program for a space ride, only $12 million?).

Sample Subjects:
DC-X will it save us/Galileo antenna problems and questions/Terraforming Mars

FAQ ▶ The following FAQs are available via FTP from RTFM.MIT.EDU in the directory:
pub/usenet/sci.space:
Space_FAQ_06_13_-_Addresses
Space_FAQ_07_13_-_Mission_Schedules
Space_FAQ_08_13_-_Planetary_Probe_History
Space_FAQ_09_13_-_Upcoming_Planetary_Probes
Space_FAQ_10_13_-_Controversial_Questions
Space_FAQ_11_13_-_Interest_Groups_&_Publications
Space_FAQ_12_13_-_How_to_Become_an_Astronaut
Space_FAQ_13_13_-_Orbital_and_Planetary_Launch_Services

Space News
sci.space.news **L**

Get the latest information on specific space programs, like the repair of the Hubble Space Telescope, and current status reports on unmanned space probes.

Sample Subjects:
Two-line orbital element sets/Spacewarn bulletin/Ulysses MOS report #190

Space Shuttle Discussion Group
sci.space.shuttle **HI**

Find out everything about the Space Shuttle. Participants go way beyond the information you typically see in the media. For example, recent posts even give you inside information on how to get Space Shuttle launch passes so you can see the real thing up close.

Sample Subjects:
Hubble's solar panel distorted/NASA needs better PR

▲ *Astronaut Buzz Aldrin of Apollo 11, photo downloaded via Internet FTP from* **wuarchive.wustl.edu**

Academia

18th-Century Studies
bit.listserv.c18-l **L**

Resource group for graduate students and academics interested in 18th-century literature and history.

Library Circulation Issues
bit.listserv.circplus **M**

Librarians discuss how to better serve their patrons.

Sample Subjects:
Study carrels/Lockers/Barcodes on the outside of books/Books with disks

Control Systems
bit.listserv.csg-l **M**

Researchers discuss control theories in living organisms, feedback loops, etc.

Sample Subjects:
Purposeful evolution/Dynamics and attractors/What PCT says about control

Administrative Computing
bit.listserv.cumrec-l **L**

Discussions on topics relating to the use of computers in academic administration.

Sample Subjects:
Electronic forums/Impact of SLDC methodology/Charging for printing

Government Documents
bit.listserv.govdoc-l **M**

Reference librarians in charge of government document collections trade information about various government publications. This is a great resource group to check if you have to do research on congressional or federal agencies.

Sample Subjects:
Thomas hearings errata sheets/GOA's report on SEC's EDGAR/HCFA and other regulatory manuals on CD's

Gutenberg Project
bit.listserv.gutnberg **L**

Professor Michael Hart searches out books and documents in the public domain (mostly classics with expired copyrights) and scans them into digital form. He has just completed his 100th book.

Sample Subjects:
Hearings on longer U.S. copyrights/Editing standards/Looking for text of U.S. treaties

History Discussion Forum
bit.listserv.history **L**

Professors, students and amateur historians debate issues of historical significance.

Sample Subjects:
Currency valuations—past and present/Maritime museums/Kennedy assassination papers

Law Students Discussion Group
bit.listserv.lawsch-l **L**

Law students, as well as those contemplating a law career, trade info, complaints and comments about going through law school, law books, lawyer's salary ranges and current legal controversies.

Library Reference Issues
bit.listserv.libref-l **L**

Discussion group for reference librarians and patrons of reference libraries. Participants are extremely helpful to researchers posting queries.

Sample Subjects:
Engineering publications needed/E-mail addresses for the Library of Congress/What are the eight natural wonders of the world?

Writing: Presenting Ideas With Words
bit.listserv.mbu-l **M**

Teachers of the written word discuss what constitutes good writing. This is a good forum if you're a teacher looking for writing projects for your class.

Sample Subjects:
Audience and purpose/Query about history of grading/ Privilege of textuality

NOTIS Library Software
bit.listserv.notis-l **M**

Users group for the popular NOTIS library software system.

Sample Subjects:
PsychLit issues/Recall fines/Loading CRL tapes/Keeping a paper shelf list

Public Access Computer Systems (PACS)
bit.listserv.pacs-l **M**

Public Access Computer systems are spreading throughout the country. In this forum, administrators of these grassroots organizations trade information about operations and funding.

Sample Subjects:
Infrastructure and society/Good bibliography formatter sought/Conference room design summary

Qualitative Research for Human Science
bit.listserv.qualrs-l **L**

Forum for the discussion of qualitative research methods such as interviews, focus group meetings and literature/fiction reviews.

Sample Subjects:
Right-brain constructions/Technicism vs wholeness/ Dance in a trance

Medical Students Discussion Group
bit.listserv.medforum **L**

Med school students engage in serious discussion of their medical educations, doctors' ethical issues, the U.S. health-care system and other items of mutual interest. Also features online American Medical Association newsletters, press releases and other information of interest to doctors.

Sample Subjects:
The effects of current hospital-based training/Medline and bioethics/Charging for residencies

Psychology Students Discussion Group
bit.listserv.psycgrad **M**

Grad students in psychology discuss sample cases, theories and real-life intervention stories with their fellow students. This might be a good place to go for

▲ *Kids in school, downloaded from* **wuarchive.wustl.edu**

answers to self-help psychology and emotional questions.

Sample Subjects:
Internship application process/50 ways to fail your final/ Sleep deprivation

Education

Education of the Disabled
alt.education.disabled **L**

Parents and teachers of disabled persons and disabled persons gather to trade information. Recent topics include mouse-operated word processors and Macintosh sign language software. Many queries are answered by researchers at prestigious research institutes. California State University at Northridge is the home for the Center On Disabilities, which holds the largest annual conference on issues related to the disabled. This year's keynote speaker is science fiction writer Ray Bradbury, who will speak on the application of virtual reality to problems of the disabled. Announcements for this and other conferences are frequently seen in this group.

Sample Subjects:
National symposium for the hearing impaired/Autisim, FC and related studies/Sex education and the disabled

Distance Education
alt.education.distance **L**

Now you can earn college credit from fully accredited

colleges and universities by taking interactive courses over the Net. One organization, the Mind Extension University (affiliated with 26 colleges and universities) will allow students to complete substantially all of their coursework for an undergraduate degree via the Internet.

Sample Subjects:
Request for pen pals for computer literacy class/Spaced Odyssey 2005/Adult education program on motion pictures

International Baccalaureate Students' Group

alt.education.ib **L**

This is truly an international group where students from Mexico and Canada respond to queries from students in the United States and Singapore. Students write well and appear to work extremely hard on their various programs. With any student-oriented newsgroup, you expect to get a large amount of idle chatter. There is some in this group, but the high quality of writing quickly drowns it out. Participants discipline each other to stay focused on the issues at hand.

Sample Subjects:
An alumnus' sentiment/New list for IB students in economics/Calculators in IB Math exams

Education Research

alt.education.research **L**

You'll love this: The National Association of Rocketry Standards has a real rocket motor they would like to donate to some educational institution. This is the real thing, 30 feet long and 4.5 feet in diameter. One stipulation is that the receiving school must *use* the rocket, not just take it apart. Other postings are more down-to-earth, like looking for dissertation abstracts and researching issues related to Attention Deficit Disorder.

Sample Subjects:
Asia-Pacific education conference/Seeking people with bulimia stories/Post-doc programs in Australia

Education & the Disabled

bit.listserv.dsshe-l **L**

Educators of the disabled help each other with the many challenges of their profession. Parents of disabled children receive prompt and informative answers to their questions.

Educational Technology

bit.listserv.edtech **M**

Using technology in education—covers everything from the use of CD-ROMs as teaching aids for foreign languages to information on NASA's SpaceLink project. Recent discussions include whether we should continue to teach students with QWERTY

keyboards and whether students should be given homework.

Sample Subjects:
Dynamically linked syllabus/English literature on disk/Free TQM SPC software

Educational Research

bit.listserv.erl-l **L**

Teachers debate whether the introduction of technology (i.e. computers) really helps education or whether it is just a distraction covering up some of the fundamental problems of education in America. Research projects are frequently posted, such as projects funded by the Annenberg/CPB Foundation to develop a database of innovative reform efforts in math and science education.

Sample Subjects:
Hammers and educational innovation/AERA Virtual Conference 1994/Software advice wanted

Education News

clari.tw.education **M**

News stories about education, K12 through university level, and stories about research findings at major universities.

Sample Subjects:
Florida researchers invent blood test for AIDS/ UPenn scraps controversial speech code/Sigoloff top choice for California education post.

Artificial Intelligence in Education

comp.ai.edu **L**

Although artificial intelligence applications are the main themes in this group, topics cover other areas of technology in education, such as the Carnegie-Mellon Software Engineering Institute's (SEI) new television series being broadcast over the National Technological University (NTU) Satellite Network.

Sample Subjects:
Desperately seeking an Authorware guru/AI CD-ROM Revision 2/Physics multimedia CD

Computers & Composition

comp.edu.composition **M**

This group is for educators trying to teach writing skills in a computer-based environment. This is also the home of Computer and Composition Digest (C&CD), a service provided by one helpful Net participant. Rather than wait for relevant messages to be posted to the group, he actively searches other groups for discussions relating to computers and composition and excerpts them for the Digest. A great service!

Sample Subjects:
Megabyte University/Grammar and style checkers/Writing across the curriculum

Elementary Chat Group
k12.chat.elementary (M)

Elementary school children post and respond to messages. This forum gives students practice at the keyboard and e-mail, but don't look for any great insights in this group.

Junior High Chat Group
k12.chat.junior (M)

Junior high school students practice their online skills.

Senior High Chat Group
k12.chat.senior (HI)

Senior high school students practice their online skills.

Teachers Chat Group
k12.chat.teacher (HI)

Teachers trade information about subjects near and dear to their hearts—students, parents and grading.

Business Curriculum
k12.ed.business (L)

Students post queries related to their Junior Achievement projects. It seems that a number of students misinterpret the function of the group and post "get rich quick" schemes like chain letters.

Sample Subjects:
White boards needed/Business communications curriculum/Correspondence schools

Computer Literacy
k12.ed.comp.literacy (M)

Teachers and students discuss the mechanics of wiring their classrooms for LANs, finding computers and getting good software.

Sample Subjects:
Network cabling/MIDI interface software/FDD or not to FDD

Health & Physical Education
k12.ed.health-pe (L)

Teachers and coaches trade information about coaching various sports. Women coaches post some interesting stories about what they have to put up with. Try this for a tough coaching assignment: a

▲ *Cretaceous period dinosaurs, downloaded from Smithsonian picture archives at* **sunsite.unc.edu**

woman coaching a boys' French Canadian hockey team.

Sample Subjects:
Coaching hockey/Soccer coaching tips/Teaching program on alcohol and drugs

Mathematics
k12.ed.math (M)

Participants post math problems and help each other find software and textbooks. As with most of the education groups, Netters really go out of their way to help each other.

Sample Subjects:
MathMagic/The "Monty Hall Paradox"/Sloppy math textbooks

Music Students' Discussion Group
k12.ed.music (L)

Students ask for and get advice on pursuing their musical careers and education. Lots of discussions on the use of high technology in teaching and composing music.

Sample Subjects:
Elementary music curiculum/MIDI interface software/ Dramatic Duo

School Science Activities
k12.ed.science (M)

Find out how to care for your bacteria, sign up for a real dinosaur dig and enter a bridge-building contest. Some of the most active participants are from small remote schools trying to overcome the problem of limited local resources.

Sample Subjects:
Adopt-a-river/Shuttle Report #13/Ribbon snakes

Social Studies Teachers' Discussions
k12.ed.soc-studies (L)

Teachers share ideas about innovative ways to teach various aspects of Social Studies. Where else could a student from Virginia post a question about Eskimos and get the answer from an Aleut teacher in Alaska? (hope the kid gets an "A").

Sample Subjects:
Revolutionary war/The Oregon Trail Project/Ino on Ireland

Special Education
k12.ed.special (L)

A teacher finds out she will be teaching a student with Angelman's Syndrome. She's never heard of it. She posts a message and gets an informative answer from a parent of a child with the syndrome. The Net really shines on the tough questions.

Sample Subjects:
Re: aggressive kids/Inclusion in regular activities/The Big Picture

Talented & Gifted Programs

k12.ed.tag **L**

A mother has a son who has been diagnosed with Attention Deficit Hyperactive Disorder but he demonstrates a strong aptitude for math. Should she try to get him into a TAG (talented and gifted) program? TAG teachers give her encouragement and practical advice.

Sample Subjects:
Flexible progression in schools/Martial arts/Education Dept. study on gifted and talented programs

Technical Education

k12.ed.tech **L**

Teachers discuss their attempts to integrate technology (or at least technical topics) into the curriculum. Questions posted from Ohio may be answered from Finland or New Zealand.

Sample Subjects:
New technology curriculum/Opinions on "Gifted and Talented" programs/School Internet access

Language Arts

k12.lang.art **M**

Teachers trade projects that inspire kids to write. Here's an interesting question: What's the best font for teaching kids to read?

Sample Subjects:
Wanted: D'Nealian Alphabet/Science poetry composition/High school grammar books

German & English Chat

k12.lang.deutsch-eng **M**

Native English speakers are supposed to help native German speakers with their German, and vice versa. So how *do* you say rock 'n roll in German?

Sample Subjects:
Brieffreundschaft/Converting English to German/Help—I took Spanish

Spanish & English Chat

k12.lang.esp-eng **M**

Native Spanish speakers help native English speakers with their Spanish, and vice versa.

Sample Subjects:
Hola de Nueva York/Que tal la tortilla/Buscamos acentos diferentes

French & English Chat

k12.lang.francais **M**

Native French speaking participants help native English speakers with their French.

Sample Subjects:
French people, places and culture/Respondez, S.V.P./Need address of university in France

Russian & English Chat

k12.lang.russian **L**

Native Russian speakers help native English speakers with their Russian.

Sample Subjects:
Mit'kovanie v Bostone/Pis'mo iz naroda/Washington hints

Education Across the Board

misc.education **HI**

If it involves education, it's discussed here—everything from computerized testing to the debate about multiculturalism. Someone who was frustrated with the Foothill/De Anza Community College School District in Cupertino, California decided to post a listing of all the lawsuits that had been filed against the district since 1992. It's all fair game on the Net. On a less litigious note, California voucher proponents plot strategy for a comeback after the Proposition 174 school voucher proposal defeat, and the effectiveness of test preparation courses is debated.

Sample Subjects:
Evaluation of K-8 Schools/Math 3 at Dartmouth/Why students hate school

Kids & Computers

misc.kids.computer **M**

Troubleshooting tips, software and advice directed primarily to parents and educators concerning PC-based educational software and games.

The Science of Education

sci.edu **HI**

Theoretically, this group is about the science of education. In reality it's mostly about the use of computers in education. A discussion that started as "computers in the workplace" changes to "the relationship between automation and structural unemployment." Well, that's what happens on the Net—a classic case of topic drift. We suspect things will get back to education when some frustrated Netter posts the message: "What the hell does GM's Saturn plant have to do with the science of education?"

Sample Subjects:
Teacher's pet program/Directory of undergraduate research/High school physics books

Science, Technology & Education

Chapter 10: Computers & Telecommunications

Millions of computer experts access the Internet's computer- and software-related newsgroups each day, making it by far the largest and best source for valuable technical help on computers, peripherals, software, applications and troubleshooting for novices, power users and developers alike.

Get Your Computer-Related Questions Answered Quickly on the Net

When you're relying upon fellow users for answers, the bigger the readership of the newsgroups, the better. Fact is, computer groups on the Net garner huge readership. An automatic program to analyze the readership of newsgroups pegs the readership of **comp.lang.c** at 180,000 readers per *day*. On the Net, the easy questions get answered in hours, the tougher ones may take a few days. Only a few computer companies maintain an official presence in any of the computer-related newsgroups, but their technical people often drop into the groups and check out the activity. It's not unusual to see postings from employees of Microsoft, IBM and Apple. You won't see the party line on these Internet groups. A bug is a bug, not an "undocumented feature."

State-of-the Art Technology on the Net

With participants from schools such as Berkeley, Carnegie-Mellon and MIT, these groups are the best place to check out the latest in cutting-edge computer technology, such as artificial reality, advanced visualization systems and neural nets. The academic orientation of many participants is reflected in the helpful manner in which they respond to most queries. There are many fewer flame wars in the computer groups than in the more political **alt.** and **soc.** forums.

Internet Shareware Resources

The shareware archives on the Net are massive, and are being updated and duplicated on hundreds of individual Internet-linked computer facilities (**servers**) throughout the world. If one server site is down or too slow, you can switch to another site in Finland or Taiwan and grab the file you're looking for.

The range of topics is enormous. There's not just one artificial intelligence forum, there are six. There are newsgroups about everything from IBM mainframes to 8-bit Ataris. Whatever your information need, there's a group here that can help you.

Artificial Intelligence

AI (Artificial Intelligence) Discussion Group

comp.ai **HI**

Discussions of any and all things related to artificial intelligence, including a researcher who programmed a computer to write like the 1960s novelist Jacqueline Susann.

FAQ ▶ The following FAQs are available via FTP from RTFM.MIT.EDU in the directory:

pub/usenet/comp.ai:
FAQ:_AI_Newsgroups_and_Mailing_Lists_2_6_[Monthly_posting]
FAQ:_Artificial_Intelligence_Bibliography_3_6_[Monthly_posting]
FAQ:_Artificial_Intelligence_FTP_Resources_4_6_[Monthly_posting]
FAQ:_Artificial_Intelligence_FTP_Resources_5_6_[Monthly_posting]
FAQ:_Artificial_Intelligence_Questions_&_Answers_1_6_[Monthly_posting]
FAQ:_Expert_System_Shells_6_6_[Monthly_posting]

Fuzzy Logic Talk Group

comp.ai.fuzzy **M**

Discussions related to fuzzy logic, an AI technique intended to allow computers to act more flexibly. This technology is being used to control railway traffic in Japan, among other things.

FAQ ▶ The following FAQs are available via FTP from RTFM.MIT.EDU in the directory:

pub/usenet/comp.ai.fuzzy:
FAQ:_Fuzzy_Logic_and_Fuzzy_Expert_Systems_1_1_[Monthly_posting]

Genetic Systems & AI

comp.ai.genetic **M**

Net participants try to find better AI algorithms by looking at natural systems.

FAQ ▶ The following FAQs are available via FTP from RTFM.MIT.EDU in the directory:

pub/usenet/comp.ai.genetic:
FAQ:_comp.ai.genetic_part_1_3_(A_Guide_to_Frequently_Asked_Questions)
FAQ:_comp.ai.genetic_part_2_3_(A_Guide_to_Frequently_Asked_Questions)
FAQ:_comp.ai.genetic_part_3_3_(A_Guide_to_Frequently_Asked_Questions)
FAQ:_genetic-faq_part1_(A_Guide_to_Frequently_Asked_Questions)
FAQ:_genetic-faq_part2_(A_Guide_to_Frequently_Asked_Questions)
FAQ:_genetic-faq_part3_(A_Guide_to_Frequently_Asked_Questions)

AI on Neural Nets

comp.ai.neural-nets **HI**

Neural nets (or NN's as they are called in this group), are another AI programming technique. Group topics include NN applications from telecommunications to music generation.

FAQ ▶ The following FAQs are available via FTP from RTFM.MIT.EDU in the directory:

pub/usenet/comp.ai.neural-nets:
changes_to__FAQ_in_comp.ai.neural-nets__—_monthly_posting
FAQ_in_comp.ai.neural-nets_—_monthly_posting
Frequently_Asked_Questions_—_weekly_reminder
Neural_Net_Patent_Posting_-_77_new_patents
Periodic_neural_network_patent_posting

Philosophy of AI

comp.ai.philosophy **HI**

Forum addresses the burning issue of the day: Will

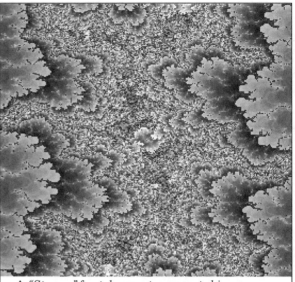

▲ *"Stream," fractal computer-generated image, downloaded via Internet FTP from* **grind.isca.uiowa.edu**

AI work? Participants, being computer experts, are naturally biased in favor of AI.

Shells for AI

comp.ai.shells **L**

Discussions of programming languages and tools for artificial intelligence applications.

Bulletin Board Systems

BBS (Bulletin Board Systems)

alt.bbs **HI**

Wide-ranging discussion group covers everything from what software to use for BBS operations to legal issues surrounding the operations of a BBS.

FAQ ▶ The following FAQs are available via FTP from RTFM.MIT.EDU in the directory:

pub/usenet/alt.bbs:
Changes_to_UNIX_BBS_Software_FAQ_with_Answers_(v_0.6)
Nixpub_Posting_(Long)
Nixpub_Posting_(Short)
UNIX_BBS_Software_FAQ_with_Answers
UNIX_BBS_Software_FAQ_with_Answers_(v_0.6)

BBS Ads & Announcements

alt.bbs.ads **HI**

If you start your own new BBS, you can advertise it here on the Internet. Ads for cheap or free BBS services seem to be about the only kind of advertising tolerated on the Net.

Sysops (System Operators) Discussion Group

alt.bbs.allsysop **M**

Many of the messages posted to this group are the same as posted to **alt.bbs**. If you only have time to read one, read **alt.bbs**.

BBSs & the Internet

alt.bbs.internet **HI**

Discussions about getting cheap or free access to the Internet via local BBS's.

FAQ ▶ The following FAQ is available via FTP from RTFM.MIT.EDU in the directory:
pub/usenet/alt.bbs.internet:
Updated_Internet_Services_List

BBS Directory: Areas & Subjects

alt.bbs.lists **M**

Many BBS operators take it upon themselves to compile lists of BBSs by area code or specialized interest. When new lists are compiled, they're often announced in this group.

FAQ ▶ The following FAQs are available via FTP from RTFM.MIT.EDU in the directory:
pub/usenet/alt.bbs.lists:
PDIAL_#013:_Public_Dialup_Internet_Access_List
THE_BBS_List_9-93_-_1500_phone_#_s
Updated_Inter-Network_Mail_Guide

BBS Bulletin Board Systems

comp.bbs.misc **HI**

Technical discussion group for various BBS system software packages, including PCBoard, Renegade and Waffle.

Waffle BBS Software

comp.bbs.waffle **HI**

Extremely active and very technical group for Waffle software, one of the most popular applications used to implement an Internet-accessible BBS on a PC.

FAQ ▶ The following FAQ is available via FTP from RTFM.MIT.EDU in the directory:
pub/usenet/comp.bbs.waffle:
Waffle_Frequently_Asked_Questions_(FAQ)

UNIX BBS Tech Tips

alt.bbs.unix.bbs **L**

Technical tips and tricks related to use and operation of UNIX-based bulletin board systems.

Sample Subjects:
Problems with Zmodem/UNIX bbs software frequently asked questions/Internet public access UNIX providers

Online Services

alt.online-service **HI**

Any online service is fair game for this group, including Prodigy, the service Netters love to hate.

You can find some good pointers about many of the new commercial Internet access providers.

PCBoard BBS System

alt.bbs.PCboard **HI**

Power users and novices trade information on the PCBoard BBS software package.

uuPCB BBS Software

alt.bbs.pcbuucp **L**

Technical support group for users of the uuPCB BBS software package.

FAQ ▶ The following FAQ is available via FTP from RTFM.MIT.EDU in the directory:
pub/usenet/alt.bbs.pcbuucp:
[FAQ]_alt.bbs.pcbuucp_(monthly_posting)

Sounds & Pictures

Multimedia Shareware

alt.binaries.multimedia **HI**

Multimedia is sound, text and images combined in one application. This group features many Windows MPEG files for programmers and users of multimedia systems. Users trade info on the hot new products and downloadable multimedia files available on the Internet.

Picture Shareware

alt.binaries.pictures **HI**

Users trade pictures, online, of everything from Henry David Thoreau to supermodels. Officially this group is for picture files only, and text-based files should be posted to **alt.binaries.pictures.d**.

Picture Shareware Discussion

alt.binaries.pictures.d **HI**

Get help with picture-viewing utilities or find that picture you've always wanted.

FAQ ▶ The following FAQs are available via FTP from RTFM.MIT.EDU in the directory:
pub/usenet/alt.binaries.pictures.d:
alt.binaries.pictures_FAQ_-_General_Etiquette
alt.binaries.pictures_FAQ_-_General_info
alt.binaries.pictures_FAQ_-_OS_specific_info
JPEG_image_compression:_Frequently_Asked_Questions

Picture Shareware—Fractals

alt.binaries.pictures.fractals **HI**

Fractals are being used to speed up computer-generated animation This is where you'll find the latest fractal software and techniques.

Computers & Telecommunications

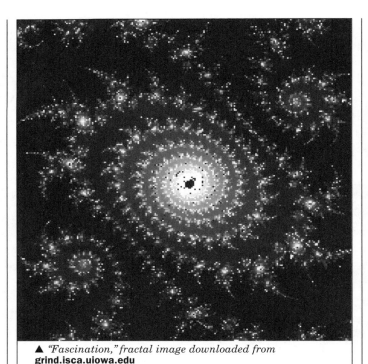

▲ *"Fascination," fractal image downloaded from*
grind.isca.uiowa.edu

Picture Shareware—Miscellaneous
alt.binaries.pictures.misc **HI**
People post picture files of just about anything in this group—logos of various sports teams, supermodels, covers to rock albums, etc.

Picture Shareware—Utilities
alt.binaries.pictures.utilities **HI**
Find the latest software for viewing all the picture files you find on the Net.

Sounds Shareware—Discussion
alt.binaries.sounds.d **HI**
Where else but the Net could you find a complete collection of Beavis & Butt-Head sound files? For those with a more, shall we say, "classical" taste, this group also features the collected sounds of the Three Stooges.
FAQ ▶ The following FAQs are available via FTP from RTFM.MIT.EDU in the directory:
pub/usenet/alt.binaries.sounds.d:
Changes_to:_FAQ:_Audio_File_Formats
FAQ:_Audio_File_Formats_(part_1_of_2)
FAQ:_Audio_File_Formats_(part_2_of_2)

Sounds Shareware—Miscellaneous
alt.binaries.sounds.misc **HI**
More must-have sound files, like Homer Simpson's answering machine, the Michigan fight song and the "Barney Song."

Apple II Shareware
comp.binaries.apple2 **L**
Software and graphic files for the Apple II—still popular after all these years.

IBM PC Shareware—Discussion
comp.binaries.ibm.pc.d **M**
Participants look for software and help each other with bugs in DOS software. A good bit of discussion on DOS 6.0 and related application programs as well.

IBM PC Shareware—Wanted
comp.binaries.ibm.pc.wanted **HI**
Users post queries and get help in finding PC programs to make their lives easier.

MAC Shareware
comp.binaries.mac **M**
Announcements and files of new Macintosh shareware posted here, directly from their authors.

OS2 Shareware
comp.binaries.os2 **L**
Shareware for OS2.

Computer Aided Design

CAD (Computer Aided Design)
alt.cad **M**
Covers the full range of Computer Aided Design topics—from requests for specific modeling packages to tips on fixing bugs in CAD software applications.

AutoCAD (Computer Aided Design)
alt.cad.autocad **M**
Very active group for the users of the most popular Computer Aided Design package.

Cadence Systems
comp.cad.cadence **L**
A discussion group for Cadence's popular Computer Aided Design software.

LSI (Large Scale Integration)
comp.lsi **M**
Technical discussions about getting more transistors on a chip. Good place to spot announcements for upcoming LSI (Large Scale Integration) conferences.
FAQ ▶ The following FAQs are available via FTP from RTFM.MIT.EDU in the directory:
pub/usenet/comp.lsi:
comp.lsi.cad_Frequently_Asked_Questions_With_Answers_(Part_1_4)_[LONG]

comp.lsi.cad_Frequently_Asked_Questions_With_Answers_(Part_2_4)_[LONG]
comp.lsi.cad_Frequently_Asked_Questions_With_Answers_(Part_3_4)_[LONG]
comp.lsi.cad_Frequently_Asked_Questions_With_Answers_(Part_4_4)_[LONG]

Computer Aided Design in LSI
comp.lsi.cad **M**

Using computer aided design to lay out Large Scale Integration (LSI) computer chips.

LSI—Testing
comp.lsi.testing **L**

Highly technical group where LSI chip builders discuss various testing procedures.

BRL's Solid Modeling Software
info.brl-cad **L**

For users of BRL's solid modeling CAD software.

CD-ROMS

CD-ROM Buyer's Advice
alt.cd-rom **HI**

Find out which CD-ROM readers are the best buys, resolve installation problems and find out about the hottest new interactive media CD-ROM titles.

FAQ ▶ The following FAQ is available via FTP from RTFM.MIT.EDU in the directory:
pub/usenet/alt.cd-rom:
alt.cd-rom_FAQ

CD-ROM on LANs
bit.listserv.cdromlan **M**

CD-ROMs are spreading fast, especially in academic libraries. Participants trade information on the latest networkable devices (like platter drives) and the availability of hot new library titles like the 1990 Census on CD-ROM.

CD-ROM Software Installation Tips
comp.publish.cdrom.software **L**

Users help each other install the most recent CD-ROM equipment and software.

Databases

dBase Discussion Group
bit.listserv.dbase-l **L**

Although formally labelled dBase, this group

▲ *Sun workstation, downloaded from* **wuarchive.wustl.edu**

discusses all dialects of Xbase database programming languages.

Databases: General Discussions
comp.databases **HI**

Anything and everything related to databases: Paradox, Gupta's SQLwindows 4.0, Clipper, FoxPro and more.

FAQ ▶ The following FAQ is available via FTP from RTFM.MIT.EDU in the directory:
pub/usenet/comp.databases:
comp.databases.sybase_Frequently_Asked_Questions_(FAQ)

Informix
comp.databases.informix **HI**

Online user group for Informix database software. Corporate users and consultants trade tips, tricks and workarounds.

Ingres
comp.databases.ingres **HI**

User group for Ingres database software.

Oracle
comp.databases.oracle **HI**

Online user group for the very popular Oracle database software.

Sybase
comp.databases.sybase **HI**

In addition to discussion on Sybase database software, participants engage in theoretical discussions of very large databases (VLDB).

Database Theory
comp.databases.theory **M**

Participants discuss database-related topics such as Object Oriented Database Management Systems (OODMS) vs. Relational Database Management Systems (RDMS).

Data Communications

Telecommunications Applications

alt.dcom.telecom **HI**

Find the best deal on 900 number services, find what services are available for ISDN or get the inside scoop on Caller ID Blocking.

Cell Relay Telecom Discussion Group

comp.dcom.cell-relay **M**

Forum for Cell Relay and ATM (Asynchronous Transmission Method). Based on recent announcements by AT&T, Sprint and other telecommunications companies, these technologies will be used to build the backbone of the new national information infrastructure.

FAQ ► The following FAQ is available via FTP from RTFM.MIT.EDU in the directory:
pub/usenet/comp.dcom.cell-relay:
comp.dcom.cell-relay_FAQ:_ATM,_SMDS,_and_related_technologies

Fax Software & Modems

comp.dcom.fax **HI**

Fax modems, gateways, software and more are discussed in this forum.

FAQ ► The following FAQs are available via FTP from RTFM.MIT.EDU in the directory:
pub/usenet/comp.dcom.fax:
De_Facto_Class2_fax_modem_Command_Scorecard_part_0b_of_6
De_Facto_Class2_fax_modem_Command_Scorecard_part_0_of_6
De_Facto_Class2_fax_modem_Command_Scorecard_part_1_of_6
De_Facto_Class2_fax_modem_Command_Scorecard_part_2_of_6
De_Facto_Class2_fax_modem_Command_Scorecard_part_3_of_6
De_Facto_Class2_fax_modem_Command_Scorecard_part_4_of_6
De_Facto_Class2_fax_modem_Command_Scorecard_part_5_of_6
De_Facto_Class2_fax_modem_Command_Scorecard_part_6_of_6
ZyXEL_modem_FAQ_List_v3.0,_July_26,_1993_Edition
ZyXEL_modem_FAQ_List_v3.1,_August_16,_1993_Edition
ZyXEL_modem_FAQ_List_v3.2,_September_20,_1993_Edition

ISDN (Integrated Services Digital Network)

comp.dcom.isdn **M**

Will ISDN ever be widely implemented, or have the local telephone companies missed the boat? This and other ISDN telecom issues are debated here.

Modem Technical Discussions

comp.dcom.modems **HI**

For the time being, at least, modems are the critical links to the Internet, and in this forum every modem-related topic imaginable is discussed. Topics include Zyxel modems, Winfax, V.32bis protocols and more.

▲ *Display of early telephones, photo image file downloaded via Internet FTP from Smithsonian photo archives at* **sunsite.unc.edu**

FAQ ► The following FAQs are available via FTP from RTFM.MIT.EDU in the directory:
pub/usenet/comp.dcom.modems:
MS-Windows_COM_and_Ns16550A_UART_FAQ
ZyXEL_U1496_series_modems_resellers_FAQ_(bi-monthly)

Cisco Products Discussion

comp.dcom.sys.cisco **M**

Discussion group for Cisco network router products.

Telecommunications: General Discussions

comp.dcom.telecom **HI**

Discussion relating to anything and everything about current news in the turbulent telecommunications industry. Topics include cellular phones, personal communication devices, 900 numbers and more.

FAQ ► The following FAQ is available via FTP from RTFM.MIT.EDU in the directory:
pub/usenet/comp.dcom.telecom:
About_This_Newsgroup_and_Telecom_Digest

Banyan

bit.listserv.banyan-l **HI**

Banyan Vines has always been the favorite network operating system for large networks. Users trade information on installing applications and devices on this networking software.

Novell

bit.listserv.novell **HI**

Novell is a big LAN force on college campuses, based on the high level of college-user activity in this newsgroup. Commercial users of Novell software can also easily find answers to their questions here.

Ethernet

comp.dcom.lans.ethernet **HI**

Technical discussion related to Ethernet LANs. Topics include: 3Com routers, 10Base-T recommendations, IBM routers and more.

FDDI

comp.dcom.lans.fddi **M**

FDDI-based LANs: Topics include bridging FDDI Networks, FDDI analyzers, EIFO switching hubs and more.

FAQ ► The following FAQ is available via FTP from RTFM.MIT.EDU in the directory:
pub/usenet/comp.dcom.lans.fddi:
FAQ

LANs: Miscellaneous Discussions

comp.dcom.lans.misc **M**

This group covers LAN topics that don't fit neatly into the other categories. Topics include ATM simulations, connecting to T1 links and general interoperability questions.

Digital Equipment Corp.

DEC's Alpha Chip

vmsnet.alpha **M**

Discussion relating to DEC's Alpha chip.

VMS Internals

vmsnet.internals **M**

Internals, MACRO-23, etc.

MX E-mail

vmsnet.mail.mx **M**

The e-mail system from RPI.

VMS: Miscellaneous

vmsnet.misc **M**

VMS topics not covered elsewhere.

Pathworks

vmsnet.networks.desktop.pathworks **HI**

For users of Pathworks, DEC's desktop integration software.

Multinet TCP/IP

vmsnet.networks.tcp-ip.multinet **M**

For users of TGV's Multinet TCP/IP software.

PDP-11

vmsnet.pdp-11 **L**

Hardware and software for DEC's venerable PDP-11 system.

DEC VMS Discussion

vmsnet.sources.d **L**

Discussion about DEC VMS software.

VMS System Managers

vmsnet.sysmgt **L**

Discussion group for DEC's VMS system managers.

VMS Test

vmsnet.test **M**

Group for test messages coming from VMSNet.

Computers: For Sale

Computer Hardware Marketplace

biz.comp.hardware **M**

Computer equipment bought and sold here. Equipment advertised includes modems, full systems and even a used TI channel bank.

Computer Services Marketplace

biz.comp.services **L**

A full range of computer services are offered here, with an emphasis on telecommunications services such as Gateways and Anonymous News/Mail servers.

For Sale: Computers

misc.forsale.computers **M**

Loaded with ads from Netters selling a wide variety of computers, printers, peripherals, software, chips and more.

FAQ ▶ The following FAQ is available via FTP from RTFM.MIT.EDU in the directory:
pub/usenet/misc.forsale.computers:
misc.forsale.computers.d_FAQ

Computers for Sale Discussion Group

misc.forsale.computers.d **M**

Participants ask for advice on which used equipment to buy and post their own "computer wanted"-type ads.

Other Computer Equipment for Sale

misc.forsale.computers.other **HI**

A broad category on the Net. Recent postings include requests for dead/damaged 386/486 chips and ads for "fried" motherboards.

Workstations Marketplace

misc.forsale.computers.workstation **HI**

Workstations (Sun, HP, etc.) bought and sold.

Free Software Society

BASH (Bourne Again Shell)

gnu.bash.bug **L**

Bug reports for the Bourne Again Shell.

GNU Chess

gnu.chess **L**

Discussion group for GNU, a popular freeware

version of UNIX.

GDB Bugs
gnu.gdb.bug **M**

Bug reports and suggested fixes for the GNU C/C++ debugger.

Ghostscript Bugs
gnu.ghostscript.bug **M**

Bug reports for the Ghostscript interpreter.

GNUsenet Testing
gnu.gnusenet.test **L**

For users of GNU's Not Usenet alternative sub-network testing.

GNU Miscellaneous
gnu.misc.discuss **HI**

All about GNU and recently created software.

GNU Utility Bugs
gnu.utils.bug **HI**

Bug reports for the GNUtilities.

Lucid Emacs
alt.lucid-emacs.bug **L**

Emacs is a UNIX-based text processing program developed at MIT. Lucid is one of the more popular variations of the program.

Emacs Help
alt.lucid-emacs.help **M**

Users help one another installing Lucid Emacs on everything from DECStations to Solbournes.

Emacs Editor
comp.emacs **HI**

Forum for discussion of various implementations of the Emacs editor.

Emacs Bugs
gnu.emacs.bug **HI**

Emacs is a UNIX-compatible text processing language developed at MIT. As with any software, it doesn't always work as planned, and this group tracks its idiosyncrasies.

GNU Emacs
gnu.emacs.gnus **M**

News-reading software running under GNU Emacs.

Emacs Help
gnu.emacs.help **HI**

Questions and answers relating to Emacs.

Emacs Sources
gnu.emacs.sources **M**

Discussion about the actual source code for GNU Emacs.

Emacs VM Bugs
gnu.emacs.vm.bug **L**

Bug reporting and resolution group for Emacs VM mail package.

G++ bugs
gnu.g++.bug **HI**

G++ is the GNU version of C++, and this group tracks and resolves the bugs therein.

G++ Help
gnu.g++.help **M**

G++ object-oriented help.

G++ Bugs
gnu.g++.lib.bug **M**

For discussion of G++ library bugs.

GCC Bugs
gnu.gcc.bug **HI**

Group for reporting and resolving GNU C Compiler bugs.

GCC Help
gnu.gcc.help **HI**

Questions and answers related to the GNU C Compiler.

Graphics

3D Graphics
alt.3d **M**

Participants discuss the use of 3D in games, rayshading programs, 3D glasses and more.

Picture Utilities
alt.graphics.pixutils **M**

Users trade information on the latest compression and decompression utilities for picture files. A great place to pick up the latest utilities while they're still in their beta-testing phase.

FAQ ▶ The following FAQ is available via FTP from RTFM.MIT.EDU in the directory:

pub/usenet/alt.graphics.pixutils:
(28feb93)_Welcome_to_alt.graphics.pixutils_-
_automated_posting.

Graphics: General

comp.graphics **HI**

Anything and everything on computer-based graphics. Topics include: 3D representation, B-splines, linear transformations, light simulation programs and more.

FAQ ▶ The following FAQs are available via FTP from RTFM.MIT.EDU in the directory:
pub/usenet/comp.graphics:

(07Sep93)_comp.graphics_Frequently_Asked_Questions_(FAQ)
(14_Oct_93)_Computer_Graphics_Resource_Listing_:_BIWEEKLY_[part_1_4]
(14_Oct_93)_Computer_Graphics_Resource_Listing_:_BIWEEKLY_[part_2_4]
(14_Oct_93)_Computer_Graphics_Resource_Listing_:_BIWEEKLY_[part_3_4]
(14_Oct_93)_Computer_Graphics_Resource_Listing_:_BIWEEKLY_[part_4_4]
(26_Sep_93)_Computer_Graphics_Resource_Listing_:_BIWEEKLY_[part_1_4]
(26_Sep_93)_Computer_Graphics_Resource_Listing_:_BIWEEKLY_[part_2_4]
(26_Sep_93)_Computer_Graphics_Resource_Listing_:_BIWEEKLY_[part_3_4]
(26_Sep_93)_Computer_Graphics_Resource_Listing_:_BIWEEKLY_[part_4_4]
(27Sep93)_comp.graphics_Frequently_Asked_Questions_(FAQ)
(9_Sep_93)_Computer_Graphics_Resource_Listing_:_BIWEEKLY_[part_1_4]
(9_Sep_93)_Computer_Graphics_Resource_Listing_:_BIWEEKLY_[part_2_4]
(9_Sep_93)_Computer_Graphics_Resource_Listing_:_BIWEEKLY_[part_3_4]
(9_Sep_93)_Computer_Graphics_Resource_Listing_:_BIWEEKLY_[part_4_4]

▲ *"Ladybugs" computer graphic, downloaded from* **wuarchive.wustl.edu**

Animation Developers Forum

comp.graphics.animation **HI**

This is the place on the Net where the computer animators hang out. A wide range of interesting topics include: Disney animation techniques, Studio 3D, films produced entirely with computer graphics and more.

AVS (Artificial Visualization Systems)

comp.graphics.avs **L**

Forum for AVS researchers. Users discuss the latest software running on high-performance platforms. Good pointers about resource materials and conferences for researchers in virtual reality.

Explorer Graphic Software

comp.graphics.explorer **L**

Forum for users of the IRIS Explorer graphic software program.

Gnuplot

comp.graphics.gnuplot **M**

User group for this popular shareware graphics utility.

FAQ ▶ The following FAQ is available via FTP from RTFM.MIT.EDU in the directory:
pub/usenet/comp.graphics.gnuplot:
comp.graphics.gnuplot_FAQ_(Frequent_Answered_Questions)

Visualization

comp.graphics.visualization **M**

Participants help each other with visualization software and programs. Topics include raytracing programs, topographical images, holographic illusions ("holusions") and more.

Khoros

comp.soft-sys.khoros **M**

Discussion group for Khoros, an integrated software development environment for information processing and visualization.

FAQ ▶ The following FAQ is available via FTP from RTFM.MIT.EDU in the directory:
pub/usenet/comp.soft-sys.khoros:
Khoros_FAQ:_The_Meta-FAQ

Internet-Related

Gopher I

alt.gopher **L**

Gopher is a user-friendly interface developed at the University of Minnesota for information systems on the Net. Participants of this group trade technical information about implementing and using Gopher software.

Computer Administration Policy

comp.admin.policy **HI**

Discussion group for Internet system administrators. Topics include acceptable activity on the local servers and protecting local servers from computer hackers.

■ Computers & Telecommunications

Large Information Systems

comp.infosystems **M**

Discussions covering general themes for big information systems, such as the Internet, the Sabre airline reservation system and medical information systems.

Geographic Information Systems

comp.infosystems.gis **HI**

The use of GIS has exploded in the last ten years. Topics include: Global Positioning Systems (GPS), navigators for cars and the government's TIGER system.

Gopher Talk Group II

comp.infosystems.gopher **HI**

Forum for discussion of the Gopher software developed at the University of Minnesota to provide an easy user interface for information stored on campus-wide information systems and the Internet.

FAQ ▶ The following FAQ is available via FTP from RTFM.MIT.EDU in the directory:
pub/usenet/comp.infosystems.gopher:
Gopher_(comp.infosystems.gopher)_Frequently_Asked_Questions_(FAQ)

WAIS

comp.infosystems.wais **M**

User group for the full-text retrieval software WAIS (Wide Area Information Servers).

FAQ ▶ The following FAQ is available via FTP from RTFM.MIT.EDU in the directory:
pub/usenet/comp.infosystems.wais:
comp.infosystems.wais_Frequently_asked_Questions_[FAQ]_(with_answers)

Computers & Society

comp.society **L**

Netters discuss the impact of computers on society. Covers such topics as "telework" and the growing trend toward contract work.

IETF (Internet Engineering Task Force)

info.ietf **HI**

(IETF) Internet Engineering Task Forces are groups of computer scientists/engineers who work on specific issues for the benefit of the Internet community. This is the group where they exchange information on the status of various projects.

SMTP (Simple Mail Transfer)

info.ietf.smtp **HI**

Discussion group for Internet Mail protocols.

PEM (Private E-mail Encryption)

info.pem-dev **M**

We'd love to tell you what this group is about, but most of the people who post messages here also encrypt them!

Languages

COBOL

alt.cobol **M**

For users of COBOL, one of the first high-level languages developed for business applications.

Assembly Language

alt.lang.asm **L**

Technical questions and answers for assembly language programmers.

BASIC

alt.lang.basic **M**

BASIC is one of the more popular high-level languages. Visual Basic, Microsoft's dialect for Windows, is one of the most popular topics of discussion.

ADA Defense Department Software

comp.lang.ada **HI**

Forum for users of the Defense Department-sponsored software ADA. The software tools available in the commercial sector may be better than ADA, but the Pentagon is willing to pay big bucks to have applications coded in its language.

FAQ ▶ The following FAQs are available via FTP from RTFM.MIT.EDU in the directory:
pub/usenet/comp.lang.ada:
comp.lang.ada_FAQ_1_2
comp.lang.ada_FAQ_2_2
Public_Ada_Library_FAQ

APL

comp.lang.apl **M**

An active group devoted to APL (A Programming Language), a high-level interactive scientific programming language.

ASM370

comp.lang.asm370 **L**

For users of IBM's Assembly language for the 370.

C Programmer's Discussion Group

comp.lang.c **HI**

The most active computer newsgroup on the Net. Discussions include anything and everything relating to the C programming language.

FAQ ▶ The following FAQs are available via FTP from RTFM.MIT.EDU in the directory:
pub/usenet/comp.lang.c:
C-FAQ-list
C-FAQ-list.abridged
C-FAQ-list.diff
Diffs_to_Index_of_free_C_or_C++_source_code_for_numerical_computation
index
Part_1_of_2:_Free_C,C++_for_numerical_computation
Part_2_of_2:_Free_C,C++_for_numerical_computation

▲ *Artist rendering of Saturn, as viewed from one of its moons, downloaded from* **wuarchive.wustl.edu**

C++

comp.lang.c++ [HI]

Forum for users of object-oriented C language compilers by Borland, Smalltalk, Symantec and Microsoft.

FAQ ▶ The following FAQs are available via FTP from RTFM.MIT.EDU in the directory:
pub/usenet/comp.lang.c++:
C++_FAQ:_posting_#1_4
C++_FAQ:_posting_#2_4
C++_FAQ:_posting_#3_4
C++_FAQ:_posting_#4_4
comp.lang.c++_FAQ_(part_1_of_4)
comp.lang.c++_FAQ_(posting_2_of_4)
comp.lang.c++_FAQ_(posting_3_of_4)
comp.lang.c++_FAQ_(posting_4_of_4)
FAQ_for_g++_and_libg++,_plain_text_version_[Revised_01_Oct_1993]
FAQ_for_g++_and_libg++,_plain_text_version_[Revised_01_Sep_1993]
FAQ_for_g++_and_libg++,_texinfo_version_[Revised_01_Oct_1993]
FAQ_for_g++_and_libg++,_texinfo_version_[Revised_01_Sep_1993]

CLOS

comp.lang.clos [L]

Discussion group for user of CLOS, the object-oriented LISP programming language.

FAQ ▶ The following FAQ is available via FTP from RTFM.MIT.EDU in the directory:
pub/usenet/comp.lang.clos:
FAQ:_Object-oriented_Programming_in_Lisp_5_7_[Monthly_posting]

Dylan

comp.lang.dylan [M]

Users group for discussion of the Dylan software language.

Eiffel

comp.lang.eiffel [M]

For users of Eiffel, an advanced object-oriented programming language that emphasizes the construction of high-quality and reusable software.

FAQ ▶ The following FAQ is available via FTP from RTFM.MIT.EDU in the directory:
pub/usenet/comp.lang.eiffel:
comp.lang.eiffel_Frequently_Asked_Questions_(FAQ)

Forth

comp.lang.forth [HI]

Group for users of Forth, a threaded interpretive language. Users are passionate about this language, but question whether they will ever get jobs as Forth programmers.

FAQ ▶ The following FAQs are available via FTP from RTFM.MIT.EDU in the directory:
pub/usenet/comp.lang.forth:
Forth_FAQ:_ANS_Forth_Standard_Info._(l_m_22.Jul.93)
Forth_FAQ:_Applications_done_with_Forth._(l_m_22.Jul.93)
Forth_FAQ:_CASE,OF,ENDOF,ENDCASE._(l_m_30.Jan.93)
Forth_FAQ:_FAQ_Overview._(l_m_27.Aug.93)
Forth_FAQ:_ForthNet:_What_and_how?_(l_m_27.Aug.93)
Forth_FAQ:_Forth_Implementations._(l_m_27.Aug.93)
Forth_FAQ:_General_Internet_info._(l_m_30.Jan.93)
Forth_FAQ:_Libraries:_Where_and_how?_(l_m_31.Mar.93)
Forth_FAQ:_Organizations_and_Publications._(l_m_30.Jan.93)
Forth_FAQ:_Programmable_BBS_Information._(l_m_05.Jun.93)
Forth_FAQ:_What_is_Forth?_(l_m_30.Jan.93)

■ **Computers & Telecommunications**

FORTRAN
comp.lang.fortran **HI**

Discussions related to all aspects of FORTRAN, the programming language of choice for most engineering applications. Although the language has been around for years, apparently not all the questions have been asked.

Functional
comp.lang.functional **M**

For users of the Functional programming language.

Idl PV-WAVE
comp.lang.idl-pvwave **M**

For users of VNI's PVWAVE software.

FAQ ▶ The following FAQ is available via FTP from RTFM.MIT.EDU in the directory:
pub/usenet/comp.lang.idl-pvwave:
IDL_(Interactive_Data_Language)_FAQ

LISP
comp.lang.lisp **M**

For users of LISP, a language used extensively in artificial intelligence research.

FAQ ▶ The following FAQs are available via FTP from RTFM.MIT.EDU in the directory:
pub/usenet/comp.lang.lisp:
FAQ:_Lisp_Frequently_Asked_Questions_1_7_[Monthly_posting]
FAQ:_Lisp_Frequently_Asked_Questions_2_7_[Monthly_posting]
FAQ:_Lisp_Frequently_Asked_Questions_3_7_[Monthly_posting]
FAQ:_Lisp_FTP_Resources_6_7_[Monthly_posting]
FAQ:_Lisp_Implementations_and_Mailing_Lists_4_7_[Monthly_posting]
FAQ:_Lisp_Window_Systems_and_GUIs_7_7_[Monthly_posting]
FAQ:_Scheme_Frequently_Asked_Questions_1_1_[Monthly_posting]

LISP MCL
comp.lang.lisp.mcl **M**

For users of the MCL dialect of LISP.

Modula2
comp.lang.modula2 **M**

For users of Modula2, the enhanced version of Pascal by Nicklaus Wirth.

FAQ ▶ The following FAQ is available via FTP from RTFM.MIT.EDU in the directory:
pub/usenet/comp.lang.modula2:
comp.lang.modula2:_Answers_to_Common_Questions__-__v1.5_93.05.03

Modula3
comp.lang.modula3 **M**

For users of Modula3, the new and improved version of Modula2.

FAQ ▶ The following FAQ is available via FTP from RTFM.MIT.EDU in the directory:
pub/usenet/comp.lang.modula3:
Modula-3_Frequently_Asked_Questions_(FAQ)

Objective C Language
comp.lang.objective-c **M**

Very active group for users of Objective C, the object-oriented C language (not to be confused with C++).

FAQ ▶ The following FAQs are available via FTP from RTFM.MIT.EDU in the directory:
pub/usenet/comp.lang.objective-c:
comp.lang.objective-c_FAQ,_part_1_3:_Answers
comp.lang.objective-c_FAQ,_part_2_3:_ClassWare_Listing
comp.lang.objective-c_FAQ,_part_3_3:_A_Sample_Program

Pascal
comp.lang.pascal **HI**

Pascal is a high-level programming language developed by Swiss mathematician Nicklaus Wirth. Most of the discussions in this group relate to Borland's popular Turbo Pascal.

Perl
comp.lang.perl **HI**

UNIX utility for manipulating text, files and processes.

FAQ ▶ The following FAQs are available via FTP from RTFM.MIT.EDU in the directory:
pub/usenet/comp.lang.perl:
comp.lang.perl_FAQ_(part_0_of_2)
comp.lang.perl_FAQ_(part_1_of_2)
comp.lang.perl_FAQ_(part_2_of_2)
Frequently_asked_questions_about_Perl_(revised_11_30_92)
Perl_Frequently_Asked_Questions,_part_0_of_4
Perl_Frequently_Asked_Questions,_part_1_of_4
Perl_Frequently_Asked_Questions,_part_2_of_4
Perl_Frequently_Asked_Questions,_part_3_of_4
Perl_Frequently_Asked_Questions,_part_4_of_4

PostScript
comp.lang.postscript **HI**

Discussion group for Adobe's PostScript, the standard printer control language for desktop publishing.

FAQ ▶ The following FAQs are available via FTP from RTFM.MIT.EDU in the directory:
pub/usenet/comp.lang.postscript:
PostScript_monthly_FAQ_v2.1_05-21-93_[01-04_of_11]
PostScript_monthly_FAQ_v2.1_05-21-93_[05-06_of_11]
PostScript_monthly_FAQ_v2.1_05-21-93_[07-10_of_11]
PostScript_monthly_FAQ_v2.1_05-21-93_[11_of_11]

PROLOG
comp.lang.prolog **M**

Discussion group for users of PROLOG (PROgramming LOGic), the high-level language used for artificial intelligence applications.

FAQ ▶ The following FAQs are available via FTP from RTFM.MIT.EDU in the directory:
pub/usenet/comp.lang.prolog:
FAQ:_Prolog_Implementations_2_2_[Monthly_posting]
FAQ:_Prolog_Resource_Guide_1_2_[Monthly_posting]

REXX Programming Discussion Group
comp.lang.rexx **M**

For users of REXX, the computer command language.

SCHEME

comp.lang.scheme **M**

A LISP dialect developed at MIT and used primarily for artificial intelligence applications.

Smalltalk

comp.lang.smalltalk **HI**

Smalltalk is a popular object-oriented version of the C computer language that was originally developed at Xerox PARC. One participant/advocate describes Smalltalk as "C++ for mere mortals."

FAQ ▶ The following FAQ is available via FTP from RTFM.MIT.EDU in the directory:
pub/usenet/comp.lang.smalltalk:
Smalltalk_Frequently-Asked_Questions_(FAQ)

TCL

comp.lang.tcl **HI**

Group for discussion of the TCL programming language and related tools.

FAQ ▶ The following FAQs are available via FTP from RTFM.MIT.EDU in the directory:
pub/usenet/comp.lang.tcl:
FAQ:_comp.lang.tcl_Frequently_Asked_Questions_(1_5)__(Last_updated:_August_10,_1993)
FAQ:_comp.lang.tcl_Frequently_Asked_Questions_(1_5)__(Last_updated:_September_20,_1993)
FAQ:_comp.lang.tcl_Frequently_Asked_Questions_(2_5)__(Last_updated:_August_10,_1993)
FAQ:_comp.lang.tcl_Frequently_Asked_Questions_(2_5)__(Last_updated:_September_20,_1993)
FAQ:_comp.lang.tcl_Frequently_Asked_Questions_(3_5)__(Last_updated:_August_10,_1993)
FAQ:_comp.lang.tcl_Frequently_Asked_Questions_(3_5)__(Last_updated:_September_20,_1993)
FAQ:_comp.lang.tcl_Frequently_Asked_Questions_(4_5)__(Last_updated:_August_10,_1993)
FAQ:_comp.lang.tcl_Frequently_Asked_Questions_(4_5)__(Last_updated:_September_20,_1993)
FAQ:_comp.lang.tcl_Frequently_Asked_Questions_(5_5)__(Last_updated:_August_10,_1993)
FAQ:_comp.lang.tcl_Frequently_Asked_Questions_(5_5)__(Last_updated:_September_20,_1993)

Verilog

comp.lang.verilog **L**

Software for Computer Aided Engineering (CAE).

VHDL

comp.lang.vhdl **M**

Very technical group for discussion of VHDL (Very High Density Logic).

Visual Basic

comp.lang.visual **M**

Programmers' discussion group for users of Microsoft's Visual Basic.

Object-Oriented Languages

comp.object **HI**

All about object-oriented languages and applications.

FAQ ▶ The following FAQs are available via FTP from RTFM.MIT.EDU in the directory:
pub/usenet/comp.object:
Comp.Object_FAQ_Version_1.0.2_(10-12)_Part_4_7
Comp.Object_FAQ_Version_1.0.2_(10-12)_Part_5_7
Comp.Object_FAQ_Version_1.0.2_(10-12)_Part_6_7
Comp.Object_FAQ_Version_1.0.2_(10-12)_Part_8_8
Comp.Object_FAQ_Version_1.0.2_(9-93)_Part_1_7
Comp.Object_FAQ_Version_1.0.2_(9-93)_Part_2_7

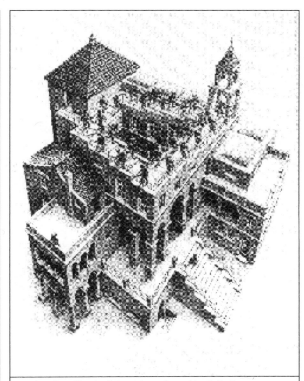

▲ *Escher "Stairs" drawing, downloaded via Internet FTP from* **grind.isca.uiowa.edu**

Comp.Object_FAQ_Version_1.0.2_(9-93)_Part_3_7
Comp.Object_FAQ_Version_1.0.2_(9-93)_Part_4_7
Comp.Object_FAQ_Version_1.0.2_(9-93)_Part_5_7
Comp.Object_FAQ_Version_1.0.2_(9-93)_Part_6_7
Comp.Object_FAQ_Version_1.0.2_(9-93)_Part_7_7
Comp.Object_FAQ_Version_1.0.3_(10-12)_Announcement
Comp.Object_FAQ_Version_1.0.3_(10-12)_Part_7_8

C Language Q&A

comp.std.c **M**

Queries and answers on the C programming language.

C++ Language Q&A

comp.std.c++ **HI**

Questions and answers on C++, the object-oriented version of the C programming language.

E-mail

Elm

comp.mail.elm **HI**

Popular e-mail program used on UNIX-based systems.

FAQ ▶ The following FAQs are available via FTP from

RTFM.MIT.EDU in the directory:
pub/usenet/comp.mail.elm:
Changes_to_the_Monthly_Elm_Posting_from_the_Elm_Development_Group
Monthly_Elm_Posting_from_the_Elm_Development_Group

MH Mail Handler
comp.mail.mh **M**

This group discusses Mail Handlers, the general class of programs that sort and distribute mail across a network.

FAQ ▶ The following FAQ is available via FTP from RTFM.MIT.EDU in the directory:
pub/usenet/comp.mail.mh:
MH_Frequently_Asked_Questions_(FAQ)_with_Answers

MIME
comp.mail.mime **HI**

For people interested in MIME (Multi-purpose Internet Mail Extensions), a specification that offers a way to interchange text in languages with different character sets and multi-media e-mail among many different computer systems.

FAQ ▶ The following FAQ is available via FTP from RTFM.MIT.EDU in the directory:
pub/usenet/comp.mail.mime:
comp.mail.mime_frequently_asked_questions_list_(FAQ)

E-Mail: Miscellaneous
comp.mail.misc **HI**

Anything and everything related to e-mail, from how to survive e-mail "bombing attacks" to proper Netiquette on e-mail signatures.

FAQ ▶ The following FAQs are available via FTP from RTFM.MIT.EDU in the directory:
pub/usenet/comp.mail.misc:
FAQ:_How_to_find_people_s_E-mail_addresses
Mail_Archive_Server_software_list
UNIX_Email_Software_Survey_FAQ

Multimedia E-Mail
comp.mail.multi-media **L**

You can send sound—and even video—on the Internet with your e-mail using some of the new Internet standards. This group tracks the latest developments.

MUSH (Mail User's Shell)
comp.mail.mush **M**

Discussion group for users of the Mail User's Shell.

Sendmail
comp.mail.sendmail **HI**

Discussion group for the Sendmail Utilities implemented on various platforms.

UUCP
comp.mail.uucp **M**

Discussion about UUCP (UNIX to UNIX CoPy), the most common way to mail files between UNIX-based systems.

FAQ ▶ The following FAQ is available via FTP from RTFM.MIT.EDU in the directory:
pub/usenet/comp.mail.uucp:
UUCP_Internals_Frequently_Asked_Questions

Organizations

Association for Computing Machinery
comp.org.acm **M**

ACM is one of the more venerable computer organizations. Most of the activity in this group relates to conference announcements and "calls for papers."

DECUS
comp.org.decus **M**

Newsgroup for users of Digital Equipment systems.

FAQ ▶ The following FAQs are available via FTP from RTFM.MIT.EDU in the directory:
pub/usenet/comp.org.decus:
DECUS_Questions_Answered_(last_modified_24-Aug-93)
Monthly_info_posting:_What_is_VMSnet?

Electronic Frontier Foundation
comp.org.eff.talk **HI**

EFF is a not-for-profit organization formed to explore the political, social and legal issues surrounding the Net. Topics include cryptography, legal liability of sysops and much more.

IEEE
comp.org.ieee **M**

Newsgroup for members of IEEE (Institute of Electrical and Electronic Engineers). Includes conference announcements on specific technical issues and "calls for papers."

UNIX Users Group
comp.org.usenix **M**

Most of the activity in this group revolves around the various USENIX-sponsored conferences that take place throughout the country on various UNIX-related topics.

FAQ ▶ The following FAQ is available via FTP from RTFM.MIT.EDU in the directory:
pub/usenet/comp.org.usenix:
FAQ:_SAGE,_The_System_Administrators_Guild

Operating Systems—BSD

BSD (Berkely Standard Distribution)
comp.os.386bsd.bugs **M**

Group for discussions on BSD, one of the more popular versions of UNIX.

BSD (Berkeley Standard Distribution)

comp.os.386bsd.development **M**

Discussion group for BSD on the 386 platform. BSD is one of the more popular versions of UNIX developed at UC Berkeley.

BSD—Questions

comp.os.386bsd.questions **HI**

Questions on BSD (Berkeley Standard Distribution) version of UNIX. Covers everything from FreeBSD to setting up bidirectional comm ports.

Operating Systems—DOS

Microsoft DOS

alt.msdos.programmer **M**

Programmers help each other find the latest bugs in Microsoft's recent releases of C, C++, etc.

4DOS

comp.os.msdos.4dos **M**

Discussion group for the 4DOS command processor for MS-DOS.

MS-DOS Applications

comp.os.msdos.apps **HI**

MS-DOS 6.2 dominates the discussion here, as well as talk about the Stacker 3.1 compression utility.

DesqView

comp.os.msdos.desqview **HI**

Users of Quarterdeck's DesqView operating environment trade information about getting DesqView to work with the most recent release of DOS 6.2.

FAQ ▶ The following FAQ is available via FTP from RTFM.MIT.EDU in the directory:
pub/usenet/comp.os.msdos.desqview:
DESQview_QEMM_Frequently_Asked_Questions:_READ_BEFORE_POSTING

MS-DOS Miscellaneous

comp.os.msdos.misc **HI**

Miscellaneous MS-DOS questions cover a broad range of topics, including the MS-DOS 6.2 "upgrade" and problems with the disk compression utility Doublespace.

MS-DOS Programming

comp.os.msdos.programmer **HI**

Programmers trade technical information about such DOS utilities as Smartdrive and the Microsoft extension for CD-ROM drives.

FAQ ▶ The following FAQs are available via FTP from RTFM.MIT.EDU in the

directory:
pub/usenet/comp.os.msdos.programmer:
comp.os.msdos.programmer_FAQ_diffs
comp.os.msdos.programmer_FAQ_part_1_of_4
comp.os.msdos.programmer_FAQ_part_2_of_4
comp.os.msdos.programmer_FAQ_part_3_of_4
comp.os.msdos.programmer_FAQ_part_4_of_4
The_Serial_Port,_rel._8,_part_1_3
The_Serial_Port,_rel._8,_part_2_3
The_Serial_Port,_rel._8,_part_3_3

Operating Systems-OS/2

OS/2 Advocacy

comp.os.os2.advocacy **HI**

Proponents and detractors of IBM's OS/2 fight it out in this group. Includes quite a bit of discussion about Windows NT, OS/2's main competitor.

OS/2 Applications

comp.os.os2.apps **HI**

Users comment on and review new applications as they become available on OS/2.

FAQ ▶ The following FAQs are available via FTP from RTFM.MIT.EDU in the directory:
pub/usenet/comp.os.os2.apps:
OS_2_Frequently_Asked_Questions_List_Rel._2.1C_(1_of_4)
OS_2_Frequently_Asked_Questions_List_Rel._2.1C_(2_of_4)
OS_2_Frequently_Asked_Questions_List_Rel._2.1C_(3_of_4)
OS_2_Frequently_Asked_Questions_List_Rel._2.1C_(4_of_4)

OS/2 Beta Testing

comp.os.os2.beta **M**

Tracks the most recent OS/2 features being tested at beta sites. Participants have started an unofficial wish list for the next release of OS/2.

OS/2 Miscellaneous

comp.os.os2.misc **HI**

For OS/2 topics not covered elsewhere. Most questions relate to getting peripherals, such as CD-ROMs and soundboards, to work with OS/2.

OS/2 Networking

comp.os.os2.networking **HI**

Users trade information on using OS/2 in a networked environment—for example, getting Ethernet cards and NetWare servers to work with OS/2.

OS/2 Programming

comp.os.os2.programmer **L**

Programmers trade information on the latest development tools for OS/2. CA's Realizer is a hot topic, as well as Borland's C++ for OS/2.

■ **Computers & Telecommunications**

Operating Systems—Other

Coherent UNIX Talk Group
comp.os.coherent **HI**

A commercial version of UNIX, developed to run on PCs.

FAQ ▶ The following FAQs are available via FTP from RTFM.MIT.EDU in the directory:
pub/usenet/comp.os.coherent:
Mark_Williams_BBS_Contents_(part_1_2)
Mark_Williams_BBS_Contents_(part_2_2)

CP/M (Control Program for Microcomputers)
comp.os.cpm **M**

The microcomputer operating system that preceded MSDOS. Apparently there are people still using it on their ancient Kaypros. Some of the postings wax nostalgic about the good ole days: "Gary Kildall, where ARE you?"

Linux
comp.os.linux **HI**

Freeware version of UNIX. This software is very popular and the group is quite active.

FAQ ▶ The following FAQs are available via FTP from RTFM.MIT.EDU in the directory:
pub/usenet/comp.os.linux:
Linux_Frequently_Asked_Questions:_TABLE_OF_CONTENTS_[monthly_posted]
Linux_Frequently_Asked_Questions_1_6_[monthly_posted]
Linux_Frequently_Asked_Questions_2_6_[monthly_posted]
Linux_Frequently_Asked_Questions_3_6_[monthly_posted]
Linux_Frequently_Asked_Questions_4_6_[monthly_posted]
Linux_Frequently_Asked_Questions_5_6_[monthly_posted]
Linux_Frequently_Asked_Questions_6_6_[monthly_posted]
Linux_INFO-SHEET
Linux_META-FAQ
Linux_NET-2-FAQ
PC-Clone_UNIX_Hardware_Buyer_s_Guide
PC-clone_UNIX_Software_Buyer_s_Guide
Welcome_to_the_comp.os.linux.*_hierarchy!
[comp.os.linux.announce]_Guidelines_for_posting
[comp.os.linux.announce]_Welcome_to_comp.os.linux.announce!

Linux II
comp.os.linux.announce **M**

Discussion group for Linux, a shareware version of UNIX.

FAQ ▶ The following FAQs are available via FTP from RTFM.MIT.EDU in the directory:
pub/usenet/comp.os.linux.announce:
Linux_Electronic_Mail_HOWTO
Linux_Frequently_Asked_Questions_with_Answers
Linux_FTP_and_BBS_List_#29_(LONG)
Linux_FTP_and_BBS_List_#30_(LONG)
Linux_INFO-SHEET
Linux_META-FAQ
Linux_News_HOWTO
Linux_UUCP_HOWTO
PC-Clone_UNIX_Hardware_Buyer_s_Guide
PC-clone_UNIX_Software_Buyer_s_Guide
[comp.os.linux.announce]_Guidelines_for_posting

Mach
comp.os.mach **M**

Operating system developed at Carnegie-Mellon.

FAQ ▶ The following FAQ is available via FTP from RTFM.MIT.EDU in the directory:
pub/usenet/comp.os.mach:
comp.os.mach_Frequently_Asked_Questions

Minix
comp.os.minix **M**

For users of the Minix operating system.

FAQ ▶ The following FAQs are available via FTP from RTFM.MIT.EDU in the directory:
pub/usenet/comp.os.minix:
Changes_to_MINIX_Information_Sheet
MINIX_Frequently_Asked_Questions_(Last_Changed:_30_June_1993)
Minix_Information_Sheet_(Last_Changed:_28_August_1993)
M_F_A_Q_(L_C:_30_J_1993)
M_I_S_(L_C:_30_J_1993)

Operating Systems: Miscellaneous
comp.os.misc **L**

For discussion of general operating system issues not found elsewhere.

OS9
comp.os.os9 **L**

OS9 is a real-time, multi-user, multi-tasking operating system developed by Microware Systems Corp. and Motorola for the 6809 microprocessor.

Operating System Research
comp.os.research **M**

For developers and researchers of operating systems. In addition to technical discussions on various aspects of operating systems, there are many conference announcements and "calls for papers."

VMS
comp.os.vms **HI**

For users of VMS, DEC's operating system for their VAX line of minicomputers.

FAQ ▶ The following FAQs are available via FTP from RTFM.MIT.EDU in the directory:
pub/usenet/comp.os.vms:
Info-VAX:_How_to_find_VAX_VMS_software.
Info-VAX:_Introduction_to_Info-VAX
Info-VAX:__Advanced__Common_Questions
Info-VAX:__Basic__Common_Questions
Monthly_info_posting:_vmsnet.sources_archive_sites
Monthly_info_posting:_VMSnet_on_Bitnet

Vxworks
comp.os.vxworks **M**

For users of Wind River Systems' VxWorks, a software development environment for a wide range of real-time programming applications.

▲ *"Waves" computer graphic, downloaded via Internet FTP from* **wuarchive.wustl.edu**

Operating Systems—UNIX

AIX I

bit.listserv.aix-l **M**

Very active group for users of IBM's version of UNIX.

Systems Administration

comp.unix.admin **HI**

Being a UNIX system administrator can be a thankless task, but this group makes it a little easier. Recent topics include setting up MMDF for the SMTP Channel and setting of time zones in SunOS 4.1.1.

AIX II

comp.unix.aix **HI**

More discussion, all about IBM's version of UNIX.

FAQ▶ The following FAQs are available via FTP from RTFM.MIT.EDU in the directory:
pub/usenet/comp.unix.aix:
AIX_Frequently_Asked_Questions_(Part_1_of_3)
AIX_Frequently_Asked_Questions_(Part_2_of_3)
AIX_Frequently_Asked_Questions_(Part_3_of_3)

UNIX on the Amiga

comp.unix.amiga **M**

All about the various versions of UNIX for the Amiga, including Minix and SYSV4.

AUX: Apple UNIX

comp.unix.aux **HI**

Discussions relating to Apple's Macintosh version of UNIX.

FAQ▶ The following FAQ is available via FTP from RTFM.MIT.EDU in the directory:
pub/usenet/comp.unix.aux:
Apple_A_UX_FAQ_List_(1_2)

BSD (Berkeley Standard Distribution)

comp.unix.bsd **M**

For users of BSD, one of the most widely used versions of UNIX, developed at the University of California's Berkeley campus.

FAQ▶ The following FAQ is available via FTP from RTFM.MIT.EDU in the directory:
pub/usenet/comp.unix.bsd:
X_on_Intel-based_UNIX_Frequently_Asked_Questions_[FAQ]

Cray UNIX Discussions

comp.unix.cray **L**

UNIX for the Cray.

UNIX Internals

comp.unix.internals **M**

Highly technical discussion for those who want to get down to the kernel level of UNIX.

UNIX Miscellaneous

comp.unix.misc **HI**

General discussion of UNIX issues not found elsewhere.

UNIX for i386

comp.unix.pc-clone.32bit **HI**

UNIX for the Intel i386 and i486 architecture.

FAQ▶ The following FAQs are available via FTP from RTFM.MIT.EDU in the directory:
pub/usenet/comp.unix.pc-clone.32bit:
SCO_Enhanced_Feature_Supplements_[summary_of_recent_changes]
SCO_Support_Level_Supplements_[summary_of_recent_changes]

UNIX Programmers

comp.unix.programmer **HI**

If you can't find the answer to your UNIX question in this group, you're in deep trouble.

FAQ ▶ The following FAQ is available via FTP from RTFM.MIT.EDU in the directory:
pub/usenet/comp.unix.programmer:
Csh_Programming_Considered_Harmful

New UNIX Users Group
comp.unix.questions **HI**

Theoretically this group is for new UNIX users' questions, but some of the questions and related answers are quite technical. If you can't get your questions answered here, check out the **comp.unix.wizards** group.

FAQ ▶ The following FAQs are available via FTP from RTFM.MIT.EDU in the directory:
pub/usenet/comp.unix.questions:
Changes_to__Welcome_to_comp.unix.questions__[Frequent_posting]
UNIX_-_Frequently_Asked_Questions_(1_7)_Digest_[Frequent_posting]
UNIX_-_Frequently_Asked_Questions_(2_7)_Digest_[Frequent_posting]
UNIX_-_Frequently_Asked_Questions_(3_7)_Digest_[Frequent_posting]
UNIX_-_Frequently_Asked_Questions_(4_7)_Digest_[Frequent_posting]
UNIX_-_Frequently_Asked_Questions_(5_7)_Digest_[Frequent_posting]
UNIX_-_Frequently_Asked_Questions_(6_7)_Digest_[Frequent_posting]
UNIX_-_Frequently_Asked_Questions_(7_7)_Digest_[Frequent_posting]
UNIX_-_Frequently_Asked_Questions_(Contents)_[Frequent_posting]
Welcome_to_comp.unix.questions_[Frequent_posting]

UNIX Shell
comp.unix.shell **HI**

Most UNIX programmers will have their favorite shell such as Bourne or C-shell. In this group, the technical pros and cons of the various shells are discussed and debated.

FAQ ▶ The following FAQs are available via FTP from RTFM.MIT.EDU in the directory:
pub/usenet/comp.unix.shell:
Changes_to__Welcome_to_comp.unix.shell__[Frequent_posting]
index
rc-FAQ
Welcome_to_comp.unix.shell_[Frequent_posting]
Z-shell_Frequently-Asked_Questions

Solaris
comp.unix.solaris **HI**

UNIX operating system for the Sun Microsystem family (and others).

FAQ ▶ The following FAQ is available via FTP from RTFM.MIT.EDU in the directory:
pub/usenet/comp.unix.solaris:
Solaris_2_Porting_FAQ

UNIX System5 Release 3
comp.unix.sys5.r3 **M**

Discussion group for UNIX System 5 Release 3, the official version of UNIX now owned by Novell.

UNIX System 5 Release 4
comp.unix.sys5.r4 **HI**

More discussions on the official version of UNIX now owned by Novell.

Ultrix
comp.unix.ultrix **HI**

DEC's (Digital Equipment Corp.'s) version of UNIX.

UNIX Wizards
comp.unix.wizards **HI**

If you're really stumped on a UNIX question, this is the group to visit.

FAQ ▶ The following FAQ is available via FTP from RTFM.MIT.EDU in the directory:
pub/usenet/comp.unix.wizards:
Intro_to_comp.unix.wizards_-
_read_before_posting!_(last_change:_Wed_Jul_28_9:50:52_EDT_1993)

XENIX SCO
comp.unix.xenix.sco **HI**

XENIX is a popular version of UNIX by SCO (Santa Cruz Operation).

FAQ ▶ The following FAQs are available via FTP from RTFM.MIT.EDU in the directory:
pub/usenet/comp.unix.xenix.sco:
Welcome_to_comp.unix.xenix.sco_[changes_from_previous_version]
Welcome_to_comp.unix.xenix.sco_[monthly_FAQ_posting]

Microsoft Windows

Windows 3.0
bit.listserv.win3-l **HI**

Microsoft Windows 3.0 forum. Users find out about the latest upgrades, trade bug reports and help each other with application problems.

FAQ ▶ The following FAQ is available via FTP from RTFM.MIT.EDU in the directory:
pub/usenet/bit.listserv.win3-l:
Windows_Programmer_FAQ:_How_to_get_it

WordPerfect for Windows
bit.listserv.wpwin-l **L**

All new software has bugs and WordPerfect for Windows is no exception. This is a great place to get help from other knowledgeable users.

Microsoft Windows Advocacy
comp.os.ms-windows.advocacy **HI**

For discussions of Microsoft Windows.

FAQ ▶ The following FAQ is available via FTP from RTFM.MIT.EDU in the directory:
pub/usenet/comp.os.ms-windows.advocacy:
Mac_&_IBM_Info-Version_1.8.9

Windows Applications Programming
comp.os.ms-windows.apps **HI**

Programming in the Windows environment.

Sample Subjects:
MS Windows

Windows: Miscellaneous Discussions

comp.os.ms-windows.misc **HI**

MS Windows discussions not found elsewhere.

Microsoft Windows Programming

comp.os.ms-windows.programmer.misc **HI**

The large number of participants in this group make it a great place to post queries about Microsoft Windows. Visual Basic is also a frequent topic of discussion in this group.

FAQ ▶ The following FAQ is available via FTP from RTFM.MIT.EDU in the directory:
pub/usenet/comp.os.ms-windows.programmer.misc:
INFO:_A_guide_to_the_Windows_newsgroups

Microsoft Windows Development Tools

comp.os.ms-windows.programmer.tools **HI**

Visual Basic and Borland's C++ 4.0 are the leading topics in this group.

Microsoft Win32

comp.os.ms-windows.programmer.win32 **HI**

This is the group to follow for programming tips on Microsoft Windows NT.

Microsoft Windows Setup

comp.os.ms-windows.setup **HI**

Participants trade tips on installing and configuring Windows. Everything from trying to get Windows for Workgroups to run in a TCP/IP environment to swapping information on device drivers.

Windows Sockets

alt.winsock **HI**

Winsock discussion group.

Protocols

TCP/IP

bit.listserv.ibmtcp-l **L**

Forum for systems managers working with the TCP/IP protocol.

Appletalk

comp.protocols.appletalk **HI**

For discussions relating to Apple's networking system for the Macintosh.

FAQ ▶ The following FAQ is available via FTP from RTFM.MIT.EDU in the directory:
pub/usenet/comp.protocols.appletalk:
CAP_FAQ

IBM Mainframe Networks

comp.protocols.ibm **L**

Covers such topics as SNA protocols and x3270.

ISO

comp.protocols.iso **M**

Discussions on the various ISO and other widely implemented standards, such as ISO 9004, the X.500 specification and GOSIP.

FAQ ▶ The following FAQ is available via FTP from RTFM.MIT.EDU in the directory:
pub/usenet/comp.protocols.iso:
comp.protocols.iso_FAQ

ISO X.400

comp.protocols.iso.x400 **M**

Discussion about the X.400 e-mail addressing scheme and its relationship to the Internet.

Kerberos

comp.protocols.kerberos **M**

User authentication program developed at MIT.

FAQ ▶ The following FAQ is available via FTP from RTFM.MIT.EDU in the directory:
pub/usenet/comp.protocols.kerberos:
Kerberos_Users__Frequently_Asked_Questions_1.6

Protocols: Miscellaneous

comp.protocols.misc **L**

Discussion about protocols not covered elsewhere, such as the popular telecommunication transfer protocol ZModem.

NFS (Network File System)

comp.protocols.nfs **HI**

Users trade information about implementing and "tuning" Network File Systems.

PPP (Point to Point Protocol)

comp.protocols.ppp **M**

For users of the popular Internet PPP connection protocol.

FAQ ▶ The following FAQs are available via FTP from RTFM.MIT.EDU in the directory:
pub/usenet/comp.protocols.ppp:
comp.protocols.ppp_frequently_wanted_information
comp.protocols.ppp_part1_of_8_of_frequently_wanted_information
comp.protocols.ppp_part1_of_frequently_wanted_information
comp.protocols.ppp_part2_of_8_of_frequently_wanted_information
comp.protocols.ppp_part2_of_frequently_wanted_information
comp.protocols.ppp_part3_of_8_of_frequently_wanted_information
comp.protocols.ppp_part3_of_frequently_wanted_information
comp.protocols.ppp_part4_of_8_of_frequently_wanted_information
comp.protocols.ppp_part4_of_frequently_wanted_information
comp.protocols.ppp_part5_of_8_of_frequently_wanted_information
comp.protocols.ppp_part5_of_frequently_wanted_information
comp.protocols.ppp_part6_of_8_of_frequently_wanted_information
comp.protocols.ppp_part6_of_frequently_wanted_information

■ Computers & Telecommunications

comp.protocols.ppp_part7_of_8_of_frequently_wanted_information
comp.protocols.ppp_part7_of_frequently_wanted_information
comp.protocols.ppp_part8_of_8_of_frequently_wanted_information
comp.protocols.ppp_part8_of_frequently_wanted_information

SNMP (Simple Network Management Protocol)

comp.protocols.snmp 【M】

For users of SNMP, the popular Internet connection protocol.

【FAQ】▶ The following FAQ is available via FTP from RTFM.MIT.EDU in the directory:
pub/usenet/comp.protocols.snmp:
comp.protocols.snmp_[SNMP]_Frequently_Asked_Questions_(FAQ)

TCP/IP

comp.protocols.tcp-ip 【HI】

Most of the users in this group have connected or are trying to connect their own network to the Internet using the TCP/IP protocol.

TCP/IP Domains

comp.protocols.tcp-ip.domains 【L】

All nodes on TCP/IP must be identified with a unique name, or domain. This group discusses the ins and outs of the TCP/IP domain-naming structure.

TCP/IP IBM PC

comp.protocols.tcp-ip.ibmpc 【HI】

You can connect your IBM PC directly to the Internet with the right software. Participants in this group will help you get started.

【FAQ】▶ The following FAQ is available via FTP from RTFM.MIT.EDU in the directory:
pub/usenet/comp.protocols.tcp-ip.ibmpc:
comp.protocols.tcp-ip.ibmpc_Frequently_Asked_Questions_(FAQ)

NTP (Network Time Protocol)

comp.protocols.time.ntp 【M】

Local time zones can really be annoying when dealing with the international activity that takes place over the Net. Users of this group discuss and advocate the adoption of the UTC (Universal Time Code) used by pilots and navigators.

FSP File Transport Protocol

alt.comp.fsp 【L】

For users of the FSP file transfer protocol and associated utilities. According to the users, FSP is a more robust way of transmitting files than FTP.

【FAQ】▶ The following FAQ is available via FTP from RTFM.MIT.EDU in the directory:
pub/usenet/alt.comp.fsp:
FSP_Frequently_Asked_Questions_(Read_This_Before_Posting!)

SNMP (Simple Network Mangement Protocol)

info.snmp 【M】

SNMP (Simple Network Management Protocol) may

be simple, but there are quite a few questions posted (and answered) in this group.

Security

Technical Privacy Issues

alt.privacy 【HI】

Privacy is always a hot topic on the Net. Participants trade the latest info on cryptography techniques and how to change your Social Security number. You can also find out about private (anonymous) mailbox operators.

【FAQ】▶ The following FAQs are available via FTP from RTFM.MIT.EDU in the directory:
pub/usenet/alt.privacy:
Anonymity_on_the_Internet_FAQ_(2_of_4)
Anonymity_on_the_Internet_FAQ_(3_of_4)
Anonymity_on_the_Internet_FAQ_(4_of_4)
Privacy_&_Anonymity_on_the_Internet_FAQ_(1_of_3)
Privacy_&_Anonymity_on_the_Internet_FAQ_(2_of_3)
Privacy_&_Anonymity_on_the_Internet_FAQ_(3_of_3)
RIPEM_Frequently_Asked_Questions
Social_Security_Number_FAQ
The_Great_Usenet_Piss_List_Monthly_Posting

Computer Security Forum

alt.security 【HI】

Get the latest information on hacking incidents around the world. Users trade information on how to protect their sites and close recently discovered "trap doors" in their computer systems.

【FAQ】▶ The following FAQs are available via FTP from RTFM.MIT.EDU in the directory:
pub/usenet/alt.security:
FAQ:_Computer_Security_Frequently_Asked_Questions
RIPEM_Frequently_Noted_Vulnerabilities

PGP (Pretty Good Privacy)

alt.security.pgp 【HI】

PGP is a privately developed encryption technique that has the government a little upset. Theoretically, law enforcement officials would not be able to read e-mail messages encrypted with PGP. The debate on whether PGP should be used rages on the Net.

Security

comp.security.misc 【HI】

Security is such a challenge on the Internet that the user community set up a Center for Emergency Response (CERT). Read this group to stay abreast of their activities.

Computer Viruses & Security

comp.virus 【HI】

The major drawback of connecting to the

Internet is the exposure to computer viruses and other system security violations. This group helps system administrators bolster their defenses.

FAQ ▶ The following FAQs are available via FTP from RTFM.MIT.EDU in the directory:
pub/usenet/comp.virus:
Amiga_Anti-viral_archive_sites_last_changed_04_August_1993
Anti-viral_Documentation_archive_sites_last_changed_18_July_1993
Apple_II_Anti-viral_archive_sites_last_changed_04_August_1993
Apple_II_Anti-viral_archive_sites_last_changed_07_July_1992
Archive_access_without_anonymous_ftp_last_changed_05_October_1993
Archive_access_without_anonymous_ftp_last_changed_11_July_1992
Atari_ST_Anti-viral_archive_sites_last_changed_04_August_1993
Atari_ST_Anti-viral_archive_sites_last_changed_07_July_1992
Brief_guide_to_files_formats_last_changed_05_February_1993
IBMPC_Anti-viral_archive_sites_last_changed_05_October_1993
IBMPC_Anti-viral_archive_sites_last_changed_18_July_1993
Introduction_to_the_Anti-viral_archives_listing_of_01_August_1993
Introduction_to_the_Anti-viral_archives_listing_of_05_October_1993
Macintosh_Anti-viral_archive_sites_last_changed_05_October_1993
UNIX_security_archive_sites_last_changed_18_July_1993
VIRUS-L_comp.virus_Frequently_Asked_Questions_(FAQ)

Shareware & Programs

Shareware Forum
alt.sources **HI**
A mixed bag of shareware programs. You may be better off trying to locate shareware in one of the other specific archives on the Net if you know what you're looking for.

FAQ ▶ The following FAQ is available via FTP from RTFM.MIT.EDU in the directory:
pub/usenet/alt.sources:
Welcome_to_alt.sources!_(biweekly_posting)

Shareware Wanted I
alt.sources.d **L**
Users post requests for shareware they're trying to locate.

Shareware Wanted II
alt.sources.wanted **M**
This is the place to visit if you're trying to locate an obscure piece of software.

FAQ ▶ The following FAQ is available via FTP from RTFM.MIT.EDU in the directory:
pub/usenet/alt.sources.wanted:
How_to_find_sources_(READ_THIS_BEFORE_POSTING)

Shareware Archives: General
comp.archives **M**
Archives are where you can download the latest shareware. This is also the forum for announcements of major shareware archive additions.

MS-DOS Shareware Archives
comp.archives.msdos.announce **HI**
This is the group to track if you want to see the latest additions to MS-DOS shareware archives on the

Internet.

FAQ ▶ The following FAQ is available via FTP from RTFM.MIT.EDU in the directory:
pub/usenet/comp.archives.msdos.announce:
comp.archives.msdos.{announce,d}_FAQ_(Frequently_Asked_Questions)

MS-DOS Archives Discussion Group
comp.archives.msdos.d **HI**
Participants request assistance in finding specific software. Archive managers point out various specialized FTP sites.

FAQ ▶ The following FAQs are available via FTP from RTFM.MIT.EDU in the directory:
pub/usenet/comp.archives.msdos.d:
Useful_MSDOS_Programs_at_SIMTEL20_and_Garbo_(Part_1_of_2)
Useful_MSDOS_Programs_at_SIMTEL20_and_Garbo_(Part_2_of_2)

Software Sources Discussion
comp.sources.d **M**
Postings from people looking for specific kinds of software. Anything from X-based paint programs to software for bar code generation.

FAQ ▶ The following FAQs are available via FTP from RTFM.MIT.EDU in the directory:
pub/usenet/comp.sources.d:
arbitron_program_(v2.4.4—last_updated_20_Oct_1989)
CSR_FAQ_and_Status_message
v40INF1:__Introduction_to_comp.sources.misc
_inpaths.c__(last_updated_Jan_28_1993)
_inpaths.c__(last_updated_Sep_17_18:20)

Shareware Sources
comp.sources.misc **M**
Netters post shareware programs to this group, which covers a wide area of software applications, from a "self-descriptive music sheet" to a program that performs network traffic accounting.

FAQ ▶ The following FAQs are available via FTP from RTFM.MIT.EDU in the directory:
pub/usenet/comp.sources.misc:
v39INF1:__Introduction_to_comp.sources.misc
v39INF2:__Index_for_comp.sources.misc,_Volume01_through_Volume07
v39INF3:__Index_for_comp.sources.misc,_Volume08_through_Volume14
v39INF4:__Index_for_comp.sources.misc,_Volume15_through_Volume21
v39INF5:__Index_for_comp.sources.misc,_Volume22_through_Volume27
v39INF6:__Index_for_comp.sources.misc,_Volume28_through_Volume33
v39INF7:__Index_for_comp.sources.misc,_Volume34_through_Volume38
v39INF8:__Index_of_Patches_posted_to_comp.sources.misc
v40INF2:__Index_for_comp.sources.misc,_Volume01_through_Volume07
v40INF3:__Index_for_comp.sources.misc,_Volume08_through_Volume14
v40INF4:__Index_for_comp.sources.misc,_Volume15_through_Volume21
v40INF5:__Index_for_comp.sources.misc,_Volume22_through_Volume27
v40INF6:__Index_for_comp.sources.misc,_Volume28_through_Volume33
v40INF7:__Index_for_comp.sources.misc,_Volume34_through_Volume39
v40INF8:__Index_of_Patches_posted_to_comp.sources.misc

Software Sources Wanted
comp.sources.wanted **HI**
If you're having trouble finding that special piece of software, post a query here. Users post queries like "Wanted: GIF/Targa animation" and "Wanted: Simple architectural

drawing package."

Shareware for X Windows

comp.sources.x **L**

Participants post shareware for the X Windows environment.

Amiga & Commodore Shareware

alt.sources.amiga **L**

Good group to visit if you still have a Commodore C64 or C128 kicking around.

Specific Software

EndNote & EndLink Users Forum

bit.listserv.endnote **L**

For users of EndNote and EndLink citation software.

Innopac

bit.listserv.innopac **L**

Discussion group for users of Innopac library management software.

Notabene

bit.listserv.notabene **M**

Very active group for users of the popular academic word processing and document processing software.

PageMaker User's Group I

bit.listserv.pagemakr **M**

Many people are working on their "next" books and publishing it themselves with the help of PageMaker. Good practical advice for users of this popular desktop publishing package.

PageMaker User's Group II

alt.aldus.pagemaker **HI**

More tips and techniques for power users of Aldus's popular PageMaker desktop publishing package.

FAQ ▶ The following FAQs are available via FTP from RTFM.MIT.EDU in the directory:
pub/usenet/alt.aldus.pagemaker:
Pagemaker_Frequently_Asked_Questions,_part_1_2
Pagemaker_Frequently_Asked_Questions,_part_2_2

Asymetrix Toolbook Product Discussions

bit.listserv.toolb-l **M**

Asymetrix's Toolbook is one of the more popular graphic tools for developing Windows multimedia applications. Participants in this group trade useful information about getting the program to work with various applications.

Word Perfect Products Discussion Group

bit.listserv.wpcorp-l **M**

This is a very active group, and, although WordPerfect Corporation does not maintain an official presence, most of the queries get quick answers by other knowledgeable WP users.

Spreadsheets Discussion Group

comp.apps.spreadsheets **M**

Discussions cover all the big spreadsheets: Excel, Lotus and Quattro Pro as well as some not-so-well-known ones.

Groupware Forum

comp.groupware **M**

Discussion group for users of software for shared interactive environments.

FAQ ▶ The following FAQ is available via FTP from RTFM.MIT.EDU in the directory:
pub/usenet/comp.groupware:
Introduction_to_comp.groupware_(Periodic_informational_Posting)

Matlab

comp.soft-sys.matlab **HI**

For users of MathWork's Matlab, a programming language for interactive numeric computation, data analysis and graphics.

Opendesktop

biz.sco.opendesktop **M**

An active group for technical discussion of SCO's Opendesktop software.

Systems—Acorn

Acorn: General

comp.sys.acorn **HI**

For users of Acorn computers. The Acorn is a British computer, and it's enjoyable to watch the Brits flame one another: "You bloody twit!"

FAQ ▶ The following FAQs are available via FTP from RTFM.MIT.EDU in the directory:
pub/usenet/comp.sys.acorn:
Acorn_ftp_and_mail-server_archives_(fortnightly_posting)
Comp.Sys.Acorn_FAQ_List_Posting_(Automatic)

Acorn Advocacy

comp.sys.acorn.advocacy **L**

Why you should run right out and buy an Acorn computer.

Acorn Technical

comp.sys.acorn.tech **HI**

Hardware and software discussion for the Acorn and ARM Pro.

Systems—Amiga

Amiga Demos
alt.sys.amiga.demos **M**

Amiga users (A1200 and A4000) trade multimedia demos. Suprisingly, Germany appears to be a hotbed of multimedia programming activity.

UUCP for Amiga
alt.sys.amiga.uucp **M**

Good group to visit if you're trying to figure out how to connect your Amiga to the Net. UUCP is the protocol for connecting to the Internet, and with the resurgence of the Amiga as a platform for video processing, this group has become very active.

FAQ ▶ The following FAQs are available via FTP from RTFM.MIT.EDU in the directory:
pub/usenet/alt.sys.amiga.uucp:
alt.sys.amiga.uucp_Frequently_Asked_Questions_(FAQ_1_2)_-_AmigaUUCP_general_information
alt.sys.amiga.uucp_Frequently_Asked_Questions_(FAQ_2_2)_-_AmigaUUCP_technical_information

Amiga Users Talk
bit.listserv.i-amiga **HI**

Amiga users love their machines and have a lot to say about Commodore's inability to market what they think is a very slick box.

Amiga Advocacy
comp.sys.amiga.advocacy **HI**

Why you should run right out and buy a Commodore Amiga. This group is particularly interesting because some of Commodore's technical staff post replies to Netter questions.

Amiga Announcements
comp.sys.amiga.announce **L**

This is where you will find out about the latest releases of Amiga software, hardware and conferences.

Amiga Applications
comp.sys.amiga.applications **HI**

Almost all the software that runs on the Amiga is quite specialized, and therefore users tend to stick together and help each other. This very active group trades everything from word processing programs to CD ROM catalogs.

FAQ ▶ The following FAQ is available via FTP from RTFM.MIT.EDU in the directory:
pub/usenet/comp.sys.amiga.applications:
[comp.sys.amiga.applications]_Answers_about_Science,School,UNIX_software

Amiga Audio
comp.sys.amiga.audio **M**

Amigas have become one of the preferred platforms for game and multimedia developers. Users in this group trade information on the audio aspect of the machine.

Amiga Telecommunications
comp.sys.amiga.datacomm **HI**

Amiga users trade information about connecting to the Internet and other online services.

FAQ ▶ The following FAQs are available via FTP from RTFM.MIT.EDU in the directory:
pub/usenet/comp.sys.amiga.datacomm:
Amiga_Point_Manager_Frequently_Asked_Questions_(FAQ)
[comp.sys.amiga.datacomm]:_AmigaNOS_Frequently_asked_questions

Amiga Emulations
comp.sys.amiga.emulations **HI**

The Amiga is great on the multimedia stuff, but most of the users find they have to run some kind of emulator, such as Emplant, for access to the tremendous amount of shareware available for the PC. Users discuss their emulation options in this group.

Amiga Games
comp.sys.amiga.games **HI**

Games and multimedia are the strong points of the Amiga, and it's reflected in the high activity level of this group.

Amiga Graphics
comp.sys.amiga.graphics **HI**

Users discuss the latest graphics cards and programs for the Amiga.

Amiga Hardware
comp.sys.amiga.hardware **HI**

Users discuss all the hot new boards and peripherals for the Amiga such as Newtek's Video Toaster, used for professional-quality video editing.

Amiga Introduction
comp.sys.amiga.introduction **M**

Group for new Amiga users.

Amiga Marketplace
comp.sys.amiga.marketplace **HI**

Active group for the trading of new and used Amiga equipment.

Amiga Miscellaneous
comp.sys.amiga.misc **HI**

Amiga issues not discussed elsewhere.

FAQ ▶ The following FAQ is available via FTP from

▲ *Steve Wozniak, co-founder of Apple Computer, downloaded from* **wuarchive.wustl.edu**

RTFM.MIT.EDU in the directory:
pub/usenet/comp.sys.amiga.misc:
Amiga-FAQ_(Biweekly_posting)

Amiga: Multimedia

comp.sys.amiga.multimedia **M**

Multimedia is the combination of text, sound, graphics and video, and Amigas are a solid and affordable platform to begin multimedia experimentation. Amiga owners trade info on using the latest multimedia boards and peripherals.

Amiga: Programmer's Group

comp.sys.amiga.programmer **HI**

Developers and intense hobbyists trade information on programming the newest version of the Amiga.

Systems—Apple

Apple II

comp.sys.apple2 **HI**

General talk group for users of the venerable Apple II, still popular after all these years.

FAQ ▶ The following FAQs are available via FTP from RTFM.MIT.EDU in the directory:
pub/usenet/comp.sys.apple2:
comp.sys.apple2_-
_Frequently_Asked_Questions_(and_answers)_part_1_of_2
comp.sys.apple2_-
_Frequently_Asked_Questions_(and_answers)_part_2_of_2

Apple II GNO

comp.sys.apple2.gno **M**

For users of the Apple IIgs GNO multi-tasking environment.

Systems—Atari

Atari 8-bit

comp.sys.atari.8bit **M**

Technical discussion for users of Atari's 8-bit microcomputers.

Atari Advocacy

comp.sys.atari.advocacy **HI**

The pros and cons of using Atari computers.

Atari ST

comp.sys.atari.st **HI**

For users of Atari's popular 16-bit micros.

FAQ ▶ The following FAQs are available via FTP from RTFM.MIT.EDU in the directory:
pub/usenet/comp.sys.atari.st:
Welcome_to_comp.sys.atari.st!
Welcome_to_comp.sys.atari.st!_(Hardware)
Welcome_to_comp.sys.atari.st!_(Software)

Atari ST II

comp.sys.atari.st.tech **HI**

For users of Atari's ST hardware and software.

Systems—DEC

DEC (Digital Eqiupment Corp.)

comp.sys.dec **HI**

General discussion about DEC computer systems.

FAQ ▶ The following FAQs are available via FTP from RTFM.MIT.EDU in the directory:
pub/usenet/comp.sys.dec:
comp.unix.ultrix_Common_Frequently_Asked_Questions
comp.unix.ultrix_DEC_OSF_1_Frequently_Asked_Questions
comp.unix.ultrix_ULTRIX_Frequently_Asked_Questions

DEC Micros

comp.sys.dec.micro **L**

Discussion group for DEC PCs, including the Rainbow and Professional 350/380.

Systems—HP

HP General

comp.sys.hp **HI**

General discussion about Hewlett-Packard computer equipment.

FAQ ▶ The following FAQ is available via FTP from RTFM.MIT.EDU in the directory:
pub/usenet/comp.sys.hp:
comp.sys.hp_FAQ

HP48 & HP20
comp.sys.hp48 **HI**
> Technical discussion on the HP48 and HP20 calculators.

Systems—IBM Mainframe

IBM Mainframes
bit.listserv.ibm-main **L**
> Contrary to what you read in the popular press, IBM mainframes are not dead yet. Users in this group help one another with the foibles of Big Blue's "Big Iron."

Systems—Macintosh

Mac Advocacy
comp.sys.mac.advocacy **HI**
> The pros and cons of using the Macintosh computer.

Mac Applications
comp.sys.mac.apps **HI**
> If you're looking for a specific application for your Mac, post your query here in this extremely active group.
> **FAQ** ▶ The following FAQs are available via FTP from RTFM.MIT.EDU in the directory:
> **pub/usenet/comp.sys.mac.apps:**
> Introductory_Macintosh_frequently_asked_questions_(FAQ)
> Macintosh_application_software_frequently_asked_questions_(FAQ)

Mac Communications
comp.sys.mac.comm **HI**
> Communications stuff for the Mac—the best modems to buy, the best fax software and internal modems for the Powerbook.
> **FAQ** ▶ The following FAQs are available via FTP from RTFM.MIT.EDU in the directory:
> **pub/usenet/comp.sys.mac.comm:**
> comp.sys.mac.comm_Frequently_Asked_Questions_[1_4]
> comp.sys.mac.comm_Frequently_Asked_Questions_[2_4]
> comp.sys.mac.comm_Frequently_Asked_Questions_[3_4]
> comp.sys.mac.comm_Frequently_Asked_Questions_[4_4]

Mac Games
comp.sys.mac.games **HI**
> Talk on games for the Mac, such as SimCity 2000, F/A-18, Warlords and more.
> **FAQ** ▶ The following FAQs are available via FTP from RTFM.MIT.EDU in the directory:
> **pub/usenet/comp.sys.mac.games:**
> New_Mac_Games_List_(Full),_8_13_93
> New_Mac_Games_List_(Updates),_8_13_93

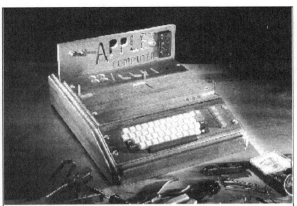

▲ *First Apple I personal computer, downloaded via Internet FTP from Smithsonian photo archives at* **sunsite.unc.edu**

Mac Hardware
comp.sys.mac.hardware **HI**
> Talk and referrals on hardware and peripherals for your Mac: video frame grabbers, slide scanners, audio boards, etc.
> **FAQ** ▶ The following FAQ is available via FTP from RTFM.MIT.EDU in the directory:
> **pub/usenet/comp.sys.mac.hardware:**
> Macintosh_PowerPC_FAQ

Mac HyperCard
comp.sys.mac.hypercard **HI**
> All about HyperCard—how to use it and what stacks are available. Some recent topics include adding charts to HyperCard, vocabulary flash card stacks, educational chess and software stacks.

Mac Databases
comp.sys.mac.databases **M**
> Tips, tricks and talk on databases for the Mac such as FileMaker Pro and FoxBase.

Mac & Apple Miscellaneous
comp.sys.mac.misc **HI**
> Covers the waterfront, but leans heavily toward discussions about Apple the company. Current topics include talk of Apple executives and the status of pending Apple licensing lawsuits.
> **FAQ** ▶ The following FAQ is available via FTP from RTFM.MIT.EDU in the directory:
> **pub/usenet/comp.sys.mac.misc:**
> Miscellaneous_Macintosh_frequently_asked_questions_(FAQ)

Mac OOP (Object-Oriented Programming)

comp.sys.mac.oop.macapp3 **M**

Populated by programmers looking for the latest development tools for the Mac. Frequently mentioned software includes the MacApp development suite that will help programmers develop software for the new PowerPC-based Macs.

Mac Portables

comp.sys.mac.portables **HI**

Find the best accessories for your Powerbook and other topics of general interest, like what a library book detector machine will do to your PowerBook (you don't want to know!).

Mac Programmer

comp.sys.mac.programmer **HI**

Mac programmers trade information on the newest development tools. Theirs is a special niche, so they tend to stick together and help each other.

FAQ ▶ The following FAQs are available via FTP from RTFM.MIT.EDU in the directory:
pub/usenet/comp.sys.mac.programmer:
Comp.Sys.Mac.Programmer_FAQ_Part_1_2_(1_12_93)
The_Mac_Programming_Public_Domain_FAQ_Answer_sheet.

Mac System Software

comp.sys.mac.system **HI**

Get all the latest information on System 7 and other development tools for the Mac.

FAQ ▶ The following FAQ is available via FTP from RTFM.MIT.EDU in the directory:
pub/usenet/comp.sys.mac.system:
Macintosh_system_software_frequently_asked_questions_(FAQ)

Mac Equipment: Wanted

comp.sys.mac.wanted **HI**

New and used Macs and accessories. SIMMs, PowerBooks, hard drives and more.

Mac Equipment: For Sale

misc.forsale.computers.mac **HI**

Mac (and Apple) systems, peripherals, software and accessories for sale.

Systems—Motorola

Motorola 6809

comp.sys.m6809 **L**

For users of Motorola's 6809 chip. This is the place to look for freeware and shareware versions of software to run on the chip.

Motorola 68000

comp.sys.m68k **L**

Good place to look for software and compatible systems for Motorola's 68000 chip.

Motorola 88000

comp.sys.m88k **L**

Users of Motorola's 88000 chip trade information.

Systems—Next

Next Advocacy

comp.sys.next.advocacy **HI**

Now it's a software company and NextStep is its flagship product. Users in this group really love the operating system, which gathered a large following of system guys in Wall Street firms.

Next Announcements

comp.sys.next.announce **L**

Track the latest official and unofficial announcements about Next and its products.

Next Hardware

comp.sys.next.hardware **HI**

Discussion group for Next hardware. Although the company has discontinued the product, this remains a very active group for getting information about accessories and peripherals for the Next Cube.

Next Marketplace

comp.sys.next.marketplace **M**

Buy and sell equipment and software for Next computers. You can even see an occasional job posting float by.

Next Miscellaneous

comp.sys.next.misc **HI**

Information on Next not found elsewhere, like trying to get a CD-ROM file system working with the machine or converting between Mac and Next fonts.

Next Programming

comp.sys.next.programmer **HI**

Programmers help each other with the latest development tools for the NextStep environment, such as implementing Xmosaic, or using Shape on the Next machine.

FAQ ▶ The following FAQ is available via FTP from RTFM.MIT.EDU in the directory:
pub/usenet/comp.sys.next.programmer:
comp.sys.next.programmer_Frequently_Asked_Questions_(FAQ)

Next Software

comp.sys.next.software **HI**

Users help each other find software to run on the Next Cube or in the NextStep environment.

Next System Administrator

comp.sys.next.sysadmin **HI**

System administrators running NextStep trade information on everything from installing CD-ROMs to doing memory upgrades on their Next Cubes.

Systems—Other

Intergraph

alt.sys.intergraph **M**

Users of the Intergraph's high-end workstations trade information on the company and its products.

ATT 3B1

comp.sys.3b1 **HI**

For users of the AT&T 7300/3B1/UNIXPC.

FAQ ▶ The following FAQs are available via FTP from RTFM.MIT.EDU in the directory:
pub/usenet/comp.sys.3b1:
comp.sys.3b1_FAQ_part1
comp.sys.3b1_FAQ_part2

Apollo

comp.sys.apollo **M**

For users of Apollo workstations.

FAQ ▶ The following FAQs are available via FTP from RTFM.MIT.EDU in the directory:
pub/usenet/comp.sys.apollo:
comp.sys.apollo_monthly_FAQ_(part1_2)
comp.sys.apollo_monthly_FAQ_(part2_2)

ATT Microcomputers

comp.sys.att **M**

Technical discussion about AT&T microcomputers. They're old, but still in use—mainly in the federal government.

FAQ ▶ The following FAQs are available via FTP from RTFM.MIT.EDU in the directory:
pub/usenet/comp.sys.att:
AT&T_3B2_Frequently_Asked_Questions_-_Part_1_2
AT&T_3B2_Frequently_Asked_Questions_-_Part_1_2_DIFFS
AT&T_3B2_Frequently_Asked_Questions_-_Part_2_2

Commodore Micros

comp.sys.cbm **HI**

Discussion about Commodore's micros.

Hand held PCs & PDAs

comp.sys.handhelds **M**

Discussion covers the broad range of handhelds from Psion, Sharp, HP and a few companies you've never even heard of.

Intel Systems

comp.sys.intel **HI**

Intel actually assembles complete systems, mostly for OEM sales. This group covers all aspects of their hardware and subcomponents. It also includes some interesting debates on the legal battles between AMD and Intel.

Laptops

comp.sys.laptops **HI**

Road warriors trade information on topics ranging from what they think is the best laptop to the hottest PCMCIA cards. Excellent group to visit before you buy the laptop of your dreams.

Mentor Graphics

comp.sys.mentor **L**

For users of Mentor Graphics and the Silicon Compiler System.

MIPS

comp.sys.mips **L**

For users of MIPS chips and products based on MIPS chips.

Miscellaneous Systems

comp.sys.misc **L**

For discussion of computer systems not found elsewhere. For example, Apple's Newton and Radio Shack's TRS-80.

NCR

comp.sys.ncr **M**

For users of NCR computers like the NCR 3000 series or the NCR UNIX SVR4.2 MP-RAS.

Novell Netware

comp.sys.novell **HI**

Novell's Netware is still by far the most popular Networking software, and this popularity is reflected in the high volume of activity in this group. Not too much gossip in this group, just hard technical info about tuning Netware networks.

Palmtops

comp.sys.palmtops **HI**

Anything and everything relating to palmtop computers such the HP95LX, the Psion and Sharp Wizard.

■ **Computers & Telecommunications**

Pen Systems

comp.sys.pen **HI**

They're a hot topic for discussion, but do they really work? Users review and debate the Zoomer, the Newton and the Simon.

FAQ ▶ The following FAQs are available via FTP from RTFM.MIT.EDU in the directory:
pub/usenet/comp.sys.pen:
Canonical_List_of_Newton_Q&A_0.0.3_part_1
Canonical_List_of_Newton_Q&A_0.0.3_part_2

Prime

comp.sys.prime **L**

For users of Prime computers (there are still a few left).

Sequent

comp.sys.sequent **L**

Discussion group for users of Sequent systems.

Tandy Systems

comp.sys.tandy **M**

Interesting topics, ranging from the Tandy TRS-80 to the new PDA (Personal Digital Assistant), the Zoomer.

Texas Instruments

comp.sys.ti **L**

Laptops are the only full computer systems TI is currently manufacturing since they sold their desktop and UNIX computer operations to HP. A lot of the discussion in this group revolves around the discontinued TI machines.

Transputer Systems

comp.sys.transputer **L**

Discussion group for this British-based computer company and its OCCAM language.

Unisys

comp.sys.unisys **L**

Unisys seems to be an expert at collecting old computer companies. This group covers computers originally made by Sperry, Burroughs, Convergent and, of course, Unisys.

Zenith

comp.sys.zenith **L**

Discussion group for Zenith Data System products like the Z-Lite laptop. Also includes occasional postings regarding the old Heathkit terminals and computers.

Systems—IBM PCs

IBM PC Action Games

comp.sys.ibm.pc.games.action **HI**

For users of arcade-style games for the IBM PC.

IBM PC Adventure Games

comp.sys.ibm.pc.games.adventure **HI**

Discussion of adventure games for the IBM PC.

IBM PC Hardware

comp.sys.ibm.pc.hardware **HI**

Technical discussion on PC/XT/AT/EISA hardware.

FAQ ▶ The following FAQ is available via FTP from RTFM.MIT.EDU in the directory:
pub/usenet/comp.sys.ibm.pc.hardware:
M_&_I_I-V_1.8.8_{r}

IBM PC: Miscellaneous

comp.sys.ibm.pc.misc **HI**

For IBM PC-related topics not discussed elsewhere, and therefore a very active group.

IBM RT

comp.sys.ibm.pc.rt **L**

Technical discussion on IBM's RT series computers.

FAQ ▶ The following FAQ is available via FTP from RTFM.MIT.EDU in the directory:
pub/usenet/comp.sys.ibm.pc.rt:
COMP.SYS.IBM.PC.RT:_IBM_RT_-_Hardware_-_Frequently_Asked_Questions

IBM Soundcard

comp.sys.ibm.pc.soundcard **HI**

Very active group for discussion of technical issues relating to IBM's soundcard.

FAQ ▶ The following FAQs are available via FTP from RTFM.MIT.EDU in the directory:
pub/usenet/comp.sys.ibm.pc.soundcard:
Generic_IBM_PC_Soundcard_FAQ_periodic_posting
IBM_MOD_Players_Compared!
Ultrasound_Internet_Archives_-_New_Files_Validated_-_Aug._31,_93

IBM PS/2 Hardware

comp.sys.ibm.ps2.hardware **M**

Covers all aspects of IBM's PS/2 microchannel hardware.

PC Clones For Sale

misc.forsale.computers.pc-clone **HI**

PC systems, peripherals, software and accessories for sale.

Systems—SGI

SGI (Silicon Graphics) System Administrators

comp.sys.sgi.admin **HI**

Silicon Graphics makes the hot graphics workstations like the Iris and the new Indy. Virtually no chitchat on this group, just terse exchange of technical information on tuning those graphic boxes.

FAQ ▶ The following FAQs are available via FTP from RTFM.MIT.EDU in the directory:
pub/usenet/comp.sys.sgi.admin:
SGI_admin_Frequently_Asked_Questions_(FAQ)
SGI_apps_Frequently_Asked_Questions_(FAQ)
SGI_graphics_Frequently_Asked_Questions_(FAQ)
SGI_hardware_Frequently_Asked_Questions_(FAQ)
SGI_misc_Frequently_Asked_Questions_(FAQ)

Silicon Graphics Applications

comp.sys.sgi.apps **M**

Software applications for the Iris and Indy workstations.

Silicon Graphics: Bugs

comp.sys.sgi.bugs **M**

Bugs found in the IRIX operating system.

High-Level Graphics Software

comp.sys.sgi.graphics **M**

Discussion of graphics packages running on the SGI machines, like Inventor and Glprof.

Silicon Graphics Hardware

comp.sys.sgi.hardware **M**

Base systems, peripherals and accessories for SGI machines.

Silicon Graphics Miscellaneous

comp.sys.sgi.misc **HI**

Discussion of SGI (Silicon Graphics) related topics not found elsewhere. Recent topics include voice recognition for the Indigo and a surcharge slapped on systems for export.

FAQ ▶ The following FAQ is available via FTP from RTFM.MIT.EDU in the directory:
pub/usenet/comp.sys.sgi.misc:
SGI_Anonymous_FTP_archives_(monthly)

Systems—Sun

Sun Microsystem Products

alt.sys.sun **L**

Discussion of Sun Microsystems hardware and software. The more official groups such as

comp.sys.sun may be better for reading and querying.

FAQ ▶ The following FAQ is available via FTP from RTFM.MIT.EDU in the directory:
pub/usenet/alt.sys.sun:
FAQ:_OPEN_LOOK_UI:_04_04:_List_of_programs_with_an_OPEN_LOOK_UI

Sun System Administrators

comp.sys.sun.admin **HI**

For system administrators running Sparcstation and Solaris Networks.

FAQ ▶ The following FAQs are available via FTP from RTFM.MIT.EDU in the directory:
pub/usenet/comp.sys.sun.admin:
FAQ:_Sun_Computer_Administration_Frequently_Asked_Questions
Master_Sun_format.dat
Solaris_2.1_Frequently_Answered_Questions_(FAQ)_$Revision:_1.22_$
Solaris_2_Frequently_Asked_Questions_(FAQ)_$Revision:_1.28_$

Sun Applications

comp.sys.sun.apps **M**

Software running on Sun systems and under Solaris. Recent topics include Netware use with the Sun and Sybase on the SparcStation.

Sun Hardware

comp.sys.sun.hardware **HI**

Base systems, peripherals and accessories for the Sun environment.

FAQ ▶ The following FAQ is available via FTP from RTFM.MIT.EDU in the directory:
pub/usenet/comp.sys.sun.hardware:
comp.sys.sun.hardware_FAQ

Sun Miscellaneous

comp.sys.sun.misc **HI**

For Sun-related topics not discussed elsewhere. This is where you will find gossip about Sun Microsystems, but the discussion is still dominated by technical matters.

Sun Hardware & Software Wanted

comp.sys.sun.wanted **M**

Sun systems, software and related products bought and sold.

Sun System Manager

info.sun-managers **HI**

All about Sun systems and networks.

Computer Theory

Computer Architecture

comp.arch **HI**

Forum for the discussion of computer architecture.

FAQ ▶ The following FAQ is available via FTP from RTFM.MIT.EDU in the directory:
pub/usenet/comp.arch:
A_reminder_about_posting_to_comp.arch_(last_mod_06_14_90)

Storage Technologies & Formats

comp.arch.storage **M**

Participants discuss flash file systems, holographic storage, the use of video tapes as storage and more.

Client Server Issues

comp.client-server **M**

Users request and receive information on resources to help them implement client-server design concepts.

Compiler Design Group

comp.compilers **HI**

Group for the discussion of compiler design and research. Computer architecture is also a frequent topic of discussion.

FAQ ▶ The following FAQs are available via FTP from RTFM.MIT.EDU in the directory:
pub/usenet/comp.compilers:
Comp.compilers_1990_Annual
comp.compilers_monthly_message_and_Frequently_Asked_Questions

Compression Techniques

comp.compression **HI**

Discussion group for compression algorithms and techniques for compressing voice, graphics, video and data.

FAQ ▶ The following FAQs are available via FTP from RTFM.MIT.EDU in the directory:
pub/usenet/comp.compression:
comp.compression_FAQ_(reminder)
comp.compression_Frequently_Asked_Questions_(part_1_3)
comp.compression_Frequently_Asked_Questions_(part_2_3)
comp.compression_Frequently_Asked_Questions_(part_3_3)

Compression Research

comp.compression.research **L**

Discussion on cutting-edge compression such as 3D and diatomic compression.

Human Factors in Design

comp.human-factors **HI**

The group covers usability and human factors, but discussion is not limited to computers. Topics include design considerations for money and coins, ATM cards, and computer furniture.

FAQ ▶ The following FAQs are available via FTP from RTFM.MIT.EDU in the directory:
pub/usenet/comp.human-factors:
FAQ:_Typing_Injuries_(1_5):_Changes_since_last_month_[monthly_posting]
FAQ:_Typing_Injuries_(2_5):_General_Info_[monthly_posting]
FAQ:_Typing_Injuries_(3_5):_Keyboard_Alternatives_[monthly_posting]
FAQ:_Typing_Injuries_(4_5):_Software_Monitoring_Tools_[monthly_posting]
FAQ:_Typing_Injuries_(5_5):_Furniture_Information_[monthly_posting]

Parallel Processing

comp.parallel **HI**

Parallel processing discussions, from PCs to massively parallel machines like those manufactured by Thinking Machines.

Supercomputers

comp.sys.super **L**

All about supercomputers (Cray, Thinking Machines, etc.) and related applications like parallelizing weather prediction models.

Theoretical Computer Science

comp.theory **M**

Very technical discussion of theoretical computer issues. Recent topics include polyadic pi-calculus and 2-isomorphisms of planar graphs. This group is not for mere mortals.

Cellular Automata

comp.theory.cell-automata **L**

All about complexity and chaos theory. Participants review books on the field and discuss innovative applications.

Dynamic Systems

comp.theory.dynamic-sys **L**

All about modelling dynamic systems (such as emulating the dynamics of a bouncing ball).

Text Processing

Text Editors

comp.editors **HI**

Discussion group for UNIX text editors. You've heard of VI, but have you heard of the new enhanced version VILE? LaTeX, troff and other popular UNIX text editing topics are also discussed.

FAQ ▶ The following FAQs are available via FTP from RTFM.MIT.EDU in the directory:
pub/usenet/comp.editors:
comp.editors_-_VI_Archives_;
Introduction_to_comp.editors_(July_29_1993)

Fonts: Technical Help Group

comp.fonts **HI**

Looking for the perfect font or just trying to get your old fonts working in a new environment? This group may have the answer you're looking for.

FAQ ▶ The following FAQs are available via FTP from RTFM.MIT.EDU in the directory:
pub/usenet/comp.fonts:
comp.fonts_FAQ.1A.General-Info_(1_3)
comp.fonts_FAQ.1B.General-Info_(2_3)
comp.fonts_FAQ.1C.General-Info_(3_3)

```
comp.fonts_FAQ.2.Mac-Info
comp.fonts_FAQ.3.MS-DOS-Info
comp.fonts_FAQ.4.OS_2-Info
comp.fonts_FAQ.5.UNIX-Info
comp.fonts_FAQ.6.Sun-Info
comp.fonts_FAQ.7.NeXT-Info
comp.fonts_FAQ.8.X-Info
comp.fonts_FAQ.9.Utilities
comp.fonts_FAQ.A.VendorList
comp.fonts_FAQ:_Amiga_Info
comp.fonts_FAQ:_Diffs_from_last_posting
comp.fonts_FAQ:_General_Info_(1_3)
comp.fonts_FAQ:_General_Info_(2_3)
comp.fonts_FAQ:_General_Info_(3_3)
comp.fonts_FAQ:_Macintosh_Info
comp.fonts_FAQ:_MS-DOS_Info
comp.fonts_FAQ:_OS_2_Info
comp.fonts_FAQ:_Sun_Info
comp.fonts_FAQ:_UNIX_Info
comp.fonts_FAQ:_Utilities
comp.fonts_FAQ:_Vendor_List
comp.fonts_FAQ:_X11_Info
```

Text Processing: General Discussions
comp.text **M**

Text processing discussion. Participants look for esoteric software such as a Portuguese word processor or a freeware thesaurus.

FAQ ▶ The following FAQ is available via FTP from RTFM.MIT.EDU in the directory:
pub/usenet/comp.text:
comp.text_Frequently_Asked_Questions

Desktop Publishing
comp.text.desktop **M**

PageMaker, Ventura and WordPerfect dominate this general-interest desktop publishing discussion group.

FrameMaker Discussion Group
comp.text.frame **HI**

For users of FrameMaker, the high-end software for desktop publishing.

FAQ ▶ The following FAQs are available via FTP from RTFM.MIT.EDU in the directory:
pub/usenet/comp.text.frame:
FrameMaker_FAQ_(Frequently_Asked_Questions)
FrameMaker_FAQ_(Frequently_Asked_Questions)_1_2
FrameMaker_FAQ_(Frequently_Asked_Questions)_2_2

Interleaf
comp.text.interleaf **M**

For users of Interleaf software, the high-end desktop publishing software.

FAQ ▶ The following FAQ is available via FTP from RTFM.MIT.EDU in the directory:
pub/usenet/comp.text.interleaf:
Interleaf_FAQ_—_Frequently_Asked_Questions_for_comp.text.interleaf

SGML (Standard Generalized Markup Language)
comp.text.sgml **M**

All about encoding your documents so they can be intelligently interpreted by presentation software. SGML, ISO standard (8879), is now a hot topic because publishers are using it to prepare their text-

based products for multimedia applications.

TEX: UNIX-Based Text Processors
comp.text.tex **HI**

All about TeX and LaTeX, the UNIX-based text processing languages.

FAQ ▶ The following FAQs are available via FTP from RTFM.MIT.EDU in the directory:
pub/usenet/comp.text.tex:
Diffs_to_Frequently_Asked_Questions_about_TeX_and_LaTeX_[monthly]
TeX,_LaTeX,_etc.:_Frequently_Asked_Questions_with_Answers_[Monthly]
TeX-FAQ-supplement_(part_1_of_3)
TeX-FAQ-supplement_(part_2_of_3)
TeX-FAQ-supplement_(part_3_of_3)
TeXhax_Digest_V93_#013
TeXhax_Digest_V93_#014

X Window

InterViews
comp.windows.interviews **M**

For users of InterViews, the object-oriented windowing system.

Windowing Systems: Miscellaneous
comp.windows.misc **M**

General discussion about all aspects of windowing systems, not just Microsoft's.

FAQ ▶ The following FAQs are available via FTP from RTFM.MIT.EDU in the directory:
pub/usenet/comp.windows.misc:
(FAQ)_Portable_GUI_Development_Kits
Comp.windows.misc_Frequently_Asked_Questions_(FAQ)

NeWS
comp.windows.news **L**

Discussion group for Microsystem's NeWS windowing system.

Open-Look
comp.windows.open-look **M**

For users of Open-Look Graphical User Interface.

X Windows Systems
comp.windows.x **HI**

Discussion group for X Windows-based systems.

FAQ ▶ The following FAQs are available via FTP from RTFM.MIT.EDU in the directory:
pub/usenet/comp.windows.x:
comp.windows.x.intrinsics_Frequently_Asked_Questions_(FAQ)
comp.windows.x:_Getting_more_performance_out_of_X._FAQ
comp.windows.x_Frequently_Asked_Questions_(FAQ)_1_5
comp.windows.x_Frequently_Asked_Questions_(FAQ)_2_5
comp.windows.x_Frequently_Asked_Questions_(FAQ)_3_5
comp.windows.x_Frequently_Asked_Questions_(FAQ)_4_5
comp.windows.x_Frequently_Asked_Questions_(FAQ)_5_5

■ **Computers & Telecommunications**

list_of_X_consultants
X_Terminal_List_-_Quarterly_posting_(Q3_93)

X Windows Applications

comp.windows.x.apps **HI**

Tips and tricks on implementing various X windows applications. Recent topics include implementing X mosiac and reviews of Zinc++, a graphical toolkit.

X Windows for the i386

comp.windows.x.i386unix **HI**

X Windows for machines running Intel i386 architecture.

X Intrinsics

comp.windows.x.intrinsics **M**

Discussion regarding X Toolkit for the X Windows environment.

Motif

comp.windows.x.motif **HI**

For users of the Motif Graphical User Interface for the X Windows system.

FAQ ▶ The following FAQs are available via FTP from RTFM.MIT.EDU in the directory:
pub/usenet/comp.windows.x.motif:
Motif_FAQ_(Part_1_of_5)
Motif_FAQ_(Part_2_of_5)
Motif_FAQ_(Part_3_of_5)
Motif_FAQ_(Part_4_of_5)
Motif_FAQ_(Part_5_of_5)

X Pex

comp.windows.x.pex **L**

The PHIGS extension of the X Window System

FAQ ▶ The following FAQ is available via FTP from RTFM.MIT.EDU in the directory:
pub/usenet/comp.windows.x.pex:
(13sep93)_Welcome_to_comp.windows.x.pex!_(FAQ)

Computer-Related—Other

Amateur Computerist Newsletter

alt.amateur-comp **M**

This group is supposed to be for discussion of computer-related issues, but of late most of the discussion is of Russian economics.

Hypertext Discussion Group

alt.hypertext **M**

By definition, hypertext is dynamically crosslinking elements of a textual database. Discussion covers applications and popular software like HyperCard.

FAQ ▶ The following FAQ is are available via FTP from RTFM.MIT.EDU in the directory:
pub/usenet/alt.hypertext:
WWW_(World_Wide_Web)_FAQ

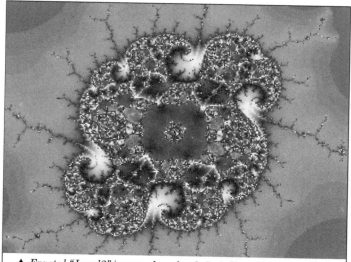

▲ *Fractal "Jewel2" image, downloaded via Internet FTP from* **grind.isca.uiowa.edu**

Sound Blaster Board

alt.sb.programmer **L**

Programmer advice for the popular Sound Blaster board.

Xview Toolkits

alt.toolkits.xview **L**

Users trade information on the most recent release of X Windows Xview 3.3 toolkit.

FAQ ▶ The following FAQs are available via FTP from RTFM.MIT.EDU in the directory:
pub/usenet/alt.toolkits.xview:
FAQ:_OPEN_LOOK_UI:_02_04:_Sun_OpenWindows_DeskSet_Questions
OPEN_LOOK_GUI_frequently_asked_questions

EDI (Electronic Data Interchange)

bit.listserv.edi-l **L**

Processing electronic transactions via the Net. A topic sure to grow as the Internet reaches a wider audience.

Public Mail Distribution Format

bit.listserv.pmdf-l **M**

Discussion of PMDF, Public Mail Distribution Format.

Sample Subjects:
POP3 server problem/Mailpatch for V6.0/UIC based fax security

VM Utilities

bit.listserv.vm-util **L**

Forum for utilities that run on IBM's VM (Virtual Machine) operating system.

SCO (Santa Cruz Operation) XENIX

biz.sco.general **HI**

For users of SCO's XENIX. Most of the discussion relates to technical implementation issues, but there is also a fair amount of gossip about the company.

FAQ ▶ The following FAQs are available via FTP from RTFM.MIT.EDU in the directory:
pub/usenet/biz.sco.general:
SCO_Mailing_List_Administrative_FAQ
SCO_Mailing_List_Technical_FAQ

Benchmarks

comp.benchmarks **HI**

Forum for discussion on benchmarks on various platforms: MACs, PCs and UNIX machines. Find out how your configuration performs against the rest.

FAQ ▶ The following FAQs are available via FTP from RTFM.MIT.EDU in the directory:
pub/usenet/comp.benchmarks:
[l_m_11_2_92]_good_conceptual_benchmarking_(2_28)_c.be_FAQ
[l_m_12_1_92]_TPC_Transaction_Processing_Council___(21_28)_c.be_FAQ
[l_m_1_31_92]_benchmark_source_info-Intro_—
netiquette(1_28)_c.be_FAQ
[l_m_3_17_92]_Measurement_environments__(12_28)_c.be_FAQ
[l_m_3_17_92]_Other_misc._benchmarks_(26_28)__c.be_FAQ
[l_m_3_17_92]_PERFECT_CLUB_(3_28)_c.be_FAQ
[l_m_3_17_92]_RFC_1242_—_terminology__(22_28)_c.be_FAQ
[l_m_3_17_92]_Equivalence___(20_28)_c.be_FAQ
[l_m_4_14_93]_music_to_benchmark_by_(7_28)_c.be_FAQ
[l_m_4_28_92]_References_(28_28)__c.be_FAQ
[l_m_4_6_92]_New_FAQ_scaffold_(6_28)__c.be_FAQ
[l_m_5_12_93]_NIST_source_and_.orgs_(11_28)__c.be_FAQ
[l_m_5_5_93]_Performance_metrics_(5_28)_c.be_FAQ
[l_m_7_15_93]_Linpack___(9_28)_c.be_FAQ

Computer Consultants

alt.computer.consultant **M**

Computer consultants (and wannabes) trade information on such topics as should you sign confidentiality agreements and should you use a broker to represent you when selling consulting services.

Digital Signal Processing

comp.dsp **HI**

Discussion about real-world and theoretical applications of Digital Signal Processing (DSP).

FAQ ▶ The following FAQs are available via FTP from RTFM.MIT.EDU in the directory:
pub/usenet/comp.dsp:
comp.dsp_FAQ_[1_of_4]
comp.dsp_FAQ_[2_of_4]
comp.dsp_FAQ_[3_of_4]
comp.dsp_FAQ_[4_of_4]

Education About Computers

comp.edu **M**

Mostly about educating people about computers and software.

Computer Miscellaneous

comp.misc **HI**

Miscellaneous newsgroups on the Net are usually *very* miscellaneous. Recent topics include computerized street maps, light pens and a discussion on the best night schools for learning computers.

Multimedia Applications

comp.multimedia **HI**

Very active group. Posters look for the best tools to do multimedia authoring and trade information on compression algorithms. There is even an occasional job posting announcement from start-up companies in the multimedia market.

Music PC Technical Talk Group

comp.music **HI**

For people interested in using computers to generate music and/or sound effects. Covers the full range of topics, from music interface boards to programs for automatic transcription of musical scores.

FAQ ▶ The following FAQs are available via FTP from RTFM.MIT.EDU in the directory:
pub/usenet/comp.music:
Electronic_and_Computer_Music_Frequently-Asked_Questions_(FAQ)
FAQ:_Gravis_Ultrasound_(_GUS_)_FAQ_v1.31

Peripherals

comp.periphs **M**

Discussions relating to monitors, tape drives, mice, scanners, etc.

Printers

comp.periphs.printers **HI**

Opinions sought and offered on the best printers for various tasks.

SCSI

comp.periphs.scsi **HI**

SCSI (Small Computer System Interface) is a very popular way to connect peripherals to systems and networks. Most of the discussion in this group is about resolving interface glitches.

FAQ ▶ The following FAQ is available via FTP from RTFM.MIT.EDU in the directory:
pub/usenet/comp.periphs.scsi:
comp.periphs.scsi_FAQ

Programming Theory Talk Group

comp.programming **HI**

Wide-ranging discussion covering everything from object-oriented languages to databases, and all things in between.

FAQ ▶ The following FAQ is available via FTP from RTFM.MIT.EDU in the directory:
pub/usenet/comp.programming:
_comp.programming_charter:_read_before_you_post_ (weekly_notice)

Real-Time Systems

comp.realtime **M**

Discussion about the various real-time operating systems for UNIX. Most of the discussion revolves around VxWorks, the popular real-time environment sold by Wind River Systems.

FAQ ▶ The following FAQs are available via FTP from RTFM.MIT.EDU in the directory:
pub/usenet/comp.realtime:
Comp.realtime:_A_list_of_real-time_operating_systems_and_tools_(LONG)
Comp.realtime:_Frequently_Asked_Questions_(FAQs)
Comp.realtime:_Welcome_to_comp.realtime

Japanese Research

comp.research.japan **L**

Several participants post their personal observations on the status of various research projects in Japan. Interesting because most of the posters are U.S. citizens living in Japan.

Robotics

comp.robotics **HI**

Robotics is not only for the big companies. In this group, hobbyist robot builders will use anything in their robots, including a Global Positioning System for cheap navigation.

FAQ ▶ The following FAQs are available via FTP from RTFM.MIT.EDU in the directory:
pub/usenet/comp.robotics:
comp.robotics_Frequently_Asked_Questions_(FAQ)_part_1_2
comp.robotics_Frequently_Asked_Questions_(FAQ)_part_2_2

Andrew System from CMU

comp.soft-sys.andrew **L**

For users of the Andrew system developed at Carnegie-Mellon University.

Software Engineering Discussion Group

comp.software-eng **HI**

All about good software engineering practices. How to write reliable and maintainable code.

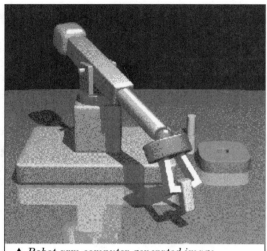
▲ *Robot arm computer-generated image, downloaded via Internet FTP from* **wuarchive.wustl.edu**

FAQ ▶ The following FAQs are available via FTP from RTFM.MIT.EDU in the directory:
pub/usenet/comp.software-eng:
Comp.software-eng_periodic_postings_and_archives
FAQ_1:_comp.software-eng_questions_and_answers
FAQ_2:_CASE_tools_summary
FAQ_3:_Software_engineering_readings
Project_Management_Programs_-_Frequently_asked_Questions_(FAQ)

Software Specification Writing

comp.specification **L**

Mostly about software tools for writing technical specifications.

Software Specification Writing II

comp.specification.z **L**

For the discussion of formal methods and standards techniques and FDTs (Formal Description Tools) such as Estelle, LOTOS, SDL, VDM and Z.

FAQ ▶ The following FAQ is available via FTP from RTFM.MIT.EDU in the directory:
pub/usenet/comp.specification.z:
comp.specification.z_Frequently_Asked_Questions_(Monthly)

Computerized Speech

comp.speech **M**

Computerized speech generation and speech recognition are the topics of this group.

FAQ ▶ The following FAQ is available via FTP from RTFM.MIT.EDU in the directory:
pub/usenet/comp.speech:
comp.speech_FAQ_(Frequently_Asked_Questions)

International Standards

comp.std.internat **L**

Discussions regarding proposed and existing OSI standards.

Terminals

comp.terminals **M**

Televideo, Wyse, Ampex and all the VT series terminals are discussed in this group.

Lab Manager

info.labmgr **M**

Managers of computer labs trade information.

Legal Issues & Computers

misc.legal.computing **M**

Is the patent system killing innovation? Should employers have the right to read employees' email? These and other legal issues related to computers are discussed.

Chapter 11: Sports, Sports Talk & News

When it comes to talk on the Net, fans of any sport can find a newsgroup devoted especially to them. There are newsgroups for all American professional sports—baseball, football, basketball, hockey (and their college counterparts) plus international sports such as soccer, rugby, and cricket.

Sports Talk Groups on the Net

Sports talk newsgroups tend to be online free-for-alls with thousands of fevered sports buffs promoting their favorite teams. This dialogue gets even hotter the morning after a big game or team-related news item.

Sports and Recreation for Active People

The Net also features many active online discussion groups covering a wide variety of outdoor, recreational and adventure activities for the active participant. Newsgroups here range from skydiving, windsurfing, skiing and fencing to bowling, backpacking and running. There are also newsgroups covering most every aspect of bicycling.

The Internet also contains dozens of ClariNet new service features with up-to-the-minute sports news and information.

Spectator Sports

Sports on the Net: Baseball, Basketball, Football and More

There are a large number of very busy discussion groups for just about any sport—for spectators, fans and active amateur players of all skill levels.

Baseball

rec.sport.baseball **HI**

Friendly, spirited fans talk about the latest pro baseball news. Baseball trivia, local boosterism and the typical barroom-style sports banter.

College Baseball

rec.sport.baseball.college **M**

Active little newsgroup for college baseball fans discussing college teams, local/regional playoffs and favorite players.

Fantasy Baseball League

rec.sport.baseball.fantasy **M**

Fantasy Baseball League fanatics pick out favorite players, make trades, put together rosters and engage in Fantasy League gaming techniques.

▲ *Michael Jordan, photo image file downloaded from* **grind.isca.uiowa.edu**

Pro Basketball

rec.sport.basketball.pro **HI**

Intense discussion among loyal fans of local basketball teams, heavily oriented toward fantalk about the usual superstar players.

College Basketball

rec.sport.basketball.college **HI**

College basketball schedules, comments and intense fan talk covering all major and minor college teams and tournaments.

Pro Football

rec.sport.football.pro **HI**

The hot group for pro football fanatics. Contains individual team injury reports, local team news and the usual banter by local team boosters.

▲ *Wayne Gretzky, downloaded from* **ftp.sunet.se**

College Football

rec.sport.football.college **HI**

Fans hold forth on their favorite teams, player prospects and conferences with lots of spirited collegiate discussions.

Football: General

rec.sport.football.misc **M**

Catch-all group largely dominated by Fantasy Football League players.

Pro Hockey

rec.sport.hockey **HI**

U.S. and Canadian hockey fans carry on about favorite teams, divisions and hockey schedules.

FAQ ▶ The following FAQs are available via FTP from RTFM.MIT.EDU in the directory:
pub/usenet/rec.sport.hockey:
rec.sport.hockey_FAQ_Part_1_of_2
rec.sport.hockey_FAQ_Part_2_of_2

Pro Tennis

rec.sport.tennis **HI**

Mostly a fan-oriented discussion group for talk about pro tennis tournaments, players, matches and a few hands-on tennis tips.

FAQ ▶ The following FAQs are available via FTP from RTFM.MIT.EDU in the directory:
pub/usenet/rec.sport.tennis:
FAQ_for_rec.sport.tennis_(1_4)_-_Tournaments
FAQ_for_rec.sport.tennis_(2_4)_-_Rankings
FAQ_for_rec.sport.tennis_(3_4)_-_Player_Information
FAQ_for_rec.sport.tennis_(4_4)_-_Miscellaneous

Pro Wrestling

rec.sport.pro.wrestling **L**

Endless talk for fans of pro wrestling (otherwise known as "fake" wrestling).

Soccer

rec.sport.soccer **HI**

Active soccer fans' discussion group with comments from participants around the world on World Cup soccer teams and players.

Australian Soccer

rec.sport.football.australian **M**

For fans of various Australian soccer teams and championships.

The Olympics

rec.sport.olympics **HI**

This is the place to get advance information on the Summer Olympic Games. Includes talk of TV broadcast availability, Olympic scheduling, and inside info on Olympic tickets and accommodations.

Active Sports/Recreation

Sports: General

rec.sport.misc **M**

A catch-all newsgroup for sports not covered in other major newsgroups, such as boxing, track and field, billiards and (believe it or not) luge.

Rugby

rec.sport.rugby **M**

A popular rugby fans' newsgroup concentrating mainly on European, Australian and New Zealand teams, game schedules, players and game reports with fans' comments from these countries.

Archery Tips, Techniques, Talk & Gear

alt.archery **M**

Talk, tips, and techniques for all things related to the sport of archery. Group includes discussions of bow tuning, shooting techniques, good products and suppliers and notices of shooting events.

Sample Subjects:
Tuning a compound bow/Draw length/Info on archery shoots/Bow for sale

FAQ ▶ The following FAQs are available via FTP from RTFM.MIT.EDU in the directory:
pub/usenet/alt.archery:
FAQ:_Archery_Books
FAQ:_Archery_Organizations
FAQ:_Asian_Turkish_Bow_Construction
FAQ:_General_Archery
FAQ:_General_Bow_Construction
FAQ:_Target_Archery
FAQ:_Traditional_Archery

Hiking & Backpacking

rec.backcountry **HI**

Newsgroup covering the great outdoors—everything from backpacking to mountain climbing, camping and casual touring in national parks. Backpackers share their comments and experiences on specific wilderness adventure locations, good hiking/camping products and gear to buy, recent mountain climbing adventures and current outdoor environmental news and issues. Also features solid info and advice from experienced hikers for those of you planning extended wilderness trips.

Sample Subjects:
Backpacking menus/Double sleeping bags/Alaska questions/Info needed on West Coast trail

FAQ ▶ The following FAQs are available via FTP from RTFM.MIT.EDU in the directory:
pub/usenet/rec.backcountry:
[l_m_10_7_93]_Questions_on_conditions_and_travel_DW_(13_28)_XYZ
[l_m_12_7_92]_summary_of_past_topics_Distilled_non-wisdom_(5_28)_XYZ
[l_m_1_26_93]_Lyme_Disease:__Distilled_Wisdom_(19_28)_XYZ
[l_m_2_11_93]_Rachel_Carson_s_Words:_Distilled_Wisdom_(10_28)_XYZ
[l_m_4_15_91]_Netiquette:__Distilled_Wisdom_(12_28)_XYZ
[l_m_4_15_92]_Eco-warriors__Distilled_Wisdom_(22_28)_XYZ
[l_m_4_15_92]_High_tech_employment,_a_romantic_notion__DW_(25_28)_XYZ
[l_m_4_15_92]_Information_on_bears:__Distilled_Wisdom_(17_28)_XYZ
[l_m_4_15_92]_Oak_Ivy__Distilled_Wisdom_(18_28)_XYZ
[l_m_4_15_92]_Words_from_Colin_Fletcher_Distilled_Wisdom_(8_28)_XYZ

Sports

[l_m_4_22_93]_rec.backC_DISCLAIMER_—
_Distilled_wisdom_(1_28)___XYZ
[l_m_4_23_93]_Related_news_groups:_Distilled_Wisdom_(26_28)_XYZ
[l_m_4_27_93]_Questions_on_conditions_and_travel_DW_(13_28)_XYZ
[l_m_5_11_93]_Water_filters_&_Giardia_Distilled_Wisdom_(9_28)_XYZ
[l_m_5_14_93]_Snake_bite:_Distilled_Wisdom_(11_28)_XYZ
[l_m_5_18_1993]_Morbid_backcountry_memorial:_Distilled_Wisdom_(16_28)_XYZ
[l_m_5_24_93]_Song___Distilled_Wisdom_(23_28)_XYZ
[l_m_6_20_91]_Leopold_s_post_Distilled_Wisdom_(15_28)_XYZ
[l_m_6_7_93]_summary_of_one_past_topic_Not_Distilled_wisdom_(6_28)_XYZ
[l_m_6_8_93]_learning_(2)_Distilled_wisdom_(4_28)_XYZ
[l_m_7_15_93]_AMS___Distilled_Wisdom_(21_28)_XYZ
[l_m_7_27_93]_Film_Cinema__Distilled_wisdom_(27_28)_XYZ
[l_m_7_29_93]_Telling_questions_r.b._Turing_test_DW:_(20_28)_XYZ
[l_m_8_19_93]_Leopold_s_Land_Ethic_Distilled_Wisdom_(14_28)_XYZ
[l_m_8_19_93]_References___Distilled_Wisdom_(28_28)_XYZ
[l_m_8_29_92]_What_is__natural?__Distilled_Wisdom_(24_28)_XYZ
[l_m_8_2_93]_Backcountry_Ethics_Distilled_Wisdom_(2_28)_XYZ
[l_m_8_30_93]_Phone_address_list_Distilled_Wisdom_(7_28)_XYZ
[l_m_8_30_93]_rec.backC_DISCLAIMER_—
_Distilled_wisdom_(1_28)___XYZ
[l_m_9_13_93]_Phone_address_list_Distilled_Wisdom_(7_28)_XYZ
[l_m_9_13_93]_summary_of_one_past_topic_Not_Distilled_wisdom_(6_28)_XYZ
[l_m_9_17_92]_learning_(l)_Distilled_wisdom_(3_28)_XYZ
[l_m_9_2_93]_References___Distilled_Wisdom_(28_28)_XYZ
[l_m_9_30_93]_summary_of_past_topics_Distilled_non-
wisdom_(5_28)_XYZ

Boomerang Throwing Tips

alt.boomerang **L**

There's actually a discussion group for people who throw boomerangs. **alt.boomerang** tells you more than you'd ever want to know about boomerangs—throwing them, building them, buying them, talking to other people about them, etc.

Sample Subjects:
Throwing boomerangs/IJA nationals/Address list update

Improving Your Bowling Game

alt.sport.bowling **M**

Enthusiastic, serious bowlers have a place on the Net, too. An active discussion group containing

▲ *Bowling computer graphics PIXAR image, downloaded via Internet FTP from* **grind.isca.uiowa.edu**

▲ *Rock climber, downloaded from* **wuarchive.wustl.edu**

valuable tips and techniques for improving your game. Discussion and advice on ball technique, pin strategy and professional league news and comments.

Sample Subjects:
League formats/Brunswick World Open/Leaving one pin/ Carey Power/Question about pros

Mountaineering & Rock Climbing

rec.climbing **M**

Enthusiastic mountaineers and rock climbers swap information on climbing techniques and gear. Also discussions and personal observations on recent climbing adventures, places to climb and emergency mountaineering situations.

Sample Subjects:
Crosscountry climbing/Info. about new climbing gym/ Climbing shoe questions

Cricket

rec.sport.cricket **HI**

Cricket fans in this newsgroup from England, Australia, Asia and around the world prove they can be just as intense in their fan talk as we Americans.

Dart-Throwing Tips & Talk

alt.sport.darts **L**

If you'd like to improve your dart game (even after that sixth beer), you will find serious players online to help you here. Everything from dart tourneys to where to find top-notch dart supplies.

Ultimate & Disc Golf Frisbee Games
rec.sport.disc **M**

Two brand-new sports cooked up on college campuses, Ultimate and Disc Golf involve a frisbee-like disc, opposing teams and individual power and skill. Ultimate is played by two teams of seven players each, with the object of the game being to pass the disc from player to player all the way up the field to the opposing team's end zone. Disc Golf involves individual players on a golf course-like field, testing each player's throwing ability to reach numerous targets. In this group, players discuss college tournaments for these two games, recent exhibitions at NFL games and new leagues starting up around the world.

FAQ ▶ The following FAQs are available via FTP from RTFM.MIT.EDU in the directory:
pub/usenet/rec.sport.disc:
rec.sport.disc_FAQ_-_Part_1
rec.sport.disc_FAQ_-_Part_2

▲ *Little girl with horse, photo downloaded via Internet FTP from* **wuarchive.wustl.edu**

Horse Owners & Riders
rec.equestrian **HI**

Invaluable resource for horse owners and riders. Horse lovers on the Net trade useful information on all aspects of owning horses, from care and feeding to exercises and treatment of specific medical conditions. Also features buy/sell horse and equipment listings, places to ride and stable rentals.

Sample Subjects:
Mouseborne disease/Horse van for sale/Horse spray/ Buying a saddle

Fencing
rec.sport.fencing **M**

Insider tactics and techniques for all kinds of fencing-related sports—foil, épée and sabre. Also a good place for beginners to get useful starting-out tips.

FAQ ▶ The following FAQ is available via FTP from RTFM.MIT.EDU in the directory:
pub/usenet/rec.sport.fencing:
Fencing_FAQ

Fishing: Sport & Gear
rec.outdoors.fishing **M**

Covers the entire scope of sport fishing, tackle, techniques and banter, for river, inland and ocean fishermen. Good info on fishing techniques and fishing gear setup, great places to fish and, of course, great fish stories.

Sample Subjects:
Ocean fishing reel/Big Minnesota bass/Half Moon Bay fishing report

Fitness & Sports Nutrition
misc.fitness **HI**

In-depth group for runners, weight lifters and others interested in physical fitness and optimal sports training and nutrition. Detailed comments on body fat measurements and protein needs, workout advice and injury treatment tips.

Sample Subjects:
Bodily proportions chart/How to avoid overtraining/Enzyme supplements/Incline bench question

FAQ ▶ The following FAQs are available via FTP from RTFM.MIT.EDU in the directory:
pub/usenet/misc.fitness:
STRETCHING:_Frequently_Requested_Information__(part_1_of_3)
STRETCHING:_Frequently_Requested_Information__(part_2_of_3)
STRETCHING:_Frequently_Requested_Information__(part_3_of_3)
Stretching_FAQ_(part_1_of_3)__***LONG***
Stretching_FAQ_(part_2_of_3)__***LONG***
Stretching_FAQ_(part_3_of_3)__***LONG***

Golfers Group
rec.sport.golf **M**

Golfers will find this newsgroup irresistible. Duffers discuss play on well-known golf courses, techniques, good putters/clubs to buy and professional golf tournaments on TV.

FAQ ▶ The following FAQ is available via FTP from RTFM.MIT.EDU in the directory:
pub/usenet/rec.sport.golf:
rec.sport.golf_Golf_FAQ

■ **Sports**

Laser Tag Electronic Games Group

alt.sport.lasertag **L**

Group for players and enthusiasts of various live and virtual reality-type electronic shooting participation games such as Laser Tag, Laser Quest and MegaZone.

Paintball

rec.sport.paintball **M**

Active group for enthusiastic paintball players. paintball strategy, semi-automatic and full-automatic guns evaluated as well as good discussions on paintball tactics, strategy, rules and sportsmanship. Participants are also quite eager to answer beginners' questions.

Rowing

rec.sport.rowing **M**

For college and amateur rowing/crew enthusiasts, with a focus on coaching, events and college rowing activities.

Running: Fitness & Sport

rec.running **HI**

Useful newsgroup oriented toward serious long-distance runners. Topics include treatment of running injuries, news of major running events in the United States, running books, software and major running event race results.

Sample Subjects:
Shinsplints/Roger Bannister book/Losing motivation/Triathlon World Champ results

FAQ ▶ The following FAQs are available via FTP from RTFM.MIT.EDU in the directory:
pub/usenet/rec.running:
rec.running_FAQ_part_1_of_3
rec.running_FAQ_part_2_of_3
rec.running_FAQ_part_3_of_3

▲ *Arnold Schwarzenegger, downloaded from* **grind.isca.uiowa.edu**

Scuba Diving Tips & Gear

rec.scuba **HI**

Primarily focused on equipment and techniques for advanced divers, **rec.scuba** features comments from scuba divers around the world, including good feedback on new diving accessories and electronic products, advanced diving techniques, safety tips and a small number of buy/sell listings.

Sample Subjects:
Drysuit question/Maui diving info wanted/Cayman dive operations rated

FAQ ▶ The following FAQ is available via FTP from RTFM.MIT.EDU in the directory:
pub/usenet/rec.scuba:
[rec.scuba]_FAQ:_Frequently_Asked_Questions_about_Scuba,_Monthly_Posting

Scuba Divers Talk

bit.listserv.scuba-l **M**

Another scuba diving-oriented group on the Net dominated by college students who relate their various diving experiences (night diving, etc.) and trade tips on gear.

Skateboarding Group

alt.skate-board **M**

Tips, techniques, hardware and accessories for hard-core skateboard fanatics.

Skating: Ice, Roller & Roller Blade

rec.skate **HI**

Hodgepodge covering equipment, culture and techniques for ice skaters, moms of young skaters and figure skaters as well as recreational roller bladers and roller skaters. Serious ice skaters will have to search this newsgroup carefully for the few good bits of information available here.

FAQ ▶ The following FAQs are available via FTP from RTFM.MIT.EDU in the directory:
pub/usenet/rec.skate:
Rec.skate_FAQ:_(Roller)Hockey_(3_9)
Rec.skate_FAQ:_In-line_Skate_reviews_(5_9)
Rec.skate_FAQ:_Skating_Tricks_and_Moves_(9_9)
Rec.skate_FAQ:_What_and_Where_to_Buy_(4_9)
Rec.skate_FAQ:_Where_to_Skate_(Indoors)_(6_9)
Rec.skate_FAQ:_Where_to_Skate_(Outdoors)_Sec._1_(7_9)
Rec.skate_FAQ:_Where_to_Skate_(Outdoors)_Sec._2_(8_9)
Rec.skate_FAQ:__Wheels,_Bearings,_and_Brakes_(2_9)
Rec.skate_Frequently-Asked_Questions:_General_Info_(1_9)

Skiing

rec.skiing **HI**

Expert skiers give advice to novices here. Includes large numbers of questions and answers on best ski conditions, accommodations, inside info on ski resorts around the world, ski-lodge banter and broken leg stories.

Sample Subjects:
Skiing Calgary/Tahoe info/Buying new boots

FAQ ▶ The following FAQs are available via FTP from RTFM.MIT.EDU in the directory:
pub/usenet/rec.skiing:
Southern_US_Skiing_FAQ
Southern_US_Skiing_FAQ_(REPOST_due_to_posting_problems)

Skydiving

rec.skydiving **M**

Macho skydivers relate their skydiving experiences in a rather over-postured way. Unfortunately, contains little in the way of useful advice for skydivers.

FAQ ▶ The following FAQ is available via FTP from RTFM.MIT.EDU in the directory:
pub/usenet/rec.skydiving:
rec.skydiving_FAQ_(Frequently_Asked_Questions)

Triathlon
rec.sport.triathlon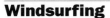

Training and conditioning tips, competitive advice, upcoming events info and good companionship for gung-ho Triathlon and Ironman event competitors.

Volleyball
rec.sport.volleyball **M**

Fans discuss their own amateur volleyball games and tournaments, as well as the emerging professional volleyball sport.

FAQ ▶ The following FAQs are available via FTP from RTFM.MIT.EDU in the directory:
pub/usenet/rec.sport.volleyball:
rec.sport.volleyball_Frequently_Asked_Questions
rec.sport.volleyball_Frequently_Asked_Questions_(FAQ)

Windsurfing
rec.windsurfing **M**

Windsurfing enthusiasts discuss local beach conditions around the U.S., windsurfing vacations, the latest in boards and sails, maintenance and repair advice and best secret windsurfing spots. Also contains a small number of windsurfing-related equipment buy/sell postings.

Surfing Tips, Talk & Gear
alt.surfing **M**

Surfers from California to Hawaii and Australia talk about their best waves, cool new gear, surf conditions, new waves to catch and other surfing-related stuff.

Sample Subjects:
Big wave scare at Kowie/Bodyboard prices

Swimming
rec.sport.swimming **M**

Useful group with good practical advice and technical pointers for active swimmers and competitors. Also contains good physical conditioning tips, resources and news of upcoming swimming events.

Table Tennis
rec.sport.table-tennis **L**

For college table tennis (Ping-Pong) tournament players.

FAQ ▶ The following FAQs are available via FTP from RTFM.MIT.EDU in the directory:
pub/usenet/rec.sport.table-tennis:
rec.sport.table-tennis_Frequently_Asked_Questions_(FAQ)_[Part_1_7]
rec.sport.table-tennis_Frequently_Asked_Questions_(FAQ)_[Part_2_7]

◀ *Bicycle racer, downloaded from* **wuarchive.wustl.edu** ▲ *Amateur bicycle racers, downloaded via Internet FTP from* **grind.isca.uiowa.edu**

rec.sport.table-tennis_Frequently_Asked_Questions_(FAQ)_[Part_3_7]
rec.sport.table-tennis_Frequently_Asked_Questions_(FAQ)_[Part_4_7]
rec.sport.table-tennis_Frequently_Asked_Questions_(FAQ)_[Part_5_7]
rec.sport.table-tennis_Frequently_Asked_Questions_(FAQ)_[Part_6_7]
rec.sport.table-tennis_Frequently_Asked_Questions_(FAQ)_[Part_7_7]

Bicycling

Bicycles & Cycling Gear

Bicycles have sure come a long way from that cute little Schwinn or the banana-seat model you pulled wheelies with as a kid. Bicycling-related groups on the Net cover the entire range of cycling interests, putting you in instant communication with thousands of fellow cycling enthusiasts from around the world—everything from favorite bicycle traffic accident stories to good "what-to-buy" cycling gear advice, cycling tour info and the latest news on racing events.

Bicycles for Sale/Wanted
rec.bicycles.marketplace **M**

Bicycles, gear and services for sale/wanted-to-buy; advice on availability, service and repair; and comments on various companies' products.

Bicycle Riding Workshop

rec.bicycles.misc

Good tips on riding technique, physical training, diet and nutrition for serious cyclists, care and treatment of injuries and general comments on cycling.

FAQ ▶ The following FAQs are available via FTP from RTFM.MIT.EDU in the directory: **pub/usenet/ rec.bicycles.misc:**
Rec.Bicycles_Frequently_Asked_Questions_Posting__Part_1_5
Rec.Bicycles_Frequently_Asked_Questions_Posting__Part_2_5
Rec.Bicycles_Frequently_Asked_Questions_Posting__Part_3_5
Rec.Bicycles_Frequently_Asked_Questions_Posting__Part_4_5
Rec.Bicycles_Frequently_Asked_Questions_Posting__Part_5_5

▲ *Tour de France bicycle race map, downloaded from* **wuarchive.wustl.edu** ▶ *Bicycle shop PIXAR computer graphic, downloaded via Internet FTP from* **grind.isca.uiowa.edu**

Bicycle Racing

rec.bicycles.racing **M**

Up-to-date news on racing results around the world, advice from participants on good racing techniques and schedules of organized events.

Bicycle Tours & Vacations

rec.bicycles.rides **M**

The latest info on bicycling tours and trips and comments on using bicycles for commuting and dealing with traffic.

Bicycle Advocacy

rec.bicycles.soc **M**

Social issues related to cycling, including comments by users on local/national cycling-related news and regulations, advocacy, conduct and manners of cyclists and drivers, road hazards and other comments, naturally, from a pro-cycling point of view.

Bicycle Repair & Performance

rec.bicycles.tech **HI**

Good tips on bike repair, performance/speed modifications and the latest advances in engineering and materials for high performance cycling gear.

ClariNet News Services

Sports Feature Stories
clari.sports.features

Top Sports News
clari.sports.top

Other Sports, Plus General Sports News
clari.sports.misc

Racing & Motor Sports
clari.sports.motor

Baseball Scores, Stories & Stats
clari.sports.baseball

Baseball Games & Box Scores
clari.sports.baseball.games

Basketball Coverage
clari.sports.basketball

College Basketball Coverage
clari.sports.basketball.college

NHL Coverage
clari.sports.hockey

Pro Football Coverage
clari.sports.football.college

Pro Football Coverage
clari.sports.football.college

The Olympic Games
clari.sports.olympic

Tennis News & Scores
clari.sports.tennis

Chapter 12: Local, University & International Newsgroups

The Internet is often touted as the global information superhighway, but there are also large numbers of Net newsgroups that are purely local in scope.

Local Connections for Net Citizens

On the Internet, a large number of newsgroups have been organized around cities, states, colleges and universities in "local nets," many of which have grown into sizeable newsgroups with large followings of their own.

You can use local metro Internet newsgroups in two ways. If you live in the city covered by the newsgroup, local Internet newsgroups give you access to online classifieds for selling used items, plus the opportunity to chat with other local residents online to discuss and debate local issues, news items and controversies and get access to online employment/help wanted listings. If you're from out of town, residents in these Net newsgroups can provide you with great tips on local restaurants, activities and places to see. Also, if you're thinking about relocating to a new city, that city's collection of local Internet newsgroups can be a good source of insider information on employment opportunities, good neighborhoods and other key aspects of moving to a new town.

University and College Internet Newsgroups

The origins of the Internet can be traced to colleges and universities across the U.S. Accordingly, large numbers of local university-based newsgroups are accessible on the Internet and their content and subject area reflects those of many locally oriented newsgroups. For example, most of these Internet university-based groups contain online classified advertising newsgroups, campus news and announcement newsgroups and even newsgroups for specific college courses. University-based groups can be another good way to soak up local color prior to a visit and can also be a good tool for high school seniors in their college search.

Laszlo and Andrea Kiss "met" on an Internet forum devoted to their home country, Hungary. From Japan, where he was conducting physics research, he transmitted to the forum a satirical essay on feminism; she, reading it from Purdue University, where she was working on a doctorate, responded with comments of her own. As Internet users often do, they then began exchanging electronic mail privately. Soon they discovered that they shared a deeply religious bent. They began courting—sometimes 10 messages a day flew across the Pacific. After exchanging photographs and $3,000 worth of phone calls, they decided to get married. "Everybody told me that we were mad," Laszlo recalled...."Without the Internet, it would not have happened." They now live in Sweden with their 5-month-old son and remain on "the net."

John Burgess, "Internet Creates A Computer Culture Of Remote Intimacy," *The Washington Post* (6/28/93)

Because of the increased need for reliable and timely information from the Commonwealth of Independent States (CIS), companies and individuals will try to formulate businesses and services to meet that need. The Internet is fast becoming a recognized and invaluable resource for many searchers.

Cynthia Schoenbrun, "From Russia, With Love: Unique Sources of Electronic Information on the Commonwealth of Independent States," *Database* (8/93)

International Newsgroups

Citizens of almost any country on Earth can find at least one newsgroup on the Net devoted to them. In most cases there are even hundreds of individual foreign-language newsgroups on the Internet devoted to a single country's interests, culture, news and social activities. For example, the **relcom.** newsgroups are the "Russian Internet," consisting of hundreds of Russian-language newsgroups for business connections, news, talk and online social activity.

In this Chapter of *What's on the Internet* we've covered many significant international and foreign-language groups, but, like everything else on the Internet, international newsgroups are expanding rapidly in number and scope: For every one newsgroup covered here, there may be dozens—or hundreds—more on the Net. See the Index and Chapter 14, "Newsgroup Alpha Directory," for listings of additional foreign-language newsgroups.

Local and International News Wire Feeds

ClariNet News Services are also available on the Internet, providing AP and Reuters news wire feeds for metro area and international news.

Metro Area U.S. Groups

Alaska News Talk Group
alt.culture.alaska **M**

Alaska residents and others discuss local Alaskan issues such as native rights, wildlife conservation and educational opportunities, including advice on how to make a living as a fisherman in Alaska.

Atlanta, GA: 1996 Olympics
atl.olympics **L**

News, info, events and ticket information for the 1996 Olympics in Atlanta, Georgia.

Atlanta, GA: General Info
atl.general **L**

Items for sale/wanted, local announcements and more for students and faculty of Georgia Tech and other Atlanta colleges.

Atlanta, GA: Help Wanted
atl.jobs **M**

Jobs wanted/available (full/part-time, mostly computer programming-related) for the Atlanta, Georgia, area.

Atlanta, GA: Resumes Online
atl.resumes **L**

Post your resume here for access by potential Atlanta-area employers.

Austin, TX: Classified Ads/For Sale
austin.forsale **M**

Merchandise of all kinds for sale or wanted in the Austin area. Computers, cars, bikes, airline tickets, etc.

Austin, TX: General Info & Announcements
austin.announce **L**

Contains general announcements relating to Austin newsgroups on the Net and news of local events in the Austin area.

Austin, TX: Local Chatter
austin.general **HI**

Austin residents swap tips on good local services and stores, look for roommates and share useful advice.

Austin, TX: Local News
austin.news **L**

Postings of local news and news discussions for Austin residents.

Boulder, CO: General Info & Classifieds
boulder.general **L**

Boulder, Colorado, residents talk about local news issues and controversies, post buy/sell listings and debate local politics.

Austin, TX: Music Events
austin.music **M**

News of Austin concerts and groups and other info on the Austin music scene.

Austin, TX: Politics
austin.politics **L**

Austin residents discuss local and national politics.

Austin, TX: Talk & Debate
austin.talk **L**

Heated debates about political correctness, gay/lesbian issues, etc.

Austin, TX: Telecommunications Issues
austin.eff **L**

News and information on emerging telecom and on electronic freedom, privacy and public policy issues.

What Every New California Resident Needs to Know
alt.california **M**

Even though U-Haul reports a larger number of moving vans leaving the state than arriving, you'd never know from the high amount of interest shown in this discussion group about California. A good place to post an inquiry or a question about California, whether you're interested in visiting or moving there. Useful advice from knowledgeable California residents. Comments relating to current California news, political issues in the state, tourist attractions and more. Also discussion about the California legislature, political issues relating to the state of California from a conservative point of view, a lot of talk about highways in California and the inside dope about living there. (For example, did you know that the reason some interstate highways in

California are six lanes wide is that they were intended to be used as emergency landing strips by B-52 bombers in the event of a war emergency?).

Sample Subjects:
California secession issue/Interstate exit numbers/ California/Moving to Bay Area/Housing needed/Car for sale/How much do hotels cost in Anaheim?

California Talk & Info: Environmental Activism
ca.environment **L**

Debate group for California-based environmental activists.

FAQ ▶ The following FAQs are available via FTP from RTFM.MIT.EDU in the directory:
pub/usenet/ca.environment:
Electric_Vehicles_FAQ_Part_1_3
Electric_Vehicles_FAQ_Part_2_3
Electric_Vehicles_FAQ_Part_3_3

California Talk & Info: General
ca.general **L**

Californians debate and complain about local news and political issues. Also features question-and-answer postings on most any subject.

California Talk & Info: Political Debate Group
ca.politics **M**

California Netters discuss hot local political issues, news items, and debate amongst themselves in usual Net fashion.

California Talk & Info: Earthquake News
ca.earthquakes **L**

Weekly earthquake activity reports from the USGS office at the California Institute of Technology, plus speculations by Netters. Should be *very* busy if the Big One comes.

California Talk & Info: Cars, Roads & Drivers
ca.driving **M**

California drivers discuss road issues, speeding tickets, accidents, insurance and the DMV.

Chicago, IL: General Info
chi.general **M**

Chicago locals discuss community news, the Bulls/Bears and good places to eat.

Chicago, IL: Classified Ads
chi.forsale **M**

Merchandise of all types—computers, electronics, musical instruments, cars and more—for sale in the Chicago area.

Chicago, IL: Consumer Referrals
chi.places **L**

Chicago residents trade advice on local businesses providing good service, based on their own personal experiences.

Chicago, IL: Local Weather Reports
chi.weather **L**

Excellent Chicago and vicinity weather forecasts posted throughout the day, from the National Weather Service.

Cleveland, OH: Sports Talk
cle.sports **HI**

Cleveland sports fanatics talk about the Browns, college teams and the Tribe.

San Diego, CA: for Sale
sdnet.forsale **M**

Online classifieds of used household items and vehicles for sale in the San Diego area.

Dallas/Fort Worth, TX: General Info
dfw.general **L**

Dallas/Fort Worth residents discuss national and local news items of interest.

San Luis Obispo, CA: Discussion & General Interest
slo.general **M**

General discussions and announcements of local events, primarily for students and residents near Cal Poly State University.

Detroit, MI: General Info
mi.misc **L**

Miscellaneous postings and announcements, mostly from students at the University of Michigan.

Seattle, WA: Talk Group
seattle.general **M**

Seattle residents actively debate and discuss local environmental, safety (gun control) and city planning issues and controversies in this popular group.

Michigan/Great Lakes Talk Group

alt.great-lakes **L**

Residents of Detroit, Michigan, and other areas around the Great Lakes of the Midwest discuss deer sightings, college sports and hockey.

Upstate New York: General Info

capdist.misc **L**

Inquiries, Q&A, and local info for residents of upstate New York towns and cities.

▲ *Locomotive "City of Los Angeles," downloaded via Internet FTP from Smithsonian photo archives at* **sunsite.unc.edu**

Florida: for Sale & General Info

fl.forsale **L**

A chat group, with for-sale listings for the Florida area.

Houston, TX: General Info & For Sale

houston.forsale **L**

Online classifieds offering merchandise (mostly computers and related equipment) for sale.

Texas: For Sale

tx.forsale **M**

Online classified ad listings of merchandise and vehicles for sale, primarily in and around major cities in Texas.

Huntsville, AL: General Info & For Sale

hsv.forsale **M**

For-sale listings offering used computers and merchandise in the Huntsville, Alabama, area.

Texas: General Info/Talk

tx.general **L**

Local residents (primarily in Austin and San Antonio) discuss good restaurants, local news, rumors, etc., in their areas.

Los Angeles, CA: General Info

la.general **M**

L.A. residents and University of Southern California students talk about local news items and controversies, exchange information and make

referrals on local attractions.

Los Angeles, CA: Merchandise for Sale

la.forsale **L**

Local listings of computers, cars, motorcycles, plane tickets, merchandise and more for sale/wanted in the L.A./Southern California area.

Los Angeles, CA: Restaurant Advice

la.eats **M**

L.A. residents offer their recommendations for best restaurants in and around the city—all-you-can-eat sushi, best blueberry pancakes, etc.

New Jersey: General Info

nj.general **M**

New Jersey Net residents swap info and answer questions on items of local interest—traffic laws, good local stores, etc.

FAQ ▶ The following FAQ is available via FTP from RTFM.MIT.EDU in the directory: **pub/usenet/nj.general:** Bookstores_in_New_York_City_(NYC)_List_(rec.arts.books)

New Orleans, LA: General Info

neworleans.general **L**

Announcements, general info and comments for New Orleans residents.

New York City: General Info/Discussion

nyc.general **M**

Eclectic talk group for New Yorkers.

▲ Statue of Liberty at dusk, photo downloaded via Internet FTP from **grind.isca.uiowa.edu**

Announcements of city events, social messages, for-sale listings and more. Good resource for tour, travel and "what's new" information.

New York State: For Sale
ny.forsale **M**

Online classified ad listings of merchandise for sale, posted by New York state and residents.

New York State: General Info & Discussion
ny.general **M**

New York residents from across the state engage in general discussions on state issues and the Internet.

Ontario, Canada: General Info
kw.general **M**

Events, messages and info for local residents and students from the University of Waterloo, Ontario, Canada.

Oregon: General Info & Discussions
or.general **M**

Oregon residents (mostly from Portland) discuss local news items and social activities in the area.

Pennsylvania: Discussion & General Info
pa.general **L**

Local residents (mostly from the Pittsburgh and Philadelphia areas) post local event announcements and discuss national news items.

Portland, OR: For Sale (Tektronix)
tek.forsale **L**

Online classifieds featuring a variety of items for sale, posted by employees of Tektronix Corporation who live in and around Portland, Oregon.

Research Triangle, NC: For Sale
triangle.forsale **M**

Active online classifieds with for-sale listings for computers, electronics, vehicles, appliances, etc., for the Raleigh, Durham, and Charlotte, North Carolina, Research Triangle area.

Research Triangle, NC: General Info & Talk
triangle.general **M**

Residents of the Research Triangle area (Raleigh, Durham, and Charlotte, North Carolina), engage in active, heated discussions on gun control, political correctness, and local area issues.

We Love Rhode Island Fan Club
alt.rhode_island **M**

An offbeat look at our nation's diminutive state, containing discussions about coffee milk, quahogs and other items and places of interest to Rhode Islanders and expatriates.

SF/Bay Area Newsgroups

SF/Bay Area, CA: Announcements & Local Events
ba.announce **L**

Active postings of general and special-interest club events, classes, social activities and support group events in the San Francisco Bay Area.

SF/Bay Area, CA: Autos & Trucks for Sale
ba.market.vehicles **M**

Cars, trucks, parts and accessories wanted/for sale in the Bay Area.

SF/Bay Area, CA: Classifieds
ba.market.misc **HI**

Online classified ads listing a wide variety of merchandise for sale/wanted. Cars, stereos, bikes, tickets, etc.

SF/Bay Area, CA: Commercial & Amateur Radio Events
ba.broadcast **L**

Combination newsgroup for ham radio enthusiasts and postings of local radio station events and concerts.

SF/Bay Area, CA: Computers for Sale
ba.market.computers **M**

Many listings of items for sale/wanted for all brands of

▲ *San Francisco skyline, downloaded via Internet FTP from* **grind.isca.uiowa.edu** ▲ *Golden Gate Bridge, downloaded via Internet FTP from* **wuarchive.wustl.edu**

used computers, peripherals, boards, etc. in the Bay Area.

SF/Bay Area, CA: Gay Info
ba.market.motss **HI**

News and talk for gays and lesbians.

SF/Bay Area, CA: Help Wanted (Misc.)
ba.jobs.misc **M**

Companies post (mostly) computer-oriented job openings for the Bay Area.

SF/Bay Area, CA: Help Wanted & Employment
ba.jobs.offered **M**

Active newsgroup featuring extensive help wanted listings in the Bay Area, mostly in the computer and electronics fields.

SF/Bay Area, CA: Hill Residents
ba.mountain-folk **L**

Residents who live in the hills around San Francisco and the Bay Area swap stories and tips about home repairs, fire issues and local government.

SF/Bay Area, CA: Houses & Apartments for Rent
ba.market.housing **M**

Listings of apartment and house rentals, rooms available and wanted, etc. in the Bay Area.

SF/Bay Area, Ca: Internet Access
ba.internet **M**

Postings of services providing access to the Internet and tech questions and answers.

SF/Bay Area, CA: Internet Usage
ba.news.stats **L**

Contains usage data for various Bay Area Internet links.

SF/Bay Area, CA: Local Color
ba.general **M**

Bay Area residents discuss most anything, trading tips on local hot spots, laws, activities, etc. Good place for prospective visitors and potential residents.

FAQ ▶ The following FAQs are available via FTP from RTFM.MIT.EDU in the directory:
pub/usenet/ba.general:
Bookstores_in_San_Francisco_Bay_Area_(SF)_List_(rec.arts.books)
Fair_and_Festival_Weekly_Posting
[l_m_1_29_93]_How_to_cancel_news_articles
[l_m_6_1_92]_A_short_note_on_posting,_cross-posting
[l_m_8_31_93]_Reminders_for_old_hands_and_new_readers_([blc]a.general)

SF/Bay Area, CA: Local News Talk
ba.politics **L**

Intense, polarized discussions of national and local political and current events by Bay Area residents.

SF/Bay Area, Ca: Local Transportation Issues
ba.transportation **L**

Heated political debate on various car, subway and airport-related Bay Area transportation controversies.

SF/Bay Area, CA: Motorcycles
ba.market.motorcycles **M**

Bay Area motorcycle enthusiasts trade tips

and riding advice, post bikes wanted and for-sale listings.

SF/Bay Area, CA: Music Scene
ba.music **M**

Concert info, tickets wanted/for sale, auditions, equipment and other music-related news of interest to Bay Area residents.

SF/Bay Area, CA: Restaurant Reviews
ba.food **M**

Bay Area residents swap tips on their favorite eating places in this popular discussion group.

SF/Bay Area, CA: Seminars, Meetings & Events
ba.seminars **L**

Postings of announcements for local seminars, club meetings, support groups and academic events of interest to Bay Area residents.

SF/Bay Area, CA: Singles
ba.singles **HI**

Singles chat and plan events in the Bay Area.

SF/Bay Area, CA: Sporting Events
ba.sports **L**

Postings of local sporting events, games and activities.

SF/Bay Area, Ca: Weather Reports
ba.weather **L**

Excellent, up-to-date daily and extended weather forecasts for the Bay Area, California and the U.S.

University Groups

MIT Regional Newsgroup: Housing Wanted
athena.misc **L**

Apartments and housing for rent/wanted for Massachusetts Institute of Technology students and faculty.

Ohio State University: For Sale
osu.for-sale **L**

Ohio State University students and local residents post a wide variety of used household items and vehicles for sale.

Stanford University: Events
su.events **L**

Listings of seminars, workshops and other activities at the campus of Stanford University.

Berkeley: University Events
uc.general **L**

Local campus announcements and talk for the University of California at Berkeley.

Berkeley: General Info & Talk
ucb.general **L**

Local residents in and around the Berkeley, California area talk about local and national issues—local socialists meet the rebukes of area conservatives.

University of Maryland: Info & Talk
um.general **L**

Local talk, inquiries and consumer info for students at the University of Maryland.

University of Minnesota: Info & Talk
umn.general.misc **L**

Talk group for students at the University of Minnesota in Minneapolis/St. Paul.

University of Toronto: Info & Talk
ut.general **M**

General announcements and for-sale listings for students at the University of Toronto, Canada.

University of Waterloo: Info & Talk
uw.general **M**

Local talk group for students at the University of Waterloo, Ontario, Canada.

University of Wisconsin: For Sale
uwisc.forsale **L**

Items for sale by University of Wisconsin students.

Marquette University: Talk
wi.general **L**

Talk group for students at Marquette University in Milwaukee, Wisconsin.

ClariNet News—Local

Various Local Headline Summaries
clari.local.headlines

Local News (New York City)
clari.local.nyc

Stories Datelined San Francisco Bay Area
clari.local.sfbay

Main Stories for the SF Bay Area
clari.sfbay.general

Shorter General Items for the SF Bay Area
clari.sfbay.misc

Very Short Items for the SF Bay Area
clari.sfbay.short

Stories from Fire Depts. of the SF Bay Area
clari.sfbay.fire

SF Bay Area & California Weather Reports
clari.sfbay.weather

Reports from Caltrans & the CHP
clari.sfbay.roads

Reviews & Entertainment News for the SF Bay Area
clari.sfbay.entertain

Twice Daily News Roundups for the SF Bay Area
clari.sfbay.briefs

Stories from the Police Depts. of the SF Bay Area
clari.sfbay.police

International Newsgroups

Australian Newsgroups: Amateur Radio
aus.radio **L**

Signal condition reports and other info of interest to Australian ham radio enthusiasts.

FAQ ▶ The following FAQs are available via FTP from RTFM.MIT.EDU in the directory:
pub/usenet/aus.radio:
Daily_IPS_Report_-_10_Oct_93
Daily_IPS_Report_-_11_Oct_93
Daily_IPS_Report_-_12_Oct_93
Weekly_IPS_Report_-_10_Sep_93
Weekly_IPS_Report_-_15_Oct_93
Weekly_IPS_Report_-_17_Sep_93
Weekly_IPS_Report_-_24_Sep_93
Weekly_IPS_Report_-__8_Oct_93

Australian Newsgroups: Amiga Computers
aus.computers.amiga **L**

Active discussion group with plentiful tech and troubleshooting info on Amiga and other Commodore computers for Aussie owners and enthusiasts.

Australian Newsgroups: Aussie Jokes & Humor
aus.jokes **M**

Aussies love a bawdy joke, as shown in this very popular newsgroup. Check it out for an interesting taste of Down Under humor!

Australian Newsgroups: Australia Politics
aus.politics **M**

Heated debates about current events, economic conditions and society in Australia.

Australian Newsgroups: Australian News and Talk
aus.general **HI**

Australians discuss national news issues of the day, government policies and politics.

Australian Newsgroups: Bicycling
aus.bicycling **L**

Buy/sell listings, bicyclist's tips, events and other cycling-related info of interest to bicyclists Down Under. Good if you're planning a cycling vacation in Australia.

Australian Newsgroups: China Culture
aus.culture.china **L**

News digests and telecom development issues posted by Chinese students.

Australian Newsgroups: Classifieds/For Sale
aus.forsale **M**

Mostly computer, peripherals and electronic gear buy/sell listings posted by Net users in major Australian cities.

Australian Newsgroups: Computers
aus.computers **L**

Miscellaneous discussions related to personal computers and tech questions/tips for Australian PC users.

Australian Newsgroups: Films
aus.films **L**

Australian film fans discuss American films and movie theater technology.

Australian Newsgroups: Flames Galore!
aus.flame **M**

A funny, active and interesting newsgroup. Learn Australian cuss words and flame phrases as Aussie Netters go at it.

Australian Newsgroups: Games
aus.games **L**

For players of sci-fi and role-playing games in Australia.

Australian Newsgroups: FAQs & General Information
aus.aarnet **L**

Informational newsgroup containing FAQs of interest to new users of very active Net newsgroup access throughout Australia.

Australian Newsgroups: Help Wanted
aus.jobs **M**

Job opportunity postings for (mostly) computer-related and academic positions in Australia and East Asia.

Australian Newsgroups: Hi-Fi Enthusiasts
aus.hi-fi **L**

For Aussie owners and enthusiasts of high-end audio, CDs, and stereo.

Australian Newsgroups: Information Wanted
aus.wanted **L**

Group for exchange of information on just about anything: consumer products, household hints, etc.

Australian Newsgroups: Macintosh User Group
aus.mac **L**

Hardware, software and peripherals discussion group for Mac/PowerBook/Newton users in Australia.

Australian Newsgroups: Motorcycles
aus.motorcycles **L**

Aussie Harley, BMW, motocross and other bike enthusiasts swap bike talk and tips.

Australian Newsgroups: PC/Compatible Computers
aus.computers.ibm-p **L**

Tech tips, info and troubleshooting for Australian-based owners of PCs, compatibles and software.

Australian Newsgroups: Pop Music
aus.music **M**

Australian rock and alternative music fans discuss their favorite (mostly Australian) performers, bands and albums.

FAQ ▶ The following FAQs are available via FTP from RTFM.MIT.EDU in the directory:
pub/usenet/aus.music:
CHART:_The_ARIA_top_60_singles_chart_-_Australia_(15_10_93)
CHART:_The_ARIA_top_60_singles_chart_-_Australia_(17_9_93)
CHART:_Top_10_albums_->_Australia_(15_10_93)
CHART:_Top_10_albums_->_Australia_(17_9_93)
CHART:_Top_10_albums_->_Australia_(1_10_93)

Australian Newsgroups: Railroad Enthusiasts
aus.rail **L**

Fans and riders of various railroads in Australia discuss favorite trains, equipment stories, rides, etc.

Australian Newsgroups: Role-Playing Games
aus.games.roleplay **L**

For players of Dungeons & Dragons-style strategy games.

Australian Newsgroups: Science Fiction
aus.sf **L**

Aussies discuss favorite science fiction games, books and movies.

Australian Newsgroups: Sex
aus.sex **L**

A rather tame group for discussions by Australians on the subject of sex.

Australian Newsgroups: Ski Reports
aus.snow **L**

Skiers and hikers report the latest ski conditions in Australia and New Zealand.

Australian Newsgroups: Sports
aus.sport **L**

Get the latest on the Perth Wildcats, Canberra Cannons and Adelaide 36ers on this active newsgroup for talk of all Aussie sporting activities—soccer, rugby, etc.

Australian Newsgroups: *Star Trek*
aus.star-trek **M**

Trekkers from Down Under discuss all aspects of Trekiana: the TV series, the movies, Trek tech, fan club, rumors, etc.

Australian Newsgroups: Statistics
aus.stats.s **L**

Australian students discuss various statistical problems and statistical applications software.

Australian Newsgroups: Telecommunications
aus.comms **L**

Technical-oriented newsgroup all about modems and data communications services of interest to Aussie Net users.

FAQ ▶ The following FAQs are available via FTP from RTFM.MIT.EDU in the directory:
pub/usenet/aus.comms:
The_NetComm_Modem_FAQ_v1.1
The_NetComm_Modem_FAQ_v1.2

Britain: General Info & Talk
uk.misc **HI**

United Kingdom-based talk group for all kinds of discussions of local news items, inquiries and chatter of interest, mostly to city dwellers in the U.K.

Britain: Media Talk
uk.media **L**

Brits discuss their national newspapers and television services from their own culture's conservative and liberal points of view.

Britain: Political Talk Group
uk.politics **HI**

Intense and highly polarized discussions of U.K. politics and legal issues. Topics include gun control, drug legalization and privatizing U.K. government functions.

Britain: Singles Chat Group
uk.singles **M**

Long-winded and rather dull chat group for British singles.

BC, Canada: Local Weather
bc.weather **HI**

Updated coastal and inland daily and extended weather forecasts for the British Columbia, Canada, area.

BC, Canada: Talk & News Group
bc.general **L**

Eclectic chat group for all kinds of local British Columbia events and announcements, local news discussions and debate.

Canada News & Info: French-Speaking Group
can.francais **L**

French-speakers' group covering a wide variety of subjects of interest to residents of Quebec, Canada.

Canada News & Info: General News Talk
can.general **M**

Heated discussions of local and national Canadian political issues.

Canada News & Info: Help Wanted
can.jobs **L**

Online classifieds for computer programming-related positions available and positions wanted.

Canada News & Info: Internet
can.canet.stats **M**

Technical group containing postings of Internet usage and network traffic statistics for Canada and provinces.

Canada News & Info: Internet Access
can.uucp.maps **L**

Extensive files listing Internet access sites in Canada, plus tech info connecting sites to the Internet using IP.

Canada News & Info: Political Discussion
can.politics **HI**

Polite political debate and discussion by Canadians on political and news issues. Tame compared to similar U.S. Net newsgroups.

Chinese Students' Discussion Group
alt.chinese.txt **L**

A Chinese-language online discussion group with many participants from universities in China.

Chinese Students' Discussion Group II
alt.chinese.text.big5 **HI**

Another Chinese-language discussion group.

FAQ ▶ The following FAQ is available via FTP from RTFM.MIT.EDU in the directory:
pub/usenet/alt.chinese.text.big5:
Chinese_BIG5_environment:_FAQ_of_alt.chinese.text.big5

Conversational French Language Chat Group

alt.nick.sucks **L**

An informal online French-language discussion group on a variety of subjects relating to places of interest, food and sports.

Japanese Culture & Language Q&A

alt.japanese.text **L**

In this (mostly) Japanese language newsgroup, participants discuss current news events in Japan. Even though most of the communications in this group are in unreadable Kanji characters (requiring special software to make them appear on your PC screen), some of the postings are in English, making this group a useful resource if you have any questions relating to Japanese language or culture.

London, England: General Info

lon.misc **L**

Local info and announcements from residents and students at the University of London.

New Zealand: General Info & Discussion

nz.general **M**

New Zealanders discuss national political issues, kangaroo meat (we're serious!) and many of the usual Net flaming issues.

Netherlands Net

nlnet.misc **HI**

Dutch-language general Net discussion group based in the Netherlands.

Norway Net

no.general **M**

Norwegian-language general discussion and social group, based in Norway.

Ontario, Canada: General Info & Discussions

ont.general **M**

General news talk and current events discussions for the Ontario, Canada area.

▲ *Winston Churchill U.S. commemorative stamp, downloaded from* **grind.isca.uiowa.edu**

Ottawa, Canada: Discussion & General Info

ott.general **L**

Active and informative discussion group in the Ottawa, Canada, area, covering a broad range of local and general informative topics.

Sweden: Info/Talk Group

swnet.general **L**

A Swedish-language general-interest discussion group.

Switzerland: European Particle Physics Lab

cern.computing **M**

Computer center and seminar announcements for the CERN European Lab for Particle Physics in Switzerland.

Toronto, Canada: General Talk & Info

tor.general **M**

Local talk group, consumer advice and local hotspots for residents in and around the Toronto, Canada, area.

ClariNet News—International

Almanac, Ottawa Special, Arts
clari.canada.features

Canadian Business Summaries
clari.canada.biz

Crimes, the Courts & the Law
clari.canada.law

Government Related News (All Levels)
clari.canada.gov

Mishaps, Accidents & Serious Problems
clari.canada.trouble

Political & Election Items
clari.canada.politics

Regular Newscast for Canadians
clari.canada.newscast

Short Items on Canadian News Stories
clari.canada.general

Chapter 13: Off the Wall, Singles & Adult

Here are all the offbeat, tasteless, strange and out-of-bounds newsgroups we could find— and what a weird place it is! There are newsgroups for UFO abductees, Spam lovers, cross-dressers and tattoo fetishists. This is also the place you'll find the adult, singles and sexually oriented newsgroups.

Many of the Internet's most freewheeling newsgroups owe their very existence to a rebellion against censorship. In 1987, Bay Area programmer John Gilmore and some friends wanted a forum for discussion of drug policy, but were blockaded by the "Backbone Cabal," as the informal, slightly secretive group of network administrators was known at the time. So Gilmore started a new category of newsgroups, known as the "alt" group, now one of the busiest in the system.

Lee Gomes, "Internet Wasteland Communication," *Dallas Morning News* (5/31/93)

According to *Wired* Magazine, May 1993 readership of the newsgroup misc.jobs.offered tied with alt.sex at 190,000 readers each.

Off The Wall

The Grossest Jokes on the Planet
alt.tasteless **HI**

The most downright, down and dirty, hilarious newsgroups on the Net are **alt.tasteless** and **alt.tasteless.jokes**. We're ashamed to admit that we laughed until we had tears in our eyes at some of the material posted here (most of it too scatological to excerpt in print). What can we say?—in **alt.tasteless.jokes**, participants tell their grossest and more pungent jokes, and in **alt.tasteless**, Netters share commentaries on current events, interesting (but obscene) news items, personal observations and miscellany from an utterly depraved perspective. Some of this writing has to be read to be believed!

Sample Subjects:
Ground horse/Rabbits eating fecal droppings/Gopher hunting/Why pick on Barney?

FAQ ▶ The following FAQ is available via FTP from RTFM.MIT.EDU in the directory:
pub/usenet/alt.tasteless:
Welcome_to_alt.tasteless!_(Monthly_Posting)

Online Watering Hole
alt.callahans **HI**

If there ever could be the online equivalent to a local neighborhood bar, this would be it! Think of it as an electronic gathering place for good humor, socializing and general banter. The difference between this being an online bar and a real one is that here you won't get a hangover the next day.

Sample Subjects:
The big day!/Assorted silliness/Hello to all/Ocelot goes to London

How to Set Up A Pirate Radio Station
alt.radio.pirate **M**

Holding true to the individualistic and somewhat anarchistic nature of Net culture, wouldn't you know that there's a very active newsgroup about pirate radio stations. For those of you who are daring enough to attempt this illegal activity and who have a knack for homegrown electronics, you'll find everything you need: advice on how to set up a pirate radio station, comments on existing pirate radio stations in various cities and, of course, the necessary talk about the legality of such operations. An interesting and fun-to-read discussion group showing that there are many people who have a strong desire to broadcast their own views and information.

Sample Subjects:
NYC free radio workshop/Seattle area stations/FM kits

▲ *Artist rendering of UFO over mountain, downloaded via Internet FTP from* **grind.isca.uiowa.edu**

UFOs & Alien Visitors
alt.alien.visitors **HI**

An offbeat group for discussions and speculations about aliens, ancient civilizations, UFOs and other phenomena.

Sample Subjects:
Nixon meets a spaceman/Nuclear holocaust/How does a UFO operate?/Pyramids=Aliens?/Alien bases on dark side of moon/Martian structures

When You've Had A Very Bad Day
alt.angst **M**

Feeling agitated? Need to blow off some steam? Need to hear calming voices on the Net? This group's for you! Spirited, off-the-edge chatter about life's phobias, daily complaints, impending birthdays and anything else that's bugging you.

Weird Talk
alt.basement.graveyard **L**

Just can't understand this one: Seems to be a group where people talk about dying and coming back from the dead.

People Who Like Breakfast Cereal
alt.cereal **L**

Would you believe there is actually a discussion group all about breakfast cereal on the Net? Of course there is! Participants here wax eloquently about their breakfast cereal experiences (for whatever that's worth). One gets the feeling that the subject of cereal here is just a cover for the usual online banter that goes on endlessly over the Net.

Sample Subjects:

Cat food? Yum/Hot and sticky/I hate Shredded Wheat/I want my Pop Tarts/Space aliens ate my Pop Tarts

People Who Like Radioactive Stuff

alt.cesium **M**

College students discuss cesium. We don't know why they're doing it, but they seem to like it. Probably another excuse for blowing off steam over the Net.

Sample Subjects:
Tons of cesium

Cow Collectibles

alt.cows.moo.moo.moo **M**

A cute little discussion group for people who like to decorate their rooms with pictures of cows, wear cow T-shirts and talk about cows. If that's you, you'll be very *moooved!*

Create Your Own Conspiracy Theory

alt.discordia **HI**

Is Microsoft a tool of an international conspiracy of Freemasons? Did the world end on May 18th, 1993? Join Lee Harvey Oswald, Jesus Christ on XTC and other off-the-wall characters in discussions of offbeat conspiracy theories, bioenergy and other offbeat subjects.

Drug Legalization Advocacy Group

alt.drugs **HI**

Visiting this group, you would think it was still 1968 and not the 1990s. Many discussions relating to using drugs, manufacturing drugs and growing drugs. Also discussions of recent current events related to the war on drugs and drug enforcement activities. Obviously, participants in this newsgroup take a permissive view of drug use, so don't be offended if you feel otherwise. Topics range from LSD manufacture to marijuana growing techniques and recent DEA drug busts.

Sample Subjects:
LSD synthesis/Is marijuana psychedelic?

FAQ ▶ The following FAQs are available via FTP from RTFM.MIT.EDU in the directory:
pub/usenet/alt.drugs:
FTP_INSTRUCTIONS_(biweekly_post)
natural_highs_faq
[l_m_10_30_92]_ADDRESSES_FAQ_(biweekly_post)
[l_m_10_5_93]_NATURAL_HIGHS_FAQ_(biweekly_post)
[l_m_6_5_92]_NATURAL_HIGHS_FAQ_(biweekly_post)
_Blue_Star__LSD-laced_tattoo_transfer_rumor_FAQ

Coffee Talk Mild & Wild

alt.drugs.caffeine **M**

Off-the-wall coffee lovers chat about their favorite hot beverage. Topics range from favorite brands of exotic bean blends, to caffeine in its more pharmaceutical forms (Vivarin or No-Doz). At this extreme, it starts reading like a coffee addict's worst nightmare.

▲ *Jolt Cola bottlecap, downloaded via Internet FTP from* **ftp.sunet.se**

Sample Subjects:
Favorite coffee/Kicking the habit/Caffeine in chocolate/Vivarin or No-Doze

Out-Of-Body & Paranormal Experiences Group

alt.out-of-body **M**

Had an out-of-body experience lately? Serious discussion here about out-of-body experiences and similar New Age topics. Not for us to say if all of this is for real, but this group provides useful and intriguing speculation on the subject for those of you who are interested.

Sample Subjects:
Astral friends/Monroe out-of-body technique/Losing astral ability?

UFO Abductees Discussion Group

alt.perinet.abduct **L**

This newsgroup is for believers and speculators on the subject of alien UFO abductions. Participants describe their alleged UFO abduction experiences and are willing to invest considerable time in attempting to explain how and why alien UFO abductions occur (that is, *if* they occur). Comments also cover a range of conspiracy theories involving top members of the U.S. government, the NSA and the military. Whether or not you believe in all this, it does make for interesting reading.

Sample Subjects:
Abductee questionnaires/Abduction explanation/Intelligence behind it all/The controllers

UFO Skeptics Discussions

alt.perinet.skeptic **L**

Have gray men from outer space visited our planet? Or are flying saucers just a part of the delusion of crowds? This online group is for skeptics on the UFO issue, featuring debate on why and how UFOs could not exist. It gets far less usage than the UFO-oriented group (which already tells you where most people on the Net stand). Worth a look from time to time, because it helps cool off some of the hot speculation occurring in many of the far more active UFO advocate groups on the Net.

Sample Subjects:
Ball lightning/Hoaxes with mostess/ Skeptic news

UFOs & Aliens: News, Talk and Speculation

alt.perinet.ufo **L**

One of the biggest groups on the Net for discussions on UFOs, flying saucers and related phenomena. Discussion and extensive speculation on present and past UFO sightings, historical UFO information and alleged government cover-ups. No matter how you feel about UFOs, you have to give participants in this group credit for their dedication to gathering and communicating this information on the Net. All in all, a fascinating and intriguing online discussion group. Recent topics have included discussions on a UFO hoax on Long Island, New York, revelations on government cover-up policies and procedures and excerpts from UFO publications.

Sample Subjects:
How does a UFO operate?/Kids and UFOs/Center for UFO studies/Government cover stories/U.K. sighting

ESP & Paranormal Events Talk

alt.paranormal **M**

Online discussions of ESP, paranormal phenomenan, and mind-over-matter issues. Recent topics have included mind-oriented pain relief, ESP in pregnancy and notices of upcoming parapsychology conferences.

Sample Subjects:
Learning mind over body/About pain tolerance

Party News & Talk from Around the World

alt.party **M**

If you want to find out about parties in Finland or acid rooms in Berlin, this is the place. A small but intense discussion group featuring talk about party-

▲ *Zippy the Pinhead, downloaded via Internet FTP from* **wuarchive.wustl.edu**

ing, parties around the world and miscellaneous banter by people who like to party.

Tell Us Your Pet Peeves

alt.peeves **HI**

Feeling a little P.O.'ed about something lately? Want to get something off your chest? **alt.peeves** is a busy, humorous repository of funny personal experiences, opinions and reactions to life's little speed bumps. Entertaining write-ups by people about their personal experiences. Recent comments include long discourses about experiences with credit cards, waiting in line, mothers and babies and the battle of the sexes.

Sample Subjects:
Swindling car dealers!/Bean counter peeve/Cry over spilled milk/Knee deep in the Mississippi/Sandles

Cascade "Poetry" & Ramblings

alt.cosuard **M**

Netters post satirical "cascades," a form of amateurish and insipid indented-format verse that is exclusively a product of the Net. Interspersed between poems are funny comments, scanned pictures and graphics created with ASCII text characters.

Elvis Sightings

alt.elvis.sighting **L**

Seen The King lately? Netters attempt to outdo one another with their funniest Elvis-sighting stories. This group is also an excuse for Netters to post their own wild, tongue-in-cheek Elvis stories and speculations.

More Hacker Flames

alt.fan.john-palmer **M**

Flamers' group for avid Net hackers.

"Bash Bill Gates" Group

alt.fan.bill-gates **L**

From its name, you would think this would be an online fan club for Bill Gates and Microsoft. Well, it's not—it's really an online gathering spot for anyone with a beef against Bill Gates and/or Microsoft. Plenty of lively discussion, odd speculations and catty remarks about the richest man in America.

Sample Subjects:
Bill's happy household/Microsoft and the illumati/Bill's traffic ticket

More Weird Theories

alt.slack **HI**

Far-out but popular newsgroup related to some of the other offbeat groups in the alt. category, **alt.slack** picks up on such weirdness as "Microsoft: a Masonic Conspiracy?" and "Barney the Dinosaur Worship."

Hallucinogenic Drugs Discussion Group

alt.psychoactives **M**

Talk on a wide range of synthetic and natural substances that are supposed to enhance mental ability, as well as better-known drugs such as marijuana and LSD. Participants also relate their experiences with so-called "smart" drugs and trade their own tips and referrals. Topics include discussion and debate on organic brain function-enhancing substances and holdover drugs from the 1960s, such as LSD and Peyote.

Sample Subjects:
Bio-energy/LSD dosages/DMAE-H3 experience

Practical Jokes: Stories & Tips

alt.shenanigans **M**

Definitely the place to go if you've just pulled off a major practical joke. Net participants relate their latest, biggest practical joke, stunt, trick or revenge technique. Recent topics and stories have included bachelor party pranks, tricks with telephones, how to catch a thief and U.S. Postal Service shenanigans told by such Net characters as Danno, Rude Boy, Lazlo Nibble and Thunderthumbs.

Sample Subjects:
To catch a thief/Teasing single guys/Stereo shenanigans

FAQ ▶ The following FAQ is available via FTP from RTFM.MIT.EDU in the directory:
pub/usenet/alt.shenanigans:
alt.shenanigans_-_FAQ_and_guidelines_for_posting

Spam Fan Club

alt.spam **L**

Wouldn't you know it, but there is even a place to go on the Net to talk about everybody's favorite mystery

▲ *Lee Harvey Oswald, downloaded via Internet FTP from* **ftp.netcom.com**

meat. Participants describe their personal experiences with Spam in all of its variations including Army Spam, Spam Sushi (evidently a popular item in Hawaii) and other tasty Spam recipes.

Stories About "Roommates from Hell"

alt.flame.roommate **M**

A mutual support group for people who have just gotten rid of their roommates from hell: Disgruntled tenants (mostly college and graduate students) bitch about their worst experiences with roommates.

Sample Subjects:
Roommates who don't do dishes/Roommate table manners/Roommates, who needs them anyway?

FAQ ▶ The following FAQ is available via FTP from RTFM.MIT.EDU in the directory:
pub/usenet/alt.flame.roommate:
The_ALT.FLAME.ROOMMATE_FAQ!!!

Thrash Music

alt.thrash **M**

Alternative, bummed-out rock music discussion group for burnouts who like thrash music. With groups having names like Pungent Stench, Atrocity, Carcass and "God Flesh," you probably already know what to expect here.

Parents' "I Hate Barney" Group

alt.barney.dinosaur.die.die.die **HI**

Participants dream up many novel (and unprintable) punishments for the popular PBS weenie-in-a-dinosaur-suit. Just about everyone here is in agreement about their contempt for public television's favorite dinosaur. Feel free to join in if you agree or even if you must defend your lumpy purple friend!

Sample Subjects:
Barney IS Rush Limbaugh/Toddler dies while watching *Barney*/Barney unmasked

Skinheads & Hate Groups

alt.skinheads **HI**

Group consisting mainly of angry young men who are generally pro-skinhead, which makes this group a pretty frightening one to read.

FAQ ▶ The following FAQ is available via FTP from RTFM.MIT.EDU in the directory:
pub/usenet/alt.skinheads:
F:_S_(a.m.s)_F_A_Q

Crazy Evangelist Stalks the Net

alt.brother-jed **M**

In this group a crazy evangelist named Brother Jed holds forth, chastising other Net participants. Brother Jed's over-the-top version of fire and brimstone preaching is not for everybody (in fact, it's made him a famous Net laughingstock).

All Hail Kibo!

alt.religion.kibology **HI**

A very active group of people, followers of a God named Kibo (who, in mortal form, is one James Parry, a 26-year-old graphic designer living in Boston). Actually, there isn't anything religious about this group at all, just a silly excuse for people to joke online, advance their own comical pet theories and post articles about UFO abductions and space aliens typed in from tabloid newspapers at the grocery store checkout.

Satirical Looks at Satanism

alt.evil **HI**

Participants discuss and debate the meaning and definition of evil in modern society. A mixture of serious discussion and satire make this group a way for amateur philosophers to spend many hours in endless, semi-serious discussion.

Sample Subjects:
Definition of evil/Atheism/Satan/Problem of the good

Zen & the Art of Parody

alt.buddha.short.fat.guy **L**

This newsgroup is what happens when you put several hundred Generation X-ers in an online discussion group to talk about religion, Zen and the art of humor. It seems like half of this group wants to know more about Buddhism and the other half wants to make fun of it. The result is a bizarre mix of Zen philosophy and satire. There is a slight possibility that those of you interested in finding out more about Zen might be able to get questions answered here.

Sample Subjects:
Following the ox/Taoist apocalypse/A random poem

FAQ ▶ The following FAQs are available via FTP from RTFM.MIT.EDU in the directory:
pub/usenet/alt.buddha.short.fat.guy:
alt.buddha.short.fat.guy_Frequently_Asked_Questions_(FAQ)_1_of_2
alt.buddha.short.fat.guy_Frequently_Asked_Questions_(FAQ)_2_of_2

Consciousness, Time, Reality & Space Discussions

alt.consciousness **M**

Discussion on issues relating to consciousness, intelligence, reality, time and space, where Net participants promote their own pet theories.

Sample Subjects:
Start of consciousness/Objective reality?/Absolute zero theory

How to Interpret Your Dreams

alt.dreams **M**

Had an interesting, unusual or disturbing dream lately? Do you believe your dreams can predict your future? Need help interpreting a recent dream? That's what this discussion group is for! Very active group where people

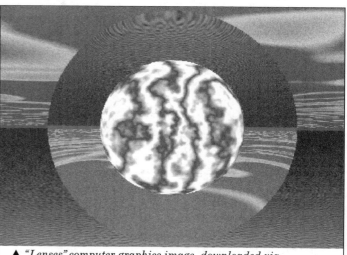

▲ *"Lenses" computer graphics image, downloaded via Internet FTP from* **wuarchive.wustl.edu**

post descriptions of their recent dreams and others engage in online interpretations and analysis of those dreams. A fun, interesting and insightful discussion group.

Sample Subjects:
Interested in your dreams/Falling and flying/My dreams are back

Lucid Dreams Talk Group

alt.dreams.lucid **M**

Participants discuss and analyze recent dreams and comment on various devices purported to induce dreams and altered states of consciousness.

Personality & IQ Tests Discussion Group

alt.psychology.personality **M**

Newsgroup participants discuss ins, outs and ramifications of various administered psychological personality tests such as handwriting and IQ tests. Participants also describe their own personal experiences and observations in taking, administering and evaluating these kinds of personality tests and add in their own speculations and assessments on various psychological traits profiled in such tests.

Sample Subjects:
Mind over body (really?)/Handwriting/MBTI test available as Hypercard

Assisted Suicide Group

alt.suicide.holiday **M**

A thoroughly depressing place where bummed-out Net participants go to talk about their problems and contemplate the unthinkable. Also contains comments from "right-to-die" followers and Hemlock Society people.

FAQ ▶ The following FAQs are available via FTP from RTFM.MIT.EDU in the directory:
pub/usenet/alt.suicide.holiday:
alt.suicide.holiday_periodic_Methods_File_posting_(FAQ,_sort_of)
Periodic_Methods_File_posting_(alt.suicide.holiday_FAQ,_sort_of)

Only the Lonely

alt.whine **L**

You guessed it! A small group of Net singles moan and groan about missing their Significant Others ("SOs" in Net lingo). If you don't have somebody to cry about, this group is probably not for you.

How You Tell When It's Time to "Get a Life"

alt.religion.monica **M**

This group is what happens when too many computer programmers work too long with too little rest. A comical religion, based on a (possibly) real-life, tanned beauty named Monica, who was once spotted playing volleyball at the Santa Monica Beach Pier. Obsessed followers of this religion use it as a pretext for endless wisecracks and other humorous endeavors.

The World of Underground Magazines

alt.zines **M**

Over the past several years, there has been an explosion of independently produced, very small circulation, special (and sometimes cult-oriented) magazines ('zines). This newsgroup gives you an eye-opening look at this exciting publishing phenomenon where just about anyone with an attitude and a Xerox machine can become a 'zine publisher. 'Zines cover the entire horizon of human and cultural interests, from horror comics to revolution to science fiction, environmentalism, poetry, technology and the absurd. Contains tips and info, and (sometimes) free 'zines, as well as comments on this exciting grassroots publishing movement.

Sample Subjects:
Militant Vegans Unite!/E 'zines archive/Cyber magazines

Nudism & Naturism

rec.nude **HI**

Another group that proves that the Net truly has a place for everyone. Nudists/naturists talk about buff sunbathing, nudist clubs, encounters with local police and other items of interest to the "au naturel" set.

FAQ ▶ The following FAQs are available via FTP from RTFM.MIT.EDU in the directory:
pub/usenet/rec.nude:
REC.NUDE_FAQ—Clubs_and_Publications,_Part_II_of_III
REC.NUDE_FAQ—Electronic_Access,_Part_III_of_III
REC.NUDE_FAQ—The_Questions,_Part_I_of_III
REC.NUDE_FAQ:_Naturist_Site_Reports:_Australasia
REC.NUDE_FAQ:_Naturist_Site_Reports:_California
REC.NUDE_FAQ:_Naturist_Site_Reports:_Europe
REC.NUDE_FAQ:_Naturist_Site_Reports:_North_America

Fireworks & Pyrotechnics

rec.pyrotechnics **M**

We're not responsible for your injuries if you take any tips from this hard-core newsgroup for makers of homemade fireworks and other pyrotechnics! Participants exchange their favorite fireworks and rocket recipes, ingredients and other info.

FAQ ▶ The following FAQ is available via FTP from RTFM.MIT.EDU in the directory:
pub/usenet/rec.pyrotechnics:
rec.pyrotechnics_FAQ

Pierced Nipples, Tattoos & Other Mutilations

rec.arts.bodyart **M**

Net characters discuss their experiences (and really gross medical problems) having various unusual body parts pierced, bejeweled and tattooed. This colorful crew discusses everything from erasable tattoos to exotic forms of genital piercings.

Sample Subjects:
Ankle tattoos/Fake tattoos/Legal anesthetics

FAQ ▶ The following FAQs are available via FTP from RTFM.MIT.EDU in the directory:
pub/usenet/rec.arts.bodyart:
rec.arts.bodyart:_Tattoo_FAQ
rec.arts.bodyart_piercing_FAQ_—_address_list
rec.arts.bodyart_piercing_FAQ_part_1_—_address_list
rec.arts.bodyart_Tattoo_FAQ:_Intro_&_Part_I_4:_Getting_a_tattoo
rec.arts.bodyart_Tattoo_FAQ:_Part_2_4_Artist_&_Shop_List
rec.arts.bodyart_Tattoo_FAQ:_Part_3_4_Caring_for_a_new_tattoo
rec.arts.bodyart_Tattoo_FAQ_Part_4_4:_Miscellaneous_Information

Cross-Dressers

alt.transgendered **M**

It sure is wild out here on the Net. Why, they even have a newsgroup for cross-dressers, gender-benders and male UNIX programmers who like to dress up in women's clothing.

Obsessives Talk about Fashion Supermodels

alt.supermodels **HI**

Net participants (all of whom are desperately in need of female companionship) discuss their favorite supermodels in typical computer-nerd-y, obsessive-compulsive fashion.

Bizarre Talk

talk.bizarre **HI**

Disjointed, disgusting and (sometimes) sexually oriented but mostly sophomoric contributions by weirded-out participants.

FAQ ▶ The following FAQ is available via FTP from RTFM.MIT.EDU in the directory:
pub/usenet/talk.bizarre:
Welcome_to_talk.bizarre!__(Monthly_Posting)

Odd Net Poetry

alt.cascade **M**

A rather odd category that seems to have attracted a quirky assortment of industrial music fanatics, post-industrial poets, and people who want pictures of Barney the dinosaur in compromising positions.

Sample Subjects:
Definition of evil/Need a picture of Barney

Mensans Go Slumming

rec.org.mensa **HI**

What a letdown——this newsgroup, purportedly a discussion center for high-IQ members of the Mensa organization, consists mainly of irrelevant and immature back-and-forth flaming.

FAQ ▶ The following FAQs are available via FTP from RTFM.MIT.EDU in the directory:
pub/usenet/rec.org.mensa:
Mensa_-_FAQ:_Do_I_qualify_for_Mensa?_How_do_I_Join?_[BiWeekly]
Mensa_-_FAQ:_What_famous_people_are_members_of_Mensa?_[Monthly]
Mensa_-_FAQ:_What_is_Mensa?_[BiWeekly]
Mensa_-_FAQ:_What_is_the_Mensa_test_like?_[Monthly]
Mensa_-_FAQ:_What_other_high-IQ_societies_are_there?_[Monthly]

Cyberpunks on the Loose

alt.cyberpunk **HI**

Out there on the cutting edge of pop culture, the cyberpunk movement attempts to merge computers, communications and rock 'n' roll into a re-ordering of the nature of humanity. That's the official definition, but check out this newsgroup and you'll find a chaotic blend of comments and observations (using that term loosely) on music, drugs, computers, Rush Limbaugh and technology. Think of a cyberpunk as the 1990s version of the 1980s hacker. Once you wade through the signal-to-noise ratio of this discussion group you'll find it's a good place to get insight into cutting edge technological issues plus a large dose of conser-

vative and liberal political debate, some of it quite good. Topics range from music and Rush Limbaugh, to leading-edge cyberpunk magazines, drugs and religious fundamentalism.

Sample Subjects:
Women and modems/Mondo's drugs/Rush Limbaugh—another view/Ads in space/Eco violence/Billy Idol computer disk

FAQ ▶ The following FAQ is available via FTP from RTFM.MIT.EDU in the directory:
pub/usenet/alt.cyberpunk:
alt.cyberpunk_Frequently_Asked_Questions_list

Cyberpunk Amateur Online Fiction

alt.cyberpunk.chatsubo **M**

Another group oriented toward the cyberpunk movement, with a focus on cyberpunk science fiction, futurism and interactive cyberpunk storytelling. The interactive storytelling part of this group features self-published contributions by would-be cyberpunk authors (remember that on the Net anybody can be a published author). Very enjoyable reading if you're interested in cyberpunk, future worlds and science fiction in general, since most of the contributors on this newsgroup make a very good effort.

Sample Subjects:
Shadow talk archive/Cognos: search and rescue

Handsome Bloodsuckers

alt.vampyres **M**

The world of vampires and other related creatures of the night goes far beyond Dracula, as you'll find out here. This is the place for hard-core devotees of vampire (if you're *really* cool, you spell it "vampyre") legends. Discussions of vampire movies, books past and present, vampire lore and even a few homemade vampire tales.

Sample Subjects:
Vampyre encyclopedia/Vampyre comics for action/Horrible Tom Cruise rumor

Singles & Adult Content

Love & Lust in the New World Order

alt.polyamory **HI**

In case you didn't know, "polyamory" is the dogma of a (very close) group that believes in "marriages" between more than two people: a wife with two husbands, several men cohabitating with several women and numerous other combinations. Participants wax endlessly about the joys of being married or heavily involved with a roomful of people (the rest of us call this *bigamy*).

Sample Subjects:
Strange "fidelity mindsets"/Real love versus being in love/ Primary, secondary, tertiary labels/Is polyamory "more natural?"

Advice for the Net Lovelorn

alt.romance **HI**

These two categories, **alt.romance** and **alt.romance.chat** combine somewhat risque but innocent dialogue and massive, ongoing debate concerning the war between the sexes. **alt.romance** is a sort of online lonely hearts club that can best be thought of as an online Ann Landers column with dozens of Net participants providing their unsolicited advice on someone's romantic problem. **alt.romance.chat** is a freewheeling dialogue among groups of chatters. All in all, these two groups would be rather disappointing to would-be romance seekers since they seem to be dominated by computer science grad students who would probably be better off if they just turned off their computer screens and got a life. Best use of these two groups would be for soliciting anonymous and objective advice about a relationship. In this respect, you might end up with some useful advice on your problems.

Sample Subjects:
Lifestyle revised/Women are bitches/Songs for precipitation

FAQ ▶ The following FAQs are available via FTP from RTFM.MIT.EDU in the directory:
pub/usenet/alt.romance:
alt.romance__FAQ__(part_1_of_2)__[posted_monthly]
alt.romance__FAQ__(part_2_of_2)__[posted_monthly]

▲ *Nelson Eddy and Jeannette MacDonald, downloaded from* **wuarchive.wustl.edu**

Romantic Advice

alt.soulmates **L**

Netters provide advice on romance, relationships and friendships.

FAQ ▶ The following FAQ is available via FTP from RTFM.MIT.EDU in the directory:
pub/usenet/alt.soulmates:
FAQ_for_alt.soulmates

Singles Talk Group

soc.singles **HI**

Far from being anything resembling an online personals listing, discussions here continue the same "war between the sexes" thread found in feminist and men's groups on the Net. However, participants do seem to enjoy the endless and somewhat tedious debate that goes on here.

FAQ ▶ The following FAQ is available via FTP from RTFM.MIT.EDU in the directory:
pub/usenet/soc.singles:
soc.singles_Frequently_Asked_Questions_(FAQ);_monthly_posting

Sex Newsgroups on the Net

(various newsgroups)

It never ceases to amaze us that there's truly something for everyone on the Net—you just have to take a look at all the **alt.sex** categories to prove it to yourself: There are over a dozen groups (just in the **alt.** category) to meet the demand: **alt.sex** is a general-interest discussion group with a lot of political discussion spillover ("is homosexuality genetic," etc.); **alt.sex.bestiality**, as its name implies, is for grown-up farmboys who still can't leave cows alone; **alt.sex.bondage** is a pretty intense group for hard-core bondage and domination fanatics and gives dates and locations of S&M conventions; **alt.sex.fetish.feet** is for (you guessed it!) those whose sex drives go below the ankles; **alt.sex.fetish.hair** is also pretty self-explanatory; **alt.sex.homosexual** and **alt.sex.motss** are two adult-oriented groups for gays; and **alt.sex.masturbation**, **alt.sex.movies** and **alt.sex.wanted** cover these respective interests. There's always a fair amount of hype surrounding the **alt.sex** groups on the Net, and we should add that much of the dialogue on these overwhelmingly male-dominated groups sounds like it comes from either   A) sugar-shocked computer programmers who should really get a life, or B) fourteen-year-old boys desperate for any thrill they can get.

Chapter 14: Newsgroup Alpha Directory

The complete listing of over 7,000 newsgroups on the Internet, in alphabetical order (magnifying glass not included).

This Chapter contains all USENET newsgroups established on the Internet up to the print date of **What's on the Internet**. Newsgroups featured in **What's on the Internet** are also listed, along with page numbers where their descriptions can be found.

A

a.bsu.programming
a.bsu.religion
a.bsu.talk
ab.general
ab.jobs
ab.politics
abg.acf-jugend
abg.acf-termine
abg.acf-vor
abg.amiga
abg.atari
abg.biete
abg.dfue
abg.diskussion
abg.gewerblich
abg.gruesse
abg.intern
abg.kultur
abg.mampf
abg.member
abg.ms-dos
abg.suche
abg.test
abg.tip-info
abg.unix
abg.uucp
abg.uucp.sta
abg.uucp.waffle
abg.witziges
ac.c.455.reviews
acadia.bulletin-board
acadia.chat
acs.magnus
acs.nntp
acs.notices
acs.osu-mentor
afmc.logdis.cm
afmc.logdis.sts
air.unix
ak.admin
ak.bushnet.thing
ak.config
ak.test
alc.alc.bier.pils
alc.alc.c2h5oh
alc.archive
alc.general
alc.market
alc.stat
alc.suicide
alc.test
alt.1d
alt.2600
alt.2d
alt.3d 148
alt.abortion.inequity 48
alt.abuse.offender.recovery
alt.abuse.recovery
alt.abuse-recovery 60
alt.activism 46
alt.activism.d 46
alt.activism.death-penalty
alt.adjective.noun.verb.verb.verb
alt.adoption 61
alt.aeffle.und.pferdle
alt.agriculture.fruit

alt.agriculture.misc 59
alt.aldus.freehand
alt.aldus.misc
alt.aldus.pagemaker 162
alt.alien.vampire.flonk.flonk.flonk
alt.alien.visitors 196
alt.allsysop
alt.als
alt.alt
alt.amateur-comp 30, 172
alt.amazon-women.admirers
alt.amiga.demos
alt.amiga.slip
alt.andy.whine.whine.whine
alt.angst 196
alt.angst.xibo.sex
alt.animation.warner-bros
alt.anonymous
alt.answers 33
alt.appalachian 87
alt.aquaria 84
alt.archery 177
alt.architecture 125
alt.architecture.alternative
alt.artcom 74
alt.arts.nomad
alt.ascii-art
alt.asian-movies
alt.astrology 89
alt.atari.2600
alt.atheism 70
alt.atheism.moderated 70
alt.ato
alt.authorware
alt.autos.antique 82
alt.autos.karting
alt.autos.rod-n-custom 82
alt.bacchus
alt.backrubs 89
alt.bad.clams
alt.badgers.rose.rose.rose
alt.baldspot
alt.banjo
alt.barney.dinosaur.die.die.die 199
alt.basement.graveyard 196
alt.bbs 32, 142-143
alt.bbs.ads 142
alt.bbs.allsysop 143
alt.bbs.allsysup
alt.bbs.doors
alt.bbs.first-class
alt.bbs.internet 32, 143
alt.bbs.lists 143
alt.bbs.lists.d
alt.bbs.majorbbs
alt.bbs.metal
alt.bbs.pcboard 143
alt.bbs.pcbuucp 143
alt.bbs.searchlight
alt.bbs.unixbbs
alt.bbs.unixbbs.uniboard
alt.bbs.uupcb
alt.bbs.waffle
alt.bbs.watergate
alt.bbs.wildcat
alt.beadworld
alt.beadwrld
alt.beer 75

alt.beer.like-molson-eh
alt.best.of.internet 30
alt.bigfoot
alt.binaries.clip-art
alt.binaries.multimedia 143
alt.binaries.pictures 143-144
alt.binaries.pictures.ascii
alt.binaries.pictures.cartoons
alt.binaries.pictures.d 143
alt.binaries.pictures.erotica
alt.binaries.pictures.erotica.blondes
alt.binaries.pictures.erotica.d
alt.binaries.pictures.erotica.female
alt.binaries.pictures.erotica.male
alt.binaries.pictures.erotica.orientals
alt.binaries.pictures.fine-art.d
alt.binaries.pictures.fine-art.digitized
alt.binaries.pictures.fine-art.graphics
alt.binaries.pictures.fractals 143
alt.binaries.pictures.furniture
alt.binaries.pictures.furry
alt.binaries.pictures.misc 144
alt.binaries.pictures.supermodels
alt.binaries.pictures.tasteless
alt.binaries.pictures.utilities 144
alt.binaries.sounds.d 144
alt.binaries.sounds.erotica
alt.binaries.sounds.midi
alt.binaries.sounds.misc 144
alt.binaries.sounds.mods
alt.binaries.sounds.movies
alt.binaries.sounds.music
alt.binaries.sounds.tv
alt.binaries.sounds.utilities
alt.binaries.sounds-armpit.noises
alt.birthright
alt.bitch.pork
alt.bitterness
alt.bob-packwood.tongue.tongue.tongue
alt.bogus.group
alt.bonehead.dave-clayton
alt.bonehead.dave-potts
alt.bonsai 75
alt.books.anne-rice 98
alt.books.deryni 99
alt.books.isaac-asimov
alt.books.m-lackey
alt.books.reviews 98
alt.books.technical 125
alt.books.toffler
alt.boomerang 178
alt.boostagogo
alt.brother-jed 200
alt.bruce.it.was.just.an.accident
alt.buddha.short.fat.guy 200
alt.business.misc 37
alt.business.multi-level 37
alt.business.multi-level.scam.scam.scam
alt.butt.harp
alt.butt-keg.marmalade
alt.buttered.scones
alt.cabal
alt.cable-tv.re-regulate
alt.cad 144
alt.cad.autocad 144
alt.california 185
alt.callahans 196
alt.captain.sarcastic

alt.cascade 202
alt.ccds
alt.cd-rom 145
alt.celebrities
alt.cellular
alt.censorship 51
alt.cereal 196
alt.cesium 197
alt.chess.bdg
alt.chess.ics
alt.child-support 61
alt.chinchilla
alt.chinese.text 66, 193-194
alt.chinese.text.big5 66, 193-194
alt.choad
alt.christnet
alt.christnet.atheism
alt.christnet.bible
alt.christnet.bible-thumpers.convert.convert.conve
alt.christnet.christianlife
alt.christnet.christnews
alt.christnet.comp.dcom.telecom
alt.christnet.crybaby.mine.mine.mine
alt.christnet.dinosaur
alt.christnet.dinosaur.barney
alt.christnet.ethics
alt.christnet.eucharist.eat-me.eat-me.eat-me
alt.christnet.evangelical
alt.christnet.hypocrisy
alt.christnet.manga
alt.christnet.philosophy
alt.christnet.prayer
alt.christnet.public
alt.christnet.religion
alt.christnet.second-coming.real-soon-now
alt.christnet.sex
alt.christnet.theology
alt.clearing.aquaria
alt.clearing.homer-w-smith
alt.clearing.scam.scam.scam
alt.clearing.technology 71
alt.clubs.compsci
alt.clueless
alt.co-evolution
alt.co-ops
alt.cobol 150
alt.collecting.autographs 74
alt.college.college-bowl
alt.college.food
alt.college.us
alt.colorguard
alt.com
alt.comedy.british 119
alt.comedy.firesgn-thtre
alt.comedy.vaudeville
alt.comics.alternative
alt.comics.batman
alt.comics.buffalo-roam
alt.comics.elfquest
alt.comics.lnh 100
alt.comics.superman 100
alt.comp.acad-freedom.news
alt.comp.acad-freedom.talk 51
alt.comp.compression
alt.comp.databases.xbase.clipper

alt.comp.fsp 160
alt.comp.hardware.homebuilt
alt.computer.consultants
alt.computer.workshop.live
alt.conference-ctr
alt.config 31
alt.config.control-freaks
alt.consciousness 200
alt.conspiracy 53
alt.conspiracy.jfk 53
alt.control-theory
alt.corel.graphics
alt.cosuard 198
alt.cows.moo.moo.moo 197
alt.crackers
alt.craig.hulsey.rack.rack.rack
alt.cult-movies 114-115
alt.cult-movies.rhps
alt.cult-movies.rocky-horror 115
alt.culture.alaska 185
alt.culture.argentina 63
alt.culture.austrian
alt.culture.electric-midget
alt.culture.hawaii 87
alt.culture.indonesia 66
alt.culture.internet 31
alt.culture.karnataka 66
alt.culture.kerala 66
alt.culture.ny.upstate
alt.culture.ny-upstate 88
alt.culture.oregon 88
alt.culture.tamil
alt.culture.theory
alt.culture.tuva
alt.culture.us.asian-indian 50
alt.culture.us.southwest
alt.culture.usenet 31
alt.current-events.blizzard-of-93
alt.current-events.bosnia
alt.current-events.clinton.whitewater
alt.current-events.flood-of-93
alt.current-events.haiti
alt.current-events.inet92
alt.current-events.la-quake
alt.current-events.russia
alt.current-events.somalia
alt.current-events.usa
alt.current-events.wtc-explosion
alt.cyb-sys
alt.cyberpunk 80, 112, 202
alt.cyberpunk.chatsubo 202
alt.cyberpunk.movement 112
alt.cyberpunk.tech 80
alt.cyberspace 111-112
alt.cybertoon
alt.dads-rights 61
alt.dan.david-arkstar
alt.data.bad.bad.bad
alt.dcom.catv
alt.dcom.telecom 146
alt.dcom.telecom.ip
alt.dean-adams.pathetic-loser
alt.dear.whitehouse 48
alt.death-of-superman
alt.dec.athena
alt.decathena
alt.delete.this.newsgroup
alt.desert.shield

alt.desert.storm.its.not.scud.its.al-hussein.dammi
alt.desert.toppings
alt.desert-shield
alt.desert-storm
alt.desert-storm.facts
alt.desert-thekurds
alt.destroy.the.earth
alt.deutsche.bundesbahn.kotz.kotz.kotz
alt.dev.null
alt.devilbunnies
alt.dice-man
alt.discordia 197
alt.discrimination 49
alt.divination
alt.dragons-inn
alt.dreams 200
alt.dreams.lucid 200
alt.drooling.animation.fandom
alt.drugs 197
alt.drugs.caffeine 197
alt.drugs.caffeine.ctl
alt.drugs.usenet
alt.drumcorps
alt.drunken.bastards
alt.drwho.creative
alt.duke.basketball.sucks.sucks.sucks
alt.earth_summit
alt.eckankar
alt.education.bangkok
alt.education.bangkok.cmc
alt.education.bangkok.databases
alt.education.bangkok.planning
alt.education.bangkok.research
alt.education.bangkok.student
alt.education.bangkok.theory
alt.education.disabled 136
alt.education.distance 136
alt.education.ib 137
alt.education.ib.econ
alt.education.ib.tok
alt.education.research 137
alt.eff-talk
alt.elvis.king
alt.elvis.sighting 198
alt.emulators.ibmpc.apple2
alt.emusic 113
alt.engr.dynamics
alt.engr.explosives
alt.ensign.wesley.die.die.die 122
alt.ernie-pook
alt.etc.passwd
alt.etext
alt.eunuchs.questions
alt.evil 200
alt.exotic-music
alt.exploding.barney
alt.exploding.kibo
alt.extropians
alt.extropians.forbidden.topics
alt.fan.addams
alt.fan.albedo
alt.fan.alok.vijayvargia
alt.fan.amy-fisher
alt.fan.andrew-beal
alt.fan.asprin
alt.fan.async-gang
alt.fan.ben-elton
alt.fan.bgcrisis
alt.fan.BIFF
alt.fan.bill-fenner
alt.fan.bill-gates 198
alt.fan.billcunningham
alt.fan.blues-brothers
alt.fan.brian_reid
alt.fan.brian-ellis
alt.fan.british-accent
alt.fan.bruce.woodcock
alt.fan.bruce-becker
alt.fan.buaf
alt.fan.bugtown
alt.fan.chaki.chaki.chaki
alt.fan.charles-lasner
alt.fan.chris-elliott
alt.fan.christopher.grawburg
alt.fan.clarence.thomas
alt.fan.conan-obrien
alt.fan.dale-bass

alt.fan.dall-agata
alt.fan.dall-agata.ctl
alt.fan.dan-quayle 46
alt.fan.dan-wang
alt.fan.dave_barry 98
alt.fan.dave.blumenthal
alt.fan.dave-williams
alt.fan.david-arkstar
alt.fan.david-bowie
alt.fan.david-lawrence
alt.fan.debbie.gibson
alt.fan.devo
alt.fan.dice-man
alt.fan.dick-depew
alt.fan.dimitri-vulis
alt.fan.disney.afternoon 118
alt.fan.doctor.bashir.grind.thrust.drool
alt.fan.don.no-soul.simmons
alt.fan.don-n-mike
alt.fan.douglas-adams 98
alt.fan.dragons
alt.fan.dune 99
alt.fan.ecsd
alt.fan.edding
alt.fan.eddings 98
alt.fan.eddings.creative
alt.fan.elvis-presley
alt.fan.enya 110
alt.fan.eric.oehler
alt.fan.eric-dynamic
alt.fan.frank-zappa 107
alt.fan.g-gordon-liddy
alt.fan.gbloom.putz.putz.putz
alt.fan.gene-scott
alt.fan.gooley
alt.fan.goons
alt.fan.greaseman 115
alt.fan.harry-mandel
alt.fan.hofstadter
alt.fan.holmes 98
alt.fan.howard-stern 115
alt.fan.howard-stern.fartman
alt.fan.hurricane.yip
alt.fan.hyena
alt.fan.itchy-n-scratchy
alt.fan.ivor-cutler
alt.fan.jai-maharaj
alt.fan.james-bond 114
alt.fan.jeff-witty
alt.fan.jen-coolest
alt.fan.jesus.monroy.jr
alt.fan.jik
alt.fan.jim_whitehead
alt.fan.jimmy-buffett 107
alt.fan.jiro-nakamura
alt.fan.joe-baptista
alt.fan.joel-furr
alt.fan.john.line
alt.fan.john-palmer 198
alt.fan.jokke
alt.fan.jwz
alt.fan.kali.astarte.inanna
alt.fan.karl-hagen
alt.fan.karl-malden.nose
alt.fan.karla-homolka
alt.fan.ken-arromdee.babble.babble.babble
alt.fan.ken-johnson
alt.fan.kent-montana
alt.fan.kevin-darcy
alt.fan.kevin-walsh
alt.fan.laurie.anderson
alt.fan.lemurs
alt.fan.lemurs.cooked
alt.fan.letterman 116
alt.fan.lightbulbs
alt.fan.lila-feng
alt.fan.madonna 107
alt.fan.maria-callas
alt.fan.mark.wang
alt.fan.marla-thrift
alt.fan.mary-chungs
alt.fan.matt.welsh
alt.fan.meredith-tanner
alt.fan.michael.deignan
alt.fan.michael-bolton
alt.fan.mike-dahmus

alt.fan.mike-jittlov
alt.fan.monty-python 117
alt.fan.mst3k
alt.fan.mts
alt.fan.naked-guy
alt.fan.nathan.brazil
alt.fan.noam-chomsky
alt.fan.oingo-boingo
alt.fan.pern 99
alt.fan.peter.hammill
alt.fan.piers-anthony
alt.fan.piete.brooks
alt.fan.poris
alt.fan.pratchett 99
alt.fan.Priss.and.the.Replicants
alt.fan.q
alt.fan.rachel-perkins.bah.bah.bah
alt.fan.rama-krishna
alt.fan.ren-and-stimpy
alt.fan.ricking-ball
alt.fan.riscos
alt.fan.rita-rudner
alt.fan.robbie.pink.tutu
alt.fan.robert.mcelwaine
alt.fan.robert-jordan
alt.fan.roger.david.carasso
alt.fan.ronald-reagan
alt.fan.rumpole
alt.fan.run-dmc
alt.fan.rush-limbaugh
alt.fan.rush-limbaugh.transcripts
alt.fan.rush-limbaugh.tv-show
alt.fan.schwaben
alt.fan.scott
alt.fan.scott-tai
alt.fan.sean.corey.dewme
alt.fan.serdar-argic
alt.fan.shedevil
alt.fan.shostakovich
alt.fan.shub-interne
alt.fan.skf-jones
alt.fan.skinny
alt.fan.spinal-tap 107
alt.fan.steve-zellers
alt.fan.suicide-squid
alt.fan.tania.bedrax
alt.fan.tank-girl
alt.fan.ted.thearp.dough.dough.dough
alt.fan.thunder-thumbs
alt.fan.tim-pierce.control.control.control
alt.fan.TinyTIM
alt.fan.tna
alt.fan.tolkien
alt.fan.tom_peterson
alt.fan.tom-robbins
alt.fan.TTBS
alt.fan.tuan
alt.fan.tuan.die.die.die
alt.fan.tuan.god.god.god
alt.fan.u2
alt.fan.vic-reeves
alt.fan.vicki.robinson
alt.fan.vladimir.zhirinovsky
alt.fan.wal-greenslade
alt.fan.wang-chung
alt.fan.warlord
alt.fan.warren.burstein
alt.fan.wedge
alt.fan.wodehouse
alt.fan.woody-allen
alt.fan.zeke
alt.fandom.cons 119
alt.fandom.misc
alt.fans.david.davidian.fascist.fascist.fascist
alt.fans.surak
alt.fashion 75
alt.fax
alt.fax.bondage
alt.feminism
alt.fether.die.die.die
alt.filepro
alt.filesystems.afs
alt.finals.suicide
alt.fishing 76
alt.flack
alt.flame 199
alt.flame.abortion
alt.flame.australian.net.cops

alt.flame.bmug-boston
alt.flame.bmug-worldwide
alt.flame.dan.gannon.nazi.scum
alt.flame.eternal
alt.flame.faggots
alt.flame.fucking.faggots
alt.flame.gigantic.sigs
alt.flame.hairy-douchebag.meredith-tanner
alt.flame.hairy-douchebag.roger-david-carasso
alt.flame.hall-of-flame
alt.flame.hannigan
alt.flame.hirai.cs.dork
alt.flame.joe-hofmeister
alt.flame.karen.kolling.fascist.fascist.fascist
alt.flame.landlord
alt.flame.marshal.perlman.weenie
alt.flame.mike-steiner
alt.flame.mud
alt.flame.net-cops
alt.flame.parents
alt.flame.pizza.greasy
alt.flame.psu
alt.flame.psuvm
alt.flame.rikiya.asano.stooooopid.putz.hahahaha
alt.flame.roommate 199
alt.flame.sean-ryan
alt.flame.spelling
alt.flame.those.nasty.little.hangnails-ouch
alt.flame.tim-gilman
alt.floorit
alt.floors.de
alt.floors.fr
alt.floors.it
alt.floors.uk
alt.folklore.college 57
alt.folklore.computers 57
alt.folklore.ghost-stories 57
alt.folklore.herbs
alt.folklore.info
alt.folklore.military
alt.folklore.science 57
alt.folklore.urban 57
alt.fondle.vomit
alt.foo.bar
alt.food
alt.food.cocacola
alt.food.dennys
alt.food.fat-free
alt.food.mcdonalds
alt.food.sugar-cereals
alt.foolish.users
alt.forever.linette
alt.forgery
alt.fractal-design.painter
alt.fractals 125
alt.fractals.pictures
alt.freaks
alt.freedom.of.information.act
alt.french.captain.borg.borg.borg
alt.fruchti.xload.glotz.glotz.glotz
alt.fun.with.tob
alt.funk-you
alt.fusion
alt.galactic-guide
alt.gambling
alt.games.air-warrior
alt.games.doom
alt.games.frp.dnd-util
alt.games.frp.live-action
alt.games.galactic-bloodshed
alt.games.gb
alt.games.ibmpc.shadowcaster
alt.games.lynx
alt.games.mk
alt.games.mornington.cresent
alt.games.mtrek
alt.games.netrek.paradise
alt.games.omega
alt.games.pabu
alt.games.sf2
alt.games.test2
alt.games.tiddlywinks
alt.games.torg
alt.games.vga-planet
alt.games.vga-planets
alt.games.video.classic

alt.games.whitewolf
alt.games.xpilot
alt.games.xtrek
alt.gathering.rainbow
alt.gbloom.putz.putz.putz
alt.geek
alt.genealogy
alt.get.a.life.nintendo.addicts
alt.gobment.lones
alt.gonzalas.jaimi.escalante.hese.hese.hese
alt.good.morning
alt.good.news
alt.gopher 149
alt.gorby.coup.coup.coup
alt.gorby.gone.gone.gone
alt.gorets
alt.gothic
alt.gourmand
alt.gourmet.chocolate.covered.onions
alt.grad.skool.sux
alt.grad-student.tenured
alt.graffiti
alt.graphics 148-149
alt.graphics.ctl
alt.graphics.pixutils 148-149
alt.great.ass.paulina
alt.great.ass.wheaton
alt.great-lakes 187
alt.grins.und.grunz
alt.guinea.pig.conspiracy
alt.guitar
alt.guitar.bass
alt.guitar.tab
alt.hackers 57
alt.hackers.cough.cough.cough
alt.hackers.malicious
alt.half.operating.system.delay.delay.delay
alt.hangover
alt.happy.birthday.to.me
alt.happynet
alt.hash.house.harriers
alt.hayco.mud.mud.mud
alt.hayco.sucks.mud
alt.health.ayurveda
alt.hemp
alt.heraldry.sca
alt.herve.villechaize.dead.dead.dead
alt.hi.are.you.cute
alt.hindu
alt.hinz.und.grunz
alt.history.living
alt.history.what-if 54
alt.homosexual
alt.horror 114
alt.horror.cthulhu
alt.horror.shub-internet
alt.horror.werewolves
alt.hotrod 82
alt.housing.nontrad
alt.humor.best-of-usenet 106
alt.humor.best-of-usenet.d
alt.humor.oracle
alt.hurricane.andrew
alt.hypertext 172
alt.hypnosis
alt.icelandic.waif.bjork.bjork.bjork
alt.illuminati 59
alt.image.medical
alt.imploding.kibo
alt.india.progressive
alt.indian.superior
alt.individualism
alt.industrial
alt.industrial.computing
alt.inet92
alt.infertility
alt.info-fest.in.tuebingen
alt.info-science
alt.info-theory
alt.internet.access.wanted
alt.internet.services
alt.internet.talk.radio
alt.internet.talk-radio
alt.iraqi.dictator.bomb.bomb.bomb
alt.irc
alt.irc.announce
alt.irc.bot
alt.irc.cori.die.die.die

alt.irc.corruption
alt.irc.corruption.log.log.log
alt.irc.hottub
alt.irc.ircii
alt.irc.lamers
alt.irc.ops.kiss.my.ass
alt.irc.questions
alt.irc.recovery
alt.irc.sleaze
alt.irc.sleaze.mark
alt.irc.undernet
alt.is.too
alt.isea
alt.japanese.text 194
alt.job.gooley
alt.job.ken-johnson
alt.journalism
alt.journalism.criticism
alt.journalism.gonzo
alt.journalism.music
alt.jubjub
alt.kalbo
alt.ketchup
alt.kids-talk
alt.kill.the.whales
alt.killfiles
alt.kodak.cd.bitch.bitch.bitch
alt.lang.apl
alt.lang.asm 150
alt.lang.awk
alt.lang.basic 150
alt.lang.cfutures
alt.lang.focal
alt.lang.intercal
alt.lang.ml
alt.lang.sas
alt.lang.teco
alt.lawyers.sue.sue.sue
alt.lefthanders
alt.lemmings
alt.letter.chain
alt.letzebuerger
alt.licker.store
alt.life.afterlife
alt.life.internet
alt.life.sucks
alt.linux.sux
alt.lit.asle
alt.lluce.sucks.sucks.sucks
alt.locksmithing
alt.lucid-emacs.bug 148
alt.lucid-emacs.help 148
alt.lwaxana-troi.die.die.die
alt.lycra
alt.machines.misc
alt.magic
alt.magick
alt.magick.sex
alt.magnus.and.ketil
alt.management.tech-support
alt.managing.techsupport
alt.manga
alt.manufacturing.misc 37
alt.maroney
alt.materials.simulation
alt.mcdonalds
alt.mcdonalds.cheese
alt.mcdonalds.drink
alt.mcdonalds.food
alt.mcdonalds.gripes
alt.mcdonalds.ketchup
alt.mcdonalds.nonUS
alt.mcdonalds.policy
alt.mcdonalds.smut
alt.mcdonalds.vegemite
alt.med.cfs
alt.med.ems
alt.meditation
alt.meditation.transcendental
alt.memetics
alt.mensa.boston
alt.messianic
alt.mfs
alt.military.cadet
alt.mindcontrol
alt.minsky.meme.meme.meme
alt.misanthropy
alt.misc

alt.missing-kids
alt.models
alt.mono.acorner
alt.motd
alt.mothergoose
alt.motherinlaw
alt.motherjones
alt.mothers
alt.mothersuperior
alt.motorcycles.harley
alt.motss.bisexua-l
alt.move.michelle.regina
alt.msdos.programmer 155
alt.mud
alt.mud.bsx
alt.mud.chupchups
alt.mud.cyberworld
alt.mud.german
alt.mud.lp
alt.mud.moo
alt.mud.t-rev.stomp.stomp.stomp
alt.mud.tiny
alt.mudders.anonymous
alt.music.a-cappella
alt.music.alternative
alt.music.amy-grant
alt.music.bela-fleck
alt.music.blues-traveler
alt.music.canada
alt.music.category-freak
alt.music.deep-purple
alt.music.ebm
alt.music.enya
alt.music.enya.puke.puke.puke
alt.music.enya.puke.puke.pukeSender:
alt.music.filk
alt.music.hardcore
alt.music.industrial
alt.music.james-taylor
alt.music.journalism
alt.music.karaoke
alt.music.machines.of.loving.grace
alt.music.marillion
alt.music.nin
alt.music.pat-mccurdy
alt.music.peter-gabriel
alt.music.pop.will.eat.itself
alt.music.pop.will.eat.itself.the.poppies.are.on.p
alt.music.pop.will.eat.itself.X.Y.and.Z.electrix.s
alt.music.prince
alt.music.progressive
alt.music.queen
alt.music.rush
alt.music.ska 110
alt.music.synthpop
alt.music.techno
alt.music.the.police
alt.music.the.police.ctl
alt.music.tmbg 110
alt.music.u2
alt.music.world
alt.my.crummy.boss
alt.my.head.hurts
alt.mythology 70
alt.national.enquirer
alt.native
alt.necktie
alt.necromicon
alt.net.personalities
alt.netgames.bolo 103-104
alt.newbie 30
alt.newbies
alt.newgroup
alt.newgroup.for.fun.fun.fun
alt.news.macedonia 93
alt.news-admins.fascist.fascist.fascist
alt.news-media 93
alt.newsgroup.creators.dork.dork.dork
alt.nick.sucks 194
alt.nodies
alt.noise
alt.non.sequitur
alt.nuke.the.USA
alt.obituaries
alt.olympics.medal-tally
alt.online-service 32, 143
alt.online-service.delphi
alt.oobe

alt.org.food-not-bombs
alt.org.pugwash
alt.org.toastmasters
alt.os.bsdi
alt.os.linux
alt.os.multics
alt.os.nachos
alt.out-of-body 197
alt.overlords
alt.pagan 70
alt.pantyhose
alt.paranet.abduct
alt.paranet.paranormal
alt.paranet.psi
alt.paranet.science
alt.paranet.skeptic
alt.paranet.ufo
alt.paranormal 198
alt.parents.analretentive.insane
alt.parents-teens 61
alt.party 198
alt.pave.the.earth
alt.pcnews
alt.peace.corps
alt.peace-corps
alt.peeves 198
alt.periphs.pcmcia
alt.personals
alt.personals.ads
alt.personals.bi
alt.personals.bondage
alt.personals.misc
alt.personals.poly
alt.personals.spanking
alt.pets.chia
alt.pets.rabbits
alt.philosophy.objectivism 70
alt.pictures.fuzzy.animals
alt.pixar.typestry
alt.pixar.typstry
alt.planning.urban
alt.plastic.utensils.spork.spork
alt.plastic.utensils.spork.spork.spork
alt.plastic.utensils.straw.straw.straw
alt.pole-shift.die.die.die
alt.politics.british
alt.politics.bush
alt.politics.clinton 47
alt.politics.correct 49
alt.politics.datahighway
alt.politics.democrats
alt.politics.democrats.clinton
alt.politics.democrats.d
alt.politics.democrats.governors
alt.politics.democrats.house
alt.politics.democrats.senate
alt.politics.drinking-age
alt.politics.ec
alt.politics.economics 50
alt.politics.elections 50
alt.politics.equality
alt.politics.europe.misc
alt.politics.gooley
alt.politics.greens 47
alt.politics.homosexuality 49
alt.politics.india.communist
alt.politics.india.progressive
alt.politics.italy
alt.politics.kibo
alt.politics.libertarian 46
alt.politics.marrou
alt.politics.media 50
alt.politics.org.batf 54
alt.politics.org.ccr
alt.politics.org.cia
alt.politics.org.covert
alt.politics.org.fbi
alt.politics.org.misc 48
alt.politics.org.nsa
alt.politics.org.suopo
alt.politics.org.un
alt.politics.perot 50
alt.politics.radical-left 47
alt.politics.reform 48
alt.politics.sex 49
alt.politics.shelfbutt
alt.politics.socialism.trotsky
alt.politics.usa.constitution 53

alt.politics.usa.misc 48
alt.politics.usa.republican 49
alt.politics.vietnamese
alt.polyamory 203
alt.postmodern 74
alt.president.clinton 47
alt.prisons 51
alt.privacy 39-40, 160
alt.privacy.anon-server
alt.privacy.clipper 39
alt.prophecies.nostradamus
alt.prose 98
alt.prose.d
alt.psychoactives 199
alt.psychology.help
alt.psychology.person
alt.psychology.personality 201
alt.pub.cloven-shield 105
alt.pub.coffeehouse.amethyst
alt.pub.dragons-inn 104
alt.pub.havens-rest 104
alt.pub-ban
alt.pub-ban.homolka
alt.pud
alt.pugwash
alt.pulp
alt.punk
alt.putz.bickering.whining.weiner
alt.ql.creative
alt.quotations 98-99
alt.radio.digital
alt.radio.internet
alt.radio.networks.npr
alt.radio.pirate 196
alt.radio.scanner 86
alt.radio-shack.bill-bixby.dead.dead.dead
alt.rap 108
alt.rap-gdead
alt.rave 111
alt.recovery 60-61
alt.recovery.codependency
alt.religion.adm3a
alt.religion.all-worlds
alt.religion.computers
alt.religion.darren.aitcheson
alt.religion.eckankar
alt.religion.emacs
alt.religion.kibology 200
alt.religion.monica 201
alt.religion.pcboard
alt.religion.sabaean
alt.religion.santaism
alt.religion.scientology 71
alt.religion.shamanism
alt.religion.vince
alt.restaurants
alt.revenge
alt.revisionism 52
alt.revolution.counter 54
alt.rhode_island 188
alt.rissa
alt.rmgroup
alt.rock-n-roll 107-108
alt.rock-n-roll.acdc 108
alt.rock-n-roll.aerosmith
alt.rock-n-roll.classic 108
alt.rock-n-roll.hard 108
alt.rock-n-roll.metal 108
alt.rock-n-roll.metal.death
alt.rock-n-roll.metal.gnr
alt.rock-n-roll.metal.heavy
alt.rock-n-roll.metal.ironmaiden 108
alt.rock-n-roll.metal.metallica
alt.rock-n-roll.metal.progressive
alt.rock-n-roll.oldies
alt.rock-n-roll.stones 108
alt.rock-n-roll.symphonic
alt.rodney.dangerfield
alt.rodney.king
alt.rodney-king
alt.romance 203
alt.romance.chat 203
alt.romance.chat.indiana.barf.barf.barf
alt.rush-limbaugh 46
alt.sadistic.dentists.drill.drill.drill
alt.satanism 71
alt.satannet
alt.satannet.barney

alt.satellite.tv.europe
alt.satellite.tv.forsale
alt.save.the.earth 47
alt.sb.programmer 172
alt.sca
alt.sci.astro.aips
alt.sci.astro.figaro
alt.sci.astro.fits
alt.sci.image-facility
alt.sci.physics.acoustics 81
alt.sci.physics.new-theories 125
alt.sci.physics.plutonium
alt.sci.physics.spam
alt.sci.planetary 134
alt.sci.sociology
alt.sci.tech.indonesian
alt.scientology.scam.scam.scam
alt.scooter
alt.scooter.classic
alt.sect.ahmadiyya
alt.sect.telecom
alt.security 39, 160
alt.security.index
alt.security.keydist
alt.security.pgp 160
alt.security.ripem
alt.sega.genesis 102
alt.self-improve 40
alt.sewing 75
alt.sex 203
alt.sex.aluminum.baseball.bat
alt.sex.bestiality 203
alt.sex.bestiality.barney
alt.sex.bestiality.hamster.duct-tape
alt.sex.bondage 203
alt.sex.bondage.particle.physics
alt.sex.boredom
alt.sex.carasso
alt.sex.carasso.snuggles
alt.sex.enemas
alt.sex.exhibitionism
alt.sex.extropians
alt.sex.fetish.amputee
alt.sex.fetish.diapers
alt.sex.fetish.fa
alt.sex.fetish.fashion
alt.sex.fetish.feet 203
alt.sex.fetish.hair 203
alt.sex.fetish.orientals
alt.sex.fetish.waifs
alt.sex.fetish.watersports
alt.sex.graphics
alt.sex.homosexual 203
alt.sex.masturbation 203
alt.sex.motss 203
alt.sex.movies 203
alt.sex.nfs
alt.sex.NOT
alt.sex.nudels.me.too
alt.sex.pedophile.mike-labbe
alt.sex.pictures
alt.sex.pictures.d
alt.sex.pictures.female
alt.sex.pictures.male
alt.sex.prevost.derbecker
alt.sex.services
alt.sex.sonja
alt.sex.sounds
alt.sex.spanking
alt.sex.stories
alt.sex.stories.d
alt.sex.strip-clubs
alt.sex.trans
alt.sex.voyeurism
alt.sex.wanted 203
alt.sex.wanted.me-too
alt.sex.watersports
alt.sex.wizards
alt.sex.woody-allen
alt.sex.zoophilia
alt.sexual.abuse.recovery 60
alt.sexual.abuse.recovery.d
alt.sexy.bald.captains
alt.sf4m
alt.shenanigans 199
alt.showbiz.gossip
alt.shrinky.dinks
alt.shut.the.hell.up.geek

alt.sigma2.height
alt.sigma2.penis
alt.silly.group.names.d
alt.skate
alt.skate-board 180
alt.skinheads 200
alt.skunks
alt.slack 199
alt.slack.BoB.dirtbag
alt.slack.devo
alt.slick.willy.tax.tax.tax
alt.smokers
alt.smokers.cough
alt.smoking.mooses
alt.smouldering.dog.zone
alt.snail-mail
alt.snowmobiles 83
alt.soc.ethics
alt.society.anarchy 54
alt.society.ati
alt.society.civil-disob
alt.society.civil-liberties 54
alt.society.civil-liberty
alt.society.conservatism 46
alt.society.cu-digest
alt.society.etrnl-vigilanc
alt.society.foia
alt.society.futures
alt.society.generation-x
alt.society.resistance
alt.society.revolution 47
alt.society.sovereign
alt.soft-sys.corel.draw
alt.soft-sys.corel.misc
alt.soft-sys.tooltalk
alt.soulmates 203
alt.source-code
alt.sources 161-162
alt.sources.amiga 162
alt.sources.amiga.d
alt.sources.d 161
alt.sources.index
alt.sources.mac
alt.sources.patches
alt.sources.wanted 161
alt.spam 199
alt.spam.tin
alt.spleen
alt.sport.bowling 178
alt.sport.bungee
alt.sport.darts 178
alt.sport.foosball
alt.sport.lasertag 180
alt.sport.officiating
alt.sport.paintball
alt.sport.photon
alt.sport.pool
alt.sport.racquetball
alt.sport.raquetball
alt.sport.squash
alt.sports.baseball.atlanta-braves
alt.sports.baseball.balt-orioles
alt.sports.baseball.chicago-cubs
alt.sports.baseball.cinci-reds
alt.sports.baseball.col-rockies
alt.sports.baseball.fla-marlins
alt.sports.baseball.houston-astros
alt.sports.baseball.la-dodgers
alt.sports.baseball.minor-leagues
alt.sports.baseball.montreal-expos
alt.sports.baseball.ny-mets
alt.sports.baseball.ny-yankees
alt.sports.baseball.oakland-as
alt.sports.baseball.phila-phillies
alt.sports.baseball.pitt-pirates
alt.sports.baseball.sd-padres
alt.sports.baseball.sf-giants
alt.sports.baseball.stl-cardinals
alt.sports.baseball.tor-bluejays
alt.sports.basketball.nba.nj-nets
alt.sports.darts
alt.sports.football.mn-vikings
alt.sports.football.pro.buffalo-bills
alt.sports.football.pro.car-panthers

alt.sports.football.pro.dallas-cowboys
alt.sports.football.pro.gb-packers
alt.sports.football.pro.jville-jaguars
alt.sports.football.pro.miami-dolphins
alt.sports.football.pro.ne-patriots
alt.sports.football.pro.ny-giants
alt.sports.football.pro.ny-jets
alt.sports.football.pro.phoe-cardinals
alt.sports.football.pro.sf-49ers
alt.sports.football.pro.sea-seahawks
alt.sports.football.pro.tampabay-bucs
alt.sports.football.pro.wash-redskins
alt.sports.hockey.echl
alt.sports.hockey.ihl
alt.sports.hockey.nhl.buffalo-sabres
alt.sports.hockey.nhl.chi-blackhawks
alt.sports.hockey.nhl.hford-whalers
alt.sports.hockey.nhl.la-kings
alt.sports.hockey.nhl.nj-devils
alt.sports.hockey.nhl.ny-islanders
alt.sports.hockey.nhl.ny-rangers
alt.sports.hockey.nhl.sj-sharks
alt.sports.hockey.nhl.tor-mapleleafs
alt.sports.hockey.nhl.vanc-canucks
alt.sports.hockey.nhl.wash-capitals
alt.sports.hockey.nhl.winni.peg-jets
alt.sports.hockey.nhl.winnipeg.jets
alt.sports.hockey.nhl.winnipeg-jets
alt.sports.hockey.uhf
alt.sports.hockey.vhf
alt.sports.hockey.whl
alt.stagecraft
alt.starfleet.rpg
alt.startrek.creative 122
alt.startrek.klingon
alt.stupid.putz
alt.stupid.putz.BoB.BoB.BoB
alt.stupid.putz.gritzner
alt.stupid.putzkutz.putz
alt.stupidity
alt.suburbs
alt.suicide.finals
alt.suicide.holiday 201
alt.suit.att-bsdi
alt.super.nes
alt.superman.dead
alt.supermodels 202
alt.support 60, 62-63
alt.support.abuse-partners 60
alt.support.arthritis
alt.support.attn-deficit
alt.support.big-folks
alt.support.cancer 62
alt.support.diet 62
alt.support.mult-sclerosis
alt.support.spina-bifida
alt.support.step-parents 62
alt.surfing 181
alt.surrealism
alt.sustainable.agriculture 49
alt.svens.house.of.12.year-old.lust
alt.swedish.chef.bork.bork.bork
alt.swine.oink.oink.oink
alt.syntax.tactical
alt.sys.amiga.demos 163
alt.sys.amiga.uucp 163
alt.sys.amiga.uucp.patches
alt.sys.intergraph 167
alt.sys.pc-clone.gateway2000
alt.sys.pc532
alt.sys.pdp11
alt.sys.pdp8
alt.sys.perq
alt.sys.sun 169
alt.sys.unisys
alt.taiwan.republic
alt.tasteless 196
alt.tasteless.johan.wevers
alt.tasteless.jokes 196
alt.tasteless.penis
alt.tasteless.pictures
alt.technology.misc
alt.technology.mkt-failure
alt.technology.obsolete 81
alt.technology.smartcards
alt.ted.frank.troll.troll.troll
alt.tennis
alt.test

alt.test.my.new.group
alt.test.test
alt.text.dwb
alt.thinking.hurts
alt.thrash 199
alt.timewasters
alt.tla
alt.todd.green.likes.it.up.the.butt
alt.toolkits.xview 172
alt.toon-pics
alt.toys.hi-tech 81
alt.toys.lego 89
alt.toys.transformers
alt.transgendered 202
alt.travel.road-trip
alt.true.crime
alt.true-crime
alt.tv.90120.sucks.sucks.sucks
alt.tv.90210
alt.tv.animaniacs
alt.tv.antagonists
alt.tv.babylon-5 116
alt.tv.barney
alt.tv.beakmans-world
alt.tv.bh90210 116
alt.tv.dinosaur.barney.die.die.die 116
alt.tv.dinosaurs 116
alt.tv.dinosaurs.barney.die.die.die
alt.tv.eek-the-cat
alt.tv.fifteen
alt.tv.game-shows
alt.tv.infomercials 116
alt.tv.infomercials.Don-LaPre.DIE.DIE.DIE
alt.tv.kids-in-hall
alt.tv.la-law 116
alt.tv.liquid-tv 116
alt.tv.mash 117
alt.tv.max-headroom
alt.tv.melrose-place 117
alt.tv.mst3k 117
alt.tv.muppets 117
alt.tv.mwc 117
alt.tv.northern-exp 117
alt.tv.prisoner 117-118
alt.tv.red-dwarf 118
alt.tv.ren-n-stimpy 118
alt.tv.rockford-files 118
alt.tv.saved-bell 118
alt.tv.seinfeld 118
alt.tv.simpsons 118
alt.tv.simpsons.itchy-scratchy
alt.tv.sn
alt.tv.snl
alt.tv.snl.snl.snl
alt.tv.talkshows.daytime
alt.tv.talkshows.late
alt.tv.the-heights.cancelled.cancelled.cancelled
alt.tv.time-traxx
alt.tv.tiny-toon 118
alt.tv.tiny-toon.fandom
alt.tv.tiny-toon.plucky-duck
alt.tv.tiny-toon.sex
alt.tv.twin-peaks 118
alt.tv.x-files
alt.ucb.class.suicide.c169
alt.unix.wizards
alt.unsubscribe-me
alt.usage.english 99
alt.usage.german
alt.usenet.addict
alt.usenet.kooks
alt.usenet.offline-reader 30
alt.usenet.recovery
alt.uu.announce
alt.uu.comp.misc
alt.uu.comp.os.linux.questions
alt.uu.fan.newgroup.jyrki.jyrki.jyrk
alt.uu.future
alt.uu.lang.esperanto.misc
alt.uu.lang.misc
alt.uu.lang.russian.misc
alt.uu.math.misc
alt.uu.misc.misc
alt.uu.tools
alt.uu.virtual-worlds.misc
alt.uw.cs.upl
alt.vampyres 202

alt.video.games.reviews
alt.video.laserdisc 81
alt.vigilantes
alt.virtual-adepts
alt.visa.us 38
alt.wais
alt.wall
alt.wanted.mars.women
alt.wanted.moslem.gay
alt.wanted.moslem.men
alt.wanted.moslem.women
alt.wanted.muslem.bestiality
alt.war 52-53
alt.war.civil.usa 53
alt.war.vietnam 52
alt.waves
alt.wedding 40
alt.wee.willie.wisner
alt.weemba
alt.wesley.crusher.die.die.die
alt.wesley-dodd.hang.hang.hang
alt.whine 201
alt.whistleblowing
alt.who.is.bob
alt.windows.cde
alt.windows.text
alt.winsock 159
alt.wired 112
alt.wolves 86
alt.wonderment.bgjw
alt.wonderment.ctl
alt.world.taeis
alt.world.thunder-thumbs
alt.wpi.negativland.subgenii.for.rent
alt.x-headers.overboard
alt.year.1976
alt.zima
alt.zines 201
alt.znet.aeo
alt.znet.pc
americast.CaManRev
americast.daily
americast.imprimis
americast.ltimes.business
americast.ltimes.feature
americast.ltimes.homenews
americast.ltimes.overseas
americast.ltimes.sport
amiga.c.dice
amiga.dice
amiga.mach
amoco.datavision.update
amoco.microstation
apana.lists.music.the-beloved
apana.lists.rec.warhammer
apc.ctwm
apc.xmt
ar.info-ada
ar.info-snmp
ar.info-unix
ar.laser-lovers
ar.space
ar.telecom
ar.unix-wizards
arc.ccf.services
arc.ccf.super
arc.ccf.unix
arpa.sun-managers
athena.announcements
athena.forsale
athena.gamit
athena.housing
athena.misc 190
athena.test
atl.arno
atl.general 185
atl.jobs 185
atl.olympics 185
atl.resumes 185
atl.test
au.jobs
au.twin-peaks
aus.aarnet 192
aus.acs
aus.acsnet
aus.ads.commercial
aus.ads.forsale
aus.ads.forsale.computers

aus.ads.jobs
aus.ads.wanted
aus.ai
aus.archives
aus.aswec
aus.auug
aus.aviation
aus.bicycle
aus.books
aus.cars
aus.cdrom
aus.comms 193
aus.comms.fps
aus.computers 191-192
aus.computers.ai
aus.computers.amiga 191
aus.computers.cdrom
aus.computers.ibm-pc
aus.computers.linux
aus.computers.logic-prog
aus.computers.mac
aus.computers.os2
aus.computers.parallel
aus.computers.sun
aus.computers.tex
aus.conserve
aus.culture.china 191
aus.culture.ultimo
aus.education
aus.education.npit
aus.education.rpl
aus.films 191
aus.flame 192
aus.followup
aus.foodtech
aus.footy
aus.forsale 191
aus.fps
aus.games 192
aus.games.roleplay 192
aus.general 191
aus.genstat
aus.hi-fi 192
aus.jobs 192
aus.jokes 191
aus.jokes.d
aus.kermit
aus.lp
aus.mac 192
aus.mail
aus.map
aus.mbio
aus.motorcycles 192
aus.music 192
aus.net.aarnet
aus.net.acsnet
aus.net.directory
aus.net.directory.osi-ds
aus.net.directory.quipu
aus.net.mail
aus.net.news
aus.net.status
aus.netstatus
aus.news
aus.org.acs
aus.org.acs.books
aus.org.auug
aus.parallel
aus.personals
aus.photo
aus.politics 191
aus.pyramid
aus.radio 191
aus.radio.amsat
aus.radio.packet
aus.radio.wicen
aus.rail 192
aus.religion
aus.scheme
aus.sex 192
aus.sex.bondage
aus.sf 192
aus.sf.star-trek
aus.snow 192
aus.sources
aus.spearnet
aus.sport 192
aus.sport.aussie-rules

aus.stats.s 193
aus.students
aus.students.overseas
aus.sun-works
aus.tex
aus.theatre
aus.tv.community
aus.wanted 192
austin.announce 185
austin.eff 185
austin.flame
austin.followup
austin.forsale 185
austin.freenet
austin.general 185
austin.important
austin.music 185
austin.news 185
austin.news.stats
austin.personals
austin.politics 185
austin.public-net
austin.talk 185
austin.test
az.general
az.swusrgrp

B

b20.3322.10
ba.announce 188
ba.bicycles
ba.broadcast 188
ba.dance
ba.food 190
ba.forsale
ba.general 189
ba.helping-hand
ba.internet 189
ba.israelis
ba.jobs.contract
ba.jobs.misc 189
ba.jobs.offered 189
ba.market 188-189
ba.market.computers 188
ba.market.housing 189
ba.market.misc 188
ba.market.vehicles 188
ba.motorcycles
ba.motss
ba.mountain-folk 189
ba.music 190
ba.news 189
ba.news.config
ba.news.group
ba.news.stats 189
ba.politics 189
ba.seminars 190
ba.singles 190
ba.smartvalley
ba.sports 190
ba.test
ba.transportation 189
ba.wanted
ba.weather 190
ba.windows.x
backbone.announce
balt.forsale
balt.jobs
balt.misc
bc.bcnet
bc.general 193
bc.news.stats
bc.rcbc
bc.unix
bc.weather 193
bcs.activists
bcs.announce
bcs.answers
bcs.config
bcs.groups
bcs.misc
bcs.olsc
bcs.test
bionet.agroforestry
bionet.announce 133
bionet.biology.computational
bionet.biology.n2-fixation

bionet.biology.tropical
bionet.cellbiol
bionet.chlamydomonas
bionet.drosophila
bionet.general 133
bionet.genome.arabidopsis 133
bionet.genome.chrom22
bionet.genome.chromosomes
bionet.immunology
bionet.info-theory 133
bionet.jobs 133
bionet.journals.contents 133
bionet.journals.note
bionet.metabolic-reg
bionet.molbio.ageing
bionet.molbio.bio-matrix
bionet.molbio.embldatabank
bionet.molbio.evolution 134
bionet.molbio.gdb
bionet.molbio.genbank 134
bionet.molbio.genbank.updates 134
bionet.molbio.gene-linkage
bionet.molbio.gene-org
bionet.molbio.genome-program
bionet.molbio.hiv
bionet.molbio.methds-reagnts 134
bionet.molbio.news
bionet.molbio.oncogenes
bionet.molbio.pir
bionet.molbio.plant
bionet.molbio.proteins 134
bionet.molbio.rapd
bionet.molbio.swiss-prot
bionet.molbio.yeast
bionet.mycology
bionet.n2-fixation
bionet.neuroscience 134
bionet.photosynthesis
bionet.plants 134
bionet.population-bio
bionet.sci-resources 134
bionet.software 134
bionet.software.acedb
bionet.software.gcg
bionet.software.sources
bionet.technology.conversion
bionet.users.addresses 134
bionet.virology
bionet.women-in-bio
bionet.xtallography
bit.admin
bit.admin.ctl
bit.comserve
bit.general
bit.lang.neder-l
bit.listserv.3com-l
bit.listserv.9370-l
bit.listserv.aaua-l
bit.listserv.ada-law
bit.listserv.advanc-l
bit.listserv.advise-l
bit.listserv.aidsnews
bit.listserv.aix-il
bit.listserv.aix-l 157
bit.listserv.allmusic 109
bit.listserv.anthro-l
bit.listserv.anu-news
bit.listserv.apple2-l
bit.listserv.applicat
bit.listserv.arie-l
bit.listserv.ashe-l
bit.listserv.asm370
bit.listserv.autism 61
bit.listserv.autocat
bit.listserv.axslib-l
bit.listserv.banyan-l 146
bit.listserv.big-lan
bit.listserv.billing
bit.listserv.biojobs
bit.listserv.bionews
bit.listserv.biosph-l 125
bit.listserv.biotech
bit.listserv.bitnet-2
bit.listserv.bitnews
bit.listserv.blindnws 61
bit.listserv.brfc-l
bit.listserv.brs-l
bit.listserv.buslib-l

bit.listserv.c+health
bit.listserv.c-l
bit.listserv.c18-l 135
bit.listserv.c370-l
bit.listserv.candle-l
bit.listserv.catala
bit.listserv.catholic 69
bit.listserv.cdromlan 145
bit.listserv.cfs.newsletter
bit.listserv.christia 69
bit.listserv.cics-l
bit.listserv.cinema-l 114
bit.listserv.circplus 58, 135
bit.listserv.cmspip-l
bit.listserv.cmsr5-l
bit.listserv.coco
bit.listserv.comm-l
bit.listserv.commed
bit.listserv.commodor
bit.listserv.comp-cen
bit.listserv.confer-l
bit.listserv.confocal
bit.listserv.contacts
bit.listserv.csg-l 135
bit.listserv.cumrec-l 135
bit.listserv.cwis-l
bit.listserv.cyber-l
bit.listserv.dasig
bit.listserv.db2-l
bit.listserv.dbase-l 145
bit.listserv.deaf-l 62
bit.listserv.decnews
bit.listserv.dectei-l
bit.listserv.devel-l 51, 125
bit.listserv.dipl-l
bit.listserv.disarm-l
bit.listserv.domain-l
bit.listserv.down-syn
bit.listserv.drp-l
bit.listserv.dsshe-l 137
bit.listserv.earntech
bit.listserv.easi
bit.listserv.ecolog-l
bit.listserv.economy
bit.listserv.edi-l 172
bit.listserv.edpolyan
bit.listserv.edstat-l
bit.listserv.edtech 137
bit.listserv.edusig-l
bit.listserv.emflds-l
bit.listserv.emusic-l 113
bit.listserv.endnote 162
bit.listserv.envbeh-l
bit.listserv.erl-l 137
bit.listserv.esl-l
bit.listserv.ethics-l
bit.listserv.ethology
bit.listserv.euearn-l
bit.listserv.falbti-l
bit.listserv.film-l
bit.listserv.fncts-l
bit.listserv.fnord-l
bit.listserv.folklore
bit.listserv.forumbio
bit.listserv.frac-l 125
bit.listserv.free-l 61
bit.listserv.fusion
bit.listserv.future-l
bit.listserv.games-l 102
bit.listserv.gaynet 60
bit.listserv.gddm-l
bit.listserv.geodesic 125
bit.listserv.geograph
bit.listserv.gerinet
bit.listserv.gguide
bit.listserv.gis-l
bit.listserv.gmast-l
bit.listserv.gophern
bit.listserv.govdoc-l 33, 135
bit.listserv.graph-ti
bit.listserv.gutnberg 135
bit.listserv.hellas
bit.listserv.help-net
bit.listserv.helpnet
bit.listserv.hier-l
bit.listserv.hindu-d
bit.listserv.history 60, 135
bit.listserv.hit

bit.listserv.hp-28
bit.listserv.hp3000-l
bit.listserv.hytel-l
bit.listserv.i-amiga 163
bit.listserv.ibm-hesc
bit.listserv.ibm-main 165
bit.listserv.ibm-nets
bit.listserv.ibm7171
bit.listserv.ibmtcp-l 159
bit.listserv.icu-l
bit.listserv.idms-l
bit.listserv.india-d
bit.listserv.india-l 66
bit.listserv.info-gcg
bit.listserv.infonets
bit.listserv.ingrafx
bit.listserv.innopac 162
bit.listserv.ioob-l
bit.listserv.ipct-l
bit.listserv.isn
bit.listserv.ispf-l
bit.listserv.jes2-l
bit.listserv.jnet-l
bit.listserv.l-hcap
bit.listserv.l-vmctr
bit.listserv.l-vspc
bit.listserv.laser
bit.listserv.lawsch-l 135
bit.listserv.liaison
bit.listserv.libpacs
bit.listserv.libref-l 58, 135
bit.listserv.libres
bit.listserv.license
bit.listserv.linkfail
bit.listserv.lis-l
bit.listserv.literary 59
bit.listserv.lstsrv-l
bit.listserv.mac-l
bit.listserv.mail-l
bit.listserv.mailbook
bit.listserv.mba-l
bit.listserv.mbu-l 59, 136
bit.listserv.md4f
bit.listserv.mdphd-l
bit.listserv.medforum 136
bit.listserv.media-l
bit.listserv.medlib-l 58, 125
bit.listserv.mednews 93
bit.listserv.methods
bit.listserv.mexico-l
bit.listserv.mideur-l
bit.listserv.ministry-l
bit.listserv.minix-l
bit.listserv.mla-l
bit.listserv.mon-l
bit.listserv.muslims
bit.listserv.nazi-l
bit.listserv.netmon-l
bit.listserv.netnws-l
bit.listserv.netscout
bit.listserv.nettrain 31
bit.listserv.new-list 30
bit.listserv.newsb-l
bit.listserv.next-l
bit.listserv.nodmgt-l
bit.listserv.notabene 162
bit.listserv.notis-l 136
bit.listserv.novell 146
bit.listserv.omrscan
bit.listserv.online-l
bit.listserv.os2-l
bit.listserv.ozone
bit.listserv.pacs-l 136
bit.listserv.page-l
bit.listserv.pagemakr 162
bit.listserv.pakistan
bit.listserv.pcserv-l
bit.listserv.physhare
bit.listserv.pmail
bit.listserv.pmdf-l 172
bit.listserv.pns-l
bit.listserv.policy-l
bit.listserv.politics 49
bit.listserv.postcard 74
bit.listserv.power-l
bit.listserv.powerh-l
bit.listserv.preshare
bit.listserv.procom-l

bit.listserv.profs-l
bit.listserv.pscript
bit.listserv.psi-l
bit.listserv.psycgrad 136
bit.listserv.qualrs-l 136
bit.listserv.redist-l
bit.listserv.relayf-l
bit.listserv.relusr-l
bit.listserv.rexxlist
bit.listserv.rhetoric
bit.listserv.rra-l
bit.listserv.rscs-l
bit.listserv.rscsmods
bit.listserv.rscsv2-l
bit.listserv.rustex-l
bit.listserv.s-comput
bit.listserv.sas-l
bit.listserv.saw-l
bit.listserv.scce-l
bit.listserv.scifraud
bit.listserv.script-l
bit.listserv.scuba-l 180
bit.listserv.seasia-l 69
bit.listserv.security
bit.listserv.seds-l 134
bit.listserv.sedsnews
bit.listserv.servers
bit.listserv.sfs-l
bit.listserv.sganet
bit.listserv.simula
bit.listserv.slart-l 58
bit.listserv.slovak-l 65
bit.listserv.snamgt-l
bit.listserv.sos-data
bit.listserv.space
bit.listserv.spires-l
bit.listserv.sportpsy
bit.listserv.spssx-l
bit.listserv.sqlinfo
bit.listserv.stat-l
bit.listserv.std-l
bit.listserv.tbi-support
bit.listserv.tech-l
bit.listserv.techwr-l 59
bit.listserv.tecmat-l
bit.listserv.tesl-l
bit.listserv.test
bit.listserv.test-l
bit.listserv.tex-l
bit.listserv.tn3270-l
bit.listserv.toolb-l 162
bit.listserv.trafic-l
bit.listserv.trans-l
bit.listserv.transplant
bit.listserv.travel-l 88
bit.listserv.tsorexx
bit.listserv.turboc-l
bit.listserv.ucp-l
bit.listserv.ug-l
bit.listserv.uigis-l
bit.listserv.urep-l
bit.listserv.usrdir-l
bit.listserv.uus-l 70
bit.listserv.valert-l
bit.listserv.vector-l
bit.listserv.vfort-l
bit.listserv.virus-l
bit.listserv.vm-rexx
bit.listserv.vm-util 173
bit.listserv.vmesa-l
bit.listserv.vmrel6-l
bit.listserv.vmslsv-l
bit.listserv.vmvtam-l
bit.listserv.vmxa-l
bit.listserv.vnews-l
bit.listserv.vpiej-l
bit.listserv.vse-l
bit.listserv.wac-l
bit.listserv.win3-l 158
bit.listserv.word-pc
bit.listserv.words-l 59
bit.listserv.wp50-l
bit.listserv.wpcorp
bit.listserv.wpcorp-l 162
bit.listserv.wpwin-l 158
bit.listserv.wx-talk
bit.listserv.x400-l
bit.listserv.xcult-l

clari.tw.environment 42
clari.tw.health 42
clari.tw.health.aids
clari.tw.misc 42
clari.tw.nuclear
clari.tw.science 42
clari.tw.space 42
clari.tw.stocks 42
clari.tw.telecom 42
clari.world.africa
clari.world.americas
clari.world.asia
clari.world.europe.eastern
clari.world.europe.western
clari.world.mideast
cle.music
cle.sports 186
club.announce
club.general
cmh.forsale
cmh.general
cmh.groups
cmh.jobs
cmh.network
cmh.opinion
cmh.test
co.general 185
co.media.rmn
co.ocs
co.politics
co.politics.amend2.discuss
co.politics.amend2.info
co.test
comp.admin.policy 149
comp.ai 137, 142
comp.ai.digest
comp.ai.edu 137
comp.ai.fuzzy 142
comp.ai.genetic 142
comp.ai.jair.announce
comp.ai.jair.papers
comp.ai.nat-lang
comp.ai.neural-nets 142
comp.ai.nlang-know-rep
comp.ai.philosophy 142
comp.ai.shells 142
comp.ai.vision
comp.answers
comp.apps.spreadsheet
comp.apps.spreadsheets 162
comp.arch 170
comp.arch.bus.vmebus
comp.arch.storage 170
comp.archives 161
comp.archives.admin
comp.archives.msdos.announce 161
comp.archives.msdos.d 161
comp.bbs.misc 143
comp.bbs.waffle 143
comp.benchmarks 173
comp.binaries.acorn
comp.binaries.amiga
comp.binaries.apple2 144
comp.binaries.atari.st
comp.binaries.cbm
comp.binaries.ibm.pc 144
comp.binaries.ibm.pc.archives
comp.binaries.ibm.pc.d 144
comp.binaries.ibm.pc.wanted 144
comp.binaries.mac 144
comp.binaries.ms-windows
comp.binaries.os2 144
comp.bugs.2bsd
comp.bugs.4bsd
comp.bugs.4bsd.ucb-fixes
comp.bugs.misc
comp.bugs.sys5
comp.cad.cadence 144
comp.cad.compass
comp.cad.pro-engineer
comp.cad.synthesis
comp.client-server 170
comp.cog-eng
comp.compilers 170
comp.compression 170
comp.compression.research 170
comp.databases 145
comp.databases.informix 145

comp.databases.ingres 145
comp.databases.ms-access
comp.databases.object
comp.databases.oracle 145
comp.databases.paradox
comp.databases.pick
comp.databases.rdb
comp.databases.sybase 145
comp.databases.theory 145
comp.databases.xbase.fox
comp.databases.xbase.misc
comp.dcom.cell-relay 146
comp.dcom.fax 146
comp.dcom.isdn 146
comp.dcom.lans 146-147
comp.dcom.lans.ethernet 146
comp.dcom.lans.fddi 146
comp.dcom.lans.hyperchannel
comp.dcom.lans.misc 147
comp.dcom.lans.novell
comp.dcom.lans.token-ring
comp.dcom.lans.v2lni
comp.dcom.modems 146
comp.dcom.servers
comp.dcom.sys.cisco 146
comp.dcom.sys.wellfleet
comp.dcom.telecom 146
comp.dcom.telecom.digest
comp.dcom.telecom.tech
comp.doc
comp.doc.techreports
comp.dsp 173
comp.editors 170
comp.edu 137, 173
comp.edu.composition 137
comp.emacs 148
comp.fonts 170-171
comp.graphics 149
comp.graphics.algorithms
comp.graphics.animation 149
comp.graphics.avs 149
comp.graphics.data-explorer
comp.graphics.digest
comp.graphics.explorer 149
comp.graphics.gnuplot 149
comp.graphics.opengl
comp.graphics.research
comp.graphics.visualization 149
comp.groupware 162
comp.human-factors 170
comp.infosystems 150
comp.infosystems.announce
comp.infosystems.gis 150
comp.infosystems.gopher 150
comp.infosystems.wais 150
comp.infosystems.www
comp.internet.library
comp.ivideodisc
comp.lang.ada 150
comp.lang.apl 150
comp.lang.asm370 150
comp.lang.basic.misc
comp.lang.basic.visual
comp.lang.c++ 128, 142-153
comp.lang.c 150-151
comp.lang.clos 151
comp.lang.clu
comp.lang.crass
comp.lang.dylan 151
comp.lang.eiffel 151
comp.lang.forth 151
comp.lang.forth.mac
comp.lang.fortran 152
comp.lang.functional 152
comp.lang.hermes
comp.lang.icon
comp.lang.idl
comp.lang.idl-pvwave 152
comp.lang.lisp 152
comp.lang.lisp.franz
comp.lang.lisp.mcl 152
comp.lang.lisp.x
comp.lang.logo
comp.lang.misc
comp.lang.ml
comp.lang.modula2 152
comp.lang.modula3 152
comp.lang.oberon

comp.lang.objective-c 152
comp.lang.pascal 152
comp.lang.perl 152
comp.lang.pop
comp.lang.postscript 152
comp.lang.prolog 152
comp.lang.rexx 152
comp.lang.sather
comp.lang.scheme 153
comp.lang.scheme.c
comp.lang.sigplan
comp.lang.smalltalk 153
comp.lang.tcl 153
comp.lang.verilog 153
comp.lang.vhdl 153
comp.lang.visual 153
comp.laser-printers
comp.lsi 144-145
comp.lsi.cad 144-145
comp.lsi.testing 145
comp.mail 153-154
comp.mail.elm 153-154
comp.mail.headers
comp.mail.maps
comp.mail.mh 154
comp.mail.mime 154
comp.mail.misc 154
comp.mail.multi-media 154
comp.mail.mush 154
comp.mail.sendmail 154
comp.mail.uucp 154
comp.misc 173
comp.msdos.programmer
comp.mulitmedia
comp.multimedia 173
comp.music 173
comp.networks.noctools.announce
comp.networks.noctools.bugs
comp.networks.noctools.d
comp.networks.noctools.submissions
comp.networks.noctools.tools
comp.networks.noctools.wanted
comp.newprod
comp.next.misc
comp.object 153
comp.object.logic
comp.org.acm 154
comp.org.decus 154
comp.org.eff.news
comp.org.eff.talk 154
comp.org.fidonet
comp.org.ieee 154
comp.org.isoc.interest
comp.org.issnnet
comp.org.lisp-users
comp.org.sug
comp.org.uniforum
comp.org.usenix 154
comp.org.usenix.roomshare
comp.org.usrgroup
comp.os.386bsd.announce
comp.os.386bsd.apps
comp.os.386bsd.bugs 154
comp.os.386bsd.development 155
comp.os.386bsd.misc
comp.os.386bsd.questions 155
comp.os.aos
comp.os.coherent 156
comp.os.cpm 156
comp.os.cpm.amethyst
comp.os.eunice
comp.os.geos
comp.os.linux 156
comp.os.linux.admin
comp.os.linux.announce 156
comp.os.linux.development
comp.os.linux.help
comp.os.linux.misc
comp.os.lynx
comp.os.mach 156
comp.os.minix 156
comp.os.misc 156
comp.os.ms-windows.advocacy 158
comp.os.ms-windows.announce
comp.os.ms-windows.apps 158
comp.os.ms-windows.misc 159
comp.os.ms-windows.nt.misc
comp.os.ms-windows.nt.setup

comp.os.ms-windows.programmer.misc 159
comp.os.ms-windows.programmer.tools 159
comp.os.ms-windows.programmer.win32 159
comp.os.ms-windows.setup 159
comp.os.msdos.4dos 155
comp.os.msdos.apps 155
comp.os.msdos.desqview 155
comp.os.msdos.desvie
comp.os.msdos.mail-news
comp.os.msdos.misc 155
comp.os.msdos.pcgeos
comp.os.msdos.programmer 155
comp.os.msdos.programmer.turbovision
comp.os.os2 155
comp.os.os2.advocacy 155
comp.os.os2.announce
comp.os.os2.apps 155
comp.os.os2.beta 155
comp.os.os2.bugs
comp.os.os2.misc 155
comp.os.os2.multimedia
comp.os.os2.networking 155
comp.os.os2.programmer 155
comp.os.os2.programmer.misc
comp.os.os2.programmer.porting
comp.os.os2.setup
comp.os.os2.ver1x
comp.os.os9 156
comp.os.qnx
comp.os.research 156
comp.os.rsts
comp.os.v
comp.os.vms 156
comp.os.vxworks 156
comp.os.xinu
comp.parallel 170
comp.parallel.pvm
comp.patents
comp.periphs 173-174
comp.periphs.printers 173
comp.periphs.scsi 173-174
comp.privacy
comp.programming 174
comp.programming.literate
comp.protocols.appletalk 159
comp.protocols.dicom
comp.protocols.ibm 159
comp.protocols.iso 159
comp.protocols.iso.dev-environ
comp.protocols.iso.x400 159
comp.protocols.iso.x400.gateway
comp.protocols.kerberos 159
comp.protocols.kermit
comp.protocols.misc 159
comp.protocols.nfs 159
comp.protocols.pcnet
comp.protocols.ppp 159-160
comp.protocols.pup
comp.protocols.snmp 160
comp.protocols.tcp-ip 160
comp.protocols.tcp-ip.domains 160
comp.protocols.tcp-ip.ibmpc 160
comp.protocols.time.ntp 160
comp.publish.cdrom.hardware
comp.publish.cdrom.multimedia
comp.publish.cdrom.software 145
comp.realtime 174
comp.research.japan 174
comp.risks
comp.robotics 174
comp.security.announce
comp.security.misc 160
comp.security.unix
comp.sex
comp.simulation
comp.society 150
comp.society.cu-digest
comp.society.development
comp.society.folklore
comp.society.futures
comp.society.privacy
comp.society.women
comp.soft-sys.andrew 174
comp.soft-sys.khoros 149
comp.soft-sys.matlab 162

comp.soft-sys.nextstep
comp.soft-sys.sas
comp.soft-sys.shazam
comp.soft-sys.spss
comp.soft-sys.wavefront
comp.software.licensing
comp.software.testing
comp.software-eng 174
comp.sources.3b1
comp.sources.acorn
comp.sources.amiga
comp.sources.apple2
comp.sources.atari.st
comp.sources.bugs
comp.sources.d 161
comp.sources.games
comp.sources.games.bugs
comp.sources.hp48
comp.sources.mac
comp.sources.misc 161
comp.sources.postscript
comp.sources.reviewed
comp.sources.sun
comp.sources.testers
comp.sources.unix
comp.sources.wanted 161
comp.sources.x 162
comp.specification 174
comp.specification.z 174
comp.speech 174
comp.std.announce
comp.std.c++ 142-153
comp.std.c 153
comp.std.internat 174
comp.std.lisp
comp.std.misc
comp.std.mumps
comp.std.unix
comp.std.wireless
comp.sw.components
comp.sys.3b1 167
comp.sys.acorn 164
comp.sys.acorn.advocacy 162
comp.sys.acorn.announce
comp.sys.acorn.tech 162
comp.sys.alliant
comp.sys.amiga 163-164
comp.sys.amiga.advocacy 163
comp.sys.amiga.announce 163
comp.sys.amiga.applications 163
comp.sys.amiga.audio 163
comp.sys.amiga.datacom
comp.sys.amiga.datacomm 163
comp.sys.amiga.emulation
comp.sys.amiga.emulations 163
comp.sys.amiga.games 163
comp.sys.amiga.graphics 163
comp.sys.amiga.hardware 163
comp.sys.amiga.introduction 163
comp.sys.amiga.marketplace 163
comp.sys.amiga.misc 164
comp.sys.amiga.multimedia 164
comp.sys.amiga.programmer 164
comp.sys.amiga.reviews
comp.sys.amiga.software.pirate
comp.sys.amiga.tech
comp.sys.amiga.telecomm
comp.sys.amiga.unix
comp.sys.apollo 167
comp.sys.apple
comp.sys.apple2 164
comp.sys.apple2.comm
comp.sys.apple2.gno 164
comp.sys.apple2.marketplace
comp.sys.apple2.programmer
comp.sys.apple2.usergroups
comp.sys.atari.8bit 164
comp.sys.atari.advocacy 164
comp.sys.atari.chomps.the.big.one
comp.sys.atari.st 164
comp.sys.atari.st.tech 164
comp.sys.att 167
comp.sys.cbm 167
comp.sys.cdc
comp.sys.celerity
comp.sys.concurrent
comp.sys.convex
comp.sys.dec 164

comp.sys.dec.micro 164
comp.sys.encore
comp.sys.handhelds 167
comp.sys.harris
comp.sys.hp 165
comp.sys.hp.apps
comp.sys.hp.hardware
comp.sys.hp.hpux
comp.sys.hp.misc
comp.sys.hp.mpe
comp.sys.hp48 165
comp.sys.hp48.d
comp.sys.ibm.hardware
comp.sys.ibm.pc 168
comp.sys.ibm.pc.demos
comp.sys.ibm.pc.digest
comp.sys.ibm.pc.games 168
comp.sys.ibm.pc.games.action 168
comp.sys.ibm.pc.games.adventure 168
comp.sys.ibm.pc.games.announce
comp.sys.ibm.pc.games.flight-sim
comp.sys.ibm.pc.games.misc
comp.sys.ibm.pc.games.rpg
comp.sys.ibm.pc.games.strategic
comp.sys.ibm.pc.hardware 168
comp.sys.ibm.pc.hardware.cd-rom
comp.sys.ibm.pc.hardware.chips
comp.sys.ibm.pc.hardware.comm
comp.sys.ibm.pc.hardware.misc
comp.sys.ibm.pc.hardware.networking
comp.sys.ibm.pc.hardware.storage
comp.sys.ibm.pc.hardware.systems
comp.sys.ibm.pc.hardware.video
comp.sys.ibm.pc.misc 168
comp.sys.ibm.pc.programmer
comp.sys.ibm.pc.rt 168
comp.sys.ibm.pc.soundcard 168
comp.sys.ibm.pc.soundcard.GUS
comp.sys.ibm.ps2 168
comp.sys.ibm.ps2.hardware 168
comp.sys.intel 167
comp.sys.intel.ipsc310
comp.sys.isis
comp.sys.laptops 167
comp.sys.m6809 166
comp.sys.m68k 166
comp.sys.m68k.pc
comp.sys.m88k 166
comp.sys.mac 165-166
comp.sys.mac.advocacy 165
comp.sys.mac.announce
comp.sys.mac.app
comp.sys.mac.apps 165
comp.sys.mac.comm 165
comp.sys.mac.databases 165
comp.sys.mac.digest
comp.sys.mac.games 165
comp.sys.mac.graphics
comp.sys.mac.hardware 165
comp.sys.mac.hypercard 165
comp.sys.mac.misc 165-166
comp.sys.mac.oop.macapp3 166
comp.sys.mac.oop.misc
comp.sys.mac.oop.tcl
comp.sys.mac.portables 166
comp.sys.mac.programmer 166
comp.sys.mac.scitech
comp.sys.mac.system 166
comp.sys.mac.wanted 166
comp.sys.macintrash
comp.sys.masscomp
comp.sys.mentor 167
comp.sys.mips 167
comp.sys.misc 167
comp.sys.ncr 167
comp.sys.newton.announce
comp.sys.newton.misc
comp.sys.newton.programmer
comp.sys.next 166-167
comp.sys.next.advocacy 166
comp.sys.next.announce 166
comp.sys.next.bugs
comp.sys.next.hardware 166
comp.sys.next.marketplace 166
comp.sys.next.misc 166
comp.sys.next.programmer 167
comp.sys.next.software 167
comp.sys.next.sysadmin 167

comp.sys.northstar
comp.sys.novell 167
comp.sys.nsc.32k
comp.sys.palmtops 168
comp.sys.pen 168
comp.sys.pens
comp.sys.powerpc
comp.sys.prime 168
comp.sys.proteon
comp.sys.psion
comp.sys.pyramid
comp.sys.ridge
comp.sys.sequent 168
comp.sys.sgi 169
comp.sys.sgi.admin 169
comp.sys.sgi.announce
comp.sys.sgi.apps 169
comp.sys.sgi.bugs 169
comp.sys.sgi.graphics 169
comp.sys.sgi.hardware 169
comp.sys.sgi.misc 169
comp.sys.sinclair
comp.sys.stratus
comp.sys.sun 169
comp.sys.sun.admin 169
comp.sys.sun.announce
comp.sys.sun.apps 169
comp.sys.sun.hardware 169
comp.sys.sun.misc 169
comp.sys.sun.wanted 169
comp.sys.super 170
comp.sys.tahoe
comp.sys.tandy 168
comp.sys.ti 168
comp.sys.ti.explorer
comp.sys.transputer 168
comp.sys.unisys 168
comp.sys.vms
comp.sys.workstations
comp.sys.xerox
comp.sys.zenith 168
comp.sys.zenith.z100
comp.terminals 174
comp.terminals.bitgraph
comp.terminals.tty5620
comp.text 171
comp.text.desktop 171
comp.text.frame 171
comp.text.interleaf 171
comp.text.sgml 171
comp.text.tex 171
comp.theory 170
comp.theory.cell-automata 170
comp.theory.dynamic-sys 170
comp.theory.info-retrieval
comp.theory.self-org-sys
comp.unix 157-158, 164
comp.unix.admin 157
comp.unix.advocacy
comp.unix.aix 157
comp.unix.amiga 157
comp.unix.applellgs
comp.unix.aux 157
comp.unix.bsd 157
comp.unix.cray 157
comp.unix.dos-under-unix
comp.unix.i386
comp.unix.intel
comp.unix.internals 157
comp.unix.large
comp.unix.microport
comp.unix.misc 157
comp.unix.msdos
comp.unix.osf.misc
comp.unix.osf.osf1
comp.unix.pc-clone.16bit
comp.unix.pc-clone.32bit 157
comp.unix.programmer 157-158
comp.unix.questions 158
comp.unix.shell 158
comp.unix.solaris 158
comp.unix.sys3
comp.unix.sys5.misc
comp.unix.sys5.r3 158
comp.unix.sys5.r4 158
comp.unix.system_calls.brk.brk.brk
comp.unix.sysv286
comp.unix.sysv386

comp.unix.ultrix 158, 164
comp.unix.unixware
comp.unix.user-friendly
comp.unix.wizards 158
comp.unix.xenix 158
comp.unix.xenix.misc
comp.unix.xenix.sco 158
comp.virus 160-161
comp.windows.garnet
comp.windows.interviews 171
comp.windows.misc 171
comp.windows.ms
comp.windows.ms.programmer
comp.windows.news 171
comp.windows.open-look 171
comp.windows.suit
comp.windows.x 171-172
comp.windows.x.announce
comp.windows.x.apps 172
comp.windows.x.i386unix 172
comp.windows.x.intrinsics 172
comp.windows.x.motif 172
comp.windows.x.pex 172
comp.x
courts.usa.config
courts.usa.federal.supreme
courts.usa.state.ohio.appls-8th
courts.usa.state.ohio.config
courts.usa.state.ohio.supreme
cpdc.test.test
cruzio.general
cruzio.network
cs.cmsc430
cs.dept.notices
cs.robots
cs-gated.announce
cs-monolit.bank.quote
cs-monolit.bank.talk
cs-monolit.bank.tech
cs-monolit.press.business.currency
cs-monolit.press.business.law
cs-moniliter.
cscuk.news
csd.aflb
csd.bboard
csd.building
csd.cmsc818x
csd.logic
csd.machines.hp
csd.new-phd
csd.sports
csn.ads
csn.ml.com-priv
csn.ml.kids 59
csn.ml.kidsnet
csn.ml.nisus-info
csn.ml.saturn 40
csstu.general
csugrad.alt.impeach.ccaputo
ct.config
ct.events
ct.food
ct.general
ct.housing
ct.jobs
ct.market.autos
ct.market.computers
ct.market.housing
ct.market.misc
ct.misc
ct.politics
ct.test
ct.wanted
ctdl.lang.c
ctdl.lang.c++
ctdl.lang.pascal
ctdl.sys.atari.st
ctdl.sys.atari8
ctdl.sys.mac
cu.applmath
cu.courses.cs1300
cu.courses.cs2010
cu.courses.cs2250
cu.courses.cs3155
cu.courses.cs3287
cu.courses.cs5573
cu.courses.econ4999
cu.courses.epob4410

cu.cs.clim
cu.cs.grads
cu.cs.macl.info
cu.cs.srl
cu.cs.systat
cu.cs.ugrads
cu.deaf-hoh.alliance
cu.decstation.managers
cu.garnet
cu.general
cu.grads.teaching
cu.grads.teaching.leads
cu.ics
cu.netstat
cu.physics.ugrads
cu.slug
cu.test
cu.vlsi
cu-den.general
culist.netbsd.current
cv.jobs
cv.oodbms
cwo.x11.intrinsics
cwo.x11.mltalk
cwtest

D

dal.general
dartmouth.alt.DPD
dc.biking
dc.dining
dc.driving
dc.forsale
dc.general
dc.graphics.avs
dc.housing
dc.info-mac
dc.jobs
dc.music
dc.politics
dc.redskins
dc.smithsonian
dc.talk.guns
dc.test
ddn.mgt-bulletin
ddn.newsletter
de.admin.archiv
de.admin.lists
de.admin.mail
de.admin.misc
de.admin.news
de.admin.news.announce
de.admin.news.groups
de.admin.news.misc
de.admin.news.software
de.admin.submaps
de.alt.admin
de.alt.astrologie
de.alt.bbs.waffle
de.alt.bestanden.toga.toga.toga
de.alt.binaries.amigaos
de.alt.binaries.amigaos.d
de.alt.binaries.config
de.alt.binaries.msdos
de.alt.binaries.msdos.d
de.alt.binaries.next
de.alt.binaries.pictures
de.alt.binaries.pictures.comix
de.alt.binaries.pictures.d
de.alt.binaries.pictures.female
de.alt.binaries.pictures.male
de.alt.binaries.pictures.misc
de.alt.binaries.pictures.natur
de.alt.binaries.pictures.relay-party
de.alt.binaries.pictures.tech
de.alt.binaries.sounds
de.alt.binaries.sounds.d
de.alt.binaries.sounds.huge
de.alt.binaries.tos
de.alt.binaries.tos.d
de.alt.cdrom
de.alt.comm.ums
de.alt.comp.os.os9.classic
de.alt.drogen
de.alt.fan.badesalz
de.alt.fan.helgescheider
de.alt.fan.helgeschneider

de.alt.fan.lassie-singers
de.alt.fan.n8schicht
de.alt.fan.perry
de.alt.fan.perry-rhodan
de.alt.fan.pluesch
de.alt.fan.Rocktheater-N8schicht
de.alt.fan.sanni
de.alt.fan.tastische4
de.alt.fan.warlord
de.alt.flame
de.alt.flame.kuchen
de.alt.foto
de.alt.fotografie
de.alt.games.pbem
de.alt.games.starskipper
de.alt.geschichten
de.alt.megatest
de.alt.mud
de.alt.musik
de.alt.netdigest
de.alt.sources
de.alt.sources.huge.unix
de.alt.sources.next
de.alt.sport
de.alt.studienreform
de.alt.sub
de.alt.sub.config.maps
de.alt.sub.general
de.alt.subnet
de.alt.swap
de.alt.sys.amiga.nonmeta
de.alt.test
de.alt.test.create
de.alt.tv.mash
de.alt.zotty.answer
de.alt.zotty.answers
de.answers
de.comm.gatebau
de.comm.gateways
de.comm.ham
de.comm.internet
de.comm.isdn
de.comm.misc
de.comm.uucp
de.comp.databases
de.comp.dtp
de.comp.gnu
de.comp.graphik
de.comp.lang.c
de.comp.lang.c++ 146
de.comp.lang.forth
de.comp.lang.lisp
de.comp.lang.misc
de.comp.lang.pascal
de.comp.lang.perl
de.comp.misc
de.comp.os.linux
de.comp.os.minix
de.comp.os.os9
de.comp.os.unix
de.comp.os.vms
de.comp.os.xenix
de.comp.security
de.comp.sources.amiga
de.comp.sources.d
de.comp.sources.misc
de.comp.sources.os9
de.comp.sources.st
de.comp.sources.unix
de.comp.standards
de.comp.sys.amiga
de.comp.sys.amiga.advocacy
de.comp.sys.amiga.archive
de.comp.sys.amiga.misc
de.comp.sys.amiga.tech
de.comp.sys.amiga.unix
de.comp.sys.amiga.uucp
de.comp.sys.apple
de.comp.sys.ibm
de.comp.sys.misc
de.comp.sys.next
de.comp.sys.pcs
de.comp.sys.st
de.comp.tex
de.etc.finanz
de.etc.lists
de.etc.misc

de.[German-language newsgroups]
de.mag.chalisti
de.mag.chalisti.d
de.mag.misc
de.mag.misc.d
de.markt
de.markt.jobs
de.markt.jobs.d
de.markt.misc
de.newusers
de.newusers.questions
de.org.auge
de.org.ccc
de.org.dfn
de.org.dfn.d
de.org.eunet
de.org.in
de.org.sub
de.org.sub.d
de.org.xlink
de.org.xlink.d
de.rec.fahrrad
de.rec.games
de.rec.games.rpg
de.rec.mampf
de.rec.misc
de.rec.modelle
de.rec.motorrad
de.rec.music.misc
de.rec.sf.misc
de.rec.sf.perry-rhodan
de.rec.sf.startrek
de.sci.ki
de.sci.ki.announce
de.sci.ki.discussion
de.sci.ki.mod-ki
de.sci.medizin
de.sci.misc
de.soc.familie
de.soc.kontakte
de.soc.kultur
de.soc.misc
de.soc.netzwesen
de.soc.politik
de.soc.recht
de.soc.studium
de.soc.umwelt
de.soc.verkehr
de.talk.chat
de.talk.jokes
de.talk.jokes.d
de.talk.jokes.funny
de.talk.misc
de.talk.romance
de.talk.sex
de.test
delaware.nerds
demon.ip.support
demon.ip.support.atari
demon.ip.support.mac
demon.ip.support.pc
demon.ip.support.unix
demon.ip.winsock
demon.local
demon.test
demos.tass.report
depewnet.misc.legal
desy.h1.hquark
desy.h1.news
desy.h1.phan
desy.zeus.beam
desy.zeus.bmuon
desy.zeus.compute
desy.zeus.fmu_vxd
desy.zeus.general
desy.zeus.hes
desy.zeus.lumi
desy.zeus.offline
desy.zeus.physics
desy.zeus.shifts
desy.zeus.srtd
dfw.eats
dfw.flame
dfw.forsale
dfw.general 186
dfw.news
dfw.news.stats
dfw.personals

dfw.singles
dfw.test
disc-vis-graph
dk.misc
dk.politik
dmi.annonces
dn.supers
dn.supers.disc
dnet.and.sub.general
dnet.archiv
dnet.atari
dnet.backbone-news
dnet.chat
dnet.checkgroups
dnet.comp.pcs
dnet.general
dnet.graphik
dnet.ham
dnet.inet
dnet.mod-ki
dnet.news
dnet.test
dnet.witze
dnet.xnet.general
dod.jobs
dsm.network

E

ecua.deportes
ecua.news
ecua.noticias
ecua.talk.ext
ecua.talk.extdep
ed.accommodation
ed.[Edinburgh Systems newsgroups]
ed.followup
ed.general
ed.prolog
ed.review
ed.sources
ed.test
ed.unix-wizards
ed.windows.x
edm.general
edm.news.stats
edm.usrgrp
erg.general
es.mug
esp.news.admin
esp.red.eventos
essug.copt
essug.misc
essug.telco
eunet.aviation
eunet.bugs.4bsd
eunet.bugs.uucp
eunet.checkgroups
eunet.esprit
eunet.esprit.eurochip
eunet.europen
eunet.followup
eunet.general
eunet.jokes
eunet.micro.acorn
eunet.misc
eunet.newprod
eunet.news
eunet.news.group
eunet.politics
eunet.sources
eunet.test
eunet.works

F

fa.eapls
fa.technoculture
fcs.sun-managers
fhg.ilt
fido.amiga-ger
fido.c_plusplus
fido.clipper
fido.desqview
fido.eur.genealogy
fido.flea-ger
fido.ger.386
fido.ger.amiga

fido.ger.atari
fido.ger.book
fido.ger.btx
fido.ger.c_echo
fido.ger.ccc
fido.ger.clipper
fido.ger.comms
fido.ger.ct
fido.ger.dfue
fido.ger.elektronik
fido.ger.flea
fido.ger.frauen
fido.ger.frust
fido.ger.gem
fido.ger.hardware
fido.ger.ibm
fido.ger.isdn
fido.ger.jokes
fido.ger.kirche
fido.ger.kommerz
fido.ger.lan
fido.ger.mailbox
fido.ger.midi
fido.ger.motorrad
fido.ger.movie
fido.ger.musik
fido.ger.os2
fido.ger.pascal
fido.ger.pc_geos
fido.ger.pgmrs
fido.ger.politik
fido.ger.recht
fido.ger.request
fido.ger.rhodan
fido.ger.rpg
fido.ger.sat
fido.ger.shareware
fido.ger.soundkarten
fido.ger.spiele
fido.ger.storage
fido.ger.tex
fido.ger.umwelt
fido.ger.unix
fido.ger.virus
fido.ger.windows
fido.ger.windows.prog
fido.ger.wissen
fido.ger.zyxel
fido.[German-language newsgroups]
fido.hardware-ger
fido.hst
fido.jokes-ger
fido.kommerz-ger
fido.linux-ger
fido.musik-ger
fido.novell
fido.pascal-ger
fido.politik-ger
fido.sex-ger
fido.spiele-ger
fido.windows-ger
fido.wissen-ger
fido.zyxel-ger
fido7.mac
fido7.mo.airport
fido7.modem
fido7.postmasters
fido7.sex
fidonet.filk
finet.asiointi.kunnat
finet.asiointi.pankit
finet.atk.kielet
finet.atk.kielet.c
finet.atk.kielet.elisp
finet.atk.suometus
finet.atk.yllapito
finet.fan.airisto.lenita
finet.[Finnish-language newsgroups]
finet.freenet.harrastus.judo
finet.freenet.harrastus.partio
finet.freenet.keskustelu
finet.freenet.kidlink.kidcafe
finet.freenet.kidlink.kidforum
finet.freenet.kidlink.kidleadr
finet.freenet.kidlink.kidlink
finet.freenet.kidlink.kidplan
finet.freenet.kidlink.kidproj
finet.freenet.kidlink.response

finet.freenet.lastensuojelu.asiantuntijat
finet.freenet.lastensuojelu.keskustelu
finet.freenet.lastensuojelu.nimeton
finet.freenet.lists.freenet-otol
finet.freenet.lists.new-patents
finet.freenet.mediateekki.keskustelu
finet.freenet.mediateekki.kirjasto
finet.freenet.mediateekki.kirjat.uutuudet
finet.freenet.mediateekki.lasten-
osasto.kirja-uutu
finet.freenet.mediateekki.lasten-
osasto.kirjat
finet.freenet.mediateekki.lasten-
osasto.omat-jutut
finet.freenet.mediateekki.lasten-
osasto.pahkina
finet.freenet.mediateekki.lasten-
osasto.sadut
finet.freenet.mediateekki.leffat
finet.freenet.mediateekki.lukusali
finet.freenet.mediateekki.viestinta
finet.freenet.oppimiskeskus.puhe.vanhemmat
finet.freenet.partnerit.art-print
finet.freenet.partnerit.keskustelu
finet.freenet.partnerit.sak
finet.freenet.partnerit.sanoma-oy
finet.freenet.partnerit.yle
finet.freenet.patents.new
finet.freenet.test
finet.freenet.tyoryhmat.kaytannot
finet.freenet.tyoryhmat.kehitys
finet.freenet.tyoryhmat.koulutus
finet.freenet.tyoryhmat.tiedotus
finet.freenet.tyoryhmat.varainhankinta
finet.freenet.tyoryhmat.yhteydet
finet.freenet.tyoryhmat.yllapito
finet.freenet.wyn.pressiklubi
finet.freenet.wyn.uutiset
finet.general
finet.harrastus.amnesty
finet.harrastus.hamppu
finet.harrastus.olut
finet.harrastus.siideri
finet.harrastus.startrek
finet.harrastus.startrek.spocks-hut
finet.harrastus.tolkien
finet.helsinki.hankinnat
finet.helsinki.hoas
finet.helsinki.liikenne
finet.helsinki.puhe
finet.helsinki.ravintolat
finet.helsinki.tapahtumat
finet.ilmot.henkkoht
finet.ilmot.sekal
finet.keskustelu.seksuaalisuus
finet.keskustelu.yleinen
finet.kielet
finet.kielet.englanti
finet.kielet.japani
finet.kielet.suomi
finet.kielet.venaja
finet.kielet.viro
finet.korkeakoulut.atk-politiikka
finet.koti.asuminen
finet.koti.tee-se-itse
finet.koulutus.opintotuki
finet.koulutus.yliopistot
finet.kulttuurit.suomi
finet.kulttuurit.venaja
finet.kulttuurit.viro
finet.kysy.mykset
finet.kysy.osoitteista
finet.kysy.unixista
finet.markkinat.kaupalliset
finet.markkinat.menovesi
finet.markkinat.pc
finet.markkinat.tietokoneet
finet.markkinat.tietopalvelut
finet.olemisen.tarkoitus
finet.politiikka.vaalit
finet.politiikka.yk
finet.puhe
finet.ryhmat
finet.salaliitot
finet.sex
finet.taidot.kirjoittaminen
finet.testi
finet.tiedotteet.lehdisto

finet.tyo.ammattijarj
finet.unet
finet.uutiset.baltia
finet.uutiset.suomi
finet.valtiot.usa
finet.viestinta.bbs
finet.viestinta.freenet
finet.viestinta.internet
finet.viestinta.televerkot
finet.viestinta.usenet
finet.yhteiskunta.anarkismi
finet.yhteiskunta.vaikuttaminen
finet.yhteiskunta.yksilonvapaus
fj.ai
fj.announce
fj.binaries.mac
fj.binaries.misc
fj.binaries.msdos
fj.binaries.msdos.d
fj.binaries.x68000
fj.books
fj.comp.arch
fj.comp.comm
fj.comp.dsp
fj.comp.image
fj.comp.misc
fj.comp.music
fj.comp.oops
fj.comp.parallel
fj.comp.printers
fj.comp.speech
fj.comp.texhax
fj.comp.text
fj.editor.emacs
fj.editor.misc
fj.editor.mule
fj.editor.sse
fj.education
fj.followup
fj.forsale
fj.general
fj.guide.admin
fj.guide.general
fj.guide.newusers
fj.info-terms
fj.[Japan-based newsgroups]
fj.jokes
fj.junet
fj.jus
fj.kanakan.misc
fj.kanakan.wnn
fj.kanji
fj.kermit
fj.lan
fj.lang.ada
fj.lang.awk
fj.lang.c
fj.lang.forth
fj.lang.fortran
fj.lang.lisp
fj.lang.misc
fj.lang.mod2
fj.lang.perl
fj.lang.postscript
fj.lang.prolog
fj.lang.st80
fj.lectures
fj.life.in-japan
fj.living
fj.mail
fj.mail-lists.apollo
fj.mail-lists.common-lisp
fj.mail-lists.connectionist
fj.mail-lists.info-japan
fj.mail-lists.nihongo
fj.mail-lists.parallel
fj.mail-lists.reduce
fj.mail-lists.types
fj.mail-lists.x-window
fj.meetings
fj.misc
fj.misc.handicap
fj.net.misc
fj.net-people
fj.news.adm
fj.news.announce
fj.news.b
fj.news.config

fj.news.group
fj.news.group.archives
fj.news.group.comp
fj.news.group.misc
fj.news.group.net
fj.news.group.rec
fj.news.group.sci
fj.news.group.soc
fj.news.lists
fj.news.map
fj.news.misc
fj.news.newsite
fj.news.policy
fj.news.sa
fj.news.usage
fj.os.386bsd
fj.os.linux
fj.os.minix
fj.os.misc
fj.os.msdos
fj.os.os9
fj.papers
fj.ptt
fj.questions.junet
fj.questions.misc
fj.questions.unix
fj.rec.aerospace
fj.rec.animation
fj.rec.autos
fj.rec.av
fj.rec.bikes
fj.rec.comics
fj.rec.fine-arts
fj.rec.fishing
fj.rec.food
fj.rec.games
fj.rec.games.scores
fj.rec.games.video
fj.rec.games.video.arcade
fj.rec.games.video.home
fj.rec.games.video.pc
fj.rec.ham
fj.rec.idol
fj.rec.marine
fj.rec.misc
fj.rec.models
fj.rec.movies
fj.rec.music
fj.rec.music.classical
fj.rec.music.progressive
fj.rec.mystery
fj.rec.pachinko
fj.rec.pets
fj.rec.photo
fj.rec.play
fj.rec.rail
fj.rec.sf
fj.rec.sports
fj.rec.sports.american.football
fj.rec.sports.baseball
fj.rec.sports.basketball
fj.rec.sports.football
fj.rec.sports.golf
fj.rec.sports.keiba
fj.rec.sports.prowrestling
fj.rec.sports.rugby
fj.rec.sports.ski
fj.rec.sports.soccer
fj.rec.tokusatsu
fj.rec.travel
fj.rec.travel.air
fj.rec.travel.japan
fj.rec.travel.world
fj.rec.tv
fj.rec.video.arcade
fj.sci.astro
fj.sci.bio
fj.sci.chem
fj.sci.geo
fj.sci.human-factors
fj.sci.lang
fj.sci.math
fj.sci.medical
fj.sci.misc
fj.sci.physics
fj.sci.psychology
fj.soc.culture
fj.soc.culture.chinese

fj.soc.environment
fj.soc.handicap
fj.soc.history
fj.soc.law
fj.soc.media
fj.soc.men-women
fj.soc.misc
fj.soc.smoking
fj.soc.tech
fj.soc.traffic
fj.sources
fj.sources.d
fj.sources.mac
fj.std
fj.sys.ews4800
fj.sys.famicom
fj.sys.ibmpc
fj.sys.j3100
fj.sys.luna
fj.sys.mac
fj.sys.misc
fj.sys.news
fj.sys.next
fj.sys.pc98
fj.sys.rs6000
fj.sys.sgi
fj.sys.sun
fj.sys.x6800
fj.sys.x68000
fj.test
fj.unix
fj.unix.wizards
fj.wanted
fj.windows.gmw
fj.windows.misc
fj.windows.x
fl.announce
fl.attractions
fl.comp
fl.comp.rep
fl.forsale 187
fl.general
fl.jobs
fl.mail
fl.map
fl.news
fl.sources
fl.test
fl.travel
fl.uug
fl.yumyum
fnet.afuu
fnet.c3
fnet.combinatoire
fnet.common-lp
fnet.culture
fnet.followup
fnet.formel
fnet.[French-language newsgroups]
fnet.general
fnet.greco-prog
fnet.hypercubes
fnet.ia
fnet.lang
fnet.lelisp
fnet.lmastat
fnet.seminaires
fnet.sm90
fnet.sps9
fnet.test
fnet.tietoliikenne.televerkot
fr.announce.newgroups
fr.bio.biolmol
fr.bio.general
fr.bio.genome
fr.bio.logiciel
fr.comp.infosystemes
fr.comp.os.linux
fr.[French-language newsgroups]
fr.network.incidents.annonces
fr.network.incidents.tickets
fr.rec.genealogie
fr.rec.humour
fr.rec.sport
fr.res-doct.archi
fr.sci.cogni.discussion
fr.sci.cogni.incognito
fr.sci.cogni.info

fr.sci.cogni.outil
fr.sci.cogni.publication
fr.test
frmug.general
fub.general

G

ga.atl-braves
ga.forsale
ga.general
ga.test
gac.fan.pseudo-
dan.whine.whine.whine.whine
gasco.weather
gay-net.labern
gen.nativenet
geo.general
geo.test
geometry.announcements
geometry.college
geometry.forum
geometry.[geometry discussion newsgroups]
geometry.institutes
geometry.pre-college
geometry.puzzles
geometry.research
gernet.ct
git.ads
git.cc.alums
git.cc.class.1501
git.cc.class.1502
git.cc.class.150x
git.cc.class.2360
git.cc.class.2390
git.cc.class.2430
git.cc.class.3450
git.cc.class.4324
git.cc.class.4341
git.cc.class.4803a
git.cc.class.6395
git.cc.class.6752
git.cc.class.7323
git.cc.class.7390
git.cc.class.8011p
git.cc.class.8113h
git.cc.class.8113p
git.cc.class.8113r
git.cc.cscw
git.cc.general
git.cc.help
git.class.class.2360
git.club.ans
git.club.asa
git.club.guns
git.club.musicians-net
git.club.seds
git.club.sword
git.cont-ed
git.edutech
git.ee.class.1300d
git.ee.class.2510
git.ee.class.3901
git.ee.class.3902
git.ee.class.390x
git.ee.class.6180
git.ee.class.6311
git.ee.class.6418
git.ee.class.compe.3510
git.ee.compass
git.environment
git.general
git.[Georgia Institute of Technology]
git.grad
git.hideout
git.infosystems
git.isye.class.3010
git.isye.class.6221
git.isye.class.6680
git.isye.class.6761
git.isye.class.7524
git.isye.class.8102
git.isye.general
git.isye.mot
git.lcc.class.1001j
git.lcc.class.2020j2
git.lcc.class.2310p

git.lcc.class.3020.bel
git.lcc.class.3020o
git.lcc.class.4020
git.lcc.class.6103
git.lcc.class.6303a
git.math.class.1507a4
git.math.class.3012a1
git.math.class.4803a
git.math.symbolic
git.me.research
git.mechatronics
git.media-talk
git.msm.general
git.news.groups
git.ohr.jobs.digest
git.oit.availability
git.oit.questions
git.os2
git.police.parking
git.politics
git.psych.class.1010
git.psych.class.1010a
git.psych.class.1010b
git.psych.class.1010c
git.psych.class.1010d
git.psych.class.1010e
git.psych.class.1010f
git.psych.class.1010g
git.psych.class.1010h
git.quality
git.sga.usc
git.talk.abortion
git.talk.religion
git.tech.futures
git.test
git.unix.solaris
gnu.announce
gnu.bash.bug 147
gnu.chess 147-148
gnu.config
gnu.emacs 148
gnu.emacs.announce
gnu.emacs.bug 148
gnu.emacs.gnews
gnu.emacs.gnus 148
gnu.emacs.help 148
gnu.emacs.lisp.manual
gnu.emacs.sex
gnu.emacs.sources 148
gnu.emacs.vm.bug 148
gnu.emacs.vm.info
gnu.emacs.vms
gnu.epoch.misc
gnu.g++ 147-148
gnu.g++.announce
gnu.g++.bug
gnu.g++.help
gnu.g++.lib.bug
gnu.gcc 148
gnu.gcc.announce
gnu.gcc.bug 148
gnu.gcc.help 148
gnu.gdb.bug 148
gnu.ghostscript.bug 148
gnu.gnusenet.config
gnu.gnusenet.test 148
gnu.groff.bug
gnu.misc.discuss 148
gnu.smalltalk.bug
gnu.test
gnu.utils.bug 148

H

hac.usenet
hackercorp.statistics
hannet.ip
hannet.ml.test
hannet.test
harvard.science-review
harvard.test
hebron.local
hepnet.admin
hepnet.announce
hepnet.conferences
hepnet.freehep
hepnet.general
hepnet.hepix

hepnet.heplib
hepnet.[Internet administrators newsgroups]
hepnet.isdn
hepnet.jobs
hepnet.lang.c++
hepnet.remote-conf.audio
hepnet.test
hepnet.videoconf
hfx.general
hiv.actup-actnow
hiv.aids.issues
hiv.aidsweekly
hiv.alt-treatments
hiv.announce
hiv.atn
hiv.events.ny
hiv.events.sf
hiv.excerpts
hiv.icata90
hiv.informal.conversations
hiv.int-conf-aids.sixth
hiv.med.questions
hiv.netherlands
hiv.oz.aids.marc
hiv.oz-aids-marc
hiv.planning
hiv.resources.addresses
hiv.seropos-ball
hiv.south
hiv.stories-myths
hiv.test
hiv.witness-project
houston.eats
houston.efh.talk
houston.forsale 187
houston.general
houston.music
houston.news
houston.news.stats
houston.personals
houston.singles
houston.test
houston.wanted
houston.weather
hsv.flame
hsv.forsale 187
hsv.general
hsv.jobs
hsv.politics
hsv.religion
hsv.tech
hw.general
hy.opiskelu.tkol.atk-perusteet

I

ia.talk.misc
ieee.announce
ieee.config
ieee.fidonet.admin
ieee.fidonet.bbs-help
ieee.fidonet.ieee
ieee.general
ieee.net.tech
ieee.news.admin
ieee.news.announce
ieee.news.newgroup
ieee.[newsgroups for IEEE Engineering society]
ieee.pcnfs
ieee.pcnfs.lifeline
ieee.rab.announce
ieee.rab.general
ieee.region1
ieee.tab.announce
ieee.tab.general
ieee.tcos
ieee.usab.announce
ieee.usab.general
ifi.in105
iij.announce
iij.general
iij.[Japan newsgroups]
iij.mail
iij.misc
iij.newsgroup
iij.questions

iij.requests
iij.test
iijnet.arts
iijnet.chem
iijnet.cm
iijnet.databases
iijnet.dcom
iijnet.dcom.carrier
iijnet.dcom.isdn
iijnet.dcom.modem
iijnet.diy
iijnet.event
iijnet.examination
iijnet.food
iijnet.forsale
iijnet.games
iijnet.general
iijnet.internauts
iijnet.internet
iijnet.jobs
iijnet.literature
iijnet.living
iijnet.mail
iijnet.med
iijnet.mpu
iijnet.mpu.i486
iijnet.mpu.sparc
iijnet.multimedia
iijnet.music
iijnet.netnews
iijnet.os
iijnet.os.dosv
iijnet.os.msdos
iijnet.os.unix
iijnet.real-estate
iijnet.sci
iijnet.sports
iijnet.sys.ibm-pc
iijnet.travel
iijnet.wanted
imag.fan.jean-louis.roch
in.bizarre
in.general 82, 120, 188, 202
in.ham-radio
in.jobs
in.misc
in.pc.mac
in.test
in.unix
info.academic-freedom
info.admin
info.big-internet 32
info.bind
info.brl-cad 145
info.bsdi.users
info.bytecounters
info.cmu-tek-tcp
info.convex
info.csg
info.epoch
info.firearms 76
info.firearms.politics
info.gated
info.grass.programmer
info.grass.user
info.gwmon
info.ibmtcp
info.icecnet
info.ietf 150
info.ietf.hosts
info.ietf.isoc
info.ietf.njm
info.ietf.smtp 150
info.interviews
info.isi
info.isode
info.jethro-tull
info.labmgr 174
info.mach
info.mh.workers
info.ncsa-telnet
info.nets
info.novell
info.nsf.grants
info.nsfnet.cert
info.nsfnet.status
info.nupop
info.nysersnmp

info.osf
info.pcipdriver
info.pem-dev 150
info.ph
info.rfc
info.rs6000
info.sganet
info.slug
info.snmp 160
info.solbourne
info.suearn
info.sun-managers 169
info.sun-nets
info.theorynt
info.unix-sw
info.utah-toolkit
info.wisenet
iu.india

J

jmas.test

K

k12.chat.elementary 138
k12.chat.junior 138
k12.chat.senior 138
k12.chat.teacher 138
k12.ed.art
k12.ed.business 138
k12.ed.comp.literacy 138
k12.ed.health-pe 138
k12.ed.lang.esp-eng
k12.ed.life-skills
k12.ed.math 138
k12.ed.music 138
k12.ed.science 138
k12.ed.soc-studies 138
k12.ed.special 138
k12.ed.tag 139
k12.ed.tech 139
k12.lang.art 139
k12.lang.deutsch-eng 139
k12.lang.esp-eng 139
k12.lang.francais 139
k12.lang.russian 139
k12.sys.channel6
k12.sys.channel9
ks.admin
ks.misc
kso.fan.warlord
ksu.fan.ralph
kw.bb.sale
kw.birthdays
kw.cpsr
kw.eats
kw.forsale
kw.fun
kw.general 188
kw.housing
kw.internet
kw.jobs
kw.micro
kw.microvax
kw.movies
kw.networks
kw.news
kw.news.stats
kw.stats
kw.theatre
kw.uucp
kw.virtual-worlds
ky.motorcycles
ky.weather
ky.weather.d

L

la.eats 187
la.forsale 187
la.general 187
la.news
la.personals
la.seminars
la.slug
la.test
la.wanted

latech.stis
list.environment
list.framers
list.gnu-msdos
list.gnuplot
list.khoros
list.maple
list.nativenet
list.phys-l
list.sun-managers
liu.lysator.test.nyskapad
liu.lysator.test.nyskapadii
local.forsale
local.general
local.marks
lon.misc 194
lon.test
lou.general
lou.sun
ls.amnesty
ls.olnews
ls.ussr

M

m4.patriot.engrdocs
m4.patriot.general
m4.patriot.test1
mac.test.dant
mail.apps.explorer
mail.ietf.end2end
mail.sun-managers
mail.sun-nets
mail.uk-sendmail-workers
manawatu.astronomy
materialnet.test
maus.[German newsgroups]
maus.info
maus.info.d
maus.landrock
maus.os.linux
maus.os.os2.prog
maus.recht
maus.schach
maus.sys.archimedes
maus.sys.atari.okami
maus.sys.atari.talk
maus.sys.mac
maus.sys.mac.dev
maus.sys.ql.c68-int
maus.sys.ql.ger
maus.sys.ql.int
mcnc.cad
mcnc.concert.video
mcnc.dcom
mcnc.general
mcnc.ncsulab
mcnc.pc
mcnc.programmers
mcnc.rec
mcnc.systems
mcnc.talks
mcnc.teleclass
mcnc.text
mentorg.list.list-managers
mentorg.metrics
mentorg.pacer
mercury.general
mi.jobs
mi.map
mi.michnet
mi.misc 186
mi.news
mi.sources
mi.sun
mi.wanted
milw.general
milw.jobs
milw.unix
misc.activism.progressive
misc.answers 32
misc.books.technical 125
misc.consumers 39
misc.consumers.house 39
misc.education 139
misc.education.language.english
misc.emerg-services 59
misc.entrepreneurs 37

misc.fitness 179
misc.forsale 41, 147, 166, 169
misc.forsale.computers 147, 166, 169
misc.forsale.computers.d 147
misc.forsale.computers.mac 166
misc.forsale.computers.other 147
misc.forsale.computers.pc-clone 169
misc.forsale.computers.workstation 147
misc.forsale.wanted 41
misc.handicap 63
misc.headlines 93
misc.headlines.unitex
misc.health.alternative 39
misc.health.diabetes 62
misc.int-property 38
misc.invest 38
misc.invest.canada
misc.invest.funds
misc.invest.real-estate 38
misc.invest.stocks
misc.invest.technical 38
misc.jobs.contract 41
misc.jobs.misc 41
misc.jobs.offered 41
misc.jobs.offered.entry 41
misc.jobs.offered
misc.jobs.resumes 41
misc.kids 62, 139
misc.kids.computer 139
misc.kids.vacation
misc.legal 38, 174
misc.legal.computing 174
misc.legal.moderated
misc.misc 41
misc.news.east-europe.rferl 93
misc.news.southasia 93
misc.rural 40
misc.security
misc.sheep
misc.taxes 38
misc.test
misc.wanted 41
misc.writing 58-59
mit.bboard
mit.help.tex
mit.lcs.announce
mit.lcs.misc
mit.lcs.seminar
mit.test
mn.archive
mn.general
mn.map
mn.net
mn.sources
mn.test
mn.traffic
mn.uum
motrpg.pit
mscs.general
msu.general
mtl.freenet.org
mtl.general
mtl.nntp
mtl.ntp
mtl.test
mu.general
muc.bondage
muc.flame
muc.general
muc.test
mucsd.general
music.genesis

N

nas.msgs
nas.nets
nas.wks
nasa.oast
nasa.oast.supersite
nashville.general
navy.nswc.testgroup1
nbg.general
nc.charlotte.entertainment
nc.charlotte.sports
nc.general 188
nc.info-highway
ncku.talk

ncsc.chemistry
ncsc.general
ncsc.systems
ncsc.training
nctu.club.midi
nctu.club.stamp
nctu.test
ne.food
ne.forsale
ne.general
ne.housing
ne.jobs
ne.motorcycles 60
ne.motss
ne.nearnet.general
ne.nearnet.tech
ne.news
ne.org.bcs
ne.org.decus
ne.org.neci.announce
ne.org.neci.general
ne.org.neci.nsp
ne.org.neci.software
ne.politics
ne.seminars
ne.singles
ne.wanted
net157.chat157
net157.region11
netcom.general
neworleans.general 187
neworleans.info
news.admin 31
news.admin.misc 31
news.admin.policy 31
news.admin.technical
news.announce.conferences 58
news.announce.important
news.announce.newgroups
news.announce.newusers
news.answers
news.config
news.future
news.groups 178
news.lists
news.lists.ps-maps
news.members
news.misc 31, 93
news.newsites
news.newusers.questions
news.software.anu-news 31
news.software.b 32
news.software.nn 32
news.software.nntp
news.software.notes
news.software.readers 30
news.sortware.nntp
news.sysadmin
news.test
nil.general
nil.maps
nirwana.kochecke
nirwana.uni.verkehrskonzept
nj.config
nj.events
nj.followup
nj.forsale
nj.general 187
nj.market.autos
nj.market.computers
nj.market.housing
nj.market.misc
nj.misc
nj.politics
nj.test
nj.wanted
nj.weather
nlnet.aio
nlnet.announce
nlnet.comp
nlnet.culinair
nlnet.followup
nlnet.general
nlnet.markt
nlnet.misc 194
nlnet.muziek
nlnet.pico
nlnet.sport

nlnet.taal
nlnet.test
nmi.admin
nmt.fool
no.ai
no.alkohol
no.alt.arkiv
no.alt.config
no.alt.fan.alvestrand
no.alt.flame
no.alt.frustrasjoner
no.alt.gledesutbrudd
no.alt.god.jul
no.alt.mat
no.alt.pompel-og-pilt
no.alt.sjokolade
no.c
no.ef
no.embnet
no.eunet.diverse
no.general 194
no.havforskning
no.irc
no.kjemi
no.multimedia
no.net
no.news
no.news.diverse
no.nuug
no.sources.list
no.sources.wanted
no.speider
no.sport.diverse
no.test
no.tungregning
no.unix
no.vitser
no.vr
no.x
nocturnal.ufo
nordunet.edu.nfdl
nordunet.sci.nopex
nordunet.sci.nopex.kurs1
north.market
nptn.academy.eclub
nptn.academy.spotlight.people
nptn.special.special-event0
nptn.special.special-event7
nptn.special.special-event8
nptn.special.special-event9
nptn.student.inter.generation
ns.general
ns.nstn.usergroup
ny.config
ny.followup
ny.forsale 188
ny.general 188
ny.nyser.net
ny.nysernet
ny.nysernet.map
ny.nysernet.maps
ny.nysernet.nic
ny.nysernet.nysertech
ny.politics
ny.seminars
ny.test
ny.wanted
nyc.announce
nyc.food
nyc.general 187
nyc.seminars
nyc.test
nynex.trd.eslab
nyt.test
nz.archives
nz.arts
nz.comp
nz.general 194
nz.molbio
nz.netstatus
nz.rec
nz.soc
nz.soc.green
nz.wanted

O

oar.noc

oar.tech
oar.users
oau.news
oc.acm
oc.forsale
oc.general
oc.slug
oc.test
oc.wanted
ocunix.general
ocunix.mail.glove
ocunix.mail.mail.hurd-folk
ocunix.mail.space-tech
ocunix.mail.sun-home
ocunix.mail.taylor-uucp
ocunix.mail.thinknet
ogi.general
oh.cast
oh.chem
oh.general
oh.k12
oh.news
oh.osc.software
oh.test
ok.general
ont.archives
ont.conditions
ont.events
ont.events.macwator.ece
ont.followup
ont.forsale
ont.general 194
ont.jobs
ont.micro
ont.personals.whips.and.rubber.chickens
ont.sf-lovers
ont.singles
ont.test
ont.uucp
opinions.supreme-court
or.forsale
or.general 188
or.ojgse.cis641
or.politics
or.test
orst.announce
orst.cs.101
orst.cs.131
orst.cs.151x
orst.cs.162
orst.cs.211
orst.cs.212
orst.cs.213
orst.cs.215
orst.cs.251
orst.cs.261
orst.cs.311
orst.cs.312
orst.cs.315
orst.cs.317
orst.cs.318
orst.cs.319
orst.cs.321
orst.cs.324
orst.cs.325
orst.cs.326
orst.cs.361
orst.cs.381
orst.cs.391
orst.cs.401
orst.cs.405
orst.cs.406
orst.cs.410
orst.cs.411
orst.cs.416
orst.cs.417
orst.cs.419
orst.cs.420
orst.cs.430
orst.cs.431
orst.cs.438
orst.cs.440
orst.cs.450
orst.cs.460
orst.cs.470
orst.cs.471
orst.cs.480
orst.cs.481

orst.cs.482
orst.cs.501
orst.cs.503
orst.cs.505
orst.cs.506
orst.cs.507C
orst.cs.507S
orst.cs.515
orst.cs.516
orst.cs.519
orst.cs.521
orst.cs.523
orst.cs.527
orst.cs.530
orst.cs.531
orst.cs.532
orst.cs.533
orst.cs.534
orst.cs.539
orst.cs.540
orst.cs.541
orst.cs.542
orst.cs.549
orst.cs.559
orst.cs.561
orst.cs.562
orst.cs.569
orst.cs.571
orst.cs.577x
orst.cs.581
orst.cs.585
orst.cs.587
orst.cs.589
orst.cs.601
orst.cs.603
orst.cs.605
orst.cs.announce
orst.cs.comment
orst.cs.consult.reading
orst.cs.consultants
orst.cs.dynix
orst.cs.general
orst.cs.grads
orst.cs.howto
orst.cs.hpux
orst.cs.hypercube
orst.cs.jobs
orst.cs.misc
orst.cs.msgs
orst.cs.project
orst.cs.public
orst.cs.resume
orst.cs.support
orst.cs.test
orst.cs.undergrad
orst.cs.unix.reading
orst.cs.utek
orst.csos.announce
orst.csos.public
orst.ece.375
orst.ece.471
orst.ece.478
orst.ee.475
orst.engr.announce
orst.forsale
orst.general
orst.jobs
orst.mail.activist
orst.mail.firewalls
orst.mail.sca-heralds
orst.mail.skunk-works
orst.mail.texhax
orst.math.announce
orst.math.general
orst.me.413
orst.network.announce
orst.network.misc
orst.network.reports
orst.news.admin
orst.news.announce
orst.oce.cm
orst.oce.data
orst.oce.general
orst.oce.ibm
orst.oce.social
orst.oce.software
orst.oce.unix
orst.oce.vis

orst.oce.wecoma
orst.org.acm
orst.org.cpsr
orst.org.faculty-senate
orst.org.gpsa
orst.org.ucsc
orst.publications
orst.sig.ai
orst.sig.congress93
orst.sig.novell
orst.sig.politics
orst.social
orst.sports
orst.sys.dec
orst.sys.next
orst.sys.os2
orst.sys.sun
orst.test
orst.ucs
orst.ucs.test
osu.acm
osu.ai
osu.ai.aim
osu.ai.hardware.sun
osu.ai.software.ext.excl
osu.ai.software.ext.frame
osu.chinese
osu.faculty.council
osu.for-sale 190
osu.general
osu.grads
osu.ibm.pc
osu.ibmpc
osu.indian
osu.jobs
osu.lisp
osu.mac
osu.magnus
osu.music
osu.network
osu.opinion
osu.opinion.libertarian
osu.sports
osu.tex
osu.women
ott.events
ott.forsale
ott.general 194
ott.housing
ott.news
ott.online
ott.singles
ott.vietnamese
ott.weather

P

pa.admin
pa.config
pa.forsale
pa.general 188
pa.test
pa.wanted
panix.announce
pbinfo.amiga
pdaxs.ads.antiques
pdaxs.ads.apartments
pdaxs.ads.appliances
pdaxs.ads.audio_video
pdaxs.ads.boats
pdaxs.ads.books
pdaxs.ads.cars
pdaxs.ads.cars.audio
pdaxs.ads.cars.misc
pdaxs.ads.cars.rv
pdaxs.ads.cars.service
pdaxs.ads.clothing
pdaxs.ads.computers
pdaxs.ads.food
pdaxs.ads.furniture
pdaxs.ads.homes.n
pdaxs.ads.homes.ne
pdaxs.ads.homes.nw
pdaxs.ads.homes.se
pdaxs.ads.homes.sw
pdaxs.ads.hotels
pdaxs.ads.jewelry
pdaxs.ads.lostrfound

pdaxs.ads.misc
pdaxs.ads.movies
pdaxs.ads.music
pdaxs.ads.notices
pdaxs.ads.office
pdaxs.ads.personals
pdaxs.ads.printing
pdaxs.ads.real_estate
pdaxs.ads.restaurants
pdaxs.ads.sales
pdaxs.ads.sports
pdaxs.ads.tickets
pdaxs.ads.tools
pdaxs.ads.wanted
pdaxs.arts.auditions
pdaxs.arts.museums
pdaxs.arts.music
pdaxs.arts.print
pdaxs.arts.radio
pdaxs.arts.tv
pdaxs.calendar.art
pdaxs.calendar.business
pdaxs.calendar.computers
pdaxs.calendar.misc
pdaxs.calendar.music
pdaxs.calendar.volunteers
pdaxs.games.board
pdaxs.games.bridge
pdaxs.games.chess
pdaxs.games.misc
pdaxs.games.rpg
pdaxs.issues.democrats
pdaxs.issues.education
pdaxs.issues.portland
pdaxs.issues.republicans
pdaxs.jobs.clerical
pdaxs.jobs.computers
pdaxs.jobs.construction
pdaxs.jobs.delivery
pdaxs.jobs.domestic
pdaxs.jobs.engineering
pdaxs.jobs.management
pdaxs.jobs.misc
pdaxs.jobs.restaurants
pdaxs.jobs.resumes
pdaxs.jobs.retail
pdaxs.jobs.sales
pdaxs.jobs.secretary
pdaxs.jobs.temporary
pdaxs.jobs.volunteers
pdaxs.jobs.wanted
pdaxs.[Portland, Oregon newsgroups]
pdaxs.religion.christian
pdaxs.religion.jewish
pdaxs.religion.misc
pdaxs.religion.moslem
pdaxs.religion.newage
pdaxs.schools.acting
pdaxs.schools.cooking
pdaxs.schools.dance
pdaxs.schools.fitness
pdaxs.schools.kids
pdaxs.schools.martial
pdaxs.schools.misc
pdaxs.schools.music
pdaxs.schools.sports
pdaxs.services.accounting
pdaxs.services.appliance
pdaxs.services.carpentry
pdaxs.services.children
pdaxs.services.cleaning
pdaxs.services.computers
pdaxs.services.consulting
pdaxs.services.counseling
pdaxs.services.electrical
pdaxs.services.financial
pdaxs.services.fitness
pdaxs.services.gardening
pdaxs.services.graphics
pdaxs.services.insurance
pdaxs.services.int_design
pdaxs.services.landscaping
pdaxs.services.legal
pdaxs.services.massage
pdaxs.services.misc
pdaxs.services.moving
pdaxs.services.music
pdaxs.services.painting

pdaxs.services.pets
pdaxs.services.photo
pdaxs.services.plumbing
pdaxs.services.roofing
pdaxs.services.security
pdaxs.services.storage
pdaxs.services.wordproc
pdaxs.sports.baseball
pdaxs.sports.basketball
pdaxs.sports.football
pdaxs.sports.golf
pdaxs.sports.rotisserie
pdx.books
pdx.computing
pdx.forsale
pdx.games
pdx.general
pdx.golf
pdx.movies
pdx.music
pdx.online
pdx.[Portland, OR-area newsgroups]
pdx.running
pdx.singles
pdx.slug
pdx.soc
pdx.sports
pdx.telecom
pdx.test
pdx.utek
pgh.apartments
pgh.cpsr
pgh.food
pgh.forsale
pgh.general
pgh.next-users
pgh.test
phl.announce
phl.bicycles
phl.config
phl.dance
phl.food
phl.forsale
phl.misc
phl.music
phl.outdoors
phl.sports
phl.test
phl.theatre
phl.wanted
phl.weather
phri.general
pipex.dialup
pipex.tickets
pnw.foresale
pnw.forsale
pnw.general
pnw.motss
pnw.news
pnw.[Pacific Northwest regional newsgroups]
pnw.personals
pnw.sys.sun
pnw.test
portfolio
prg.jobs
psi.general
psi.nrg
psi.nwg
psi.psilink
psi.[PSILink network newsgroups]
psi.psinet
psi.stats
psi.test
psi.tickets
psu.cac.outages
pubnet.config
pubnet.nixpub
pubnet.sources
pubnet.sysops
pubnet.talk
pubnet.test
pubnet.wanted
purdue.forsale
purdue.general

Q

qtp.bulletin
qtp.general

R

rain.bsdi-users
rain.firewalls
rain.smail3
rain.sources
rain.sources.d
rec.answers 32
rec.antiques 74
rec.aquaria
rec.arts.animation 101
rec.arts.anime 101-102
rec.arts.anime.info 101
rec.arts.anime.marketplace 101
rec.arts.anime.stories 102
rec.arts.bodyart 201-202
rec.arts.bonsai 75
rec.arts.books 98-99, 187, 189
rec.arts.books.tolkien 99
rec.arts.cinema 114
rec.arts.comics 101
rec.arts.comics.info 101
rec.arts.comics.marketplace 101
rec.arts.comics.misc 101
rec.arts.comics.strips 101
rec.arts.comics.xbooks 101
rec.arts.dance 75
rec.arts.disney 87
rec.arts.drwho 119
rec.arts.erotica
rec.arts.fine 74
rec.arts.int-fiction 100
rec.arts.manga 100
rec.arts.marching.drumcorps 89
rec.arts.marching.misc 89
rec.arts.misc 74
rec.arts.movies 114
rec.arts.movies.reviews 114
rec.arts.poems 100
rec.arts.prose
rec.arts.sf.announce 119
rec.arts.sf.fandom
rec.arts.sf.marketplace 119
rec.arts.sf.misc 119
rec.arts.sf.movies
rec.arts.sf.reviews
rec.arts.sf.science 119
rec.arts.sf.starwars 119
rec.arts.sf.tv 119
rec.arts.sf.written 119-120
rec.arts.sf-lovers
rec.arts.sf-reviews
rec.arts.startrek 120-122
rec.arts.startrek.current 120
rec.arts.startrek.fandom 120
rec.arts.startrek.info 120-121
rec.arts.startrek.misc 121
rec.arts.startrek.reviews
rec.arts.startrek.tech 121-122
rec.arts.theatre 88-89
rec.arts.tv 118-119
rec.arts.tv.soaps 118
rec.arts.tv.tiny-toon
rec.arts.tv.uk 119
rec.arts.wobegon 115
rec.audio 113
rec.audio.car 113
rec.audio.high-end 113
rec.audio.pro 113
rec.auto
rec.autos 82-83
rec.autos.antique 82
rec.autos.driving 83
rec.autos.marketplace
rec.autos.misc
rec.autos.rod-n-custom 83
rec.autos.simulators
rec.autos.sport 83
rec.autos.subaru
rec.autos.tech 83
rec.autos.vw 83
rec.aviation 79-80
rec.aviation.announce
rec.aviation.answers 79
rec.aviation.homebuilt 79

rec.aviation.ifr 79
rec.aviation.military 79
rec.aviation.misc 80
rec.aviation.owning 80
rec.aviation.piloting 80
rec.aviation.products 80
rec.aviation.simulators 80
rec.aviation.soaring 80
rec.aviation.stories 80
rec.aviation.student 80
rec.backcountry 177
rec.basketball.nude
rec.bicycles 181-182
rec.bicycles.marketplace 181
rec.bicycles.misc 182
rec.bicycles.racing 182
rec.bicycles.rides 182
rec.bicycles.soc 182
rec.bicycles.tech 182
rec.birds 85
rec.boats 84
rec.boats.paddle 84
rec.chrome.dildos
rec.climbing 178
rec.collecting 74
rec.collecting.cards 74
rec.collecting.stamps
rec.crafts.brewing 75
rec.crafts.metalworking 77
rec.crafts.misc 77
rec.crafts.quilting
rec.crafts.textiles 77
rec.crafts.winemaking 78
rec.equestrian 179
rec.fart
rec.fitness
rec.folk-dancing
rec.food.cooking 78
rec.food.drink 78
rec.food.historic 78
rec.food.recipes 78
rec.food.restaurants 78
rec.food.sourdough 78
rec.food.veg 78-79
rec.gambling 89
rec.games.abstract
rec.games.backgammon 103
rec.games.board 103
rec.games.board.ce
rec.games.bolo
rec.games.bridge 103
rec.games.chess 103
rec.games.chinese-chess
rec.games.corewar
rec.games.cyber
rec.games.design
rec.games.diplomacy 103
rec.games.empire
rec.games.frp 105
rec.games.frp.advocacy 105
rec.games.frp.announce
rec.games.frp.archives
rec.games.frp.cyber 105
rec.games.frp.dnd
rec.games.frp.live-action
rec.games.frp.marketplace 105
rec.games.frp.misc 105
rec.games.go
rec.games.hack
rec.games.int-fiction
rec.games.mecha 102
rec.games.miniatures 102
rec.games.misc
rec.games.moria
rec.games.mud 104
rec.games.mud.admin 104
rec.games.mud.announce 104
rec.games.mud.bogleg.eotl.bume
rec.games.mud.diku 104
rec.games.mud.lp 104
rec.games.mud.misc 104
rec.games.mud.tiny 104
rec.games.mud.wine.bitch.moan
rec.games.netrek
rec.games.pbm 102-103
rec.games.pinball
rec.games.programmer 103
rec.games.rogue

rec.games.roguelike.angband
rec.games.roguelike.announce
rec.games.roguelike.misc
rec.games.rpg
rec.games.trivia 103
rec.games.vectrex
rec.games.video 102
rec.games.video.3do
rec.games.video.advocacy
rec.games.video.arcade 102
rec.games.video.arcade.collecting
rec.games.video.atari
rec.games.video.classic 102
rec.games.video.marketplace 102
rec.games.video.misc 102
rec.games.video.nintendo 102
rec.games.video.sega 102
rec.games.xtank.play
rec.games.xtank.programmer
rec.gardens
rec.golf
rec.guns 76
rec.ham-radio
rec.ham-radio.packet
rec.ham-radio.swap
rec.heraldry
rec.humor 106
rec.humor.d 106
rec.humor.flame
rec.humor.funny 106
rec.humor.oracle 106
rec.humor.oracle.d 106
rec.hunting
rec.juggling
rec.kibo.hunting
rec.kites
rec.mag
rec.mag.fsfnet
rec.mag.otherrealms
rec.martial-arts
rec.misc
rec.models.railroad
rec.models.rc
rec.models.rockets
rec.models.scale
rec.motorcycles 83
rec.motorcycles.dirt 83
rec.motorcycles.harley
rec.motorcycles.racing
rec.music 107-114
rec.music.a-cappella
rec.music.afro-latin 108
rec.music.beatles 107
rec.music.bluenote 108-109
rec.music.cd 113-114
rec.music.celtic
rec.music.christian 110
rec.music.classical 109
rec.music.classical.guitar
rec.music.classical.performing
rec.music.compose
rec.music.country.western 109
rec.music.dementia 110
rec.music.dylan 107
rec.music.early 109
rec.music.folk 109
rec.music.funky 108
rec.music.gaffa 109
rec.music.gdead 107
rec.music.indian.classical 109
rec.music.indian.misc 109
rec.music.industrial 109
rec.music.info 107, 109-111, 113
rec.music.makers 112-113
rec.music.makers.bass 112
rec.music.makers.guitar 112
rec.music.makers.guitar.acoustic
rec.music.makers.guitar.tablature 112
rec.music.makers.marketplace
rec.music.makers.percussion 112
rec.music.makers.synth 112-113
rec.music.marketplace 111
rec.music.misc 111
rec.music.newa-young
rec.music.newage 110
rec.music.phish 110
rec.music.reggae 108
rec.music.reviews 111

rec.music.synth 113
rec.music.video 111
rec.nude 201
rec.org.mensa 202
rec.org.mensa.flame.flame.flame
rec.org.sca 89
rec.outdoors.fishing 179
rec.parks.theme 87
rec.pets 84-86
rec.pets.birds 85
rec.pets.cats 85
rec.pets.dogs 85-86
rec.pets.herp 85
rec.pets.rabbits
rec.photo 77
rec.puzzles 77-78
rec.puzzles.crosswords 78
rec.pyrotechnics 201
rec.radio.amateur.antenna
rec.radio.amateur.digital.misc
rec.radio.amateur.equipment
rec.radio.amateur.homebrew
rec.radio.amateur.misc 86
rec.radio.amateur.packet 86
rec.radio.amateur.policy 87
rec.radio.amateur.space
rec.radio.broadcasting 87
rec.radio.cb 87
rec.radio.info 86
rec.radio.noncomm
rec.radio.scanner
rec.radio.shortwave 86-87
rec.radio.swap 87
rec.railroad 75
rec.roller-coaster
rec.running 180
rec.s
rec.scouting 59
rec.scuba 180
rec.skate 180
rec.skating
rec.skiing 180
rec.skydiving 180
rec.sport.baseball 176
rec.sport.baseball.college 176
rec.sport.baseball.fantasy 176
rec.sport.basketball 176
rec.sport.basketball.college 176
rec.sport.basketball.misc
rec.sport.basketball.pro 176
rec.sport.cricket 178
rec.sport.cricket.scores
rec.sport.disc 179
rec.sport.fencing 179
rec.sport.football 176-177
rec.sport.football.australian 177
rec.sport.football.canadian
rec.sport.football.college 176
rec.sport.football.fantasy
rec.sport.football.misc 176
rec.sport.football.pro 176
rec.sport.football.pro.liverpool
rec.sport.football.pro.spurs
rec.sport.golf 179
rec.sport.hockey 177
rec.sport.hockey.field
rec.sport.midget.tossing
rec.sport.misc 177
rec.sport.olympics 177
rec.sport.paintball 180
rec.sport.pro-wrestling
rec.sport.rowing 180
rec.sport.rugby 177
rec.sport.snowboarding
rec.sport.soccer 177
rec.sport.swimming 181
rec.sport.table-tennis 181
rec.sport.tennis 177
rec.sport.triathlon 181
rec.sport.volleyball 181
rec.sport.waterski
rec.toys.lego
rec.toys.misc
rec.travel 88
rec.travel.air 88
rec.travel.marketplace 88
rec.video 80-81
rec.video.cable-tv

rec.video.production 81
rec.video.releases 81
rec.video.satellite 81
rec.windsurfing 181
rec.woodworking 39, 77
relcom.ads
relcom.ads.comp
relcom.archives
relcom.archives.d
relcom.arts.epic
relcom.arts.qwerty
relcom.banktech
relcom.bbs
relcom.bbs.list
relcom.commerce
relcom.commerce.audio-video
relcom.commerce.chemical
relcom.commerce.computers
relcom.commerce.construction
relcom.commerce.consume
relcom.commerce.energy
relcom.commerce.estate
relcom.commerce.food
relcom.commerce.food.drinks
relcom.commerce.food.sweet
relcom.commerce.household
relcom.commerce.infoserv
relcom.commerce.jobs
relcom.commerce.machinery
relcom.commerce.medicine
relcom.commerce.metals
relcom.commerce.money
relcom.commerce.orgtech
relcom.commerce.other
relcom.commerce.software
relcom.commerce.software.demo
relcom.commerce.stocks
relcom.commerce.talk
relcom.commerce.tobacco
relcom.commerce.tour
relcom.commerce.transport
relcom.comp.animation
relcom.comp.binaries
relcom.comp.crosstools
relcom.comp.dbms.clipper
relcom.comp.dbms.foxpro
relcom.comp.demo.d
relcom.comp.gis
relcom.comp.lang.forth
relcom.comp.lang.pascal
relcom.comp.os.os2
relcom.comp.os.vms
relcom.comp.os.windows
relcom.comp.os.windows.prog
relcom.comp.security
relcom.comp.sources.d
relcom.comp.sources.misc
relcom.currency
relcom.exnet
relcom.exnet.quote
relcom.expo
relcom.fido.flirt
relcom.fido.ru.hacker
relcom.fido.ru.modem
relcom.fido.ru.networks
relcom.fido.ru.strack
relcom.fido.ru.unix
relcom.fido.su.books
relcom.fido.su.c-c++
relcom.fido.su.dbms
relcom.fido.su.general
relcom.fido.su.hardw
relcom.fido.su.magic
relcom.fido.su.softw
relcom.fido.su.tolkien
relcom.fido.su.virus
relcom.humor
relcom.internic.net-happenings
relcom.kids
relcom.lan
relcom.maps
relcom.msdos
relcom.music
relcom.netnews
relcom.netnews.big
relcom.newusers
relcom.penpals
relcom.politics

relcom.postmasters
relcom.postmasters.d
relcom.rferl
relcom.[Russian-language newsgroups]
relcom.sources
relcom.spbnews
relcom.talk
relcom.tcpip
relcom.terms
relcom.test
relcom.wtc
relcom.x
relcom-list.internic.net-happenings
relog.isdn
resif.conferences
resif.cuisine
resif.culture
resif.[French-language newsgroups]
resif.info.amiga
resif.info.atari
resif.info.divers
resif.info.mac
resif.info.msdos
resif.info.next
resif.info.unix
resif.info.vms
resif.info.x
resif.reseaux.divers
resif.reseaux.modems
rfhsm.general
ri.admin
ri.general
ri.k12.experiences
ri.k12.providers.funding
ri.k12.providers.staff
ri.k12.providers.tech
ri.k12.socialstudies
ri.politics
ri.[Rhode Island educational newsgroups]
ri.test
rmit.xx.general
rmit.xx.test
robin.[German-language networking newsgroups]
robin.lsmpf
robin.main
rpi.[Rennselaer Polytechnic Institute newsgroups]
ru.general

S

saar.alt.vga-planets
saar.org.ip.general
saar.org.ip.intern.in-info
saar.org.ip.intern.sex-am-staden
saar.org.ip.praesidium
saar.talk.lyoner
sac.general
sac.[Sacramento, CA newsgroups]
sac.swap
sac.test
sanet.adverts
sanet.config
sanet.flame
sanet.fun
sanet.ibmpc
sanet.[Internet networking groups]
sanet.lang.c
sanet.modems
sanet.monty-python
sanet.newsletters.d
sanet.radio.packet
sanet.sources.d
sanet.talk.politics
sanet.talk.religion
sanet.tech
sanet.test
sanet.uniforum
sanet.unix.questions
sanet.unix.talk
sary-arka.local_news
sary-arka.local-news
sary-arka.newspaper
schule.mathe.did
schule.verwaltung
sci 81, 125-134, 139
sci.aeronautic

sci.aeronautics 126
sci.aeronautics.airliners 126
sci.agriculture
sci.answers
sci.anthropology 126
sci.anthropology.paleo
sci.aquaria 126
sci.archaeology 126
sci.astro 126
sci.astro.fits
sci.astro.hubble
sci.astro.planetarium
sci.bio 126-127
sci.bio.ecology
sci.bio.ethology
sci.bio.evolution
sci.bio.herp
sci.bio.technology 127
sci.chaos
sci.chem 127
sci.chem.organomet
sci.classics 127
sci.cognitive 127
sci.comp-aided
sci.cryonics 127
sci.crypt 127-128
sci.data.formats
sci.econ 128
sci.econ.research
sci.edu 139
sci.electronics 128
sci.energy 128
sci.energy.hydrogen 128
sci.engr 128-129
sci.engr.advanced-tv
sci.engr.biomed 128
sci.engr.chem 129
sci.engr.civil 129
sci.engr.control 129
sci.engr.lighting
sci.engr.manufacturing
sci.engr.mech 129
sci.environment 129
sci.fractals 125, 129
sci.geo.fluid
sci.geo.fluids 129
sci.geo.geology 130
sci.geo.meteorology 130
sci.gio.geology
sci.image.processing 130
sci.lang 130
sci.lang.japan 130
sci.life-extension
sci.logic 130
sci.materials 130
sci.math 130-131
sci.math.num-analysis 130-131
sci.math.research 131
sci.math.stat 131
sci.math.symbolic 131
sci.med 131
sci.med.aids 131
sci.med.dentistry
sci.med.nursing
sci.med.nutrition 131
sci.med.occupational
sci.med.pharmacy
sci.med.physics 131
sci.med.psychobiology
sci.med.telemedicine
sci.military 131
sci.misc 132
sci.nanotech 132
sci.nonlinear
sci.op-research
sci.optics 132
sci.philosophy.meta 132
sci.philosophy.tech 132
sci.physics 81, 125, 132
sci.physics.accelerators
sci.physics.edward.teller.boom.boom.boom
sci.physics.fusion 132
sci.physics.particle
sci.physics.research
sci.polymers
sci.psychology 132
sci.psychology.digest
sci.research 133

sci.research.careers 133
sci.skeptic 133
sci.space 126, 134
sci.space.news 134
sci.space.policy
sci.space.science
sci.space.shuttle 134
sci.space.tech
sci.stat.consult
sci.stat.edu
sci.stat.math
sci.systems
sci.techniques.microscopy
sci.techniques.xtallography
sci.virtual-worlds 133
sci.virtual-worlds.apps
sco.opendesktop 162
scot.announce
scot.environment
scot.followup
scot.general
scot.[Scotland-based newsgroups]
scot.test
scruz.events
scruz.general
scruz.poetry
scruz.test
sdnet.cerfnet
sdnet.computing
sdnet.eats
sdnet.events
sdnet.forsale 186
sdnet.general
sdnet.housing
sdnet.jobs
sdnet.lit
sdnet.misc
sdnet.motss
sdnet.movies
sdnet.music
sdnet.next
sdnet.politics
sdnet.rideshare
sdnet.seminars
sdnet.sports
sdnet.talks
sdnet.test
sdnet.theatre
sdnet.waffle
sdnet.wanted
sdnet.writing
sdsu.c++
sdsu.cs520
sdsu.cs596
seattle.admin
seattle.forsale
seattle.general 186
seattle.test
seismic.general
seven.allg.bundeswehr
sfnet.akat.mtuki
sfnet.aloittelijoille
sfnet.atk
sfnet.atk.amiga
sfnet.atk.atari
sfnet.atk.cpm
sfnet.atk.flpf
sfnet.atk.flpf.tiedotukset
sfnet.atk.gnu
sfnet.atk.grafiikka
sfnet.atk.hallinto.hevi
sfnet.atk.hallinto.opintohallinto
sfnet.atk.hallinto.valma
sfnet.atk.hallinto.yleinen
sfnet.atk.hallinto.ysky
sfnet.atk.kerhot
sfnet.atk.korkeakoulujen-mikrotuki
sfnet.atk.kulttuuri
sfnet.atk.laitteet
sfnet.atk.laitteet.pc
sfnet.atk.linux
sfnet.atk.mac
sfnet.atk.mach
sfnet.atk.minix
sfnet.atk.ms-dos
sfnet.atk.nextstep
sfnet.atk.ohjelmointi
sfnet.atk.sodat

sfnet.atk.tex
sfnet.atk.turvallisuus
sfnet.atk.unix
sfnet.atk.vm
sfnet.atk.vms
sfnet.atk.yllapito
sfnet.checkgroups
sfnet.csc
sfnet.csc.tiedotukset
sfnet.eunet.tiedotukset
sfnet.[Finland-based newsgroups]
sfnet.funet.tiedotukset
sfnet.fuug.tiedotukset
sfnet.fysiikka
sfnet.harrastus
sfnet.harrastus.aseet
sfnet.harrastus.astronomia
sfnet.harrastus.audio+video
sfnet.harrastus.autot
sfnet.harrastus.biljardi
sfnet.harrastus.dx-kuuntelu
sfnet.harrastus.elektroniikka
sfnet.harrastus.elokuvat
sfnet.harrastus.ham
sfnet.harrastus.ilmailu
sfnet.harrastus.itsepuolustus
sfnet.harrastus.kalastus
sfnet.harrastus.kulttuuri
sfnet.harrastus.kulttuuri.sarjakuvat
sfnet.harrastus.kulttuuri.sf
sfnet.harrastus.lemmikit
sfnet.harrastus.mp
sfnet.harrastus.musiikki
sfnet.harrastus.partio
sfnet.harrastus.pelit
sfnet.harrastus.pelit.rooli
sfnet.harrastus.pelit.shakki
sfnet.harrastus.pelit.strategia
sfnet.harrastus.puutarha
sfnet.harrastus.retkeily
sfnet.harrastus.ruoka+juoma
sfnet.harrastus.sf
sfnet.harrastus.tanssi
sfnet.harrastus.urheilu
sfnet.harrastus.valokuvaus
sfnet.harrastus.veneet
sfnet.harrastus.viinit
sfnet.harrastus.visailu
sfnet.huuhaa
sfnet.ieee
sfnet.juoru
sfnet.keskustelu
sfnet.keskustelu.avaruus
sfnet.keskustelu.evoluutio
sfnet.keskustelu.ey
sfnet.keskustelu.filosofia
sfnet.keskustelu.foreigners
sfnet.keskustelu.huumeet
sfnet.keskustelu.huumori
sfnet.keskustelu.ihmissuhteet
sfnet.keskustelu.kieli
sfnet.keskustelu.koulutus
sfnet.keskustelu.laki
sfnet.keskustelu.lapset
sfnet.keskustelu.liikenne
sfnet.keskustelu.maanpuolustus
sfnet.keskustelu.politiikka
sfnet.keskustelu.psykologia
sfnet.keskustelu.rajatieteet
sfnet.keskustelu.seksi
sfnet.keskustelu.skeptismi
sfnet.keskustelu.talous
sfnet.keskustelu.terveys
sfnet.keskustelu.uskonto
sfnet.keskustelu.uskonto.evoluutio
sfnet.keskustelu.varaventtiili
sfnet.keskustelu.vienstinta.radio
sfnet.keskustelu.viestinta
sfnet.keskustelu.viestinta.tv
sfnet.keskustelu.vitsit
sfnet.keskustelu.yhteiskunta
sfnet.keskustelu.ymparisto
sfnet.lists.geograph
sfnet.lists.sunflash
sfnet.maantiede
sfnet.matkustaminen
sfnet.opiskelu
sfnet.opiskelu.kult

sfnet.opiskelu.sospsyk
sfnet.opiskelu.ymp.kurssit
sfnet.ruoka+juoma
sfnet.ryhmat
sfnet.sorsat
sfnet.sources
sfnet.tapahtumat
sfnet.test
sfnet.tiede
sfnet.tiede.arkeologia
sfnet.tiede.astronomia
sfnet.tiede.bio
sfnet.tiede.bio.kasviekol.info
sfnet.tiede.bio.kasviekol.j-opas
sfnet.tiede.bio.kasviekol.kesk
sfnet.tiede.bio.kasvit
sfnet.tiede.bio.kasvit.ekol.info
sfnet.tiede.bio.kasvit.ekol.j-opas
sfnet.tiede.bio.kasvit.info
sfnet.tiede.bio.kasvit.j-opas
sfnet.tiede.bio.troopp+ymp
sfnet.tiede.biologia.kasviekologia
sfnet.tiede.biologia.kasviekologia.jatko-opinto-op
sfnet.tiede.biologia.kasviekologia.kokoukset-ja-ku
sfnet.tiede.biologia.troopp+ymp
sfnet.tiede.didaktiikka
sfnet.tiede.filologia.englanti
sfnet.tiede.fysiikka
sfnet.tiede.geofysiikka
sfnet.tiede.hahmontunnistus
sfnet.tiede.historia
sfnet.tiede.kasvatus
sfnet.tiede.kehitystutkimus
sfnet.tiede.kemia
sfnet.tiede.kielitiede
sfnet.tiede.kirjastot
sfnet.tiede.kulttutk
sfnet.tiede.laake.kemia.kliininen
sfnet.tiede.maantiede
sfnet.tiede.matematiikka
sfnet.tiede.metsantutkimus
sfnet.tiede.nonlinear
sfnet.tiede.tekoaly
sfnet.tiede.tietotekniikka
sfnet.tiede.tietotekniikka.tohtorix
sfnet.tiede.tilastotiede
sfnet.tiede.tilastotiede.jatkokoul
sfnet.tiede.yt
sfnet.tiede.yt.info
sfnet.tiede.yt.kurssit
sfnet.tiede.yt.kvaltut
sfnet.tiede.yt.laitokset
sfnet.tiede.yt.metodit
sfnet.tiede.yt.yleis
sfnet.tiedotukset
sfnet.tietoliikenne
sfnet.tietoliikenne.juoru
sfnet.tietoliikenne.katko
sfnet.tietoliikenne.palvelimet
sfnet.tietoliikenne.ryhmat+listat
sfnet.tietoliikenne.tekniikka
sfnet.tietoliikenne.televerkot
sfnet.tietoliikenne.tilastot
sfnet.tietoliikenne.viestinviejat
sfnet.tohtorix
sfnet.tori
sfnet.tori.asunnot
sfnet.tori.kyydit
sfnet.tori.muut
sfnet.tori.myydaan
sfnet.tori.myydaan.atk
sfnet.tori.ostetaan
sfnet.tori.ostetaan.atk
sfnet.tori.seura
sfnet.tori.tyopaikat
sfnet.tori.uutuudet
sfnet.uskonto.evoluutio
sfnet.yt
sfnet.yt.test
sgi.bugs.newport
sgi.general
sgi.mail.explorer
sgibugs.volmgr
slac.announce.outages.lan
slac.announce.outages.mac
slac.announce.outages.network

slac.announce.outages.wan
slac.announce.scs
slac.announce.slacvm
slac.announce.slacvx
slac.announce.unixhub
slac.b-factory.2gamma
slac.b-factory.calorimeter
slac.b-factory.comp
slac.b-factory.general
slac.b-factory.ir
slac.b-factory.magnet
slac.b-factory.parameters
slac.b-factory.particleid
slac.b-factory.physics
slac.b-factory.tracking
slac.b-factory.vertex
slac.bes.status
slac.bsd.minutes
slac.building-mgr
slac.ccg.minutes
slac.cesr.news
slac.comp.fcs
slac.[Cornell University newsgroups]
slac.database.nomad
slac.database.oracle
slac.database.spires
slac.database.spires.eldreq
slac.e142.minutes
slac.eld.fbsim
slac.emergency-ops
slac.esh.escorts
slac.general
slac.group-c.general
slac.groups
slac.jobs
slac.lang.c
slac.lang.c++
slac.lang.fortran
slac.lang.maple
slac.lang.pascal
slac.lang.postscript
slac.lang.rexx
slac.library.hepths
slac.library.ppf
slac.library.ppf.string
slac.listserv.sldphy-l
slac.market
slac.markiii.general
slac.net.usenet
slac.networks
slac.newusers.unix
slac.physapps.cernlib
slac.rec.books
slac.rec.explorers
slac.rec.food
slac.rec.ham_radio
slac.rec.health
slac.rec.music
slac.scac.aug93
slac.scs.ibm-pc
slac.scs.minutes
slac.scs.sitewide
slac.scs.tigerteam
slac.scs.trips
slac.seminars.comp
slac.seminars.physics
slac.silicon.tracking
slac.slacvx
slac.slc.polariz
slac.sluo.computing.minutes
slac.sluo.minutes
slac.soc.women
slac.tau-charm.comp
slac.tau-charm.detector
slac.test
slac.text.frame
slac.text.tex
slac.users.aix
slac.users.amiga
slac.users.excel
slac.users.ibm-pc
slac.users.mac
slac.users.next
slac.users.unix
slac.users.windows.x
slac.vcg.minutes
slac.vm.pipelines
slac.www.announce

slac.www.bugs
slac.www.general
slac.www.interest
slac.www.talk
slo.club
slo.club.rose-float
slo.dept.csc
slo.flame
slo.for-sale
slo.general 186
slo.housing
slo.ibm-pc
slo.net
slo.politics
slo.punks
slo.stats
slo.sun
slo.test
slo.unix
slo.unix-questions
soc.answers 63
soc.bi 60
soc.bi.papal-bull
soc.college
soc.college.grad
soc.college.gradinfo
soc.college.graduation
soc.college.org.aiesec
soc.college.teaching-asst
soc.couples 58
soc.couples.intercultural
soc.culture.afghanistan 63
soc.culture.african 63
soc.culture.african.american 63
soc.culture.arabic 63
soc.culture.argentina
soc.culture.asean 63
soc.culture.asian.american 64
soc.culture.australia
soc.culture.australian 64
soc.culture.austria
soc.culture.baltics 64
soc.culture.bangladesh 64
soc.culture.bosna-herzgvna 64
soc.culture.brazil 64
soc.culture.british 64
soc.culture.bulgaria 64
soc.culture.burma
soc.culture.canada 64
soc.culture.caribbean 64
soc.culture.celtic 64
soc.culture.china 65
soc.culture.cis
soc.culture.croatia 65
soc.culture.czecho-slovak 65
soc.culture.ecsd
soc.culture.esperanto 65
soc.culture.europe 65
soc.culture.filipino 65
soc.culture.french 65
soc.culture.gaelic
soc.culture.german 65
soc.culture.greek 65
soc.culture.hongkong 65-66
soc.culture.indian 66
soc.culture.indian.american
soc.culture.indian.info
soc.culture.indian.telugu 66
soc.culture.indonesia 66
soc.culture.iranian 66
soc.culture.israel
soc.culture.italian 66
soc.culture.japan 66
soc.culture.jewish 66-67
soc.culture.korean 67
soc.culture.laos
soc.culture.latin-america 67
soc.culture.lebanon 67
soc.culture.maghreb
soc.culture.magyar 67
soc.culture.malaysia 67
soc.culture.mexican 67
soc.culture.misc 69
soc.culture.native 67
soc.culture.nepal 67
soc.culture.netherlands 67
soc.culture.new-zealand 68

soc.culture.nordic 68
soc.culture.pakistan 68
soc.culture.palestine
soc.culture.peru
soc.culture.polish 68
soc.culture.portuguese 68
soc.culture.romanian 68
soc.culture.scientisis
soc.culture.scientists
soc.culture.singapore 68
soc.culture.soviet 68
soc.culture.spain 68
soc.culture.sri-lanka 69
soc.culture.taiwan 69
soc.culture.tamil 69
soc.culture.thai 69
soc.culture.turkish 69
soc.culture.ukrainian
soc.culture.uruguay
soc.culture.usa 69
soc.culture.venezuela
soc.culture.vietnamese 69
soc.culture.yugoslavia 69
soc.feminism 60, 63
soc.history 52
soc.human-nets
soc.libraries.talk 58
soc.men 60
soc.misc
soc.motss 60
soc.motss.rmgroup.4.AIDS.im.a.curse
soc.net-people 58
soc.penpals 57
soc.politics
soc.politics.arms-d
soc.religion.bahai 70
soc.religion.christian 70
soc.religion.christian.bible-study 69
soc.religion.eastern 70
soc.religion.islam 70
soc.religion.quaker 58
soc.religion.shamanism
soc.rights.human 58
soc.roots 89
soc.singles 203
soc.singles.nice
soc.veterans 59
soc.women 58
spk.literary
sqnt-public.forsale
srg.drs1
srg.drs2
srg.drs3
srg.info
srg.programme
srg.[Switzerland-based media newsgroups]
srg.ticker
srg.tvdrs
sri.market
ssc.gem.comp
ssc.gem.news
ssc.news
sse.rumours
sta.general
sta.test
stgt.general
stl.general
stl.jobs
stl.news
stl.rec
stl.test
su.amiga
su.class.ce294
su.class.chem135
su.class.chem31
su.class.comm1
su.class.cs109b
su.class.cs147
su.class.cs223
su.class.cs244a
su.class.cs249
su.class.econ90
su.class.ee133
su.class.ee141
su.class.ee366
su.class.ee373
su.class.ee382

su.class.ee487
su.class.stat340
su.class.sts160
su.computers
su.computers.rcc
su.etc
su.events 190
su.gay
su.issues.china
su.issues.free-speech
su.jobs
su.library.math-cs
su.lost-and-found
su.market
su.org.acsss
su.org.india
su.org.orch
su.org.ski-club
su.org.womens-center
sub.binaries.amigados
sub.binaries.amigados.d
sub.binaries.config
sub.binaries.msdos
sub.binaries.msdos.d
sub.binaries.pictures
sub.binaries.pictures.d
sub.binaries.tos
sub.binaries.tos.d
sub.boerse
sub.comm
sub.config
sub.config.lists
sub.config.maps
sub.databases
sub.followup
sub.games
sub.gateways
sub.general
sub.gnu
sub.jokes
sub.jokes.d
sub.kultur
sub.lists
sub.mag.chalisti
sub.mag.chalisti.d
sub.mail
sub.mampf
sub.market
sub.misc
sub.newusers
sub.newusers.questions
sub.org.auge
sub.org.ccc
sub.org.in
sub.org.sub
sub.os.minix
sub.os.misc
sub.os.os9
sub.os.unix
sub.os.vms
sub.os.xenix
sub.politik
sub.security
sub.sex
sub.sources.amiga
sub.sources.d
sub.sources.misc
sub.sources.os9
sub.sources.st
sub.sources.unix
sub.studium
sub.sys.amiga
sub.sys.apple
sub.sys.ibm
sub.sys.misc
sub.sys.st
sub.test
sub.tex
sub.umwelt
sub.verkehr
sura.announce
sura.config
sura.noc.status
sura.security
sura.techs
swnet.ai.neural-nets
swnet.conferences
swnet.diverse

swnet.followup
swnet.general 194
swnet.gopher
swnet.info-gnu
swnet.jobs
swnet.lans
swnet.lans.novell
swnet.mac
swnet.mail
swnet.org.europen
swnet.org.snus
swnet.org.sunet.info
swnet.org.swipnet
swnet.org.tipnet
swnet.paintball
swnet.politik
swnet.pryltorg
swnet.sci.astro
swnet.siren
swnet.snus
swnet.sources
swnet.sources.list
swnet.sunet-info
swnet.svenska
swnet.sys.amiga
swnet.sys.dec
swnet.sys.dnix
swnet.sys.hp
swnet.sys.ibm.pc
swnet.sys.mac
swnet.sys.ncr
swnet.sys.prime
swnet.sys.pyramid
swnet.sys.sun
swnet.sys.sun.flash
swnet.test
swnet.thermo
swnet.unix
swnet.utbildning.grundbulten
swnet.wanted
sysop

T

talk.abortion 49
talk.answers
talk.bizarre 202
talk.bizarre.rabbit
talk.environment 49
talk.origins 71
talk.philosophy.misc 71
talk.politics.animals
talk.politics.china 51
talk.politics.cis
talk.politics.crypto
talk.politics.drugs 50
talk.politics.guns 46
talk.politics.medicine 50
talk.politics.mideast 51
talk.politics.misc 49
talk.politics.soviet 50
talk.politics.space 50
talk.politics.theory 50
talk.politics.tibet
talk.rape 60
talk.religion.misc 71
talk.religion.newage 71
talk.rumors 54
tamu.aasg
tamu.adex.690
tamu.amateur
tamu.cray
tamu.electronic.library.resources
tamu.entc.micro
tamu.flame
tamu.forsale
tamu.fuzzy
tamu.general
tamu.gopher
tamu.jobs
tamu.kanm.radio
tamu.micro.mac
tamu.micro.msdos
tamu.micro.os2
tamu.music
tamu.news
tamu.phil.240
tamu.phil.489h

tamu.religion.christian
tamu.sports.squash
tamu.test
tamu.[Texas A & M University
newsgroups]
tamu.unix.general
tamu.unix.sgi
tamu.vm.general
tamu.vms.general
taronga.misc
taronga.worldview
tek.foresale
tek.forsale 188
tn.flame
tn.general
tn.msdos
tn.talk
tn.test
tn.unix
tnn.admin
tnn.comm.pager
tnn.foods.kansai
tnn.forum.tron
tnn.internet.firewall
tnn.[Japan-based newsgroups]
tnn.medical
tnn.netnews.dream
tnn.netnews.inn
tnn.netnews.stats
tnn.os.bsd-on-386
tnn.os.dosv
tnn.os.msdos
tnn.religion.catholic
tnn.support.hyperad.uucp
tnn.sys.news
tnn.sys.zaurus
to.ccavax
to.cimco
to.cmcl2
to.cmx
to.cunyvm
to.grebyn
to.iggy
to.itsgw
to.kepler
to.ncs
to.netsys
to.newkodak
to.njin
to.nyser
to.one 60
to.oswego
to.pinet
to.psialb
to.psicom
to.psinntp
to.rlgvax
to.rodan
to.rpitsgw
to.rpitsmts
to.rsi
to.rutgers
to.saic-mvb
to.skidmore
to.sunic
to.tiaa
to.trie
to.uupsi
to.vax
to.wrdis01
tor.forsale
tor.general 194
tor.jobs
tor.news
tor.news.stats
tor.test
tor.uucp
tp.kso.werbung
trentu.general
trentu.seminar
trial.misc.legal.software
trial.newgroups
trial.rec.metalworking
trial.soc.culture.czechoslovak
trial.soc.culture.italian
trial.talk.politics.peace
trial.test
triangle.csnet

triangle.decus
triangle.forsale 188
triangle.freenet
triangle.gardens
triangle.general 188
triangle.graphics
triangle.jobs
triangle.libsci
triangle.movies
triangle.neural-nets
triangle.politics
triangle.radio
triangle.singles
triangle.sports
triangle.sun
triangle.systems
triangle.talks
triangle.transport
triangle.vlsi
triangle.wizards
tub.general
tub.wanted
tuia.announce
tuia.forum
tx.evolution.vs.abortion
tx.flame
tx.followup
tx.forsale 187
tx.general 186-187
tx.jobs
tx.maps
tx.motorcycles
tx.news 185
tx.news.stats
tx.politics 185
tx.test
tx.thenet.managers
tx.wanted

U

u3b.config
u3b.misc
u3b.sources
u3b.tech
u3b.test
ua.support
ualberta.general
ualberta.phys.general
uberlin.general
uc.general 190
uc.grads.union
uc.motss
uc.news
uc.test
ucb.class.chem104b
ucb.class.chem1b
ucb.class.classics28
ucb.class.cs61a
ucb.class.cs61b
ucb.class.ib286
ucb.class.mc190
ucb.class.mcb130
ucb.net.home-ip
ucd.agecon
ucd.cs.club
ucd.cs.jobs
ucd.gradgroups.abs
ucd.kiosk.jobs
ucd.life
ucd.snowboarding
ucd.talk.bugculture
uch.general
ucsb.compsci.cs160
ucsb.compsci.cs170
ucsb.compsci.cs180
ucsb.compsci.cs270b
ucsb.compsci.faculty
ucsb.compsci.grad
ucsb.general
ucsb.humanities
ucsb.net.help
ucsb.[University of California/Santa
Barbara newsgroups]
ucsc.admin.grants
ucsc.baskin.general
ucsc.class.cmp101
ucsc.class.cmp104a

ucsc.class.cmpe185
ucsc.messages
ucsc.plan
ucsc.research
ucsc.research.morph
ufra.incubus.flame
ufra.incubus.test
ug.general
uga.fan.glenn
uiuc.org.iccf
uiuc.org.tbp.projects
uiuc.soc.women
uiuc.sys.sgi
uiuc.[University of Illinois (Illini)
newsgroups]
uk.announce
uk.bcs.announce
uk.bcs.misc
uk.environment
uk.events
uk.general
uk.ikbs
uk.jips
uk.jobs
uk.jobs.d
uk.jobs.offered
uk.jobs.wanted
uk.lisp
uk.media 193
uk.misc 193
uk.net
uk.net.maps
uk.net.news
uk.news
uk.news.group
uk.news.map
uk.org.community
uk.politics 193
uk.radio.amateur
uk.singles 193
uk.sources
uk.sun
uk.support
uk.test
uk.transport
uk.ukuug
uk.wic
uk.yb-users
uka.oracle
uka.studium
um.comp-iss
um.forsale
um.general 190
um.h19
um.housing
um.music
um.network
um.test
um.tex
um.umcptalk
um.wam
um.wam.bmgt301
umiami.general
umich.eecs.announce
umich.eecs.ce.students
umich.eecs.class.270
umich.eecs.class.370
umich.eecs.class.373
umich.eecs.class.380
umich.eecs.class.381
umich.eecs.class.426
umich.eecs.class.470
umich.eecs.class.476
umich.eecs.class.481
umich.eecs.class.482
umich.eecs.class.483
umich.eecs.class.484
umich.eecs.class.486
umich.eecs.class.487
umich.eecs.class.489
umich.eecs.class.492
umich.eecs.class.498
umich.eecs.class.506
umich.eecs.class.510
umich.eecs.class.585
umich.eecs.class.586
umich.eecs.class.587
umich.eecs.class.627

umich.eecs.class.681
umich.eecs.class.682
umich.engin.eecs.489
umich.engin.eecs.class.498
umich.interesting.people
umich.itd.stats
umich.[University of Michigan
newsgroups]
umn.aem.general
umn.aem.gradst
umn.aem.net
umn.aem.seminars
umn.aem.ugrads
umn.bioc.class.5025
umn.cis.systems
umn.config
umn.cs.class.3113
umn.cs.class.3322
umn.cs.class.5181
umn.cs.class.5211
umn.cs.class.5504
umn.cs.class.5505
umn.cs.class.5511
umn.cs.class.8011-scic
umn.cs.class.8101
umn.cs.lang.misc
umn.cs.systems.mac
umn.cs.systems.misc
umn.cs.systems.status
umn.cs.systems.unix
umn.ee.class.5505
umn.ee.class.5760
umn.ioft.class.1001h
umn.law.class.5109
umn.local-lists.aci-4d
umn.local-lists.bookstore-prices
umn.local-lists.cnug-dss
umn.local-lists.disc-evidence
umn.local-lists.disc-nordlib
umn.local-lists.disc-sar
umn.local-lists.disc-tacfanout
umn.local-lists.disc-vis-graph
umn.local-lists.ethnic-theater
umn.local-lists.infotech-disc
umn.local-lists.microcomputer-news
umn.local-lists.net-people
umn.local-lists.news-stats
umn.local-lists.sgi-admins
umn.local-lists.siren
umn.local-lists.tc-backup
umn.local-lists.tc-email
umn.local-lists.tc-sgi
umn.local-lists.tc-unix
umn.local-lists.techc-admin
umn.local-lists.techc-all
umn.local-lists.techc-backup
umn.local-lists.techc-email
umn.local-lists.techc-general
umn.local-lists.techc-microlan
umn.local-lists.techc-public
umn.local-lists.techc-sgi
umn.local-lists.techc-site
umn.local-lists.techc-unix
umn.local-lists.techc-workst
umn.local-lists.users-mlre
umn.local-lists.writingc
umn.me.class.5343
umn.music
umn.org.china
umn.rhet.class.8210
umn.rhet.general
umn.rhet.gradst
umn.[University of Minnesota
newsgroups]
umontreal.cerca
umontreal.general
umontreal.[University of Montreal
newsgroups]
unicef.test
unicef.test4
unix-pc.bugs
unix-pc.general
unix-pc.sources
unix-pc.test
unix-pc.uucp
uo.cs.cis313
uo.cs.cis410-c+c++
uo.cs.cis423

uo.cs.cis451
uo.cs.cis621
uofa.bogus
us.arts.tv.soaps
us.config
us.forsale.computers
us.forsale.d
us.forsale.misc
us.groups
us.groups.announce
us.jobs.contract
us.jobs.misc
us.jobs.offered
us.jobs.resumes
us.legal
us.misc
us.politics.abortion
us.sport.baseball
us.sport.baseball.college
us.sport.basketball.college
us.sport.basketball.misc
us.sport.basketball.pro
us.sport.football.college
us.sport.football.misc
us.sport.football.pro
us.sport.misc
us.taxes
us.test
us.usenet
us.wanted.d
us.wanted.misc
usa-today.banks
users-mlre
ut.ecf.comp9T5
ut.ecf.ece242
ut.ecf.engsci
ut.general 190
utcs.[University of Texas newsgroups]
utece.general
utexas.cc.sysmod
utexas.cc.utxvm.remark
utexas.class.cs347-a
utexas.class.cs347-b
utexas.class.cs352
utexas.class.cs356
utexas.class.lis340
utexas.class.mis385
utexas.general
utexas.religion.christian
uu.cs.class.354
uunet.alternet
uunet.announce
uunet.forum
uunet.[Internet commercial network newsgroups]
uunet.products
uunet.status
uunet.tech
uw.aco.system
uw.ahs.general
uw.ahs.system
uw.ai.learning
uw.aix.support
uw.cgl
uw.cgl.software
uw.combopt
uw.computing.support.staff
uw.computing-support-staff
uw.cong.system
uw.cs.cs230
uw.cs.cs242.c++
uw.cs.cs246
uw.cs.cs330
uw.cs.cs338
uw.cs.cs342
uw.cs.cs436
uw.cs.cs498p
uw.csg
uw.dcs.gripe
uw.dcs.operations
uw.dcs.suggestions
uw.dp.staff
uw.ee.ee621
uw.ee.grad
uw.ee.opt
uw.english-usage
uw.envst.ers285
uw.envst.ers301

uw.envst.general
uw.envst.system
uw.forsale
uw.gams
uw.general 190
uw.history.hist264a
uw.history.hist264b
uw.mac-users
uw.math.tsa
uw.mathcad
uw.matlab
uw.mfcf.bugs
uw.mfcf.gripe
uw.mfcf.hardware.mac
uw.mfcf.people
uw.mfcf.software
uw.mfcf.software.mac
uw.nag
uw.network.stats
uw.os2-users
uw.outers
uw.pmc
uw.psychology
uw.shoshin
uw.stats.stat231
uw.sytek
uw.talks
uw.test
uw.unix
uw.uwinfo
uw.virtual-worlds
uw.visualization
uw.vlsi
uw.vm-migration
uwarwick.dcs.course.cs117
uwarwick.societies.amateur-radio
uwisc.general
uwm.general
uwo.biomed.engrg
uwo.biomed.inroads
uwo.comp.general
uwo.comp.ibm.announce
uwo.comp.micro
uwo.comp.nupop
uwo.comp.packet
uwo.comp.pegasus
uwo.comp.pine
uwo.comp.progress
uwo.comp.security
uwo.comp.sgi.announce
uwo.comp.sun.announce
uwo.csd.cs175
uwo.csd.cs201
uwo.csd.cs304
uwo.csd.cs305
uwo.csd.cs319
uwo.csd.cs331
uwo.csd.cs333
uwo.csd.cs346
uwo.csd.cs350
uwo.csd.cs357a
uwo.events
uwo.iaa.research
uwo.med
uwo.med.research
uwo.med.talk
uwo.physics.optics
uwo.pma
uwo.slis.c558
uwo.slis.c591
uwo.slis.c601
uwo.slis.c640
uwo.slis.c705
uwo.slis.c706
uwo.slis.c708
uwo.slis.review
uwo.ssc.network
uwo.sscl.network

V

va.general
va.test
vmsnet.admin
vmsnet.alpha 147
vmsnet.announce
vmsnet.announce.newusers
vmsnet.databases.rdb

vmsnet.decus.journal
vmsnet.decus.lugs
vmsnet.employment
vmsnet.epsilon-cd
vmsnet.infosystems.gopher
vmsnet.infosystems.misc
vmsnet.internals 147
vmsnet.mail 147
vmsnet.mail.misc
vmsnet.mail.mx 147
vmsnet.mail.pmdf
vmsnet.misc 147
vmsnet.networks.desktop.misc
vmsnet.networks.desktop.pathworks 147
vmsnet.networks.management.decmcc
vmsnet.networks.management.misc
vmsnet.networks.misc
vmsnet.networks.tcp-ip.cmu-tek
vmsnet.networks.tcp-ip.misc
vmsnet.networks.tcp-ip.multinet 147
vmsnet.networks.tcp-ip.tcpware
vmsnet.networks.tcp-ip.ucx
vmsnet.networks.tcp-ip.wintcp
vmsnet.pdp-11 147
vmsnet.sources 147, 156
vmsnet.sources.d 147
vmsnet.sources.games
vmsnet.sysmgt 147
vmsnet.tcp.multinet
vmsnet.test 147
vmsnet.tpu
vmsnet.uucp
vmsnet.vms-posix
vu.org.mac101
vuw.general

W

wa.general
wa.politics
wa.test
well.general
wi.forsale
wi.general 190
wi.transit
wny.events
wny.general
wny.news
wny.rocslug
wny.seminar
wny.test
wny.unix-wizards
wny.wanted
wny.yumyum
wolfhh.archive
wpi.clubs.hsa
wpi.faculty
wpi.library
wpi.philosophy
wpi.ranting.and.raving
wpi.spanish
wpi.techwriting
wpost
wsu.csc

X

Y

yale.[Yale newsgroups]
york.announce
york.ariel.questions
york.doc
york.general 187
york.[York University newsgroups]

Z

za.ads.jobs
za.ads.lifts
za.ads.misc
za.archives
za.culture.xhosa
za.environment
za.events
za.flame

za.humour
za.misc
za.net.maps
za.net.misc
za.net.stats
za.politics
za.schools
za.[South Africa newsgroups]
za.sport
za.test
za.und.ads
za.und.clubs.staff
za.und.misc
za.und.news
za.unix.misc
za.unix.sco
zer.fundgrube.suche
zer.[German-language newsgroups]
zer.pm-netz.diskurs
zer.pm-netz.systeminfo
zer.pm-netz.zmap

Chapter 15: Master Newsgroup Subject Index & Finder

Part of the problem with the Internet is being able to select the newsgroups which appeal to your needs and interests: Here are 3,757 well-chosen words to help you find the newsgroups relating to your specific interests and business activities.

A particularly annoying trait of newsgroups on the Internet is their widespread incoherence and disorganization. Newsgroup names reflect the Internet's tech-weenie origins and are mostly a confusing hash of truncated words, dots and dashes. Newsgroup names can *sometimes* be descriptive (**alt.barney.dinosaur.die.die.die** being a perfectly good example), but many times a newsgroup's name doesn't describe its **content** or **application** at all (for example, you'd never know from its name that **misc.misc** is a newsgroup covering a wide variety of general household information, consumer advice and do-it-yourself topics).

What we've done with the newsgroups covered in *What's on the Internet* is to assign up to six subject **keywords** which describe the content of each newsgroup covered in *What's on the Internet*. We provide you with a variety of subject terms to help you locate the newsgroups you need.

For example, the newsgroup **biz.misc** can be located in the Index under the subject keywords **business opportunities**, **connections (business)**, **entrepreneurs**, **business (information)** and **information (business)**. Alongside the subject keyword, you'll also find its corresponding newsgroup name and the page number where it can be found in *What's on the Internet*. We've also indexed some newsgroups (mostly obscure groups or foreign-language groups) which are not covered in *What's on the Internet*. These listings are identified by double asterisks (**) in the page column.

Subject	Newsgroup	Page
Amiga	comp.unix.amiga	157
ammunition (reloading)	info.firearms	76
ammunition	rec.guns	76
Amnesty International	soc.rights.human	58
amusement parks	rec.parks.theme	87
amusement parks	rec.roller coaster	89
anarchy	alt.revolution.counter	54
anarchy	alt.society.anarchy	54
ancestors (finding)	soc.roots	89
ancient civilizations	alt.mythology	70
Andrew System	comp.soft-sys.andrew	174
animals (wolves)	alt.wolves	86
animation (disney)	alt.fan.disney.afternoon	118
animation (fantasy)	(various newsgroups)	107, 203
animation (Japanese)	rec.arts.anime.info	101
animation (Japanese)	rec.arts.anime.marketplace	101
animation (Japanese)	rec.arts.anime	101-102
animation (Japanese)	rec.arts.anime.stories	102
animation	comp.graphics.animation	149
animation	rec.arts.animation	101
anime (animation)	rec.arts.anime.stories	102
Anne Rice	alt.books.anne-rice	98
anonymity (maintaining)	alt.security	39, 160
answers (finding)	bit.listserv.circplus	58, 135
Anthony, Piers	alt.fan.pier-anthony	99
antique cars	rec.autos.antique	82
antique/classic cars	alt.autos.antique	82
antiques	rec.antiques	74
antiques	rec.collecting.cards	74
antiques	rec.collecting	74
anthropology	sci.anthropology	126
apartheid (South Africa)	za.misc	**
APL	comp.lang.apl	150
Apollo	comp.sys.apollo	167
Apple II	comp.sys.apple2	164
Apple II	comp.sys.apple2.gno	164
Apple/Mac news (ClariNet news)	clari.nb.apple	**
Applebus	comp.protocols.appletalk	159
Appletalk	comp.protocols.appletalk	159
aquariums	alt.aquaria	84
aquariums	sci.aquaria	126
Arab (culture)	soc.culture.arabic	63
Arab (religion)	soc.religion.islam	70
Arab politics	talk.politics.mideast	51
archaeology	sci.archaeology	126
architecture	alt.architecture	125
Argentina (culture)	alt.culture.argentina	63
Army (news)	soc.veterans	59
art & politics	alt.artcom	74
art	alt.postmodern	74
art	rec.arts.fine	74
artificial intelligence (AI)	comp.ai	137, 142
artificial intelligence (fuzzy)	comp.ai.fuzzy	142
artificial visualization SW (AVS)	comp.graphics.avs	149
ASEAN (culture)	soc.culture.asean	63
Asia (politics)	talk.politics.china	51
Asia (Thailand)	soc.culture.thai	69
Asia	alt.culture.indonesia	66
Asian (culture)	soc.culture.asian.american	64
Asian-Indian (culture)	alt.culture.us.asian-indian	50

Subject	Newsgroup	Page
Asimov, Isaac	alt.books.isaac.asimov	99
asm370	comp.lang.asm370	150
assembly language	alt.lang.asm	150
Assoc. for Computer Machinery (ACM)		
comp.org.acm		154
astral projection	alt.out-of-body	197
astrology	alt.astrology	89
astronomy	sci.astro	126
Asymetrix (Toolbook)	bit.listserv.toolb-l	162
AT&T (micros)	comp.sys.att	167
AT&T 7300	comp.sys.3b1	167
Atari	comp.sys.atari.8bit	164
Atari	comp.sys.atari.advocacy	164
Atari	comp.sys.atari.st	164
Atari	comp.sys.atari.st.tech	164
ATF	alt.politics.org.batf	54
atheism	alt.atheism	70
atheism	alt.atheism.moderated	70
Atlanta (events)	atl.general	185
Atlanta (jobs)	atl.jobs	185
Atlanta (Olympics)	atl.olympics	185
Atlantic City (gambling)	rec.gambling	89
auctions	rec.collecting.cards	74
audio (car)	rec.audio.car	113
audio (high-end)	rec.audio.high-end	113
audio (professional)	rec.audio.pro	113
audio electronics	rec.audio	113
audio (Amiga)	comp.sys.amiga.audio	163
Austin, TX (for sale)	austin.forsale	185
Austin, TX (info)	austin.announce	185
Austin, TX (music)	austin.music	185
Austin, TX (news)	austin.news	185
Austin, TX (politics)	austin.politics	185
Austin, TX (politics)	austin.talk	185
Austin, TX (privacy)	austin.eff	185
Austin, TX (talk)	austin.general	185
Austin, TX (travel)	tx.general	186-187
Australia (Amiga computers)	aus.computers.amiga	191
Australia (bicycling)	aus.bicycling	191
Australia (computers)	aus.computers	191-192
Australia (culture)	soc.culture.australian	64
Australia (employment)	aus.jobs	192
Australia (films)	aus.films	191
Australia (for sale)	aus.forsale	191
Australia (games)	aus.games	192
Australia (games)	aus.games.roleplay	192
Australia (ham radio)	aus.radio	191
Australia (IBM PC computers)	aus.computers.ibm-p	192
Australia (Info)	aus.wanted	192
Australia (jokes)	aus.jokes	191
Australia (Mac/Apple)	aus.mac	192
Australia (motorcycles)	aus.motorcycles	192
Australia (music)	aus.music	192
Australia (news)	aus.general	191
Australia (news)	aus.politics	191
Australia (newsgroups-general)	aus.aarnet	192
Australia (politics)	aus.general	191
Australia (politics)	aus.politics	191
Australia (pop culture)	aus.flame	192
Australia (railroads)	aus.rail	192

Subject	Newsgroup	Page
Australia (science fiction)	aus.sf	192
Australia (sex)	aus.sex	192
Australia (ski reports)	aus.snow	192
Australia (sports)	aus.sport	192
Australia (Star Trek)	aus.star-trek	192
Australia (statistics)	aus.stats.s	193
Australia (stereo)	aus.hi-fi	192
Australia (telecom)	aus.comms	193
Australia (vacations)	aus.bicycling	191
Australia (video)	aus.computers.amiga	191
autism	alt.education.disabled	**
autism	bit.listserv.autism	61
auto repair	alt.autos.antique	82
auto restoration	alt.autos.antique	82
AutoCad	alt.cad.autocad	144
autographs	alt.collecting.autographs	74
automobile (racing)	rec.autos.sport	83
automobile (Saturn)	csn.ml.saturn	40
automobiles (antique)	rec.autos.antique	82
automobiles (custom)	alt.autos.rod-n-custom	82
automobiles (driving)	rec.autos.driving	83
automobiles (high performance)	alt.hotrod	82
automobiles (maintainence)	rec.autos.tech	83
automobiles (repair)	rec.autos	82-83
automobiles (street rods)	rec.autos.rod-n-custom	83
automobiles (Volkswagen)	rec.autos.vw	83
autos (custom)	alt.autos.rod-n-custom	82
AUX	comp.unix.aux	157
aviation (crashes)	rec.aviation.stories	80
aviation (equipment)	rec.aviation.owning	80
aviation (flying techniques)	rec.aviation.piloting	80
aviation (for sale)	rec.aviation.owning	80
aviation (general)	rec.aviation.answers	79
aviation (general)	rec.aviation.misc	80
aviation (gliders)	rec.aviation.soaring	80
aviation (homebuilt)	rec.aviation.homebuilt	79
aviation (instruments)	rec.aviation.ifr	79
aviation (military)	rec.aviation.military	79
aviation (product talk)	rec.aviation.products	80
aviation (software)	rec.aviation.simulators	80
aviation (stories)	rec.aviation.stories	80
aviation (student pilots)	rec.aviation.student	80
aviation news (ClariNet news)	clari.news.aviation	93
avionics	rec.aviation.products	80
avionics	rec.aviation.student	80
AVS	comp.graphics.avs	149
Ayn Rand	alt.philosophy.objectivism	70
Ayn Rand	talk.philosophy.misc	71

B

Subject	Newsgroup	Page
Babylon 5 (TV)	alt.tv.babylon-5	116
backgammon (games)	rec.games.backgammon	103
backpacking	rec.backcountry	177
backrubs	alt.backrubs	89
bad jokes	rec.humor.oracle.d	106
bad jokes	rec.humor.oracle	106
Baha'i	soc.religion.bahai	70
baking (bread)	rec.food.sourdough	78
baking (recipes)	rec.food.recipes	78
baking	rec.food.cooking	78

Subject	Newsgroup	Page
baking	rec.food.historic	78
Balkans (news)	alt.news.macedonia	93
Balkans	soc.culture.croatia	65
Baltics (culture)	soc.culture.baltics	64
bands (marching)	rec.arts.marching	89
Bangalore	alt.culture.karnataka	66
Bangladesh (culture)	soc.culture.bangladesh	64
banking (ClariNet news)	clari.biz.finance.services	42
Banyan	bit.listserv.banyan-l	146
Barbados	soc.culture.caribbean	64
Barney (hate group)	alt.barney.dinosaur.die.die.die	199
Barney (hate group)	alt.tv.dinosaur.barney.die.die.die	116
Barry, Dave (columns)	clari.feature.dave_barry	106
Barry, Dave	alt.fan.dave_barry	98
Bart Simpson (TV)	alt.tv.simpsons	118
baseball (college)	rec.sport.baseball.college	176
baseball (Fantasy League)	rec.sport.baseball.fantasy	176
baseball (pro)	rec.sport.baseball	176
baseball cards	rec.collecting.cards	74
baseball-news (ClariNet news)	clari.sports.baseball	182
baseball-scores (ClariNet news)	clari.sports.baseball.games	182
BASH (Bourne Again Shell)	gnu.bash.bug	147
BASIC	alt.lang.basic	150
basketball (college)	rec.sport.basketball.college	176
basketball (pro)	rec.sport.basketball.pro	176
basketball-college (ClariNet news)	clari.sports.basketball.college	182
basketball-news (ClariNet news)	clari.sports.basketball	182
bass fishing	rec.outdoors.fishing	179
bass guitar	rec.music.makers.bass	112
BATF	alt.politics.org.batf	54
bathing	alt.backrubs	89
BBC (Dr. Who)	rec.arts.drwho	119
BBS (ads)	alt.bbs.ads	142
BBS (directory)	alt.bbs.ads	142
BBS (Internet)	alt.bbs.internet	32, 143
BBS (lists)	alt.bbs.lists	143
BBS (setting up)	alt.bbs	32, 142-143
BBS (software)	comp.bbs.waffle	143
BBS services	alt.bbs.internet	32, 143
BBS software	alt.bbs.PCboard	143
BBS software	alt.bbs.pcbuucp	143
BBS systems	alt.bbs.lists	143
BBS	alt.bbs.allsysop	143
BBS	alt.bbs	32, 142-143
BBS	alt.bbs.lists	143
BBS	alt.bbs.pcbuucp	143
BBS	alt.bbs.unix.bbs	143
BBS	comp.bbs.misc	143
beach	alt.surfing	181
beadwork	rec.crafts.misc	77
Beatles	rec.music.beatles	107
Beavis and Butt-Head (TV)	alt.tv.liquid-tv	116
beer (brewing)	rec.crafts.brewing	75
beer	alt.beer	75
Beetle (Volkswagen)	rec.autos.vw	83
benchmarks	comp.benchmarks	173
Berkeley, CA (news & talk)	ucb.general	190
Berkeley, CA (University of CA)	uc.general	190

Subject	Newsgroup	Page
Berkeley Standard Distribution BSD	comp.os.386bsd.bugs	154
Berlin (newsgroups)	bln.announce.fub	**
Beverly Hills 90210 (TV)	alt.tv.bh90210	116
Bible study	soc.religion.christian.bible-study	69
bibliographic (software)	bit.listserv.notis-l	136
bicycles (for sale)	rec.bicycles.marketplace	181
bicycles (lifestyles)	rec.bicycles.soc	182
bicycles (racing)	rec.bicycles.racing	182
bicycles (repair)	rec.bicycles.tech	182
bicycles (riding)	rec.bicycles.misc	182
bicycles (touring)	rec.bicycles.rides	182
bigamy	alt.polyamory	203
bikes (motorcycles)	ne.motorcycles	60
bikes (motorcycles)	rec.motorcycles	83
Bill Clinton (news)	alt.news-media	93
Bill Clinton	alt.dear.whitehouse	48
Bill Clinton	alt.politics.clinton	47
Bill Clinton	alt.politics.org.misc	48
Bill Clinton	alt.politics.reform	48
Bill Clinton	alt.politics.usa.misc	48
Bill Clinton	alt.president.clinton	47
biofeedback (talk)	alt.paranormal	198
biology	sci.bio	126-127
biology	sci.bio.technology	127
bionet (announcements)	bionet.announce	133
biosphere	bit.listserv.biosph-l	125
biostasis	sci.cryonics	127
biotechnology	sci.bio.technology	127
bird watching	rec.birds	85
birding	rec.birds	85
birds (pets)	rec.pets.birds	85
bisexuals	soc.bi	60
bizarre talk	talk.bizarre	202
Blackjack (card counting)	rec.gambling	89
blacks (ClariNet news)	clari.news.group.blacks	94
blacks (discussion)	soc.culture.african.american	63
blindness (resources)	misc.handicap	63
blindness	bit.listserv.blindnws	61
blonde jokes	rec.humor	106
Blue Note (jazz albums)	rec.music.bluenote	108-109
board games	(various newsgroups)	107, 203
boating	alt.fishing	76
Bob Dylan	rec.music.dylan	107
Bob Marley	rec.music.reggae	108
body visualization	alt.support.big.folks	62
Bolo (computer game)	alt.netgames.bolo	103-104
Bond, James	alt.fan.james-bond	114
Bonsai trees	alt.bonsai	75
book news (ClariNet news)	clari.news.books	93
book publishing	misc.writing	58-59
book reviews (technical/computer)	alt.books.technical	125
book reviews	alt.books.reviews	98
books (18th Century)	bit.listserv.c18-l	135
books (Anne Rice)	alt.books.anne-rice	98
books (comics)	alt.comics.lnh	100
books (comics)	rec.arts.comics.info	101
books (computer/technical)	misc.books.technical	125
books (discussion)	bit.listserv.literary	59
books (Dune)	alt.fan.dune	99
books (fantasy)	alt.fan.pern	99

Subject	Newsgroup	Page
books (fantasy)	rec.arts.books.tolkien	99
books (horror)	alt.horror	114
books (science fiction)	alt.books.deryni	99
books (science fiction)	alt.books.isaac.asimov	99
books (science fiction)	alt.fan.pier-anthony	99
books (science fiction)	alt.fan.Pratchett	99
books (science fiction)	rec.arts.sf.written	119-120
books (self-improvement)	alt.self-improve	40
books (Sherlock Holmes)	alt.fan.holmes	98
books (technical)	alt.books.technical	125
books (technical)	biz.books.technical	98
books (technical)	misc.books.technical	125
boomerangs	alt.boomerang	178
Bosnia (crisis)	alt.news.macedonia	93
Bosnia	soc.culture.bosna-herzgvna	64
Bosnia	soc.culture.yugoslavia	69
Boulder, CO (news)	boulder.general	185
Bourne shell	comp.unix.shell	158
bowling	alt.sport.bowling	178
Boy Scouts	rec.scouting	59
brain	sci.cognitive	127
brain teasers	rec.puzzles	77-78
Brazil (culture)	soc.culture.brazil	64
Brazil (newsgroups)	brasil.anuncios	**
bread (making)	rec.food.sourdough	78
bread (making)	rec.food.veg	78-79
breakfast (talk)	alt.cereal	196
breweries	alt.beer	75
bride (wedding)	alt.wedding	40
bridge (games)	rec.games.bridge	103
Britain (news & talk)	uk.misc	193
Britain (politics)	uk.politics	193
Britain (singles)	uk.singles	193
British (culture)	soc.culture.british	64
British Columbia, CA (news)	bc.general	193
British Columbia, CA (weather)	bc.weather	193
British comedy (film/TV)	alt.comedy.british	119
BRL	info.brl-cad	145
BRL-CAD (software)	info.brl-cad	145
broadcasting (pirate radio)	alt.radio.pirate	196
broadcasting (radio)	rec.radio.broadcasting	87
Broadway (theater)	rec.arts.theatre	88-89
Brother Jed (evangelist)	alt.brother-jed	200
BSD (Berkely Standard Distribution)	comp.unix.bsd	157
BSD (UNIX)	comp.os.386bsd.questions	155
BSD	comp.os.386bsd.bugs	154
BSD	comp.os.386bsd.development	155
bubble baths	alt.backrubs	89
Buckminster Fuller	bit.listserv.geodesic	125
Buddhism (satire)	alt.buddha.short.fat.guy	200
Buddhism	soc.religion.eastern	70
Buffett (Jimmy)	alt.fan.Jimmy-Buffett	107
building (house)	misc.consumers.house	39
Bulgaria (culture)	soc.culture.bulgaria	64
bulletin board services (setting up)	alt.bbs	32, 142-143
bulletin board system	alt.bbs.ads	142
bulletin board system	alt.bbs	32, 142-143
bulletin board system	alt.bbs.unix.bbs	143

Subject	Newsgroup	Page
bulletin board system (BBS)	comp.bbs.misc	143
bulletin board system (directory)	alt.bbs.ads	142
Burroughs, William	alt.cyberpunk.movement	112
Burroughs (computers)	comp.sys.unisys	168
Bush (Kate)	rec.music.gaffa	109
business (ClariNet news)	clari.biz.top	42
business (ClariNet news)	clari.nb.business	42
business (connections)	alt.business.misc	37
business (entrepreneurship)	misc.entrepreneurs	37
business (Hong Kong)	soc.culture.hongkong	65-66
business (information)	alt.business.misc	37
business (information)	alt.business.multi-level	37
business (information)	bit.listserv.buslib-1	37
business (information)	biz.misc	38, 42
business (manufacturing)	alt.manufacturing.misc	37
business (Q & A)	bit.listserv.buslib-1	37
business (startups)	alt.business.misc	37
business bulletins (ClariNet news)	clari.biz.urgent	42
business features (ClariNet news)	clari.biz.features	42
business finance (ClariNet news)	clari.biz.finance	42
business opportunities	biz.misc	38, 42
business trends (ClariNet news)	clari.nb.trends	42
business-Canada (ClariNet news)	clari.canada.biz	194
business-mergers (ClariNet news)	clari.biz.mergers	42
business-other (ClariNet news)	clari.biz.misc	42

C

Subject	Newsgroup	Page
C++	comp.lang.c++	128, 142-153
C++	comp.os.ms-windows.programmer.tools	159
C++	comp.std.c++	142-153
C	comp.lang.c	150-151
C	comp.std.c	153
cable TV	rec.video.cable	81
CAD	alt.cad	144
CAD	alt.cad.autocad	144
CAD	comp.cad.cadence	144
CAD	comp.lsi.cad	144-145
CAD	info.brl-cad	145
Cadence Systems	comp.cad.cadence	144
CAE (Computer Aided Engineering)	comp.lang.verilog	153
caffeine (talk)	alt.drugs.caffeine	197
California (cars/driving)	ca.driving	186
California (ClariNet news)	clari.sfbay.roads	191
California (earthquakes)	ca.earthquakes	186
California (environment)	ca.environment	186
California (news)	ca.general	186-187, 189-190
California (politics)	ca.politics	186, 189
California (San Diego — for sale)	sdnet.forsale	186
California (Stanford University)	su.events	190
Callahan's (online talk)	alt.callahans	196
calligraphy (crafts)	rec.crafts.misc	77
camcorders	rec.video	80-81
cameras (movie)	rec.arts.cinema	114
cameras	rec.photo	77
campaigns (political)	alt.politics.elections	50
camping	rec.backcountry	177
Canada (ClariNet news)	clari.canada.biz	194

Subject	Newsgroup	Page
Canada (ClariNet news)	clari.canada.features	194
Canada (ClariNet news)	clari.canada.general	194
Canada (ClariNet news)	clari.canada.newscast	194
Canada (ClariNet news)	clari.news.canada	94
Canada (culture)	soc.culture.canada	64
Canada (Internet)	can.canet.stats	193
Canada (Internet)	can.uucp.maps	193
Canada (Ontario)	kw.general	188
Canada (Ottawa — information)	ott.general	194
Canada (politics)	can.general	193
Canada (politics)	can.jobs	193
Canada (Quebec)	can.francais	193
Canada (Quebec)	can.politics	193
Canada (University of Montreal)	umontreal.general	**
cancer (support)	(various newsgroups)	107, 203
cancer	alt.support.cancer	62
canoes	rec.boats.paddle	84
car (racing)	rec.autos.sport	83
car (repair)	rec.autos.vw	83
car (repairs)	rec.autos.tech	83
car (sound systems)	rec.audio.car	113
car repair	rec.autos	82-83
car restoration	alt.autos.antique	82
car stereo	rec.audio.pro	113
card games	rec.gambling	89
card games	rec.games.trivia	103
career advice	misc.jobs.misc	41
Caribbean (culture)	soc.culture.caribbean	64
carpentry	rec.woodworking	39, 77
cars (antique)	rec.autos.antique	82
cars (custom)	alt.autos.rod-n-custom	82
cars (driving)	rec.autos.driving	83
cars (high performance)	alt.hotrod	82
cars (Saturn)	csn.ml.saturn	40
cars (street rods)	rec.autos.rod-n-custom	83
cars (talk)	rec.autos	82-83
cars (Volkswagen)	rec.autos.vw	83
cars/trucks for sale (SF/Bay Area)	ba.market.vehicles	188
cartoons (fantasy)	(various newsgroups)	107, 203
cartoons (Japanese)	rec.arts.anime.info	101
cartoons (Japanese)	rec.arts.anime.marketplace	101
cartoons (Japanese)	rec.arts.anime	101-102
cartoons (Japanese)	rec.arts.anime.stories	102
cartoons (printed)	rec.arts.comics.misc	101
cartoons	alt.barney.dinosaur.die.die.die	199
cartoons	rec.arts.animation	101
cascades (poetry)	alt.cosuard	198
casting (metal)	rec.crafts.metalworking	77
Catholicism	bit.listserv.catholic	69
cats (pets)	rec.pets.cats	85
CB radio	rec.radio.cb	87
CD (music)	rec.music.cd	113-114
CD ROM software	comp.publish.cdrom.software	145
CD ROM	alt.cd-rom	145
CD-32	comp.sys.amiga.advocacy	163
CD ROM (publishing)	comp.publish.cdrom.software	145
CD ROM drives	alt.cd-rom	145
CD ROM (LANS)	bit.listserv.cdromlan	145
CDs (used)	rec.music.marketplace	111
celebrities (autographs)	alt.collecting.autographs	74

Subject	Newsgroup	Page
computers (hackers)	alt.hackers	57
computers (image proceing)	sci.image.processing	130
computers (Japan)	comp.research.japan	174
computers (kids)	csn.ml.kids	59
computers (legal issues)	misc.legal.computing	174
computers (miscellaneous)	comp.sys.misc	167
computers (molecular)	sci.nanotech	132
computers (privacy)	alt.security.pgp	160
computers (video games)	rec.games.video.arcade	102
computers (vintage)	alt.technology.obsolete	81
computers (writing)	bit.listserv.mbu-l	59, 136
computers for sale (SF/Bay Area)	ba.market.computers	188
computers	comp.misc	173
conferences (academic)	news.announce.conferences	58
conferences (professional)	news.announce.conferences	58
conflicts-world (ClariNet news)	clari.news.issues.conflict	95
connections (business)	biz.misc	38, 42
consciousness	alt.consciousness	200
conservatisim	alt.conspiracy	53
conservatism (Rush Limbaugh)	alt.rush-limbaugh	46
conservatism	alt.fan.dan-quayle	46
conservatism	alt.politics.libertarian	46
conservatism	alt.politics.usa.republican	49
conservatism	alt.society.conservatism	46
conspiracy theories	alt.conspiracy	53
conspiracy theories	alt.conspiracy.jfk	53
conspiracy theories	alt.discordia	197
conspiracy theories	alt.revisionism	52
Constitution (U.S.)	misc.legal	38, 174
Constitution (U.S.)	alt.politics.usa.constitution	53
consultants (computer)	alt.computer.consultants	**
consumer (ClariNet news)	clari.news.consumer	94
consumer electronics (audio)	rec.audio.high-end	113
consumer electronics (audio)	rec.audio	113
consumer electronics (car audio)	rec.audio.car	113
consumer electronics (laserdisc)	alt.video.laserdisc	81
consumer electronics (laserdisc)	rec.video.releases	81
consumer electronics (satellite TV)	rec.video.satellite	81
consumer electronics (video)	rec.video	80-81
consumer electronics	alt.cyberpunk.tech	80
consumer electronics	alt.toys.hi-tech	81
consumer issues	misc.consumer	39
consumers (Chicago)	chi.places	186
consumers (Saturn cars)	csn.ml.saturn	40
contract programming	misc.jobs.contract	41
control systems	bit.listserv.csg-l	135
controversy (historical)	soc.history	52
conventions (science fiction)	alt.fandom.cons	119
conventions (science fiction)	rec.arts.sf.announce	119
Convergent	comp.sys.unisys	168
conversational French	alt.nick.sucks	194
cooking (historic dishes)	rec.food.historic	78
cooking (recipes exchange)	rec.food.recipes	78
cooking (vegetarian)	rec.food.veg	78-79
cooking	rec.food.cooking	78
copyright (computers)	misc.legal.computing	174
copyright issues	misc.int-property	38
cordials	rec.food.drink	78
Cornell (newsgroups)	slac.announce.important	**
corporate earnings (ClariNet news)	clari.biz.finance.earnings	42

Subject	Newsgroup	Page
counter revolution	alt.revolution.counter	54
counter-culture (magazines)	alt.zines	201
counter-revolution (speculation)	alt.politics.usa.constitution	53
counterculture (talk)	alt.drugs	197
country living	misc.rural	40
country/western music	rec.music.country.western	109
couples	soc.couples	58
cows (collectibles)	alt.cows.moo.moo.moo	197
CPM	comp.os.cpm	156
crafts	rec.crafts.misc	77
crafts	rec.crafts.textiles	77
Cray	comp.sys.super	170
Cray	comp.unix.cray	157
creationism	talk.origins	71
credit (privacy)	alt.privacy	39-40, 160
crew (rowing)	rec.sport.rowing	180
cricket	rec.sport.cricket	178
crime (ClariNet news)	clari.news.law.crime	95
crime (ClariNet news)	clari.news.law.investigation	95
crime	alt.prisons	51
crime-drugs (ClariNet news)	clari.news.law.drugs	95
crime-sex (ClariNet news)	clari.news.law.crime.sex	95
crime-violent (ClariNet news)	clari.news.law.crime.violent	95
Croatia (culture)	soc.culture.croatia	65
Croatia	soc.culture.bosna-herzgvna	64
Croatia	soc.culture.yugoslavia	69
cross dressers	alt.transgendered	202
crossword puzzles	rec.puzzles.crosswords	78
cryonics	sci.cryonics	127
cryptology	sci.crypt	127-128
Cub Scouts	rec.scouting	59
Cuba	soc.culture.latin-america	67
cult films	alt.cult-movies	114-115
cult films	alt.cult-movies.rocky-horror	115
cult TV (The Prisoner)	alt.tv.prisoner	117-118
cult TV	alt.tv.twin-peaks	118
cults	alt.religion.scientology	71
culture (Afghanistan)	soc.culture.afghanistan	63
culture (Africa)	soc.culture.african	63
culture (Alaska)	alt.culture.alaska	185
culture (America)	soc.culture.usa	69
culture (American Indian)	soc.culture.native	67
culture (Arab)	soc.culture.arabic	63
culture (Argentina)	alt.culture.argentina	63
culture (ASEAN)	soc.culture.asean	63
culture (Asian)	soc.culture.asian.american	64
culture (Asian-Indian)	alt.culture.us.asian-indian	50
culture (Australia)	soc.culture.australian	64
culture (Baltics)	soc.culture.baltics	64
culture (Bangladesh)	soc.culture.bangladesh	64
culture (Brazil)	soc.culture.brazil	64
culture (British)	soc.culture.british	64
culture (Bulgaria)	soc.culture.bulgaria	64
culture (Canada)	soc.culture.canada	64
culture (Caribbean)	soc.culture.caribbean	64
culture (Celtic)	soc.culture.celtic	64
culture (China)	soc.culture.china	65
culture (Croatia)	soc.culture.croatia	65
culture (Czech)	soc.culture.czecho-slovak	65

Subject	Newsgroup	Page
culture (FAQs)	soc.answer	63
culture (French)	soc.culture.french	65
culture (German)	soc.culture.german	65
culture (Greece)	soc.culture.greek	65
culture (Hong Kong)	soc.culture.hongkong	65-66
culture (Hungary)	soc.culture.magyar	67
culture (India)	soc.culture.indian	66
culture (Indian)	soc.culture.indian.telugu	66
culture (Indonesian)	soc.culture.indonesia	66
culture (Internet)	alt.cyberspace	111-112
culture (Iranian)	soc.culture.iranian	66
culture (Italian)	soc.culture.italian	66
culture (Japan)	soc.culture.japan	66
culture (Jewish)	soc.culture.jewish	66-67
culture (Korean)	soc.culture.korean	67
culture (Latin America)	soc.culture.latin-america	67
culture (Lebanese)	soc.culture.lebanon	67
culture (Malaysia)	soc.culture.malaysia	67
culture (Mexico)	soc.culture.mexican	67
culture (miscellaneous)	soc.culture.misc	69
culture (Nepal)	soc.culture.nepal	67
culture (New Zealand)	soc.culture.new-zealand	68
culture (Nordic)	soc.culture.nordic	68
culture (Pakistan)	soc.culture.pakistan	68
culture (Poland)	soc.culture.polish	68
culture (Portugal)	soc.culture.portuguese	68
culture (Romania)	soc.culture.romanian	68
culture (Singapore)	soc.culture.singapore	68
culture (Soviet)	soc.culture.soviet	68
culture (Spain)	soc.culture.spain	68
culture (Sri Lanka)	soc.culture.sri-lanka	69
culture (Sri Lanka)	soc.culture.tamil	69
culture (Taiwan)	soc.culture.taiwan	69
culture (Thailand)	soc.culture.thai	69
culture (The Netherlands)	soc.culture.netherlands	67
culture (The Philippines)	soc.culture.filipino	65
culture (Turkey)	soc.culture.turkish	69
culture (Vietnam)	soc.culture.vietnamese	69
culture (Yugoslavia)	soc.culture.yugoslavia	69
culture	alt.artcom	74
culture	alt.politics.usa.republican	49
culture	alt.postmodern	74
culture	rec.arts.fine	74
cultures (ancient)	sci.anthropology	126
cultures (ancient)	sci.archaeology	126
current events (Bosnians/Serbs)	alt.news.macedonia	93
current events	alt.activism.d	46
current events	talk.politics.misc	49
custody (in divorce)	alt.dads-rights	61
cyberpunk (games)	rec.games.frp.cyber	105
cyberpunk (magazines)	alt.zines	201
cyberpunk (raves)	alt.rave	111
cyberpunk	alt.cyberpunk	80, 112, 202
cyberpunk	alt.cyberpunk.chatsubo	202
cyberpunk	alt.cyberpunk.movement	112
cyberpunk	alt.discordia	197
cyberspace	alt.cyberspace	111-112
Czech (culture)	soc.culture.czecho-slovak	65
Czechoslovakia	bit.listserv.slovak-l	65

Subject	Newsgroup	Page
D		
dad's rights	alt.dads-rights	61
Dallas/Fort Worth, TX (information)	dfw.general	186
Dan Quayle	alt.fan.dan-quayle	46
dance	rec.arts.dance	75
darkroom (photography)	rec.photo	77
darts (throwing)	alt.sport.darts	178
databases (general)	comp.databases	145
databases (theory)	comp.databases.theory	145
databases	comp.databases.informix	145
databases	comp.databases.ingres	145
databases	comp.databases.oracle	145
databases	comp.databases.sybase	145
dating	alt.romance	203
dating	soc.singles	203
Dave Barry (columns)	clari.feature.dave_barry	106
Dave Barry	alt.fan.dave_barry	98
Dave Letterman	alt.fan.letterman	116
dBase	bit.listserv.dbase-l	145
Deadheads	rec.music.gdead	107
deafness	bit.listserv.deaf-l	62
DEC (Digital Computer Corp.)	comp.sys.dec	164
DEC (Digital Equipment Corp.)	comp.sys.dec.micro	164
DEC (Digitial Equipment Corp.)	comp.os.vms	156
DEC (news)	biz.dec.decnews	**
DEC (VAX/VMS)	vmsnet.misc	147
DEC	vmsnet.alpha	147
DEC	vmsnet.internals	147
DEC users group	comp.org.decus	154
DECUS	comp.org.decus	154
defense industry (ClariNet news)	clari.tw.defense	42
deficit reduction	alt.politics.perot	50
deficit spending	alt.politics.economics	50
Deryni	alt.books.deryni	99
design	alt.cad.autocad	144
desktop publishing (PageMaker)	alt.aldus.pagemaker	162
desktop publishing	comp.text.desktop	171
desktop publishing	comp.text.frame	171
Desqview	comp.os.msdos.desqview	155
Detroit, MI (information)	mi.misc	186
development (third world)	bit.listserv.devel-l	51, 125
devil worship	alt.satanism	71
diabetes	misc.health.diabetes	62
dieting (support)	alt.support.big.folks	62
dieting (support)	alt.support.diet	62
dieting	(various newsgroups)	107, 203
Digital Equipment Corp. (VAX/VMS)	vmsnet.misc	147
digital radio	rec.radio.amateur.packet	86
digital signal processing (DSP)	comp.dsp	173
dining (reviews)	rec.food.restaurants	78
Dinosaurs (TV)	alt.tv.dinosaurs	116
diplomacy (games)	rec.games.diplomacy	103
dirt bikes	rec.motorcycles	83
disabilities (resources)	misc.handicap	63
disaster news (ClariNet news)	clari.news.disaster	94
Disc Golf	rec.sport.disc	179
discrimination	alt.discrimination	49
Disney, Walt	alt.fan.disney.afternoon	118
Disneyland	rec.arts.disney	87

Subject	Newsgroup	Page
Disneyworld	rec.arts.disney	87
display (3D graphics)	alt.3d	148
diving (scuba)	bit.listserv.scuba-l	180
diving (scuba)	rec.scuba	180
divorce (child custody)	bit.listserv.free-l	61
divorce	alt.child-support	61
divorce	alt.dads-rights	61
dogs (pets)	rec.pets.dogs	85-86
domain	comp.protocols.tcp-ip.domains	160
domestic law	alt.child-support	61
DOS	alt.msdos.programmer	155
Dr. Demento	rec.music.dementia	110
Dr. Who	rec.arts.drwho	119
Dracula	alt.vampyres	202
drama (theater)	rec.arts.theatre	88-89
dreams (analysis)	alt.dreams.lucid	200
dreams (interpreting)	alt.dreams	200
dreams (lucid)	alt.dreams.lucid	200
dreams (out of body experiences)	alt.out-of-body	197
drinking (beer)	alt.beer	75
drinking (parties)	alt.party	198
driving (California)	ca.driving	186
driving (tips)	rec.autos.driving	83
drugs (illegal)	alt.drugs	197
drugs (legalization)	alt.drugs	197
drugs (psychedelic)	alt.psychoactives	199
drum corps	rec.arts.marching	89
drummers	rec.music.makers.percussion	112
DSP	comp.dsp	173
Dune (books)	alt.fan.dune	99
Dungeons and Dragons	alt.fan.furry	103
Dylan, Bob	rec.music.dylan	107
Dylan	comp.lang.dylan	151
dynamical systems	comp.theory.dynamic-sys	170

E

Subject	Newsgroup	Page
early classical music	rec.music.early	109
earthquakes (California)	ca.earthquakes	186
Eastern Europe (ClariNet news)	clari.news.hot.east_europe	94
Eastern Europe (Czechoslovakia)	bit.listserv.slovak-l	65
Eastern Europe (discussion)	soc.culture.soviet	68
Eastern Europe (news)	misc.news.east-europe.rferl	93
eastern religions	soc.religion.eastern	70
eating (support)	alt.support.diet	62
eating disorders	alt.support.big.folks	62
ecology	alt.politics.greens	47
ecology	alt.save.the.earth	47
economic news (ClariNet news)	clari.news.economy	94
economics (ClariNet news)	clari.biz.economy	42
economics	alt.politics.economics	50
economics	sci.econ	128
economics-world (ClariNet news)	clari.biz.economy.world	42
EDI (Electronic Data Interchange)	bit.listserv.edi-l	172
Edinburgh (newsgroups)	ed.general	**
education (artificial intelligence)	comp.ai.edu	137
education (CD-ROMs)	comp.ai.edu	137
education (colleges)	soc.college	**
education (composition)	comp.edu.composition	137
education (disabled)	alt.education.diabled	**
education (disabled)	bit.listserv.dsshe-l	137

Subject	Newsgroup	Page
education (distance)	alt.education.distance	136
education (French)	k12.lang.francais	139
education (general)	misc.education	139
education (German)	k12.lang.deutsch-eng	139
education (health)	k12.ed.health-pe	138
education (home schooling)	misc.education	139
education (internat'l bacalaureate)	alt.education.ib	137
education (law school)	bit.listserv.lawsch-l	135
education (mathematics)	k12.ed.math	138
education (medical)	bit.listserv.medforum	136
education (multimedia)	comp.ai.edu	137
education (news)	clari.tw.education	42, 137
education (physical education)	k12.ed.health-pe	138
education (research)	alt.education.research	137
education (research)	bit.listserv.erl-l	137
education (Rhode Island)	ri.admin	**
education (Russian)	k12.lang.russian	139
education (Spanish)	k12.lang.esp-eng	139
education (talented and gifted)	k12.ed.tag	139
education (technology)	bit.listserv.edtech	137
education (writing)	comp.edu.composition	137
education	alt.parents-teens	61
education	comp.edu	137, 173
education	sci.edu	139
educational computing	bit.listserv.edtech	137
educational software	bit.listserv.edtech	137
educational software	misc.kids.computer	139
EFF	comp.org.eff.talk	154
Eiffel	comp.lang.eiffel	151
elections (ClariNet news)	clari.canada.politics	194
elections (ClariNet news)	clari.news.election	94
elections	alt.politics.elections	50
electronic (music)	rec.music.makers	112-113
Electronic Frontier Foundation EFF	comp.org.eff.talk	154
electronic mail (finding people on)	soc.net-people	58
electronic music	alt.emusic	113
electronic music	bit.listserv.emusic-l	113
electronic music	rec.music.makers.synth	112-113
electronic music	rec.music.synth	113
electronics (avionics)	rec.aviation.products	80
electronics (consumer)	alt.cyberpunk.tech	80
electronics (consumer)	alt.toys.hi-tech	81
electronics news (ClariNet news)	clari.tw.electronics	42
electronics	sci.electronics	128
ELM	comp.mail.elm	153-154
Elvis (sightings)	alt.elvis.sighting	198
EMACS (bugs)	gnu.emacs.bug	148
EMACS (help)	gnu.emacs.help	148
EMACS	alt.lucid-emacs.bug	148
EMACS	alt.lucid-emacs.help	148
EMACS	comp.emacs	148
EMACS	gnu.emacs.sources	148
EMACS	gnu.emacs.vm.bug	148
email	comp.mail.elm	153-154
email	comp.mail.mh	154
email	comp.mail.mime	154
email	comp.mail.misc	154
email	comp.mail.multi-media	154
email	comp.mail.mush	154
email	comp.mail.sendmail	154

Subject	Newsgroup	Page
feminism	soc.men	60
feminism	soc.singles	203
feminism	soc.women	58
feminism	talk.rape	60
fencing	rec.sport.fencing	179
ferrets (pets)	rec.pets	84-86
fetishes	(various newsgroups)	107, 203
fiber optics	comp.dcom.lans.fddi	146
fiber optics	sci.optics	132
file transfer protocols	alt.comp.fsp	160
film (processing)	rec.photo	77
film (reviews)	bit.listserv.cinema-l	114
film (reviews)	rec.arts.movies	114
film (reviews)	rec.arts.movies.reviews	114
film making	rec.arts.cinema	114
film reviews	rec.arts.movies	114
film reviews	rec.arts.movies.reviews	114
films (Australian)	aus.films	191
films (cult)	alt.cult-movies	114-115
films (cult)	alt.cult-movies.rocky-horror	115
films (horror)	alt.horror	114
films (laserdisc)	alt.video.laserdisc	81
films (talk)	bit.listserv.cinema-l	114
finance-personal (ClariNet news)	clari.biz.finance.personal	42
fine art	rec.arts.fine	74
Finland (info)	soc.culture.nordic	68
Finland (newsgroups)	finet.asiointi.kunnat	**
Finland (newsgroups)	sfnet.arkistot.ftp	**
firearms (politics)	talk.politics.guns	46
firearms	alt.law-enforcement	52
firearms	alt.war	52-53
firearms	info.firearms	76
firearms	rec.guns	76
Firesign Theater	alt.comedy.firesigntheater	106
fireworks	rec.pyrotechnics	201
fish (aquariums)	alt.aquaria	84
fish (aquariums)	sci.aquaria	126
fish tanks	alt.aquaria	84
fishing	alt.fishing	76
fishing	rec.outdoors.fishing	179
fitness	misc.fitness	179
Fleming, Ian	alt.fan.james-bond	114
flight simulation software	rec.aviation.simulators	80
flight simulator (Microsoft)	rec.aviation.simulators	80
Florida (information)	fl.forsale	187
fluid dynamics	sci.geo.fluids	129
flying (stories)	rec.aviation.stories	80
flying (technical instruction)	rec.aviation.piloting	80
flying saucers (skeptics)	alt.perinet.skeptic	198
flying saucers (talk)	alt.perinet.ufo	198
flying saucers	alt.alien.visitors	196
flying saucers	alt.perinet.abduct	197
flying saucers	alt.perinet.skeptic	198
flying	rec.aviation.student	80
FM radio	rec.radio.broadcasting	87
folk music (Bob Dylan)	rec.music.dylan	107
folk music	rec.music.folk	109
folklore (urban)	alt.folklore.urban	57
fonts	comp.fonts	170-171
food (cooking)	rec.food.cooking	78

Subject	Newsgroup	Page
food (cooking)	rec.food.historic	78
food (health)	misc.health.alternative	39
food (restaurants)	rec.food.restaurants	78
food (Spam)	alt.spam	199
football (ClariNet news)	clari.sports.football.college	182
football (college)	rec.sport.football.college	176
football (Fantasy League)	rec.sport.football.misc	176
football (pro)	rec.sport.football.pro	176
for rent (MIT)	athena.misc	190
for rent (SF/Bay Area, CA)	ba.market.housing	189
for sale (Austin, TX)	austin.forsale	185
for sale (Chicago)	chi.forsale	186
for sale (Florida)	fl.forsale	187
for sale (Houston, TX)	houston.forsale	187
for sale (Huntsville, AL)	hsv.forsale	187
for sale (Los Angeles)	la.forsale	187
for sale (miscellaneous)	misc.wanted	41
for sale (MIT)	athena.forsale	**
for sale (New York State)	ny.forsale	188
for sale (Ohio State University)	osu.for-sale	190
for sale (Portland, OR)	tek.forsale	188
for sale (Raleigh/Durham, NC)	triangle.forsale	188
for sale (San Diego, CA)	sdnet.forsale	186
for sale (SF/Bay Area, CA)	ba.market.computers	188
for sale (SF/Bay Area, CA)	ba.market.misc	188
for sale (Texas)	tx.forsale	187
for sale (University of Wisconsin)	uwisc.forsale	190
for sale (wanted)	misc.forsale.wanted	41
for sale (clones)	misc.forsale.computers.pc-clone	169
for sale (computers)	misc.forsale.computers.d	147
for sale (Macintosh)	misc.forsale.computers.mac	166
for sale (miscellaneous)	misc.forsale.computers.other	147
for sale (workstations)	misc.forsale.computers.workstation 147	
forecasting (business)	bit.listserv.buslib-1	37
foreign countries (FAQs)	soc.answer	63
foreign language (Chinese)	alt.chinese.text.big5	66, 193-194
FORTH	comp.lang.forth	151
FORTRAN	comp.lang.fortran	152
fractals	alt.binaries.pictures.fractals	143
fractals	alt.fractals	125
fractals	bit.listserv.frac-l	125
fractals	sci.fractals	125, 129
Framemaker	comp.text.frame	171
France (language discussion)	alt.nick.sucks	194
France (newsgroups)	fnet.general	**
France (newsgroups)	fr.announce.divers	**
France (newsgroups)	resif.admin	**
Frank Herbert	alt.fan.dune	99
free speech (media)	alt.censorship	51
freedom	alt.conspiracy	53
freedom	alt.society.civil-liberties	54
Freemasonry	alt.illuminati	59
French (culture)	soc.culture.french	65
French (language)	alt.nick.sucks	194
French language (Canada)	can.francais	193
French language (Canada)	can.politics	193
frequencies (radio)	alt.radio.scanner	86
Frequently Asked Questions (FAQ)	rec.answers	32

Subject	Newsgroup	Page
fringe politics	alt.revolution.counter	54
Frisbee (games)	rec.sport.disc	179
FSP (file transfer)	alt.comp.fsp	160
FSP (file transport protocol)	alt.comp.fsp	160
functional	comp.lang.functional	152
funk (music)	rec.music.funky	108
furniture (antique)	rec.antiques	74
furniture (building)	rec.woodworking	39, 77
furry (games)	alt.fan.furry	103
fusion	sci.energy.hydrogen	128
fusion	sci.physics.fusion	132
futurism (cyberpunk)	alt.cyberpunk.chatsubo	202
futuristic games	alt.pub.havens-rest	104
fuzzy AI	comp.ai.fuzzy	142

G

Subject	Newsgroup	Page
G++ help	gnu.g++.help	**
G++ Library bugs	gnu.g++.lib.bug	**
Galt, John	alt.philosophy.objectivism	70
gambling	rec.gambling	89
games (adventure/fantasy)	alt.pub.dragons-inn	104
games (arcade)	rec.games.video.arcade	102
games (backgammon)	rec.games.backgammon	103
games (board/strategy)	(various newsgroups)	107, 203
games (bridge)	rec.games.bridge	103
games (chess)	rec.games.chess	103
games (designing computer)	rec.games.programmer	103
games (diplomacy)	rec.games.diplomacy	103
games (fantasy/strategy)	rec.games.board	103
games (fantasy)	alt.fan.furry	103
games (fantasy)	rec.games.frp.advocacy	105
games (fantasy)	rec.games.frp.cyber	105
games (fantasy)	rec.games.frp.marketplace	105
games (fantasy)	rec.games.frp.misc	105
games (fantasy)	rec.games.frp.moria	105
games (general)	bit.listserv.games-l	102
games (interactive)	rec.arts.int-fiction	100
games (MUDs)	rec.games.mud.misc	104
games (multi-player)	alt.netgames.bolo	103-104
games (play-by-mail)	rec.games.pbm	102-103
games (Sega Genesis)	alt.sega.genesis	102
games (toy soldiers)	rec.games.miniatures	102
games (video)	bit.listserv.games-l	102
Garcia, Jerry	rec.music.gdead	107
gardening	misc.rural	40
Garrison Keillor	rec.arts.wobegon	115
Gates, Bill	alt.fan.bill-gates	198
gay/lesbian	soc.bi	60
gay politics	alt.politics.homosexuality	49
gay	bit.listserv.gaynet	60
gay	soc.motss	60
gays (ClariNet news)	clari.news.group.gays	94
gays (SF/Bay Area, CA)	ba.market.motss	189
gays	alt.politics.homosexuality	49
GCC	gnu.gcc.bug	148
GCC	gnu.gcc.help	148
geeks	alt.religion.monica	201
genealogy	soc.roots	89
genius (Mensa)	rec.org.mensa	202
geodesic domes	bit.listserv.geodesic	125

Subject	Newsgroup	Page
Geographic Info Systems (GIS)	comp.infosystems.gis	150
geology	sci.geo.geology	130
geometry (newsgroups)	geometry.announcements	**
George Lucas	rec.arts.sf.starwars	119
Georgia Institute of Technology	git.cc.general	**
German (culture)	soc.culture.german	65
German (networking)	robin.advocacy	**
German (newsgroups)	bln.announce.fub	**
German (newsgroups)	cl.adressen.allgemein	**
German (newsgroups)	de.admin.archiv	**
German (newsgroups)	maus.info	**
German (newsgroups)	zer.t-netz.fileserver	**
German (newsgroups)	fido.ger.lan	**
ghostscript	gnu.ghostscript.bug	148
GIS	comp.infosystems.gis	150
gliders	rec.aviation.soaring	80
GNU C/C++ debugger	gnu.gdb.bug	148
GNU Chess	gnu.chess	147-148
GNU G++	gnu.g++.bug	**
GNU	gnu.gcc.bug	148
GNU	gnu.ghostscript.bug	148
GNU	gnu.misc.discuss	148
GNU utilities	gnu.utils.bug	148
gnuplot	comp.graphics.gnuplot	149
GNUS	gnu.emacs.gnus	148
GNUSnet	gnu.gnusenet.test	148
Go (game)	rec.games.trivia	103
God	sci.philosophy.meta	132
gods and goddesses	alt.mythology	70
golf	rec.sport.golf	179
gopher	alt.gopher	149
gopher	comp.infosystems.gopher	150
GOSIP	comp.protocols.iso	159
government (agriculture)	alt.agriculture.misc	59
government (ClariNet news)	clari.canada.gov	194
government (ClariNet news)	clari.news.gov.agency	94
government (ClariNet news)	clari.news.gov	94
government (coverup)	alt.conspiracy.jfk	53
government (economics)	alt.politics.economics	50
government (libertarian)	alt.politics.libertarian	46
government (publications)	bit.listserv.govdoc-l	33, 135
Government Acctn'g. Office (GAO)	bit.listserv.govdoc-l	33, 135
government budgets (ClariNet news) clari.news.gov.budget		94
government corruption (ClariNet)	clari.news.gov.corrupt	94
government leaders (ClariNet news)	clari.news.gov.officials	94
government news (ClariNet news)	clari.nb.govt	42
Government Printing Office (GPO)	bit.listserv.govdoc-l	33, 135
government	alt.politics.elections	50
government	alt.president.clinton	47
government-federal (ClariNet news)	clari.news.gov.usa	94
government-state (ClariNet news)	clari.news.gov.state	94
governments-foreign (ClariNet news) clari.news.gov.international		94
graduate schools	soc.college.gradinfo	**
graduate students (information)	soc.college.grad	**
grants	sci.research	133
graphic novels (Japanese)	rec.arts.manga	100
graphics (3D)	alt.3d	148
graphics (computer)	alt.3d	148

Subject	Newsgroup	Page
hot rods	alt.autos.rod-n-custom	82
hot rods	alt.hotrod	82
hot rods	rec.autos.rod-n-custom	83
hotels	rec.travel	88
house (buying)	misc.consumers.house	39
house (buying)	misc.invest.real-estate	38
housing (MIT)	athena.misc	190
housing (SF/Bay Area, CA)	ba.market.housing	189
Houston, TX (information)	houston.forsale	187
HP (Hewlett-Packard)	comp.sys.hp	165
HP (Hewlett-Packard)	comp.sys.hp48	165
HP 95LX	comp.sys.handhelds	167
HP	comp.sys.hp	165
HP95LX	comp.sys.palmtops	168
Hudson Valley	alt.culture.ny-upstate	88
human factors	comp.human-factors	170
human interest (ClariNet news)	clari.news.interest	94-95
human interest (ClariNet news)	clari.news.interest.history	94
human rights	soc.rights.human	58
humor (Dave Barry)	clari.feature.dave_barry	106
humor (geeks)	alt.religion.monica	201
humor (general)	misc.misc	41
humor (Internet)	alt.humor.best-of-usenet	106
humor (Kibo)	alt.religion.kibology	200
humor (stories)	rec.humor.funny	106
humor (weird theories)	alt.slack	199
humor	(various newsgroups)	107, 203
humor	rec.humor.d	106
Hungary (culture)	soc.culture.magyar	67
hunting	alt.archery	177
Huntsville, AL (information)	hsv.forsale	187
hydrogen (energy)	sci.energy.hydrogen	128
HyperCard	comp.sys.mac.hypercard	165
hypertext	alt.hypertext	172
hypertext	bit.listserv.mbu-l	59, 136

I

Subject	Newsgroup	Page
IBM (mainframes)	bit.listserv.ibm-main	165
IBM PC (hardware)	comp.sys.ibm.pc.hardware	168
IBM PC	comp.sys.ibm.pc.misc	168
IBM PS/2	comp.sys.ibm.ps2.hardware	168
IBM RT	comp.sys.ibm.pc.rt	168
IBM soundcard	comp.sys.ibm.pc.soundcard	168
ice skating	rec.skate	180
IDL pvwave	comp.lang.idl-pvwave	152
IEEE (engineering)	ieee.announce	**
IEEE	comp.org.ieee	154
IETF	info.ietf	150
Illini (university newsgroups)	uiuc.announce	**
Illuminati	alt.illuminati	59
immigration	alt.visa.us	38
India (culture)	soc.culture.indian	66
India (news)	alt.culture.karnataka	66
India (news)	alt.culture.kerala	66
India (news)	bit.listserv.india-l	66
India (news)	misc.news.southasia	93
Indian (culture)	alt.culture.us.asian-indian	50
Indian (culture)	soc.culture.indian.telugu	66
Indian music (classical)	rec.music.indian.classical	109
Indian music (classical)	rec.music.indian.misc	109

Subject	Newsgroup	Page
individual rights	alt.society.civil-liberties	54
Indonesia	alt.culture.indonesia	66
Indonesia (culture)	soc.culture.indonesia	66
industrial music	alt.cascade	202
industrial music	rec.music.industrial	109
industry forecasts	bit.listserv.buslib-1	37
Indy (Silicon Graphics)	comp.sys.sgi.admin	169
Indy (Silicon Graphics)	comp.sys.sgi.apps	169
infant care	misc.kids	62, 139
info (Austin, TX)	austin.announce	185
info (Australia)	aus.wanted	192
infomercials (TV)	alt.tv.infomercials	116
information (business)	alt.business.misc	37
information (business)	alt.business.multi-level	37
information (business)	bit.listserv.buslib-1	37
information (business)	biz.misc	38, 42
information (colleges)	soc.college	**
information (Dallas/Fort Worth, TX)	dfw.general	186
information (Detroit, MI)	mi.misc	186
information (farming)	alt.agriculture.misc	59
information (Florida)	fl.forsale	187
information (general)	misc.misc	41
information (health)	bit.listserv.mednews	93
information (Houston)	houston.forsale	187
information (Huntsville, AL)	hsv.forsale	187
information (Internet)	rec.answers	32
information (London)	lon.misc	194
information (Los Angeles)	la.general	187
information (manufacturing)	alt.manufacturing.misc	37
information (medical)	bit.listserv.mednews	93
information (Netherlands)	nlnet.misc	194
information (New Jersey)	nj.general	187
information (New Orleans)	neworleans.general	187
information (New York City)	nyc.general	187
information (New York City)	nz.general	194
information (New York State)	ny.general	188
information (Norway)	no.general	194
information (Ontario, CA)	ont.general	194
information (Ontario)	kw.general	188
information (Oregon)	or.general	188
information (Ottawa, Canada)	ott.general	194
information (Pennsylvania)	pa.general	188
information (Sweden)	swnet.general	194
information (Toronto, CA)	tor.general	194
information (University of MD)	um.general	190
information (University of MN)	umn.general.misc	190
information (University of Toronto)	ut.general	190
information (University of Waterloo)	uw.general	190
information (Virginia)	va.general	**
information systems	comp.infosystems	150
Informix	comp.databases.informix	145
Ingres	comp.databases.ingres	145
Innopac	bit.listserv.innopac	162
INS	alt.visa.us	38
inspiration	alt.self-improve	40
insurance (health)	talk.politics.medicine	50
Integraph	alt.sys.intergraph	167
Intel i386	comp.unix.pc-clone.32bit	157
Intel	comp.sys.intel	167
intellectual property	misc.int-property	38

Subject	Newsgroup	Page
music (Indian)	rec.music.indian.classical	109
music (Indian)	rec.music.indian.misc	109
music (industrial)	rec.music.industrial	109
music (Madonna)	alt.fan.madonna	107
music (New Age)	rec.music.newage	110
music (news)	rec.music.misc	111
music (offbeat)	bit.listserv.allmusic	109
music (Phish)	rec.music.phish	110
music (pop charts)	rec.music.info	107, 109-111, 113
music (rap)	alt.rap	108
Music (reggae)	rec.music.reggae	108
music (reviews)	rec.music.reviews	111
music (rock N roll)	(various newsgroups)	107, 203
music (rock N roll)	rec.music.beatles	107
music (rock N roll)	rec.music.gdead	107
music (rock)	alt.rock-n-roll	107-108
music (rock)	alt.rock-n-roll.metallica	108
music (rock-ACDC)	alt.rock-n-roll.acdc	108
music (satire)	rec.music.dementia	110
music (SF/Bay Area, CA)	ba.music	190
music (ska)	alt.music.ska	110
music (synthesizers)	rec.music.synth	113
music (thrash)	alt.thrash	199
music (TMBG)	alt.music.tmbg	110
music (top ten lists)	rec.music.info	107, 109-111, 113
music (top ten lists)	rec.music.misc	111
music (weird)	rec.music.dementia	110
music	alt.emusic	113
musicians (electronic)	rec.music.makers	112-113
mutual funds	misc.invest	38
MX email	vmsnet.mail.mx	147
mysteries	alt.fan.holmes	98
Mystery Science Theatre 3000 (TV)	alt.tv.mst3K	117
mythology	alt.mythology	70
myths	alt.folklore.urban	57

N		
nanotechnology	sci.nanotech	132
NASA (ClariNet news)	clari.tw.space	42
NASA	alt.sci.planetary	134
NASA	talk.politics.space	50
nature (bird watching)	rec.birds	85
naturism	rec.nude	201
Navy (news)	soc.veterans	59
nazi (hate group)	alt.skinheads	200
NCR	comp.sys.ncr	167
Nepal (culture)	soc.culture.nepal	67
Netherlands (information)	nlnet.misc	194
Netiquette	alt.culture.internet	31
network	alt.bbs.internet	32, 143
network time protocol (NTP)	comp.protocols.time.ntp	160
networking (standards)	info.big-internet	32
networking	alt.amateur-comp	30, 172
networking	alt.online-service	32, 143
networking	alt.winsock	159
networks (Internet)	sanet.announce	**
networks (Internet)	uunet.announce	**
networks	alt.bbs.allsysop	143

Subject	Newsgroup	Page
networks	alt.bbs.pcbuucp	143
networks	alt.bbs.unix.bbs	143
networks	alt.bbs.waffle	**
New Age (religion)	talk.religion.newage	71
New Age music	rec.music.newage	110
New Age phenomena	alt.out-of-body	197
new business opportunities	alt.business.multi-level	37
new Internet newsgroups	bit.listserv.new-list	30
New Jersey (information)	nj.general	187
New Orleans (information)	neworleans.general	187
new products (ClariNet news)	clari.biz.products	42
new products (ClariNet news)	clari.nb.review	42
new products (electronics)	alt.cyberpunk.tech	80
New York (upstate)	capdist.misc	187
New York City (ClariNet news)	clari.local.nyc	191
New York City (information)	nyc.general	187
New York State (for sale)	ny.forsale	188
New York State (information)	ny.general	188
New Zealand (culture)	soc.culture.new-zealand	68
New Zealand (information)	nz.general	194
news & talk (Berkeley)	ucb.general	190
news & talk (Britain)	uk.misc	193
news (Austin, TX)	austin.news	185
news (Bosnians/Serbs)	alt.news.macedonia	93
news (Boulder, CO)	boulder.general	185
news (British Columbia, CA)	bc.general	193
news (California)	ca.general	186-187, 189-190
news (Chicago)	chi.general	186
news (DEC)	biz.dec.decnews	**
news (discussion)	misc.headlines	93
news (discussion)	talk.politics.misc	49
news (Eastern Europe)	misc.news.east-europe.rferl	93
news (farming)	alt.agriculture.misc	59
news (Hawaii)	alt.culture.hawaii	87
news (Michigan)	alt.great-lakes	187
news (Russia)	misc.news.east-europe.rferl	93
news (San Luis Obispo, CA)	slo.general	186
news (Seattle, WA)	seattle.general	186
news (South Asian)	misc.news.southasia	93
news (space)	alt.sci.planetary	134
news (Vietnam)	bit.listserv.seasia-l	69
news bulletins (ClariNet news)	clari.news.flash	93
news features (ClariNet news)	clari.news.features	94
news headlines-hourly (ClariNet)	clari.news.headlines	94
news media	misc.headlines	93
news readers (Internet)	news.software.readers	30
news readers	alt.usenet.offline-reader	30
news summaries (ClariNet news)	clari.news.briefs	93
news-animals (ClariNet news)	clari.news.interest.animals	94
news-baseball (ClariNet news)	clari.sports.baseball	182
news-basketball (ClariNet news)	clari.sports.basketball	182
news-funny (ClariNet news)	clari.news.interest.quirks	95
news-international (ClariNet news)	clari.news.top.world	95
news-local (ClariNet news)	clari.local.headlines	190
news-misc (ClariNet news)	clari.news.issues	95
news-NYC (ClariNet news)	clari.local.nyc	191
news-racing (ClariNet news)	clari.sports.motor	182
news-San Francisco (ClariNet news)	clari.local.sfbay	191
news-San Francisco (ClariNet news)	clari.sfbay.briefs	191

Subject	Newsgroup	Page
personals (online)	soc.penpals	57
perversion	alt.polyamory	203
pesticides (organic)	alt.sustainable.agriculture	49
pets (birds)	rec.pets.birds	85
pets (cats)	rec.pets.cats	85
pets (dogs)	rec.pets.dogs	85-86
pets (fish)	alt.aquaria	84
pets (general)	rec.pets	84-86
pets (lizards/snakes)	rec.pets.herp	85
pets (wolves)	alt.wolves	86
PEX	comp.windows.x.pex	172
PGP (encryption)	alt.privacy.clipper	39
PGP (encryption)	alt.security.pgp	160
PGP (Pretty Good Privacy)	alt.security.pgp	160
pharmaceuticals	talk.politics.drugs	50
PHIGS	comp.windows.x.pex	172
philosophy (Libertarian)	alt.philosophy.objectivism	70
philosophy (New Age)	talk.religion.newage	71
philosophy (Objectivism)	talk.philosophy.misc	71
philosophy (satire)	alt.evil	200
philosophy	alt.clearing.technology	71
philosophy	alt.consciousness	200
philosophy	sci.philosophy.meta	132
philosophy	sci.philosophy.tech	132
Phish	rec.music.phish	110
phone systems	alt.dcom.telecom	146
photography	rec.photo	77
physical fitness	rec.running	180
physics (acoustics)	alt.sci.physics.acoustics	81
physics (CERN)	cern.computing	194
physics (medicine)	sci.med.physics	131
physics (new theories)	alt.sci.physics.new-theories	125
physics (software)	bit.listserv.physhare	**
physics	alt.sci.physics.new-theories	125
physics	sci.philosophy.tech	132
physics	sci.physics.fusion	132
physics	sci.physics	81, 125, 132
picture (utilities)	alt.graphics.pixutils	148-149
pictures (discussion)	alt.binaries.pictures.d	143
pictures (files)	alt.binaries.pictures	143-144
pictures (files)	alt.binaries.pictures.misc	144
pictures (utilities)	alt.binaries.pictures.utilities	144
piercings (body)	rec.arts.bodyart	201-202
Piers Anthony	alt.fan.pier-anthony	99
pilots (private)	rec.aviation.misc	80
pilots (stories)	rec.aviation.stories	80
pinball games	rec.games.video.arcade	102
ping-pong	rec.sport.table-tennis	181
pirate radio stations	alt.radio.pirate	196
pistols	rec.guns	76
planetary exploration	alt.sci.planetary	134
planning (weddings)	alt.wedding	40
plants	alt.bonsai	75
play-by-mail (games)	rec.games.diplomacy	103
play-by-mail (games)	rec.games.pbm	102-103
plays (theater)	rec.arts.theatre	88-89
PMDF	vmsnet.mail.pmdf	**
poems (online)	rec.arts.poems	100
poetry (online)	rec.arts.poems	100

Subject	Newsgroup	Page
poetry	alt.cascade	202
Poland (culture)	soc.culture.polish	68
police (ClariNet news)	clari.news.law.police	95
police radio frequencies	alt.radio.scanner	86
police	alt.law-enforcement	52
polishing (metal)	rec.crafts.metalworking	77
political correctness	alt.politics.correct	49
political debate	alt.discrimination	49
political debate	alt.politics.usa.republican	49
political discussion (liberal/left)	alt.activism.d	46
political elections	alt.politics.elections	50
political science	soc.history	52
political science	talk.politics.theory	50
politics (anarchy)	alt.society.anarchy	54
politics (Asia)	talk.politics.china	51
politics (Austin, TX)	austin.politics	185
politics (Austin, TX)	austin.talk	185
politics (Australia)	aus.general	191
politics (Britain)	uk.politics	193
politics (California)	ca.politics	186, 189
politics (Canada)	can.general	193
politics (Canada)	can.jobs	193
politics (ClariNet news)	clari.news.politics	95
politics (ClariNet news)	clari.news.politics.people	95
politics (Clinton &)	alt.dear.whitehouse	48
politics (Clinton &)	alt.politics.clinton	47
politics (Clinton &)	alt.politics.reform	48
politics (Clinton &)	alt.politics.usa.misc	48
politics (Clinton &)	alt.president.clinton	47
politics (conservatism)	alt.society.conservatism	46
politics (discussion)	alt.activism	46
politics (discussion)	bit.listserv.politics	49
politics (drugs)	talk.politics.drugs	50
politics (feminism)	soc.couples	58
politics (fringe)	alt.revolution.counter	54
politics (gun control)	talk.politics.guns	46
politics (left wing)	alt.activism.d	46
politics (liberal)	alt.politics.correct	49
politics (Mideast)	talk.politics.mideast	51
politics (organization)	alt.politics.elections	50
politics (radical left)	alt.politics.radical-left	47
politics (radical left)	alt.save.the.earth	47
politics (SF/Bay Area, CA)	ba.politics	189
politics (space)	talk.politics.space	50
politics (talk)	talk.politics.misc	49
politics (theory)	talk.politics.theory	50
politics and media	alt.politics.media	50
politics	alt.conspiracy	53
politics	alt.dear.whitehouse	48
politics	alt.discrimination	49
politics	alt.politics.greens	47
politics	alt.politics.libertarian	46
politics	alt.postmodern	74
politics	rec.arts.fine	74
pollution	alt.politics.greens	47
polyamory	alt.polyamory	203
polygamy	alt.polyamory	203
pop culture (Austin, TX)	austin.music	185
pop culture (Australia)	aus.music	192
pop culture (raves)	alt.rave	111

Subject	Newsgroup	Page
Ross Perot	alt.politics.perot	50
routers	comp.dcom.sys.cisco	146
rowing	rec.sport.rowing	180
Royko, Mike (columns)	clari.feature.mike_royko	106
RPI (newsgroups)	rpi.announce	**
rugby	rec.sport.rugby	177
rumors	talk.rumors	54
running	misc.fitness	179
running	rec.running	180
Rush Limbaugh	alt.rush-limbaugh	46
Russia (Baltics)	soc.culture.baltics	64
Russia (ClariNet news)	clari.news.hot.ussr	94
Russia (news)	misc.news.east-europe.rferl	93
Russia (newsgroups)	relcom.archives	**
Russia (politics)	talk.politics.soviet	50

S

Subject	Newsgroup	Page
SABRE	comp.infosystems	150
Sacramento (newsgroups)	sac.general	**
sailboats	rec.boats	84
sailing	rec.boats.paddle	84
sailing	rec.boats	84
salsa (music)	rec.music.afro-latin	108
San Diego, CA (for sale)	sdnet.forsale	186
San Francisco (ClariNet news)	clari.local.sfbay	191
San Francisco (ClariNet news)	clari.sfbay.briefs	191
San Francisco (ClariNet news)	clari.sfbay.entertain	191
San Francisco (ClariNet news)	clari.sfbay.fire	191
San Francisco (ClariNet news)	clari.sfbay.general	191
San Francisco (ClariNet news)	clari.sfbay.misc	191
San Francisco (ClariNet news)	clari.sfbay.police	191
San Francisco (ClariNet news)	clari.sfbay.short	191
San Francisco (ClariNet news)	clari.sfbay.weather	191
San Luis Obispo, CA (news)	slo.general	186
Santa Cruz Operation (SCO)	comp.unix.xenix.sco	158
Santa Cruz Operation (Xenix)	biz.sco.general	173
satanism	alt.pagan	70
satanism	alt.satanism	71
satellite TV	rec.video.satellite	81
satellites (space)	alt.sci.planetary	134
satire (music)	alt.fan.spinal-tap	107
satire (music)	rec.music.dementia	110
satire (religion)	alt.evil	200
satire (talk)	alt.slack	199
satire (Zen)	alt.buddha.short.fat.guy	200
Saturn (car)	csn.ml.saturn	40
Saved By The Bell (TV)	alt.tv.saved-bell	118
savings	misc.invest	38
savings	misc.invest.technical	38
SCA	rec.org.sca	89
Scandanavia (Norway)	no.general	194
Scandinavians (info)	soc.culture.nordic	68
scanner (radio)	alt.radio.scanner	86
SCHEME	comp.lang.scheme	153
School Libraries Association (SLA)	bit.listserv.slart-l	58
schooling (home)	misc.education	139
sci.meteorology	sci.geo.meteorology	130
science (ClariNet news)	clari.tw.science	42
science (education)	k12.ed.science	138
science (physics)	alt.sci.physics.new-theories	125

Subject	Newsgroup	Page
science fiction (Australia)	aus.sf	192
science fiction (books)	alt.books.isaac.asimov	99
science fiction (books)	alt.fan.dune	99
science fiction (books)	alt.fan.pier-anthony	99
science fiction (books)	alt.fan.Pratchett	99
science fiction (books)	rec.arts.sf.written	119-120
science fiction (collectibles)	rec.arts.sf.marketplace	119
science fiction (conventions)	alt.fandom.cons	119
science fiction (conventions)	rec.arts.sf.announce	119
science fiction (cyberpunk)	alt.cyberpunk.chatsubo	202
science fiction (Douglas Adams)	alt.fan.douglas-adams	98
science fiction (Pern)	alt.fan.pern	99
science fiction (self-publishing)	rec.arts.int-fiction	100
science fiction (Star Trek stories)	alt.startrek.creative	122
science fiction (Star Trek)	rec.arts.startrek.tech	121-122
science fiction (talk)	alt.fan.eddings	98
science fiction (talk)	rec.arts.sf.misc	119
science fiction (talk)	rec.arts.sf.science	119
science fiction (TV shows)	rec.arts.sf.tv	119
science fiction	rec.arts.drwho	119
science	sci.bio	126-127
science	sci.bio.technology	127
science	sci.chem	127
science	sci.cognitive	127
science	sci.edu	139
science	sci.electronics	128
science	sci.energy	128
science	sci.engr.biomed	128
science	sci.engr.chem	129
science	sci.engr.civil	129
science	sci.engr.control	129
science	sci.engr.mech	129
science	sci.engr	128-129
science	sci.environment	129
science	sci.fractals	125, 129
science	sci.geo.fluids	129
science	sci.geo.geology	130
science	sci.image.processing	130
science	sci.lang	130
science	sci.logic	130
science	sci.materials	130
science	sci.math.num-analysis	130-131
science	sci.math.research	131
science	sci.math	130-131
science	sci.math.stat	131
science	sci.math.symbolic	131
science	sci.med.aids	131
science	sci.med.nutrition	131
science	sci.med.physics	131
science	sci.med	131
science	sci.misc	132
scientology	alt.clearing.technology	71
scientology	alt.religion.scientology	71
SCO (ODT)	biz.sco.opendesktop	162
SCO (UNIX)	biz.sco.general	173
Scotland (newsgroups)	scot.general	**
Scotland	soc.culture.celtic	64
scouting (Boy & Cub)	rec.scouting	59
SCSI	comp.periphs.scsi	173-174
scuba diving	bit.listserv.scuba-l	180

Subject	Newsgroup	Page
stock market-NYSE (ClariNet news)	clari.biz.market.ny	42
stock market-S&P (ClariNet news)	clari.biz.market.report	42
stocks (technical investing)	misc.invest.technical	38
stocks	misc.invest	38
Stones (Rolling)	alt.rock-n-roll.stones	108
stories (funny)	rec.humor.funny	106
strange phenonena	alt.alien.visitors	196
strategy (military)	alt.war	52-53
strategy games (Australia)	aus.games	192
strategy games (Australia)	aus.games.roleplay	192
strategy games	(various newsgroups)	107, 203
strategy games	rec.games.board	103
street rods	rec.autos.rod-n-custom	83
strikes (ClariNet news)	clari.biz.labor	**
strikes (ClariNet news)	clari.news.labor	95
strikes (ClariNet news)	clari.news.labor.strike	95
subways	rec.railroad	75
success stories (ClariNet news)	clari.news.goodnews	94
suicide (assisted)	alt.suicide.holiday	201
SUN (computer)	alt.sys.intergraph	167
SUN (tool talk)	alt.soft-sys-tooltalk	**
Sun Microsystems — NeWS	comp.windows.news	171
Sun Microsystems	alt.sys.sun	169
Sun Microsystems	comp.sys.sun.admin	169
Sun Microsystems	comp.sys.sun.apps	169
Sun Microsystems	comp.sys.sun.hardware	169
Sun Microsystems	comp.sys.sun.misc	169
Sun Microsystems	comp.sys.sun.wanted	169
Sun Microsystems	info.sun-managers	169
Supercomputers	comp.sys.super	170
superheroes (comics)	rec.arts.comics.misc	101
Superman	alt.comics.superman	100
supermodels (talk)	alt.supermodels	202
support group (autism)	bit.listserv.autism	61
support group (blindness)	bit.listserv.blindnws	61
support group (cancer)	alt.support.cancer	62
support group (dieting)	alt.support.diet	62
support group (disabled)	misc.handicap	63
support group (employment)	misc.jobs.misc	41
support group (general)	alt.support	60, 62-63
support group (MS)	alt.support.mult.sclerosis	62
support group (step parents)	alt.support.step.parents	63
support groups (alcoholism)	alt.recovery	60-61
support groups (cancer)	(various newsgroups)	107, 203
support groups (deafness)	bit.listserv.deaf-l	62
support groups (diabetics)	misc.health.diabetes	62
support groups (psychology)	bit.listserv.psycgrad	136
Supreme Court (ClariNet news)	clari.news.law.supreme	95
Supreme Court (U.S.)	courts.usa.federal	93
surf ski	rec.boats.paddle	84
surfing	alt.surfing	181
survival (wilderness)	rec.backcountry	177
suspended animation	sci.cryonics	127
Sweden (information)	swnet.general	194
swimming	rec.sport.swimming	181
Switzerland (newsgroups)	srg.info	**
Sybase	comp.databases.sybase	145
symbolics	sci.math.symbolic	131
symposia	news.announce.conferences	58
synthesizers (music)	rec.music.synth	113

Subject	Newsgroup	Page
synthesizers (musicians)	rec.music.makers.synth	112-113
synthesizers	alt.emusic	113
sysop	alt.bbs.allsysop	143
sysop	alt.bbs.pcbuucp	143
sysop	alt.bbs.allsysop	143
System 7	comp.sys.mac.system	166
system administration	comp.unix.admin	157
system operators	alt.bbs.allsysop	143
SYSV4	comp.unix.amiga	157

T

Subject	Newsgroup	Page
table tennis	rec.sport.table-tennis	181
tailoring	alt.sewing	75
Taiwan (culture)	soc.culture.taiwan	69
talk (bizarre)	talk.bizarre	202
talk (online)	alt.callahans	196
talk (sex)	(various newsgroups)	107, 203
talk (writers)	misc.writing	58-59
talk radio (Rush Limbaugh)	alt.rush-limbaugh	46
tall tales	alt.folklore.urban	57
Tandy	comp.sys.tandy	168
Tardis	rec.arts.drwho	119
tattoos	rec.arts.bodyart	201-202
tax (real estate)	misc.invest.real-estate	38
tax advice	misc.taxes	38
tax laws (ClariNet news)	clari.news.gov.taxes	94
taxes (politics)	alt.politics.economics	50
taxes	alt.privacy	39-40, 160
TCL	comp.lang.tcl	153
TCP/IP (IBM PC)	comp.protocols.tcp-ip.ibmpc	160
TCP/IP	bit.listserv.ibmtcp-l	159
TCP/IP	comp.protocols.tcp-ip	160
TCP/IP	comp.protocols.tcp-ip.domains	160
technical analysis (investment)	misc.invest.technical	38
technical books	alt.books.technical	125
technical books	biz.books.technical	98
technical books	misc.books.technical	125
technical writing	bit.listserv.mbu-l	59, 136
technical writing	bit.listserv.techwr-l	59
technology (education)	bit.listserv.edtech	137
technology (education)	k12.ed.tech	139
technology (new products)	alt.cyberpunk.tech	80
technology (obsolete)	alt.technology.obsolete	81
technology	sci.philosophy.tech	132
teenagers	alt.parents-teens	61
tele-operations	sci.virtual-worlds	133
Telebit (modem)	biz.comp.telebit	**
telecom-news (ClariNet news)	clari.nb.telecom	**
telecommunications	alt.bbs	32, 142-143
telecommunications (ClariNet news)	clari.tw.telecom	42
telecommunications	alt.amateur-comp	30, 172
telecommunications	alt.bbs.allsysop	143
telecommunications	alt.bbs.internet	32, 143
telecommunications	alt.bbs.lists	143
telecommunications	alt.bbs.pcbuucp	143
telecommunications	alt.bbs.waffle	**
telecommunications	alt.dcom.telecom	146

Subject	Newsgroup	Page
telecommunications	alt.online-service	32, 143
telecommunications	comp.dcom.telecom	146
telecommuting	misc.rural	40
telecommuting	comp.society	150
telephones	alt.dcom.telecom	146
television (British)	rec.arts.tv.uk	119
television (cable)	rec.video.cable	81
television (Dave Letterman)	alt.fan.letterman	116
television (Disney)	alt.fan.disney.afternoon	118
television (infomercials)	alt.tv.infomercials	116
television (laserdisc)	rec.video.releases	81
television (production)	rec.video.production	81
television (satellite)	rec.video.satellite	81
television (science fiction)	rec.arts.drwho	119
television (science fiction)	rec.arts.sf.tv	119
television (soap operas)	rec.arts.tv.uk	119
television (soaps)	rec.arts.tv.soaps	118
television (Star Trek)	rec.arts.startrek.tech	121-122
television (trivia)	rec.arts.tv	118-119
television	rec.arts.anime.stories	102
television	rec.video	80-81
telework	comp.society	150
Telnet	alt.unix.wizards	**
tennis (ClariNet news)	clari.sports.tennis	182
tennis (pro)	rec.sport.tennis	177
term limits	alt.politics.usa.constitution	53
terminals	comp.terminals	174
terrorism (ClariNet news)	clari.news.terrorism	95
Terry Pratchett	alt.fan.Pratchett	99
TeX	comp.text.tex	171
Texas (for sale)	tx.forsale	187
Texas (info & talk)	tx.general	186-187
Texas A & M (newsgroups)	tamu.general	**
text editors	comp.editors	170
text editors	comp.emacs	148
text editors	comp.fonts	170-171
text processing	alt.lucid-emacs.bug	148
text processing	comp.text	171
text processing	comp.text.tex	171
textile (crafts)	rec.crafts.textiles	77
textiles	alt.sewing	75
TGV	vmsnet.networks.tcp-ip.multinet	147
Thailand (culture)	soc.culture.thai	69
The Hobbitt	rec.arts.books.tolkien	99
The Netherlands (culture)	soc.culture.netherlands	67
The Philippines (culture)	soc.culture.filipino	65
The Prisoner (TV)	alt.tv.prisoner	117-118
The Simpsons (TV)	alt.tv.simpsons	118
The White House	alt.news-media	93
The White House	alt.politics.clinton	47
The White House	alt.politics.org.misc	48
The White House	alt.politics.reform	48
The White House	alt.politics.usa.misc	48
The White House	alt.president.clinton	47
theater	rec.arts.theatre	88-89
theatre news (ClariNet news)	clari.news.arts	93
theme parks	rec.arts.disney	87
theme parks	rec.parks.theme	87
theme parks	rec.roller coaster	89
They Might be Giants (music group)	alt.music.tmbg	110

Subject	Newsgroup	Page
Thinking Machines	comp.sys.super	170
Third-World development	bit.listserv.devel-l	51, 125
TI (Texas Instruments)	comp.sys.ti	168
time/space	alt.consciousness	200
Tiny Toon Adventures (TV)	alt.tv.tiny-toon	118
TMBG (music)	alt.music.tmbg	110
today in history (ClariNet news)	clari.news.almanac	93
Tolkien, J.R.R.	rec.arts.books.tolkien	99
Toolbook (Asymetrix)	bit.listserv.toolb-l	162
tools (woodworking)	rec.woodworking	39, 77
top ten lists (music)	rec.music.misc	111
Toronto, Canada (university info)	ut.general	190
Toronto (info)	tor.general	194
totalitarianism	alt.conspiracy	53
tourism (air travel)	rec.travel.air	88
tourism (Appalachian)	alt.appalachian	87
tourism (California)	alt.california	185
tourism (Disney)	rec.arts.disney	87
tourism (Hawaii)	alt.culture.hawaii	87
tourism (New York City)	nyc.general	187
tourism (New Zealand)	nz.general	194
tourism (SF/Bay Area, CA)	ba.food	190
tourism (SF/Bay Area, CA)	ba.general	189
tourism (Thailand)	soc.culture.thai	69
tourism (travel)	rec.food.restaurants	78
tourism	alt.culture.ny-upstate	88
tourism	alt.culture.oregon	88
tourism	bit.listserv.travel-l	88
tourism	rec.parks.theme	87
tourism	rec.travel.marketplace	88
tourism	rec.travel	88
toy soldiers	rec.games.miniatures	102
toys (high-tech)	alt.toys.hi-tech	81
toys (Lego)	alt.toys.lego	89
trademark issues	misc.int-property	38
trains	rec.railroad	75
transportation (ClariNet news)	clari.sfbay.roads	191
transportation (SF/Bay Area, CA)	ba.transportation	189
transputer	comp.sys.transputer	168
transvestites	alt.transgendered	202
travel (Apppalachian)	alt.appalachian	87
travel (dining)	rec.food.restaurants	78
travel (Europe)	soc.culture.europe	65
travel (Hawaii)	alt.culture.hawaii	87
travel (Los Angeles)	la.eats	187
travel (New York City)	nz.general	194
travel (Raleigh/Durham, NC)	triangle.general	188
travel (SF/Bay Area, CA)	ba.food	190
travel (SF/Bay Area, CA)	ba.general	189
travel (Texas)	tx.general	186-187
travel (Toronto, CA)	tor.general	194
travel	alt.california	185
travel	alt.culture.ny-upstate	88
travel	alt.culture.oregon	88
travel	bit.listserv.travel-l	88
travel	rec.arts.disney	87
travel	rec.parks.theme	87
travel	rec.travel.air	88
travel	rec.travel.marketplace	88
travel	rec.travel	88

Area Code	Public Access Provider(s) & Phone
202	PSI 703-620-6651 ■ CAPCON Library Network 202-331-5771 ■ Clark Internet Services, Inc. 800-735-2258 ■ Digital Express Group 800-969-9090 ■ Merit Network, Inc. 313-764-9430 ■ The Meta Network 703-243-6622
203	John von Neumann Computer Network 800-35-TIGER
205	Nuance Network Services 205-533-4296
206	Eskimo North 206-367-7457 ■ ■ Netcom Online 800-501-8649 ■ Northwest Nexus Inc. 206-455-3505 ■ Olympus 206-385-0464
212	Echo Communications 212-255-3839 ■ Maestro 212-240-9600 ■ MindVOX 212-989-2418 ■ PANIX Public Access Unix 212-877-4854 ■ The Pipeline n/a
213	CR Laboratories 415-381-2800 ■ DIAL n' CERF 800-876-2373 ■ KAIWAN 714-638-2139 ■ Netcom Online 800-501-8649
214	Texas Metronet 214-705-2900 ■ Netcom Online 800-501-8649
215	John von Neumann Computer Network 800-35-TIGER ■ PREPnet 412-268-7870
216	OARnet 614-292-8100 ■ APK- Public Access 216-481-9428
217	Prairienet Freenet 217-244-1962
301	PSI 703-620-6651 ■ CAPCON Library Network 202-331-5771 ■ Clark Internet Services, Inc. 800-735-2258 ■ Digital Express Group 800-969-9090 ■ Merit Network, Inc. 313-764-9430 ■ The Meta Network 703-243-6622
302	Systems Solutions 302-378-1386
303	Community News Service 719-592-1240 ■ Colorado SuperNet, Inc. 303-273-3471 ■ Netcom Online 800-501-8649 ■ Nyx none
305	CyberGate, Inc 305-428-GATE
310	CR Laboratories 415-381-2800 ■ DIAL n' CERF 800-876-2373 ■ KAIWAN 714-638-2139 ■ Netcom Online 800-501-8649
312	InterAccess 800-967-1580 ■ MCSNet 312-248-UNIX ■ Netcom Online 800-501-8649 ■ XNet Information Systems 708-983-6064
313	Merit Network, Inc. 313-764-9430 ■ MSen 313-998-4562
401	Anomaly 401-273-4669 ■ The IDS World Network 401-884-7856 ■ John von Neumann Computer Network 800-35-TIGER
403	PUCnet Computer Connections 403-448-1901 ■ UUNET Canada, Inc. 416-368-6621
404	CR Laboratories 415-381-2800 ■ Netcom Online 800-501-8649
407	CyberGate, Inc 305-428-GATE
408	Netcom Online 800-501-8649 ■ The Portal System 408-973-9111
410	CAPCON Library Network 202-331-5771 ■ Clark Internet Services, Inc. 800-735-2258 ■ Digital Express Group 800-969-9090
412	PREPnet 412-268-7870 ■ Telerama Public Access Internet 412-481-3505
415	CR Laboratories 415-381-2800 ■ DIAL n' CERF 800-876-2373 ■ Netcom Online 800-501-8649 ■ The Portal System 408-973-9111 ■ The Whole Earth 'Lectronic Link 415-332-4335
416	HookUp Communication Corporation 519-747-4110 ■ UUNET Canada, Inc. 416-368-6621 ■ UUnorth 416-225-8649
419	OARnet 614-292-8100
503	Netcom Online 800-501-8649 ■ Teleport 503-223-4245
504	NeoSoft's Sugar Land Unix 713-438-4964
508	Anomaly 401-273-4669 ■ NEARnet 617-873-8730 ■ North Shore Access 617-593-3110 voicemail ■ NovaLink 800-274-2814
510	CR Laboratories 415-381-2800 ■ DIAL n' CERF 800-876-2373 ■ HoloNet 510-704-0160 ■ Netcom Online 800-501-8649
512	RealTime Communications (wixer 512-451-0046
513	Freelance Systems Programming 513-254-7246 ■ OARnet 614-292-8100
514	Communications Accessibles Mon 514-931-0749 ■ UUNET Canada, Inc. 416-368-6621

Area Code	Public Access Provider(s) & Phone
516	John von Neumann Computer Network 800-35-TIGER
517	Merit Network, Inc. 313-764-9430
519	HookUp Communication Corporation 519-747-4110 ■ UUNET Canada, Inc. 416-368-6621 ■ UUnorth 416-225-8649
602	CR Laboratories 415-381-2800 ■ Data Basix 602-721-1988 ■ Evergreen Communications 602-955-8315 ■ Internet Direct, Inc. 602-274-0100
603	MV Communications, Inc. 603-429-2223 ■ NEARnet 617-873-8730
604	UUNET Canada, Inc. 416-368-6621
609	John von Neumann Computer Network 800-35-TIGER
613	UUNET Canada, Inc. 416-368-6621 ■ UUnorth 416-225-8649
614	OARnet 614-292-8100
616	Merit Network, Inc. 313-764-9430
617	DELPHI 800-544-4005 ■ NEARnet 617-873-8730 ■ Netcom Online 800-501-8649 ■ North Shore Access 617-593-3110 voicemail ■ NovaLink 800-274-2814 ■ The World 617-739-0202
619	E & S Systems 619-278-4641 ■ ■ CTS Network Services 619-637-3637 ■ The Cyberspace Station n/a ■ DIAL n' CERF 800-876-2373 ■ Netcom Online 800-501-8649
703	PSI (available nationwide) 703-620-6651 ■ CAPCON Library Network 202-331-5771 ■ Clark Internet Services, Inc. 800-735-2258 ■ Digital Express Group 800-969-9090 ■ Merit Network, Inc. 313-764-9430 ■ Netcom Online 800-501-8649 ■ The Meta Network 703-243-6622
704	CONCERT-CONNECT 919-248-1999 ■ Vnet Internet Access, Inc. 704-374-0779
707	CR Laboratories 415-381-2800
708	InterAccess 800-967-1580 ■ MCSNet 312-248-UNIX ■ XNet Information Systems 708-983-6064
713	The Black Box 713-480-2684 ■ South Coast Computing Services 713-661-3301 ■ NeoSoft's Sugar Land Unix 713-438-4964
714	DIAL n' CERF 800-876-2373 ■ Digital Express Group 800-969-9090 ■ KAIWAN 714-638-2139 ■ Netcom Online 800-501-8649
717	PREPnet 412-268-7870
718	Maestro 212-240-9600 ■ MindVOX 212-989-2418 ■ Netcom Online 800-501-8649 ■ PANIX Public Access Unix 212-877-4854 ■ The Pipeline n/a
719	Community News Service 719-592-1240 ■ Colorado SuperNet, Inc. 303-273-3471 ■ Old Colorado City Communicatio 719-632-4848
804	Wyvern Technologies, Inc. 804-622-4289
810	Merit Network, Inc. 313-764-9430 ■ MSen 313-998-4562
814	PREPnet 412-268-7870
815	InterAccess 800-967-1580 ■ MCSNet 312-248-UNIX ■ XNet Information Systems 708-983-6064
817	Texas Metronet 214-705-2900
818	DIAL n' CERF 800-876-2373 ■ Netcom Online 800-501-8649
905	UUNET Canada, Inc. 416-368-6621
906	Merit Network, Inc. 313-764-9430
907	University Of Alaska Southeast 907-465-6453
908	Digital Express Group 800-969-9090 ■ John von Neumann Computer Network 800-35-TIGER
910	CONCERT-CONNECT 919-248-1999
916	Netcom Online 800-501-8649
919	CONCERT-CONNECT 919-248-1999 ■ Vnet Internet Access, Inc. 704-374-0779

Notes

Notes

About the Author

Eric Gagnon is the president of GAA, a consulting firm specializing in product development and marketing for online, publishing and multimedia ventures. Mr. Gagnon has 14 years' experience as an entrepreneur in the online consumer database, software publishing and new venture development fields, including new business development for The Source, a pioneering consumer information service.

Mr. Gagnon can be reached via Internet e-mail at **p00553@psilink.com**, and welcomes your comments on this book, as well as your suggestions for additions to upcoming editions of ***What's on the Internet***.